Secret War

Billy H. Webb

Secret War

Billy G. Webb

To order additional copies of this book, contact:
Xlibris Corporation
1-888-795-4274
www.Xlibris.com
Orders@Xlibris.com
83856

Contents

Dedication

This book is dedicated to the heroes of the Secret War in Laos, and they were many.

Thousands of honorable Lao fought to keep their kingdom free from Communist rule. These men pledged their lives, fortunes, and sacred honor to the cause and often lost all three. They shall not, and should not, be forgotten.

General Vang Pao never gave up the fight, even when his own government and ours turned their backs on him. He's still fighting today, in every way he can. Thanks, VP.

The tireless efforts of Edgar "Pop" Buell and his associates saved the lives of thousands who might otherwise have perished during that bloody civil war. Pop, you left us in 1980, at the young age of 67. I hope you've found the peace you deserve.

And, we should not forget the incredibly courageous men of the CIA, and State Department. These men did their jobs with monumental effectiveness and style, standing strong against the rising tide of ignorance and dishonor as long as they were allowed to do so. If our political leaders had been as steadfast as you, gentlemen, Laos might still be free.

And of course, without the courageous American servicemen who fought and died in Laos, we could have accomplished nothing. As always, our men did their duty with bravery, skill, honor, and as always, too many of them failed to come home. Gentlemen, I thank you for your sacrifices. You make me proud to be an American.

And, last, but certainly not least, we should never forget the incredibly brave, courageous and dedicated men of Air America who flew unarmed into the teeth of death almost every single day, and never flinched. Thousands of indigenous personnel and hundreds of Americans owe their lives to these dedicated patriots. Gentlemen, wherever you are, may god bless, and keep you. You are simply the best.

Until they all come home (POW/MIA).

Introduction

For centuries, explorers have traveled the world in search of adventure, fame, wealth and knowledge. Nations have sought to increase their spheres of influence by sponsoring these explorers in their travels to various exotic locales, hitching their stars to proposals both reasonable and fantastic on the off chance that they might strike gold—sometimes literally. Upon discovering a new land with potential for development and exploitation, the explorers would naturally claim the territory for the country they represented, regardless of whether anyone else called it their own. Generally, the natives of the new land were either exterminated—sometimes by accident, in the case of introduced diseases, but often intentionally—or else shunted aside and marginalized.

The country that we now call Laos was one of those new lands. Laos was originally known as Lan Xang, "the Land of a Million Elephants," an appellation which graced the land from approximately the fourteenth century until the eighteenth century. It is believed, however, that organized societies existed in Laos as early as the ninth century. Early written documents describe ancient Laos as an agrarian society in which life revolved around subsistence agriculture, using domesticated water buffaloes.

For much of its history as a nation, Laos had been under the thumb of its neighbors. At varying times the Chinese, Vietnamese, Cambodians and Thais ruled Lan Xang, making it difficult for any national identity to become established. Left to their own devices, the indigenous population developed what most Westerners would consider an indolent lifestyle. They simply stood back, watched things happen, and in general lived life in a very relaxed state of mind. They accepted the status quo, and were happy enough to get by.

By the mid-eighteenth century, Imperial France had occupied Vietnam and Cambodia, and by approximately 1867, they had formed the two countries into a political unit they called the Indochina Union. Laos joined the Union in about 1893, whereupon the three countries then became collectively known as French Indochina. Even though they occupied Laos for the following six decades, the French never established a large presence there. They did send several hundred personnel to administer the country, but most of the day-to-day activities were overseen by Vietnamese civil servants. The French did little to improve the country during this period, but they did begin to immediately import many industrial goods from France to sell in French Indochina. Unfortunately, Laos was not rich in natural resources, so there was very little to export—except for opium. And so the French exported opium, encouraging both its growth and production. But the geography of Laos did not lend itself to extensive export of any commodity.

Laos is a landlocked country, meaning that there are no direct access points to ocean seaports. In fact, at first there were no roads to move export goods to a seaport. The only decent roads stretched between Vientiane to Luang Prabang in the north, and Savannakhet to the south. Laos is rather small, about the size of Great Britain; today, it's bordered by the countries of Thailand and Myanmar (historically, Siam and Burma) to the west, China to the north, Vietnam to the east, and Cambodia to the south. The mighty Mekong River demarks most of the western border, and acts as an important artery for transportation and trade. Unfortunately, it also provides no direct access to the ocean. The topography of Laos is mostly mountainous, with typical elevations of above five hundred meters (1,640 feet), and is dominated by steep terrain and narrow river valleys to the north. The southern panhandle, however, is generally level, and is conducive to agricultural development; though ultimately, only about four percent of the total land mass is fit for cultivation.

Laos experiences a tropical monsoon climate with heavy rains from May to October, a cool dry season from November through February, and a hot, dry season during March and April. Rainfall varies by as much as fifty percent each year, making rice production unreliable. Temperatures range from a high of 40 degrees Celsius (104 degrees Fahrenheit) in March to five degrees Celsius (41 degrees Fahrenheit) in the upland regions in January.

Three basic cultural groups make up the population of Laos. The largest group is the ethnic Lao, or Lao Loum, as they are called. This group represents about two-thirds of the population, and is composed basically of Thai peoples who migrated to Southeast Asia from China in the fifteenth century. This ethnic group is located predominately in the low lands of Laos. The second ethnic group is the Lao Theung, or mid-slope Lao. They are a dark-skinned people, possible related to the Kyaks of Borneo, who migrated to Laos in approximately the seventeenth century. At one time they were considered to be at the bottom of the social pyramid, and were referred to simply as "Kha", meaning slave. The third ethnic group is the Lao Soung, or highland Lao. The Lao Soung are a mixture of Chinese, Thai, Tibetan and Burmese mountain tribes; the indigenous Hmong are included in this group. This group prefers to live at the higher elevations and have their own distinct languages. They resent, and for the most part reject, the social values of the other Lao ethnic groups. In fact, most even reject the official religion of Laos, Theravada Buddhism, altogether.

Buddhism was officially introduced to the country in the sixteenth century by a king of Lan Xang, Photisarath. Even though Photisarath received the credit for it, there is evidence to suggest that the nation's conversion to Buddhism actually took place gradually over the centuries, with the first conversions dating back to about the ninth century. There are many beautiful temples (wats) in Laos, and Buddhism remains a stabilizing factor in a country otherwise consumed by conflict.

By the seventeenth century, Lan Xang had entered a period of decline, and in the eighteenth century Siam (now Thailand) established functional control over Laos. The Thais divided Laos into three separate states, centered around the royal capital of Luang Prabang in the north, Champassak in the south, and Vientiane in the center. The political and business capital of Laos was Vientiane. The royal capital was Luang Prabang, where the king lived prior to the Communist takeover in 1975.

On the political side of Laos, factional bickering and disharmony was a national tradition. The kingdom united only once in its history, from about A.D. 1353 to the mid-1600s. The Japanese also briefly tried to reunite the country during World War II, and the French tried to unite it again after the war.

However, by then the governing elite had become so factionalized that there was no central voice to speak for the entire country. In fact, in Luang Prabang, the king received lip service from just about everyone.

Meanwhile, in North Vietnam, Ho Chi Minh founded the Indochinese Communist Party (ICP) in 1930, and began to recruit Lao citizens into the party in 1936. Later, in 1946/47, Kaysone Phomvihan, a student from Laos, was recruited by the ICP while attending law school in Hanoi. In 1950, the Pathet Lao was formed, and recruited Prince Souphanouvong as its figurehead. France and Laos later signed the "Franco-Lao Treaty" in 1953, establishing Laos as a sovereign and independent country. The treaty established a monarchy with Sisavang Vong as its king. Three groups then emerged and contended for power. The Neutralists were led by Prince Souvanna Phouma; the Rightists by Prince Boun Oum; and the Leftists were led by Prince Souphanouvong.

Finally, two of the royal offspring, Prince Souvanna Phouma and Prince Souphanouvong, emerged to take control of the government. The older brother, Souvanna Phouma, was willing to work towards a gradual independence under the French. His younger brother by eleven years, Souphanouvong, was impatient and joined the Viet Minh. He adopted their ways and reportedly learned to fight among them, even though there is little evidence that he fought at all. Boun Oum ultimately moved to Thailand, out of frustration to escape the constant squabbling and upheaval in his native land.

The early history of the Hmong, who play an important role in the recent history of Laos, is difficult to trace. However, one thing is sure: the theories placing their origin in Mesopotamia, Siberia or Mongolia are probably false. It is known that less than 200 years ago, the Hmong lived in the Yunnan Province of southwest China, and evidence suggests that they occupied the same areas of southern China for at least 2,000 years before that. Beginning in the eighteenth century, the Hmong migrated to Southeast Asia, following the Annamite mountain ranges southward to new mountain settlements in Laos, Thailand, Burma and Vietnam. When the Hmong were still in China, Dutch and Portuguese missionaries introduced them to the only modern tools they adopted into their way of life: the steel knife and the long-barreled musket.

In his book *Nation of Sheep,* William J. Lederer describes Laos thus:

> Laos itself is not a rich land. However, strategically and politically it is the key to a treasure chest, a magic chunk of territory which borders six important nations. Laos is a corridor, and access point, to Thailand, South Vietnam, Malaya, Burma and Cambodia. It is the northern point of a natural highway the Chinese Communists hope to follow as far south as Indonesia. Laos may well be the foothold by which Red China can open the door to Southeast Asia's rice bowl. Its vast oil reserves and untapped mineral deposits, as well as a supply of labor, is greater than the United States. If Red China should gain this rich peninsula which is just south of Laos, she would also get a strategic position flanking Australia, New Zealand and India. It would allow her to snuff out Japan's Southeast Asia trade, forcing Japan to join the Communists axis. This, then, is why little Laos—a land of swamps, jungles, mountains and illiterate, sick people—is so important.[1]

As the second half of the 20th century began, Laos was in for an even more tumultuous experience as Southeast Asia tried to establish its identify. The French and British empires were beginning to lose their holds over Asia, the Japanese had been soundly defeated by the Allies, and China was bent on spreading Communism throughout Southeast Asia, with the assistance of—and in competition with—the Soviet Union. Also, in the 1960s, the U.S. Central Intelligence Agency (CIA) began to recruit the indigenous Hmong people in Laos to help the United States during the Vietnam War. The Hmong were identified as Special Guerrilla Units (SGU), and were led by General Vang Pao. During the war, over eight percent of the Hmong people in Laos were recruited to aid the United States. The CIA used the SGUs as a counterattack force to block the Ho Chi Minh Trail, or Truong Son Road, as it was officially named. The Trail was the main artery for the North Vietnamese Army (NVA) to move troops and supplies to South Vietnam.

The SGUs also assisted in the rescue of downed American pilots, and took part in frontline fighting. As a result, the Hmong suffered a high casualty rate in personnel killed, injured and disabled. It is against this backdrop that our story really begins. And now that you have been introduced to this truly unique country, please turn the page, and begin your journey into the past to discover Laos, and the wonderful people who live there—proud, hardworking people who were caught in a crossfire of war and betrayal.

Figure 1. Map of Southeast Asia
(Illustration from the Public Domain)

Chapter 1

French Occupation

As France and Great Britain built what would eventually become global empires in the post-Renaissance world, they naturally looked eastward in search of opportunities for trade and expansion. By 1600, Great Britain had established trade relations with China, following the lead of the Italian Marco Polo and his successors, and was profiting handsomely. Not surprising, the Britons didn't care to share China, and vigorously blocked any continental efforts to enter into the Oriental trade. Hence, France decided to explore an indirect approach in their efforts to open up the lucrative Chinese market.

French authorities concluded that if they could find a "back door" into China by way of Laos and the Mekong River, they could share in the vast profits that could be made in China. In addition, Laos itself offered excellent trade potential. So in order to get a feel for the terrain, in 1868 France sent an expedition up the Mekong to investigate the feasibility of using the river as a trade route into China. After two years of navigating the river and its unpredictable currents, as well as exploring jungle trails on foot, the expedition provided a report explaining the great difficulties associated with reaching China via the so-called back door.

Undeterred, the French continued to send expeditions up the Mekong River, drawing maps and gathering ore samples for roughly 18 years. The result of all these explorations was the establishment of an official French presence in Luang Prabang in 1893. Laos had officially become a part of the Empire of France, which included Tonkin (northeast Vietnam), Annam (Central Vietnam), South Vietnam, and Cambodia. Except for Tonkin, these regions were referred to collectively as the "Associated States." The official seat of the French government for this group of nations, referred to simply as Indochina, was Hanoi.

At this particular juncture in history, colonization was the order of the day for European forces occupying foreign lands. Not only did colonization give the Europeans more political influence over their territories, but they also stood to benefit economically. Vietnam's fertile deltas assured profitable returns from harvesting and selling rice, tobacco, indigo, tea and coffee, not to mention the potential of the rubber plantations. In addition, Cambodia, with its fertile deltas, produced rice, fish, rubber and timber, all of which would add to France's wealth.

And then there was the little country of Laos. Laos had no major exports, and the population consisted primarily of subsistence farmers tilling small plots of land where they grew vegetables, rice and opium. The latter was essentially the only cash crop; therefore, France took control of the opium trade, and made certain that the sale of the drug remained legal. The French military managed the business, and even used some of its profits to fund military operations; nevertheless, Laos was mostly an economic disappointment to the French.

For the people of Laos, adjusting to life under French rule was not difficult. In fact, the Lao benefited culturally from the French. Many Lao still speak French, and France left its architectural contributions behind in the form of many public and private buildings that still exist today. The French also rewarded faithful service with educational opportunities for the Lao, at schools and universities in Paris. That beneficial relationship continued until World War II. It came to an abrupt end in 1940, when France surrendered to the Nazis in Paris, and a pro-Nazi government established a seat in Vichy, France. The Vichy Government subsequently granted Japan military access to Indochina. The purpose of Japan's presence in Southeast Asia was ostensibly to blockade China, preventing it from importing arms, fuel, and tens of thousands of tons of other war materiél each month.

In September 1940, Japan and the government in Vichy signed an accord granting Japan transit rights and permission to establish military bases. The accord also authorized Japan to initially station 6,000 troops in Indochina, with an overall cap on troop strength set at 25,000 troops. The agreement barred Japanese air and naval forces from Indochina, except as allowed by the accords. True to form, Japan completely ignored the accords, and immediately began bringing in its air and naval forces. Japan's publicized goal was to ostensibly create a "Great East Asia Co-Prosperity Sphere", comprised of Japan, Manchuria, China, and parts of Southeast Asia. Great East Asia would set up a new international order seeking "co-prosperity" for Asian countries, free from Western colonialism and domination.

In other words, Asians would work with Asians to provide goods and services at low prices. In truth, Japan was only concerned with its own needs, and intended to use Great East Asia as a means to step up their aggression in Southeast Asia. The Japanese also intended to use Great East Asia as a front to manipulate local populations and economics for the benefit of Imperial Japan. But other Asian nations quickly saw through the façade to Japan's true designs, and ultimately, the plan failed miserably.

The Japanese plans in Indochina went forward, however; they occupied the region, and began exploiting the people and taking what they wanted in the same brutal fashion they had displayed in occupied Nanking, the Philippines, and elsewhere. In Laos, the Japanese were especially cruel, forcing men, women and children into slavery under the worst of conditions. For example: there was a working silver mine near the village of Ban Ban in northeastern Laos. Before the occupation by Japan, Hmong women worked the mine, and their men were paid to manage it. When the Japanese took over, the Hmong women, men and children all functioned as slave labor, and were not paid anything to work in the mine. In fact, they were even forced to sleep in the mine at night in order to be ready for work more quickly every morning. This particular mine was also known to be unsafe, and on more than one occasion, parts of the mine collapsed onto sleeping Hmong, killing many. The mine was also cold and damp, with little if any ventilation, causing continuing unsanitary conditions.

Japan's occupation of Indochina was incomplete, however, because they lacked enough trained professionals to handle the administrative issues resulting from the racial and linguistic complexity of the region. To fill the void, the Japanese allowed the French, already in-country, to stay and oversee the day-to-day affairs. Under the Vichy government, which lasted from 1941 to 1944, the French Governor-General of Laos was a man named Jean Decoux, who found himself lodged between a rock and a hard place during the early stages of the Japanese occupation. Decoux was unable to acquire aid from other sources, because all contact with the outside world was cut off by Japan, so he was forced to yield to Japan's demands—or at least pretend to.

By the end of 1941, Japan's hold on Indochina had been relaxed somewhat because of limited resources. Decoux took advantage of the situation, and began raising his own private army. He convinced Japan that it was to their advantage to support the newly-formed army, which he called *La Legion des Combattants,* by providing them with arms and ammunition. Next, Decoux set up the Mission Franco-Japanese in 1942, to reportedly act as a liaison agency between Japan and Laos. But in reality it was an added layer of government, designed to form a bottleneck to slow down any action on Japanese demands.

After 1942, Japan became wary of Decoux, and suspected that he was supporting the Allied forces. He was accused of failing to fire on American aircraft, and of harboring Allied aviators shot down over Laos. Actually, Decoux was doing both. In late 1944, the French, who were now free of the Vichy regime, secretly dropped commando forces into the mountains of northern Laos in preparation for an offensive to retake Laos. By March 1945 Japan was at war with France again, and the Japanese began combing the countryside in Indochina, rounding up French military and civilian personnel. They imprisoned the French officials and administrators, and continued the roundup into the summer of 1945. Decoux was ousted, and Japan took direct control of the government.

In order to instill fear among the Laotian public, the Japanese put on public displays of brutality. On one occasion, the Japanese paraded five French captives through the streets of Ban Ban in full sight of the villagers. The captives were tethered, and had strings run through their noses. As the Japanese soldiers herded the prisoners down the street, just as they would herd livestock, the soldiers would jerk on the strings, causing the French soldiers to jerk violently, screaming in pain, with blood pouring from their noses. Other reports indicated that the Japanese also used the French prisoners to pull plows in the fields in place of water buffalos.

The Japanese also went to extreme efforts in their attempts to eradicate the French influence in Laos. Any Laotian caught aiding the French could expect summary execution. Upon apprehension, the Lao collaborator would be led to the center of town and all the citizens would be gathered around the prisoner. A Japanese soldier would then simply walk up to the collaborator, put a gun to his head, and pull the trigger—killing him right there where he stood, for everyone to see.

By the summer of 1945, French commandos were already undertaking offensive operations in the hills and mountains with support from Hmong like young Vang Pao. With commandos in place, the French and Hmong guerrillas would ambush Japanese supply convoys coming into Laos through a mountain pass at Nong Het, blowing up the bridges and ambushing the Japanese. At one point, the commandos were so effective in their constant hit-and-run attacks that the Japanese firmly believed they came from a large secret base somewhere in the area, where thousands of French troops were assigned.

In August 1945, the United States dropped the first atomic bomb on Japan, announcing that it was only a matter of days before the Japanese would surrender. Hearing the news, Japanese troops stationed in Laos immediately began committing suicide *en masse*, both by means of hara-kiri (ritual disembowelment) and by blowing themselves up with their own grenades. Not all the Japanese troops killed themselves, however; many simply began marching towards Hanoi, an area they perceived as safe. But not very many Japanese soldiers made it out of Laos alive, with most simply vanishing along the way. The Hmong guerrillas explained the disappearances simply by saying that the Japanese were "taken away by the wind."

Meanwhile, to the east, the wily and persistent Viet Minh, under the leadership of Ho Chi Minh, were busy increasing their strength and war-fighting capabilities in the Tonkin area. They were growing stronger by the day, and weapons and ammunition were flowing freely to them from China and Russia.[2]

Shortly after World War II ended, the Chinese Kuomintang (Nationalist) Army arrived in Vietnam to oversee repatriation of the Japanese Imperial Army. And on September 2, 1945, Ho Chi Minh proclaimed formation of the Democratic Republic of Vietnam (DRV) to replace "French Indochina." The DRV, headquartered in Tonkin, quickly formed a legislature and held elections. Shortly after that, the existing government's titular head, Bao Dai, the pro-French Emperor, officially abdicated, recognizing the DRV as the legitimate government of Vietnam.

A few months later, the French, Chinese and Vietnamese met and came to a three-way understanding. The French agreed to relinquish certain rights in China, while the DRV agreed to the return of the

French, in exchange for promises of independence within the French Union. The Chinese, having achieved their goals, departed, and the French and Viet Minh continued their discussions. The talks later broke down, resulting in almost ten years of war between France and the DRV. This conflict became known as the First Indochina War.

At the beginning of the conflict, the French Army possessed a high-level of confidence that they would easily win the war against the Viet Minh. After all, France was a wealthy Western nation that boasted a modern army with tanks, aircraft, ships, guns and sophisticated communications equipment. They also had the famed Foreign Legion, whose fighting skills were legendary. Perhaps ironically, in light of their quick surrender to the Nazis, the French were convinced they knew everything related to warfare and the prosecution of war. After all, they were a sophisticated, well-armed military fighting a bunch of little guys hiding in the jungle with limited supplies of antiquated light weapons.

In hindsight, it's clear that the French approach to warfare with the Viet Minh was fatally flawed. In his 1964 book *Street Without Joy*, Bernard B. Fall[3] observes that the French did not understand the uniqueness of the war, and they failed to adapt to it. They armed, equipped and trained for the European style of warfare known as "Set-Piece Battle." Their approach was to select an objective, and then to set off for the target with all their tanks, cannons, troops and equipment. When they reached their target, they would engage the enemy, overpowering their opponents using superior firepower and a large military force. Then they would move on to the next objective.

Of course, as they learned to their chagrin (and as the Americans learned later), the Viet Minh did not accommodate the French by simply sitting and waiting to be attacked. There were no fronts to speak of, and the Communists stayed mobile at all times. Indeed, there were only two instances in which set piece battle worked to the advantage of the French. And, as Bernard Fall observed, "Terrain and people triumph over technology." In other words, French armor and firepower became a burden in rugged terrain when fighting against the highly-mobile Viet Minh troops.[4]

The fact that their mechanized army could only travel on improved road surfaces also greatly inhibited the French offensives, limiting their ability to engage the enemy in the hills and the jungle.

This chink in the armor, so to speak, allowed the Viet Minh to engage the French at a time and place of their choosing. And of course if the engagement wasn't going the way the Viet Minh wanted it to go, they would simply break off fighting, and melt away into the jungle and hills. This hit-and-run style of warfare would, in the end, be the key to victory for the Viet Minh.

Rather than adapt to the existing conditions and use tactics and equipment that allowed them to be more mobile and more directly capable of responding to the Viet Minh threat, the French continued to allow the limits of their machinery to dictate strategy. If no roads existed, the French would simply build new roads, or improve existing ones. But just beyond the roads there was tall grass, rice fields, and the ever-present and almost impenetrable jungle. Mechanized equipment simply could not perform in the rough terrain alongside the roadways, and the Viet Minh simply wouldn't cooperate by staying within sight along the roads at all times. Not far away from the roads, there were foot trails and paths lacing through the jungles and hills, and the Viet Minh used this informal network to escape from the French time after time. Often, the French would rumble along the roads, kicking up dust with all their noisy mechanized equipment as they traveled to their objectives. Meanwhile, the Viet Minh would follow along on a nearby trail on foot, invariably arriving before the French. Then the Communists troops would simply rest and wait for the perfect opportunity to attack.

Along their network of trails, the Viet Minh established strategically located way stations where they could rest, regroup, treat their injured, and re-arm as necessary for their next engagement.[5] Unlike the Viet Minh, the French did not have the luxury of aid or way stations. They were forced to take everything they needed with them, based on the expected duration of the mission. This exacted a heavy burden, because the average French soldier was weighed down with equipment and ammunition, while Viet Minh soldier carried only what he needed for that day.

However, the French did have military outposts throughout Tonkin, Annam, and, to a lesser extent Laos. The outposts were usually staffed with small military units, and often used indigenous Thai, Hmong, Vietnamese and Nung personnel as back-up. But ultimately, these outposts turned out to be more of an obstacle than an asset for the French. They were also easy targets for the Viet Minh, because they lacked staffing and supplies; it was not uncommon for the Viet Minh to launch campaigns in which they destroyed outpost after outpost, killing and capturing most of the troops. They also picked up French weapons and ammunition taken from, or left behind, by the fleeing French.

But where was French air support during all this? The French *did* have an air force, if not a particularly effective or dedicated one. Indeed, the French pilots called their airplanes *"les Pieges"*, which meant "the traps" in English. French pilots considered their aircraft to be death traps, because even if you didn't die in a crash, going down in enemy territory was considered a death sentence. Even with survival equipment, it was unlikely the pilot would survive if captured by the Viet Minh. Worse, the French lacked an organized search and rescue force.

At the beginning of the First Indochina War, the French possessed approximately sixty British-manufactured Spitfires, which were made of wood and canvas. The Spitfires were not designed for use in tropical climates, and they literally rotted away in the humid heat of Southeast Asia. In addition to the Spitfires, the French had a few German Junkers-52 tri-motors. These aircraft were used for hauling cargo, and could be used as bombers. The French also used other aircraft like the Morane L-5s, which were designed for aerial reconnaissance; in addition, Catalina Flying Boats were used for aerial surveillance along the coastal areas.

Later, in 1951, American aircraft became available to France through the U.S. Military Assistance Program (MAP). The United States provided almost 100 B-26s, 100 C-47s, more than 20 C-119s, 112 Hellcat and Bearcat fighter-bombers, and finally, less than 20 helicopters. Even with the aircraft provided by the United States, France never developed any real air capability in Indochina. However, the C-119 freighters were effectively used to move supplies and equipment into airstrips capable of receiving them. The C-47s also hauled cargo and served as medical evacuation transports, but with their limited payload capability it was more advantageous to use the C-119s.

Even though the French did have something of an air capability, the Viet Minh were able, for the most part, to work around the reconnaissance and fighter/ bomber aircraft. Their network of trails and footpaths were well-concealed from aerial view by large canopy trees, and if additional camouflage was required, it was provided by the Viet Minh logistics specialists.

And so the war continued through the late 1940s into the early 1950s. The French were constantly clanging and banging, grinding up and down the roads in clouds of dust, while the Viet Minh arrived ahead of them and patiently waited until they were ready to strike. They then surprised the French and inflicted heavy casualties, melting into the hills when they were done, leaving many dead French soldiers behind. Understandably, the human, psychological, and financial toll began to wear the French down.

In particular, France found it increasingly difficult to fund the First Indochina War, particularly as the French people grew weary of the fighting and pressured their government not to bankroll it any longer. Who else, then, could help? Well, there were Great Britain and the United States, to name two candidates. But the British were not fond of the French at all. While it is not known how much, if anything, the British contributed, we do know that in 1950 alone, the United States gave approximately $10,000,000 to the French for the prosecution of the war in Vietnam; and in the following three years, we provided the French with at least $100,000,000 each year. This is above and beyond the air fleet the U.S. provided. But wait, there's more: the United States also provided the French with over 700 armored fighting vehicles, 13,000 transport vehicles, and 253 naval vessels, in addition to thousands of lesser items.

Meanwhile, in tiny, out-of-the-way Laos, the French had not heretofore spent all that much money on the war against the Communists, because there was very little going on from a military standpoint. France did have a few military outposts scattered across the countryside, and were obligated to protect the cities of Vientiane and Luang Prabang. Their hope was that the Lao would form their own government, with assistance from Paris, of course, and take care of their own internal security problems. That did not happen, but, finally, Laos did form its own Royal Lao Government (RLG) in 1947. Later, in 1949, a Franco-Lao agreement granted the RLG authority to raise an army that they named, appropriately enough, the Lao National Army.

Now that Laos had formed a government and was granted the authority to raise an army, France facilitated the training of military leaders, and allowed the United States to provide the RLG with arms. There was a catch, however: the weapons had to pass through French hands before being provided to the RLG. Of course, the U.S. was eager to help, and sufficient quantities of M-1 Garand rifles, M-1 carbines, ammunition and other weapons, including explosives, soon began to flow. This infusion of arms allowed the French to concentrate on fighting the Viet Minh in Vietnam, but the respite did not last long.

In 1949, the Resistance Committee of Eastern Laos was formed. It was the forerunner of the Pathet Lao, and backed by the Viet Minh. With the formation of the Resistance Committee, the French began to justifiably get nervous. A year later, the Resistance Committee rallied 150 men capable of fighting for the Viet Minh in Laos. Later, in 1952, the Viet Minh began to systematically probe French and RLG units in northeastern Laos near the town of Sam Neua. Later, in April 1953, a Viet Minh force of ten battalions entered northeastern Laos and initiated battle with local forces. Some of these forces used the trails through a place called Dien Bien Phu to reach Laos.[6] Fortunately for the French and the RLG, the monsoon rains came early that year, causing the Viet Minh to retreat to North Vietnam and wait for the next dry season before initiating any large-scale attacks.

On August 13, 1953, American officials reported that the Viet Minh were using several pro-Communist Lao units in its stepped-up activities in Laos. It was also reported that the Lao units were eliminating perceived traitors, gaining the support of the local population, and conducting intensive intelligence operations against French units. A comment added to the report indicated that it was the first indication that the "Free Laos" (Pathet Lao) movement of Prince Souphanouvong was attracting support among the Lao peasants in the Sam Neua area.

By then, the war in Indochina was stalemated. But casualties continued to mount, and costs continued to spiral upwards for the French and the RLG. Something needed to be done; so the French offered the Indochina command to Lieutenant General Henri Navarre, Chief of Staff to the commander of the Northern Atlantic Treaty Organization (NATO) ground forces in Central Europe. Navarre was content with his assignment to NATO, and did not want the command; but after some coaxing he accepted, and was off to Asia on May 19, 1953.

Navarre was considered a competent and experienced officer, and he impressed government ministers as clear-sighted and intelligent. Upon arrival in Indochina, Navarre refused to get bogged down in the day-to-day operational issues. Instead, he spent his time visiting the fronts, inspecting troops and installations, and questioning subordinates and leaders alike. Navarre realized that the Viet Minh were strongly established in Tonkin, where the French Expeditionary Corps assumed a defensive role. Combined with the allied forces of the Associated States (Cambodia, Laos, and Vietnam), the Expeditionary Corps outnumbered the Viet Minh significantly. But with the troops dispersed in small outposts throughout Indochina, this strategic superiority dwindled to almost nothing.

Navarre then decided that the French strategy would be to go on the offensive rather than continue defensive operations. He created mobile strike teams and, believing that the Communists would push east into Laos in significant numbers, he sent a large number of troops to Dien Bien Phu to act as a blocking force. Navarre had two objectives. First, he hoped that he could draw the Viet Minh into a large, pitched battle so that superior French forces could wipe them out in one large engagement. Second, he believed the French occupation of Dien Bien Phu would deny the Viet Minh direct access to Laos.

When Navarre first briefed his plan to his subordinates, every single one of them objected to the idea. There were two immediate problems with Navarre's plan for Dien Bien Phu. First, the Viet Minh were not likely to allow themselves to be beaten in a set-piece European style battle, and second, Dien Bien Phu was hardly the perfect place for such a battle, because it was surrounded by hills and could be blocked off from outside support, except for aerial resupply. It seemed that the French had *still* not learned their lesson.

Navarre also decided to greatly increase the size of the French units called *Groupements Mobiles* (GMs)—"mobile groups" which normally consisted of from 2,000 to 3,000 troops—because the Viet Minh were fielding division-size units numbering approximately 20,000 troops. He also wanted to turn these division-sized GMs into highly maneuverable offensive units, unlike the previously defensive GMs. In addition, Navarre planned to use the 1954-55 campaign season to consolidate the French positions, and then go on a full-scale offensive in the summer of 1955 with a troop strength ultimately numbering nearly 100,000.

Navarre then briefed everyone in his chain of command on his proposal, the eponymous "The Navarre Plan." All along the way, his superiors endorsed the plan; so now, it was time to go and find the money to execute it. The British were still unhappy with the French, France was strapped for money at home, and its citizens had grown weary of the war. So once again, the only place left to turn was the deep pockets of the United States.

By this time, former-general Dwight D. (Ike) Eisenhower was the President of the United States, and he endorsed Navarre's plan. Ike also supported France's request for $400,000,000 to execute the Navarre Plan. After all, Ike was strongly anti-Communist, and had already developed what would come to be known as the famous "Domino Theory." Ike's theory was that if the Communists won the war in Vietnam, then the other countries in the region would fall like dominos, until the entire hemisphere was Communist-controlled—and he would go to any lengths to keep that from happening.

At any rate, the discussions began in Washington, D.C., and of course ultimately wound up being debated on the floor of Congress. Meanwhile, the United States dispatched General John W. O'Daniel, commander of the United States Army in the Pacific region, to Saigon to evaluate the French war effort. He took two officers from each branch of the service, except for the Marines, with him, and was to spend a month studying conditions on the ground.

Figure 2. General John W. O'Daniel
(Photo from the Public Domain)

The team, led by O'Daniel, dutifully spent one month on the ground in Vietnam conducting their study. He received complete briefings from Navarre, along with copies of plans and other documentation required for completion of the study. The team then returned to Hawaii, where they spent four days writing up their findings. The O'Daniel report, as it was called, was then submitted to the Pentagon, and it endorsed the Navarre Plan. The report, did state, however, that

> " . . . though the new French High Command is prepared to take certain essential and highly desirable steps in the right direction, they will not, and perhaps cannot in view of political considerations, consider undertaking military campaigns designed to achieve total victory with the forces now available."

The Joint Chiefs of Staff (JCS) also endorsed the Navarre Plan, with the stipulation that its cost not come out of funds already appropriated for the Pentagon. In other words, they said, it should be funded with new money from other government sources. In Congress, however, the Navarre Plan ran into trouble, and stalled. Ike stepped in and twisted congressional arms to get the funding approved, which it ultimately was.

With the funding in place and the arguments about "Why Dien Bien Phu?" over, the first French paratroopers, numbering approximately 1,200 men, were dropped into the area on November 20, 1953. Over the next two days, thousands of additional troops were dropped into Dien Bien Phu to establish an airhead for the French forces. This effort was called "Operation Castor" and was commanded by Brigadier General Jean Gilles, the commander of the French Airborne troops during the First Indochina War. Giles' job was to repair and lengthen the existing airstrip, and to provide security for the waves of French troops yet to come.

Dien Bien Phu is a long valley measuring nine miles long and six miles wide at its widest point. The valley is ringed with hills of varying height, and at the time of the conflict, numerous villages dotted the landscape of the valley floor. The population of the valley averaged just over 20,000 people, comprised of Vietnamese, Chinese, Thai and Hmong ethnic groups. Some of the villagers were farmers, some were shop owners and merchants, and some were traders. Of course, the primary trade at Dien Bien Phu was in opium.

With the arrival of the French troops, the villagers quickly departed the valley *en masse* and melted away into the hills. It should be noted that this was not the first time that military troops had used the valley: at various times during the First Indochina War, Viet Minh and French troops skirmished over Dien Bien Phu, with control of the valley changing hands frequently. More recently, however, the valley had not been occupied by military personnel, except for those in transit, who used the valley to rest and re-arm.

Ten days later, on November 30, 1953, the French command in Tonkin issued its basic instructions to the garrison at Dien Bien Phu. Their orders were to (1) guarantee free use of the airfield; (2) hold this position to the last man; and (3) discourage the buildup of Viet Minh forces by initiating powerful attacks out of the base at Dien Bien Phu.

*   *   *

At about this same time, a conference was taking place many miles away on the island of Bermuda. As initially envisioned, the purpose of the conference was to discuss the possibility of easing East-West tensions; but the Soviet dictator, Joseph Stalin, had died in March 1953, and it was decided that a meeting would take place between the "Big Three": Great Britain, France and the United States. There was very little structure to the meeting, and President Eisenhower used the occasion as an opportunity to pitch his belief in the use of atom bombs to deter rogue nations like Korea and China. Ike was of the firm belief that there should be no distinction between conventional and atomic weapons, and he was planning to deliver that same message to the United Nations in the near future.[7]

After Ike's speech, the conference began to deteriorate, with the French and British completely shunning each other. But some important ground was covered during the conference, nonetheless: Britain discussed their problems in Malaya, and the United States addressed their issues concerning Korea. The French discussed Indochina, and began to verbalize their desire to open negotiations relative to their war there; but President Eisenhower was against any such negotiations.

Meanwhile, when the leader of the Viet Min troops, General Võ Nguyen Giap, heard the news that the French had occupied Dien Bien Phu, his troops were already on the march in the Thai mountains. In order to engage Navarre's troops, he ordered the troops to keep marching in the direction of the French stronghold. Giap had already decided that it was time for a showdown; and actually, he was quite pleased that the French had decided on Dien Bien Phu, because he knew he could control the terrain and defeat them.

By 1953, the Viet Minh had become disciplined combat veterans with tightly-integrated formations. Their firepower had increased to equal that of the French, and they possessed sophisticated communications. They had also established an intricate support infrastructure throughout North and South Vietnam; the only issue was one of establishing supply bases near Dien Bien Phu.

In order to overcome the logistical issues of fighting the French at Dien Bien Phu, Giap enlisted the aid of over 75,000 peasants, porters and workers. He also summoned engineering units and even regular infantry soldiers where needed. With his troops in place, on November 26, 1953, General Giap issued the mobilization order: his engineers were ordered to open Provincial Road 41 to vehicular traffic all the way to Dien Bien Phu. All bridges were to be reinforced for heavy loads, and the road was to be widened and repaired as necessary. When the work was completed, it equaled sixty miles of new mountain roads.

Meanwhile, supplies for the Viet Minh were arriving in China and were being deposited at depots in Nanning and at Lang Son. To transport the supplies, over 1,000 Molotova Russian trucks were mobilized to move the equipment from China to the Tonkin area, where it would be loaded onto smaller trucks for the trip to Dien Bien Phu. The human porters and peasants would also be used to carry the supplies on their backs, or by whatever means were necessary to get them to the French Stronghold over 500 miles away. (The total weight transported during the campaign exceeded 15,600,000 lbs).

Figure 3. Molotova Trucks
(Photo from the Public Domain)

Later, as the thousands of tons of war supplies destined for the Viet Minh began to flow in the direction of Dien Bien Phu, so did thousands of Communist fighters. All through December 1953, battalions of Viet Minh troops continued to filter into the mountains surrounding the French position at Dien Bien Phu. When all the Viet Minh troops were finally in place and ready to fight, they numbered approximately 70,000—which meant that for every French soldier, there were approximately six Viet Minh fighters.

Meanwhile, the government in Paris began to grow nervous. They waited, and hoped for good news from the front in Vietnam, but it did not come. The French government then decided to send a special commission to Indochina to conduct a full study of the situation. Also growing more nervous by the day, the United States sent General O'Daniel back to Vietnam to inspect Dien Bien Phu. General O'Daniel subsequently reported that the French were in a sound position. A separate American mission of antiaircraft experts who were familiar with the capabilities of Russian antiaircraft artillery in use at the time also inspected Dien Bien Phu, and concluded that the Viet Minh would not be able to reach the airfield from the hill above the French stronghold. Several other U.S. personnel inspected Dien Bien Phu during this period, including a U.S. Military Advisory Group (MAG), Lieutenant Colonel J. C. Foster of Air Force Intelligence, and Major General Thomas J. Trapnell of the U.S. Army.

The fighting began in earnest on March 13, 1954, when the Viet Minh began firing artillery shells on the French position at a defensive position named "Beatrice" late in the afternoon. By midnight, Beatrice had fallen to the Viet Minh. The battle subsequently raged on for a total of 57 days, ending in victory for the Viet Minh on May 7. When it was over, the valley floor was littered with the bodies of thousands of soldiers from both sides, and thousands more were wounded. The following day, the Viet Minh rounded up the surviving French soldiers, who totaled over 11,000. Of that number, over 4,000 were wounded. After all was said and done, with all its might and with the assistance of the United States, the French had lost the battle for Dien Bien Phu.[8]

Most people who are knowledgeable about the French occupation of Vietnam will tell you that the First Indochina War ended at Dien Bien Phu on May 7, 1953—but that is not in fact the case. While it's true that the defeat at Dien Bien Phu symbolically ended the war, fierce fighting was still taking place in the Tonkin and the Annam regions of Vietnam. Another fact that many people did not know at the time of the battle was that the United States was considering a plan called "Operation Vulture." If that plan had been implemented to save the French, it would have included the use of atomic bombs similar to ones used against Hiroshima and Nagasaki in 1945. In fact, the troops, aircraft, and bombs were

Figure 4. Dien Bien Phu in 1954
(Photo from the Public Domain)

Figure 5. Dien Bien Phu Today
(Photo from the Public Domain)

already strategically positioned for just such a mission. But after much debate, and consultation with Britain's Sir Winston Churchill, President Eisenhower opted not to implement Operation Vulture.

After the battle of Dien Bien Phu, the French Prisoners of War (POWs) were marched off to North Vietnam, where they were incarcerated and treated harshly. Thousands died at the hands of their Viet Minh captors, and were never heard from again. Later, in mid-1954, the DRV, Cambodia, France, Laos, Communist China, South Vietnam, Russia and the United Kingdom agreed to meet in Geneva, Switzerland for peace talks.[9] The talks began on May 8, 1954 and ended on July 21, 1954, resulting in the release of thousands of French POWs. The accords reached in Geneva also essentially divided Vietnam into northern and southern countries. In addition, the talks recognized the sovereignty of Indochina, granting it independence from France. Laos and Cambodia were recognized as neutral countries. The agreements also required that all foreign nations remove their troops from Laos, with the exception of a small number of French advisory troops, and cease hostilities. An International Control Commission was also established to oversee the implementation of the Geneva Accords.

Chapter 2

Young Vang Pao

In Chapter One, I outlined the French Occupation of Southeast Asia, its impact, and its outcome; this period of Laotian history is especially important, because it would shape events that would take place in the near future. But now, however, it's necessary to digress briefly, in order to introduce an important participant in the Secret War in Laos.

The year is 1931, and the place is Nong Het, Laos, Xieng Khouang Province. Nong Het is located in northeastern Laos, along modern Route 7, near the Laotian border with North Vietnam. It's a major market town, a French outpost, and a cultural center for the Hmong. The residents of the town are primarily Hmong subsistence farmers, who relocated to Laos in the 1800s from China. Against this backdrop, in 1931 a son is born to a member of the Vang clan; he is given the name Vang Pao, and later becomes known as VP.

Vang Pao was the son of a peasant farmer whose family resided in a thatched hut adjacent to a small plot of land where vegetables, rice, and opium poppies were grown. The French encouraged opium production and maintained its legality, because they controlled the harvesting and sale of the drug to dealers from France, Vietnam, and China. Young Vang Pao's childhood was no different from that of any other boy growing up in Nong Het. As a boy, he would join in with the other boys, running around the town looking for excitement and something to do.

From the beginning, however, Vang Pao stood out from the other boys. The town elders noticed that the boy always tried harder, ran faster, and exhibited an indescribable zeal for life. The elders always looked for potential leaders from among the young men; in VP, they found one. Later, when a school opened in Nong Het, VP was invited to attend. On the appointed day, he showed up for class with a big smile on his face, but with soiled clothes and in need of a bath. The teacher took one look at the boy and sent him home to bathe, put on clean clothes, and then return to class. VP did as instructed, and then joined the other boys in the class. He did well in school, and learned much.

When World War II found its way to Southeast Asia and Japan occupied Laos, Japanese soldiers passed through Nong Het occasionally to monitor the population. The Japanese were known for their brutality for any violation of Japanese rules, meting out punishment in front of the other residents as a way to deliver a clear message and garner respect. The Hmong townspeople, desiring anonymity, tended to quietly slip away into the hills whenever the Japanese would show up. VP, however, was not afraid of the foreigners. In fact, he would greet them cheerfully and offer to perform odd jobs for them: for instance, offering to locate fresh meat and vegetables for the troops in exchange for money. VP even learned French and some Japanese along the way.

As previously mentioned, the French covertly returned to Laos in January 1945 and established an intelligence-gathering network. After their defeat by the United States in 1945, the Japanese presence slowly vanished from Laos, and the proud soldiers of the Empire either killed themselves or tried to leave the country.[10] When the French returned to take control of the country, the enterprising VP was about fourteen years old, and began to work for them as a courier. He also performed other small jobs, such as providing proper burials for French soldiers killed along the main roads. In 1947, VP joined the colonial police in Xieng Khouang Province, made corporal by 1948, and was accepted at a French Noncommissioned Officer (NCO) school. Later, in the early 1950s, VP became a soldier without rank in the Lao Territorial Army (LTA).

In 1952, the commander of the French troops in northern Laos asked VP to go out into the field and attempt to learn all the locations of the Viet Minh, who by this time had established a foothold in northern Laos. VP wasn't sure that he would be successful, however, and expressed as much to the commander. The officer listened, and reassured VP that he was confident that he would indeed be successful. So VP set out with a small squad of Hmong troops in search of the Viet Minh. After walking for several days and finding none, VP and his team focused on an area he believed might provide information as to possible locations of the Communist troops.

Upon arrival in the area, VP used his personal charm and charisma on the locals to determine the location of several Viet Minh soldiers. The LTA troops then quietly surrounded the encampment where the Communists were located, counting about a dozen men casually passing the evening. They opened fire on the unsuspecting Viet Minh and killed all but one, who escaped but was later caught. After the fight and subsequent search for intelligence information, the Hmong patrol returned to Muang Ngan, where they were praised for their excellent work. Almost immediately after returning from their first mission, VP and his men were ordered back into the field to intercept and eliminate more Viet Minh troops, who were reportedly on the march to Sop Nao to reinforce Communist troops in battle. He and his weary squad re-armed and departed again, and once more they were completely successful.

As it turned out, the French were so impressed that they arranged for VP to attend officer's school for the Lao Army, where he soon graduated as a cadet officer. Later, in November 1952, the Viet Minh moved into Dien Bien Phu, North Vietnam, and in April 1953 launched an offensive into northern Laos. After the offensive got underway, the Communists headed west towards Luang Prabang, but were cut off by VP and his troops; the enemy was forced to retreat to other areas already under their control. General Navarre, the French Commander in Chief, then took immediate action to draw up plans to eliminate the Viet Minh in Laos, because he considered it essential not to allow the Communists to get a foothold in Laos.

In October 1953 French Captain Jean Sassi, an experienced combat veteran, returned to Laos, where he was assigned to the French Special Forces *Groupe de Commandos Mixtes Aéroportés* (GCMA). His mission was to train and equip the Hmong to fight the Viet Minh. Upon his arrival, he met then-Second Lieutenant Vang Pao, who was already serving with the French. Soon after Sassi's arrival, he and VP began conducting missions together, and the Captain was impressed with the Lieutenant's prowess and skills.

By early 1954, the French were hopelessly surrounded by the Viet Minh at Dien Bien Phu, and were in a fight for their lives. Captain Sassi understood the gravity of the situation, and developed a plan to use VP and his Hmong troops to break the siege at Dien Bien Phu. Called "Operation D," the mission would require the Hmong to get as close as possible to Dien Bien Phu, whereupon VP would harass the Communists with small guerrilla actions, causing the enemy to lose focus and become engaged with the Hmong rather than the French. Sassi calculated that while the Hmong kept the Viet Minh off balance, French forces inside Dien Bien Phu would be able to escape and regroup with Vang Pao's men. Then the combined Hmong and French force would keep the Communist rear elements tied down until much larger French forces could arrive, and help repel the Viet Minh from the valley at Dien Bien Phu.

In mid-April 1954, all elements of the plan were approved, and it was time for VP, his men, and Captain Sassi to put Operation D into action. The operational elements moved out shortly thereafter, marching toward Dien Bien Phu. Meanwhile, the French hoped that the United States would launch their B-29 bombers from the Philippines and put Operation Vulture into action during the last week of April 1953. Sadly for them, that did not happen; but VP, Sassi, and the Hmong kept marching. On May 7, 1954, the troops of Operation D were still some distance away from Dien Bien Phu and were exhausted, but they continued on—until May 8, when, as they were nearing their objective, a radio message was received announcing the decisive French defeat in the valley at Dien Bien Phu.

Operation D was abruptly cancelled, and the group was issued new orders: to assist any French survivors who had been able to escape the Hell on Earth that had been Dien Bien Phu. Captain Sassi soon received new orders directing him elsewhere, and so left VP in charge to continue the process of rounding up and assisting the French escapees. During the next week, the Hmong rescued over 200 French survivors and guided them to safety. In the end, the French tried to regroup in Laos to fight another day, but as history records, it was not to be.

VP, on the other hand, emerged from the mission with valuable experience and solid leadership skills. The heroism of Vang Pao and his Hmong troops did not go unnoticed by the United States; soon, they sought his assistance as they, too, became interested in Laos. That year, 1954, became a transitional period as the French began to withdraw from Southeast Asia, and the United States began to formulate plans to establish a presence in Laos and South Vietnam. In December, VP was promoted to Captain, and placed in charge of the Hmong guerrillas of Xieng Khouang Province.

In 1958, VP was selected to attend a battalion commander's course at Chinaimo Air Base near Vientiane, and then traveled to the Philippines for counterinsurgency training. During the course of all of this training and moving around, VP was promoted to Major, and received an appointment as Director of the NCO school scheduled to open at Khang Khay. The NCO school closed not long after, however, and VP was transferred to the Plain of Jars to command a mixed Hmong and lowland Lao unit of the Royal Lao Army (RLA). The lowland Lao and the Hmong didn't get along, due to differing ethnic and cultural differences, so VP offered his support to Phoumi Nosavan, a popular RLA general. VP threw his support behind Phoumi, and stood by him when Phoumi formed his countercoup force in Savannakhet in 1960. Phoumi reciprocated in December 1960 by promoting VP to Lieutenant Colonel.

This thumbnail sketch of Vang Pao's early life brings us to the early 1960s, when the United States began to establish a serious presence in Laos to pick up where the departing French had left off. By this time, the French had left Laos and were embroiled in another conflict in Algiers. But VP had distinguished himself by his actions and initiative, and would go on to make significant contributions to his country in the Secret War. As succeeding chapters unfold, we will continue to observe this rising star on Laos' political and military stage.

Meanwhile, much was recorded about the French experience in Vietnam, and this information was made available to the U.S. military officers for study. In the succeeding chapters of this book, you'll find out whether or not the United States read and understood the information provided to them about France's debacle in Southeast Asia.

Chapter 3

The U.S. Moves In

To set the stage for the pages that follow, it's important to keep certain facts in mind. The French, defeated in Southeast Asia, were on their way out. The Geneva Accords of 1954 called for the immediate departure of all foreign troops from Laos, including the Viet Minh, although the accords did allow a small contingent of French military to remain in Laos temporarily. The Accords also allowed the Pathet Lao to regroup in the provinces of Sam Neua and Phong Saly for four months. After that grace period, the Pathet Lao were required to integrate into the Royal Lao Government (RLG). The newly appointed International Control Commission (ICC) was to make sure everyone played by the rules.

Additionally, Lao Military Regions were established to improve the military's span of control. Initially, the country was divided into four military regions. Military Region One (MR 1) covered northwestern Laos, bordering on Burma and China. MR 2 included northeastern Laos, and MR 3 consisted of central Laos, or the Panhandle as it was called. MR 4 covered southern Laos and the areas adjacent to southern Thailand and northern Cambodia. Later, MR 5 was established, including Vientiane, and bordered Regions 1 and 2.

As outlined in the introduction, Laos was still an underdeveloped country, lacking both a strong government and a strong military. Public officials were corrupt, and social status meant everything. Three princes ran the country: Souvanna Phouma, Soupannavong, and Boun Oum. Of the three, only Souvanna was trying to keep the country together.

Souphannavong was the

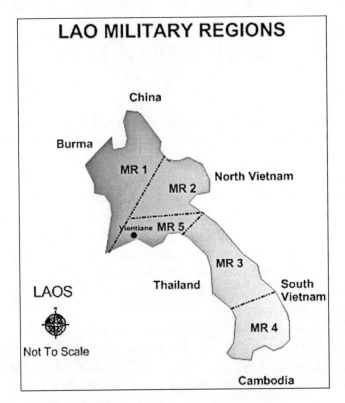

Figure 6. Lao Military Regions
(Drawing from the author's collection)

symbolic leader of the Pathet Lao. With the assistance of the Viet Minh (later renamed, the North Vietnamese Army (NVA)), the Pathet Lao planned to bring Communism to the entire country of Laos.

By this time, Vang Pao was a rising star who was dead-set against the country falling to the Communists. The United States backed VP, and was providing funding to Laos to resist the Pathet Lao. Kong Le, a neutralist and RLA Captain, had his own beliefs, which fell somewhere between those of Vang Pao and the Pathet Lao. There was also the Royal Lao Army (RLA) and the Royal Lao Air Force (RLAF), who carefully picked and chose their fights.

The United States became involved with the evolving situation in Laos early on, officially recognizing the kingdom as an independent state within the French Union in February 1950. To support the resistance against the Communists, America signed a Mutual Defense Assistance agreement with France, Cambodia, Laos and Vietnam in December 1950. Under the agreement, the U.S. increased military aid above what it was already providing through France. The agreement also expressly prohibited direct contact with the Military Assistance Advisory Group (MAAG) that the U.S. government wanted to establish in Laos.

Later, in September 1953, the United States agreed to underwrite all the funding for a French plan (Operation Lea) to directly confront the Viet Minh and reduce their numbers in Laos, to the point where local Lao troops could suppress any residual guerrilla action. As directed by the Geneva Accords, the Pathet Lao did withdraw to the Northern provinces of Phong Saly and Sam Neua. They and the RLG were to jointly administer the two provinces until a political solution could be agreed upon. Also under the Accords, Laos would keep its neutral status, and would not enter into any military alliance or seek foreign military aid except in preserving territorial defenses. The Accords did not, however, affect preexisting U.S. military and economic agreements with the RLG.

As mentioned earlier, the United States had refused to sign the agreements in Geneva, but did agree to recognize the Accords if everyone else did. Not having any faith in promises made by the North Vietnamese, however, Secretary of State John Foster Dulles began laying the groundwork for a collective defense treaty for Laos. Shortly thereafter, in September 1954, representatives from Pakistan, Thailand, the Philippines, France, Australia, New Zealand, Great Britain and the United States met in Manila and formed the Southeast Asia Treaty Organization (SEATO). One of the provisions of the alliance was that any attack on Laos would be considered an attack against all the other members of SEATO. During all this activity in Geneva and Manila, the tiny kingdom of Laos was neither consulted nor allowed to attend any of the meetings—but suddenly, they were theoretically under SEATO's protection.

After the Geneva Accords were signed, France began to reduce the number of military troops in Laos. These reductions quickly left a void in leadership in the Lao armed forces. Heretofore, France had not considered the Lao to be capable leaders, so there were very few high-ranking Lao military officers. Since the French were now incapable of providing that leadership, civilians of status and wealth (though not necessarily military competence) quickly filled the void.

With France drawing down its military presence in Laos, the United States could have helped fill the leadership void, if it had been allowed to establish an official MAAG; but again, the Geneva Accords prohibited such a move so long as France was chartered to provide that leadership. Understandably, the U.S. Department of Defense was reluctant to introduce military hardware that it could not manage. Nevertheless, the State Department wanted to build up the Lao armed forces to a level of approximately 20,000 men. That desire was fueled by the expectation that the new RLA could be a primary force for nation-building, and would act as a deterrent to any efforts made by Russia and China to introduce Communism.

In January 1955, the Eisenhower administration provided aid to the tune of $34,000,000 dollars for the modernization of the Lao military, with the U.S. Operations Mission (USOM) administering the activities. Meanwhile, the NVA had not withdrawn its troops from Laos as promised; they had merely assumed advisory and technical roles or donned Pathet Lao uniforms. Furthermore, a Pathet Lao training center and an officer candidate school were established at Son Tay, North Vietnam.

The Pathet Lao had its roots in, and stemmed from, the Indochinese Communist Party founded by Ho Chi Minh in 1930. At its inception, the ICP was entirely Vietnamese, but soon spread throughout French Indochina, establishing a small "Lao Section" in 1936. In the mid-1940s, a campaign to recruit Lao members began; and in 1946 or 1947, Kaysone Phomvihan, a law student at the University of Hanoi, was recruited, along with Nouhak Phoumsavan, a committee member of the Communist Party of Laos. The organization under the name "Pathet Lao" first appeared in 1950, when it was adopted by Lao forces under Prince Souphanouvong, the so-called "Red Prince." Souphanouvong joined the Viet Minh's revolt against the French authorities about the same time, and became the figurehead for the Pathet Lao.

The Communists soon began to make incursions into central Laos with the support of the Viet Minh, and a civil war erupted. The Pathet Lao quickly occupied large sections of the country. When the Geneva Accords required the withdrawal of foreign troops from Laos in 1954, one side-effect was that it allowed the Pathet Lao to establish itself as a regime in Laos' Northern provinces. From that time on, Sam Neua was the base of operations for the Pathet Lao, and they later held POWs there during the Vietnam War.

In December 1955, a semi-covert group known as the Program Evaluations Office (PEO) was set up as a section of USOM. The PEO was a disguise for the military mission in Vientiane, in order to conform to the rules laid out in Geneva in 1954. Retired Brigadier General Rothwell H. Brown, who reported to the U.S. Ambassador in Vientiane, first managed the office. Brown was a member of the mission's Country Team, which consisted of the U.S. Ambassador to Laos, his deputy, the CIA station chief, the PEO, the United States Agency for International Development (USAID), and various other U.S. personnel as needed.

Brigadier General John Heintges, a U.S. Army Special Forces officer with a distinguished military background, later replaced General Brown. His name mysteriously disappeared from the active military roles at about this time. U.S. military personnel in the PEO were referred to as "technicians" and everyone wore civilian clothing; but the actual purpose of the PEO was to form, train, and support a competent army completely staffed and led by Lao personnel. In order to maintain the appearance of adherence to the Geneva Accords (if only by letter, rather than spirit), a dozen or so retired and reserve U.S. military personnel in civilian status initially staffed the PEO, on a rotating basis for short periods of time. But with the constant turnover in personnel, it soon became necessary to staff the office with active duty military personnel disguised as civilian employees.

At this point, it would serve us well to define specific roles as pertained to the U.S. personnel serving in Laos. The U.S. Ambassador was the America's official representative; he was the man in charge. The CIA was responsible for overseeing the covert operations or "Secret War" in Laos as it later became known. They used Hmong guerrillas, led by rising stars like Vang Pao, to fight the NVA. Their budget and method of operation was completely controlled by the "Agency," ostensibly with oversight by the Ambassador. The Military Assistance Program (MAP) was managed by the U.S. Department of Defense, and executed by the Defense Attaché's Office (DAO), utilizing the PEO, and the many U.S. military personnel (technicians).

They also were accountable to the Ambassador. Their mission was to train and equip the RLA and RLAF.

From 1959 to 1961, the PEO was augmented by United States Army Special Forces (Green Berets), led by the legendary Colonel Arthur (Bull) Simons, who provided training and advice in counter-insurgency tactics. This effort was initially known as "Operation Hotfoot" and later as "White Star."

Between 1955 and 1958, over $200 million dollars in U.S. aid had been funneled to the kingdom of Laos—and the sudden influx of currency resulted in widespread corruption within the Lao government. Meanwhile, Prince Souphanouvong had organized the Pathet Lao into a new political party called the Neo Lao Hak Xat, or the Laotian Patriotic Front. Souphanouvong began campaigning under the banner of national unity and peace, placing emphasis on rooting out corruption.

With Vientiane's newfound wealth, U.S. Ambassador J. Graham Parsons was concerned that the rampant corruption might bolster Souphanouvong's support in the neglected Laotian backcountry. To shore up public opinion of the Lao government, Parsons came up with an economic aid program he called "Booster Shot." Under the program, nearly a hundred civic action projects were initiated, including well drilling, road repair, irrigation, construction of schools, the repair of government and religious buildings, and the improvement and resurfacing of airfields. The program also called for distribution of medical supplies, food and construction equipment to many small rural villages.

With most areas being inaccessible by roads, because they didn't exist, a method for airdrops would have to be instituted to accomplish Booster Shot. It was hoped that the RLAF could assist in the distribution of the supplies, but it was ill-equipped and ill-trained to perform the role. To satisfy the need for air support, Air Laos, a civilian contractor, was hired to deliver the supplies using their Douglas DC-3 transport aircraft. To facilitate the distribution of supplies, the U.S. and France set about improving four airfields: one in Savannakhet, one on the Plain of Jars, another at Pakse, and finally one at Vientiane.

In 1956, the United States proposed new aircraft and training for the RLAF. After much discussion, it was decided that Laos would get 30 DC-3 transports and four LT-6 armed reconnaissance aircraft.

But saying that was one thing, of course, and actually accomplishing it was another; and so by 1958, the necessary aircraft and trained RLAF pilots were still unavailable. There were also supplies sitting in warehouses that had not been delivered under Booster Shot, because Air Laos could only do so much. To fill the void, the embassy in Vientiane again turned to the U.S. Air Force (USAF).

To assist in the airdrops of food, medicine and supplies, the U.S. airbase at Ashiya, Japan was tapped to do the job, using their C-119 "Flying Boxcars" and C-130 "Hercules" transport aircraft. It was anticipated that the initial operation would take about five days, and to save fuel, the aircraft would stage out of Bangkok, Thailand. The aircraft were later moved to Bangkok, and by March 31, 1958, the mission had been completed. Having done what they were asked to do, the USAF packed and was ready to go back to Japan when Ambassador Parsons asked for and received permission from Washington to levy additional requirements on the aviators, extending the scope of Booster Shot.

The second phase of Booster Shot did not go as well as the first, however, due to lack of infrastructure and the fact that there were too many fingers in the proverbial pie. So the United States turned to Civil Air Transport (CAT).[11] CAT had been founded in China in 1946, and was an offshoot of General Claire L. Chennault's famed Flying Tigers. It had also been licensed as a CIA proprietary company called the Pacific Corporation. CAT had already been flying in Southeast Asia for quite some time, and was the best source for airdrops. The pilots of CAT were composed mostly of former U.S. military pilots who thirsted for adventure and money. They would literally go anywhere and do anything.

But, flying in Laos was extremely hazardous at best, given the weather and terrain. The thick cumulus layer inhibited accurate map reading, the sole means of navigation. Another factor was the haze of smoke that resulted from the slash-and-burn method of farming. In some cases, the haze made it difficult to see and navigate up to the 10,000-foot level. Most of Laos was also very mountainous and rugged, with limestone peaks rising to almost 10,000 feet (though the norm was about 7,000 feet). Nestled among these peaks were small valleys where the natives lived—and where the airdrops had to be made. Meanwhile, all the supplies under the second phase of Booster Shot were delivered, and the United States realized that effective air delivery would be a continuing requirement in the future.

By July 1, 1958, U.S. aid to Laos was suspended pending institution of new monetary reforms. Corruption was still rampant, and confidence in the government under Souvanna Phouma's leadership had been eroding. Behind the scenes, Major General Ouane Rathikone had been fostering dissension. Finally, on August 18, 1958, Phoui Sananikone, a pro-Western Lao diplomat, formed a new government, forcing Souvanna to resign. With a new fragile government in place, U.S. aid was soon flowing again as Phoui developed closer ties with the United States and Thailand, resulting in an increase of Western economic and military aid. As Prime Minister, Phoui believed in keeping Laos neutral, but broke with Souvanna's policy of isolation, reaching out to Saigon and Taipei to establish consular relations. Likewise, he shunned Hanoi and Peking, and let it be known that he would not hesitate to use force against the Pathet Lao and NVA.

Meanwhile, there had been little progress in setting up a viable military in Laos, even with establishment of the PEO and U.S. aid totaling over $100,000,000. The French had not been able to help either, because their war in Algeria had drained all their military resources. To shore up the Lao military, the PEO was expanded in the years 1957-1959 in what became known as the Heintges Plan. General Heintges also proposed reorganizing the PEO by staffing it with active-duty military and using them for field training of the Lao Armed Forces (FAL). The training was to be a joint US-French effort with special teams assigned to each RLA battalion. Of course, the U.S. advisors would be Green Berets, under Operation White Star.[12]

While Laos grappled with its problems, events were taking place in Vietnam that would ultimately intertwine the two countries in a way that would shape the future of Southeast Asia. Ho Chi Minh had attempted to discuss unification, but leaders in South Vietnam would have nothing to do with his overtures. NVA cadres in the south were subsequently notified that an all-out guerrilla war against the government of South Vietnam was imminent. To exercise this plan, Ho and General Giap would need a method of resupply for their forces in South Vietnam. To accomplish that, the series of footpaths and trails running from North Vietnam through Laos and into South Vietnam would have to be improved and expanded. This transportation system would later become known as the Ho Chi

Minh Trail. Of course, it would be necessary to send many thousands of NVA troops to Laos to facilitate the activity on the Trail.

At about this same time, Phoui Sananikone began talking tough in Laos, and declared that he was willing to use the RLA to clean out the Pathet Lao. To that end, he announced that his troops would be patrolling areas bordering North Vietnam. When the news of Phoui's intentions reached General Giap and Ho Chi Minh, they realized that Laos would have to be dealt with militarily in order for transport activity on the Trail to proceed without being impeded. In other words, Phoui had essentially sealed his country's fate.

Meanwhile, the rhetoric concerning the integration of the Pathet Lao into the RLA continued into May 1959. Agreements could not be reached, however, because the Pathet Lao wanted too many of its officers placed in important positions. Discussions were at an impasse. Finally, Vientiane issued an ultimatum: either accept the government's terms within twenty-four hours, surrender, or resign. Some Pathet Lao personnel agreed to the demands, but others did not. Finally, on May 19, approximately 700 Pathet Lao personnel and their families stole away at night and began a trek to a new area inside North Vietnam, about 40 miles north of Sam Neua, The troops were listed as deserters, and their leader, Prince Souphanouvong, was placed under house arrest.

Upon arrival in North Vietnam, the deserters were immediately retained by the NVA to conduct cross-border raids. By July, they had added several hundred new Pathet Lao troops to their number. Soon, patrols from this group were conducting hit-and-run attacks on isolated Lao government outposts in Phong Saly and Sam Neua provinces. These attacks became the impetus for the U.S. State Department to announce, on July 23, that an emergency training program would be initiated to increase Phoui's troop strength to approximately 30,000. But even with the reinforcements, the situation in Phong Saly and Sam Neua provinces continued to deteriorate. Shortly thereafter, Pathet Lao troops surrounded the local RLA garrison, but the government in Vientiane refused to surrender this hard-won turf, and made the decision to hold the Northern provinces at all costs.

Meanwhile, the U.S. Embassy in Vientiane worked hard to provision the desperate RLA garrison. CAT and Air Laos were contracted to make several airdrops a week to the troops, and the RLAF used the few DC-3, or "C-47" (military version) aircraft it owned to also make airdrops to the RLA. The United States quickly provided five more C-47s and several L-20 Beavers, light observation aircraft to help the beleaguered Lao garrisons in northern Laos. And, as the situation in the north remained very tense, the U.S. contemplated bringing in Joint Task Force 116 from Thailand.[13]

On September 8, 1959, the USAF Chief of Staff General Thomas D. White asked the Joint Chiefs of Staff (JCS) for approval to send USAF B-47 jet bombers from the Strategic Air Command (SAC) to Clark Air Base in the Philippines. General White wanted to be able to use the bombers to cripple Communist insurgents and their supply lines by bombing selected targets in North Vietnam, using either conventional or nuclear weapons. The JCS did not approve the request, and White's plan was shelved, probably because it mentioned nuclear weapons. Some Pentagon officials, however, considered it a viable option, believing the Communists might think twice if they knew that the United States could exercise the nuclear option.

Meanwhile, aid continued to flow to Laos, and some political leaders began to question what the long-term goals of the United States really were in Laos. President Eisenhower had made it clear that Laos would not be allowed to become another domino to fall to Communism. But the aid to Laos thus far had mostly been for military use; for every five dollars of aid received, four dollars went to the military, and only one went to economic aid. Some questioned whether more aid for social and economic programs would have helped to win hearts and minds more quickly. The logic behind that belief was that if the people had been taken care of, their loyalty to the RLG and the U.S. would have been stronger, thereby making them less likely to be duped by the Communists. To a degree, that had been the purpose of Operation Booster Shot.

On December 30, Phoui resigned as Prime Minister as a result of a rift with other Lao government officials. Immediately thereafter, a CIA asset by the name of Phoumi Nosavan staged a coup d'état. Phoumi was one of the bright young men the CIA had picked to organize the right wing in Laos, and he had been the first Lao officer to attend the French War College. He had completed that program earlier in 1959, and had returned to Laos as the commander of the newly created MR 5. Shortly thereafter, he was promoted to Brigadier General.

Phoumi's coup was short-lived and unsuccessful, and he quieted down when he was appointed as Defense Minister. However, five months later, a rigged Lao national election—organized by the CIA, and the Department of Defense, through its PEO representative— legitimized Phoumi Nosavan as Prime Minister, because they viewed him as a strong anti-Communist proponent. The Agency's plan, however, proved to be a disaster when Phoumi refused to go to the capital for his swearing in. He did, however, continue as Minister of Defense, and assumed duties as Assembly Chairman. Later, with the encouragement of the U.S., the King appointed Tiao Somsanith, Souvanna Phouma's nephew, as interim Prime Minister.

In his role as Defense Minister, Phoumi announced that he would place Prince Souphanouvong on trial based upon his activities against the RLA in the Northern provinces. Meanwhile, Souphanouvong was being held in a prison in northern Laos. He found out about Phoumi's plan, and, with inside help, slipped away on the night of May 23, 1960, and walked to Sam Neua, where the Pathet Lao received him warmly. Meanwhile, the military training provided by the PEO continued, but by the fall of 1959 training had been suspended, because the White Star soldiers were needed to supervise the elections.

Coupled with that was the fact that the Lao officers were not firmly behind the training. In fact, they did not participate for the most part, believing that their commissions in and of themselves qualified them to lead. The non-commissioned officers and other enlisted men continued to train, but this was of little value because the officers above them remained incapable. A satisfactory logistics infrastructure was also lacking. The RLA oversaw the logistics process, but requisitioned items seldom made it through the pipeline. Once U.S. military aid left PEO channels, it was beyond U.S. control, and accountability was impossible.

As training lagged, Phoumi requested that the training schedule be extended for a year. But Washington was only willing to extend the program until June 30, 1961, believing that the troops should be reasonably well trained by that date. The French also complained about the progress of the training, and offered to take over the process themselves. Phoumi was against the French proposal and wanted them out of the country as soon as possible. Certain Lao officers did not share Phoumi's feelings, and even preferred the French to the Green Berets. Of course, the problem there was that many of the White Star instructors were enlisted men, and some of the Lao officers considered them inferior for that reason.

These same officers also believed that the PEO presence was a violation of the Geneva Accords, and could be used as provocation by Laos's Communist neighbors.

Meanwhile, in June 1960, a cantankerous retired farmer from Indiana by the name of Edgar (Pop) Buell quietly entered Laos as a volunteer employee of the International Volunteer Service (IVS).[14] Little notice was given to the scruffy little middle-aged man as he deplaned at Wattay Airport in Vientiane. How could anyone guess, or even fathom, that the man would soon become the third most powerful man in Laos, behind the king and the up-and-coming Vang Pao?

At this particular juncture, the United States needed hard intelligence information about activities in northeastern Laos. To this end, they recruited indigenous personnel to act as eyes and ears for U.S. intelligence officials. The assets would be tasked to obtain information about NVA and Pathet Lao troop movements in the area or sector to which they were assigned. They would watch and listen every day, and report regularly. In exchange for the information, the assets would be paid in local currency or goods. This type of raw intelligence information was necessary, but was not without its drawbacks. In some cases the information could not be verified through other assets, and the sources were not always as aggressive or truthful as the United States would have liked.

Meanwhile, on August 8, 1960, Prime Minister Tiao Somsanith and most of his cabinet traveled to Luang Prabang to discuss funeral arrangements for the late King Sisavang Vong, who had passed away some time earlier and had been replaced by Savang Vatthana. Later that same evening Captain Kong Le, the Neutralist leader, took advantage of the power vacuum in Vientiane, and led several hundred of his men of the 2nd Paratroop Battalion in a near-bloodless coup, based on what they perceived as ill-treatment by Phoumi. First, they occupied Wattay Airport. Then they captured five RLAF C-47 aircraft. They also took control of the local radio station and several key government buildings. By morning, Kong Le controlled the entire city of Vientiane. Broadcasting from the radio station, Kong Le claimed that his purpose for the coup was to end the fighting, to bring about a truly neutral government, and to eliminate all foreign intervention in Laos. He also announced that a government under Souvanna

Figure 7. Kong Le and Vang Pao
(Photo from the Public Domain)

Phouma would end foreign interference in Laos, and he asked for the nomination of Souvanna Phouma as Prime Minister.

Kong Le instantly became a national hero in a country that had very few, and the already fragmented population became even more of a collective pawn in the international arena. Both Hanoi and the Pathet Lao tentatively congratulated Kong Le, and the Soviet Union and China quickly followed suit. The U.S. Embassy was still behind Souvanna Phouma and approved of him becoming the Prime Minister. Of course, the CIA and the PEO were still solidly behind General Phoumi, who announced over a loudspeaker that he was, in fact, also a "Neutralist." He pledged to deny all foreign interference in his country, eliminate corruption in the government, and commit Laos to a path of neutrality. This meant reinstating Prince Souvanna Phouma as a Neutralist prime minister, of course. By this time, confusion reigned supreme in Laos, even for those observers who knew the cast of characters and understood the volatile politics of the country. Meanwhile, Kong Le ignored the political waves that his coup had generated, while the U.S. Embassy began to quickly evacuate American civilians from posts around a country that would soon become very insecure.

The day the coup took place, both the U.S. Army Attaché and the Chief of the PEO sent urgent telegrams to the Secretary of State in Washington, D.C. In his telegram, the Army Attaché reported:

Situation in Vientiane now outwardly calm. Movement in town around 0800 hours local slightly hampered by guards. Movement to a few areas is not permitted, and some roadblocks are holding up traffic. Clearly, entry to town is also permitted, but exits are not. Guards are stationed many local facilities, including post offices, telephones, telegraphs, the Defense Ministry, FAL headquarters, some homes, General Ouane, Phoumi and some other officials. All army camps are under guard with troops inside apparently accepting situation. Soldiers are patrolling around town in jeeps and armored cars. The paratroops control the airport, and no flights are scheduled.

The PEO chief summed up the activity this way:

(1) *Starting about 1945 hours, Zulu time, 8 August, sporadic firing broke out in Vientiane. Nothing known of casualties.*

(2) *Contacted Colonel Kouprasith Abhay, Commander, Military Region 5 at his quarters personally. He knew nothing as his phone was out of order. He departed 2025 hours, Zulu time, for his headquarters at Chinaimo with Assistant ARMA (Army Attaché) following in a separate vehicle. Upon arrival entrance Chinaimo, Kouprasith was stopped by troops and obviously arrested. Kouprasith stated he did not know what was going on but that 2nd Parachute Battalion commanded by Captain Kong Le had seized town and Kouprasith was not allowed to leave outpost but got guards permission for Assistant ARMA to leave. (3) Indications are troops are in control of Vientiane, but lightly. King and cabinet members went to Luang Prabang, August 8, and doubt cabinet has returned to Vientiane. (4) Too early to make any assessment of Laos political factions involved, in any. Captain Kong Le is related by marriage to General Ouane.[15]*

At this point, we should mention that coups in Laos were not extraordinary events. In fact, they took place often. This particular coup was practically bloodless, and it was over within a week. To the average person on the street, there was some minor disruption to normal day-to-day activities, but for the most part, the nonviolent Lao went about their activities as they would have on any other day. In neighboring Thailand, coups were also commonplace, and are still taking place in the twenty-first century.

On August 13, the Lao National Assembly expressed "No Confidence" in Tiao Somsanith's cabinet, and it resigned *en masse*. Tiao stayed put in Luang Prabang, as he was afraid to return to Vientiane. Three days later, Souvanna Phouma was selected as Prime Minister. He pledged to unite the country, seek neutrality, respect treaties, and accept aid from any country. He proposed a new cabinet wherein he would keep the Defense and Foreign Affairs portfolios. His Interior Minister would be Quinim Pholsena, a known leftist, and the famous Hmong Touby Lyfoung would be the Minister of Justice and Religious Affairs.

This left Phoumi without an appointment in the new government, and so he refused to recognize it. He flew first to Bangkok and then to Savannakhet, where he formed a countercoup revolutionary committee. This action essentially divided the military and created new problems for the PEO. In order to support both factions, General Heintges stayed in Vientiane with most of the PEO people, and U.S. Army Colonel Alfred R. Brownfield, Jr., went to Savannakhet to set up a second PEO office to support Phoumi. In this manner, the PEO could support the rebel group as well as the established government in Vientiane. Of course, this put the U.S. Embassy at odds with Ambassador Winthrop G. Brown, who supported Souvanna. And to make things even more interesting, the PEO and CIA still supported Phoumi.

On August 16, Souvanna's government received Western recognition. That was apparently all that Kong Le had been waiting for: the next day, he announced that his coup was over, and stepped down from his provisional post as the President of the Council of Ministers. That same day, another element was added to the mix when the Pathet Lao ordered forces loyal to Souphanouvong to avoid contact with Souvanna and Kong Le's troops on the Plain of Jars, and to attack Phoumi's troops whenever they could. Hearing the news, the Pathet Lao's Second Battalion, which had fled a year earlier to North Vietnam, came out of hiding and attacked the garrison at Sam

Neua. The PEO contacted the embassy with the news of the attack, and Ambassador Brown authorized an airlift of needed supplies to the LAO government forces there. Air America (formerly CAT) utilized two C-46 cargo aircraft to transport ammunition, fuel and food to the pinned down government forces. The airlift had to be halted, however, on September 28, when the Pathet Lao overran the airstrip. After that, Air America only hauled supplies to the Plain of Jars and to Phoumi's outposts in the Savannakhet area.

By the following day, the RLA garrison was without supplies and cut-off from the outside world. In desperation, they walked away from the garrison and retreated southward. Also on September 29, a combined force of Kong Le's men and Pathet Lao troops crossed the Kading River and moved toward the city of Thakhek (pronounced "Ta-Ket"), Laos. There, Phoumi's troops fought to hold the town, and eventually forced the attackers back across the river. Shortly thereafter, King Vatthana stopped the battle, and decreed that troops could not cross the Kading River to engage Phoumi.

Vang Pao, then an RLA Major, believed that open warfare involving all three factions was imminent, and that northern Laos would be the flashpoint. This was also the area in which most of the Hmong lived. VP also believed the RLA would collapse, and the entire area would fall to the Communists. He then drew up a plan to unify, and save, many of the Hmong tribes in northern Laos. VP's plan suggested that when the critical time came, the Hmong would be formed into a guerrilla army that would encircle the Plain of Jars. Then, when it appeared the enemy was about to seize the Plain, approximately 70,000 Hmong would abandon their villages and move by foot to seven previously named mountains. The Hmong would then cut off any further enemy advance, and harass the enemy until they were driven back to the borders of North Vietnam.

During this time, Ambassador Brown was trying desperately to prevent the fighting in Laos from becoming an all-out civil war. Meanwhile, Washington was losing patience with Souvanna's wavering position. On October 12, Washington sent two State Department representatives to try to talk some sense into Souvanna, but the mission failed and only made matters worse. Later that month, the first Soviet ambassador to Laos presented his credentials, and offered aid to Laos. Souvanna, who had already gone on record as stating he would accept aid from anyone, gladly accepted the offer of aid from the Soviet Union. But in the interim, the NVA took advantage of the constant political bickering in Laos by providing military support to the Pathet Lao in Sam Neua and Xieng Khouang provinces.

Later, on November 9, in an attempt to appease the Pathet Lao, Souvanna announced a new cabinet that included two Pathet Lao representatives, and he appointed the leftist, Quinim Pholsena, as chief negotiator with the Pathet Lao. Pholsena was a former Lao government official of Chinese decent who favored contact with the Communists. But this move by Souvanna was the last straw for the Americans, and they shifted their support to Phoumi.

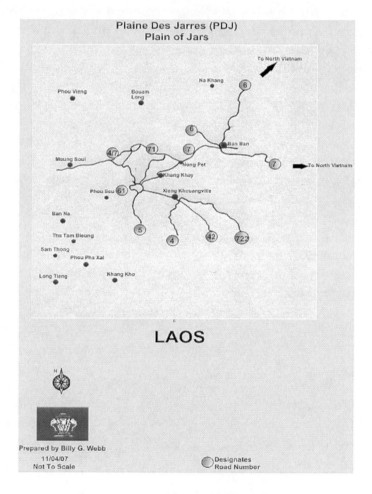

Figure 8. Roads and Towns on the PDJ
(Drawing prepared by author)

On December 4, the Soviets began airlifting food, fuel and military items from Hanoi to Vientiane, using Russian IL-14 Ilyushin aircraft. Their intention, of course, was to make sure Kong Le had all the arms and ammunition he needed, while giving the appearance of providing economic aid to all the people of Laos. On December 8, RLA Colonel Kouprasith Abhay, the MR 5 commander, seized Vientiane in yet another coup, forcing Kong Le's troops to retreat to Wattay Airport. Abhay claimed allegiance to Souvanna, and insisted on arresting Pathet Lao officials in the city. Souvanna stopped Abhay from carrying out his plan, and in anger, the colonel retreated to Chinaimo barracks outside the city. Kong Le's troops then returned to Vientiane. Not to be outdone, Colonel Abhay contacted Phoumi and pledged support in exchange for assistance in retaking Vientiane. Phoumi responded by sending about two hundred paratroopers to Chinaimo to support Abhay.

On December 9, Abhay and Phoumi's forces joined together and marched on Vientiane. Souvanna and his family quickly fled to safety in Cambodia, and the battle for the city began. Meanwhile, the leftist, anti-American Pholsena quietly left Vientiane onboard a Soviet transport bound for Hanoi. On the following day, Pholsena unilaterally reached an agreement with Hanoi to provide arms and supplies to Kong Le in exchange for the loyalty of the little paratroop captain. On December 11, Soviet transports arrived at Wattay carrying six 105mm artillery pieces and the NVA crews to man them. Sadly, it was the same equipment provided by the U.S. to the French at Dien Bien Phu. Apparently, the NVA had confiscated the guns after defeating the French in April, 1954.

Figure 9. Ilyushin IL-14 Crate
(Photo from the Public Domain)

Two days later, on December 13, the first shots were fired. For the next 76 hours, a battle was waged in the streets of Vientiane. Bullets and artillery rounds whizzed over the city and through the streets as the right-wing troops pressed in from the east. When the shooting stopped, over three hundred people had been killed and Kong Le had abandoned the airport, withdrawing with all his men and equipment to Moung Soui in northern Laos, on the northwestern edge of the Plain of Jars. There, at the town of Ban Ban, just northeast of the Plain, Pathet Lao forces rallied by Prince Souphanouvong eagerly awaited Kong Le's arrival in order to link up and seize as much territory as possible.

When Vientiane figured out Kong Le's apparent intentions of hunkering down at Moung Soui, they contacted the RLA Zone commander in the area. Vientiane directed the commander to litter Route 7 with fallen trees, in order to stop the troop advance. The commander dutifully carried out his orders. Shortly thereafter, Kong Le's forces approached the outskirts of the city. At about that same time, the Zone commander spotted literally hundreds of Neutralist paratroopers dropping into Moung Soui. Fearing for his safety, the commander marshaled his troops and fled into the surrounding hills. Meanwhile, Kong Le's troops walked into the city without opposition.

As Kong Le walked into Moung Soui, the Pathet Lao, stiffened by NVA soldiers, initiated an attack on the FAL at Nong Het. The defenders immediately radioed for reinforcements, but they didn't wait for help; instead, they began a hasty retreat southward. RLA Colonel Don Sasorith Sourith, the MR 2 commander, immediately drove to the Plain to provide leadership. Upon arrival, he met with nine PEO advisors from the Khang Khay detachment. The PEO contacted the U.S. embassy at Vientiane and requested arms, ammunition and fuel. In an hour or two, Air America C-46 transports began showing up with the equipment and supplies requested by the PEO.

As the FAL troops began to drag the equipment and supplies from the aircraft, another Air America pilot reported that a convoy of Kong Le's men was approaching. Hearing the report, the Lao defenders began disappearing, ultimately leaving only PEO advisors and Air America personnel at the airstrip. Having received word that Kong Le's men were on the northwestern edge of the Plain, newly promoted Lieutenant Colonel Vang Pao arrived at the airfield from his quarters on the southern part of the Plain. His troops, consisting mostly of lowland Lao rather than his native Hmong, fled with most of the other troops.

Working alone, Vang Pao loaded crates of explosives into his jeep and drove several kilometers north to the Nam Ngum River. There, he blew up the bridge spanning the river. With the bridge gone, Kong Le would not be able to bring heavy weapons across the river for at least a day. Having bought some valuable time, VP drove back to the airfield. He then found two 4.2-inch mortars and ammunition beside the runway. He aimed the mortar tubes to the northwest and dropped rounds down the tubes. Both misfired. Spotting some recently delivered pallets of ammunition, VP crossed the runway and quickly found fresh mortar shells. He then returned to the mortar tubes and loaded fresh rounds, firing both tubes. He watched as the rounds raced high into the sky and then rained down on the leading elements of Kong Le's advancing forces.

As conditions rapidly deteriorated on the Plain, the U.S. Embassy in Vientiane dispatched aircraft to evacuate the IVS volunteers, the PEO advisors, other Americans, and anyone else who supported the United States in Xieng Khouang Province. Among those was Pop Buell, his assistant Dick Bowman, and the U.S. Special Forces Green Berets assigned to the PEO detachment at Khang Khay. The long awaited civil war in Laos had finally erupted.

By this time, dusk was now fast approaching on the Plain of Jars, as Ron Sutphin, Air America pilot, returned to the airfield in his Helio Courier (a Short Take Off and Landing-STOL aircraft). By this time, the only friendlies left were VP, a few troops, and their families near the end of the runway. As the aircraft came to a halt near the waiting crowd, artillery rounds exploded nearby, showering the aircraft with dirt and shrapnel. Not wasting any time, VP jumped into the Helio with Sutphin and they quickly departed, flying to Xieng Khouangville, where Vang Pao got off the aircraft. Then Captain Sutphin took off again and nursed the damaged aircraft back to Wattay Airport in Vientiane. A short time later, one last Air America C-47 transport aircraft landed at Phongsavan to evacuate the last of the friendly forces. When the aircraft landed, several White Star personnel, a Frenchman, his Lao wife, their servants, various local residents, and an odd collection of farm animals and belongings emerged. When everybody and everything were finally aboard, the overloaded C-47 lumbered down the dirt runway, clawed its way into the night sky, and headed for Vientiane.

On December 31, 1960, military leaders in Washington, D.C. reported that enemy forces consisting of seven battalions were advancing rapidly on the Plain of Jars. It was also reported that NVA troops had attacked Nong Het and Ban Ban near the Plain, and that enemy troops, probably Pathet Lao, had retaken the city of Phong Saly in northeastern Laos. It was further believed the offensive might be the start of a consolidated and coordinated effort by the Pathet Lao guerrillas to reestablish control of their former strongholds of Sam Neua and Phong Saly.

With Laos now embroiled in a civil war, the United States again placed Joint Task Force (JTF-116) on alert for possible deployment to Thailand. Simultaneously, the need for accurate aerial reconnaissance of northern Laos was recognized. Unfortunately, there were no reconnaissance aircraft in Laos, so Saigon loaned a VC-47 converted transport, and its pilot, Lieutenant Colonel Butler B. Toland, to the embassy in Vientiane. Toland, who had diplomatic status in both countries and was already familiar with the terrain in Laos, flew the VC-47 to Vientiane.

The VC-47 was equipped with sophisticated K-17 and K-20 cameras, utilized on December 20 and 21 when Toland flew reconnaissance missions over northern Laos. The over-flights yielded valuable intelligence information, showing heavy enemy movement along the roads north of Vientiane and evidence of a large military presence. It was then realized that Russian involvement was much greater than first thought. Toland was also able to get high-resolution close-up pictures of the Russian aircraft. The photos of the Russian transports were later loaded onto an aircraft and taken to Washington, evaluated, and released to the media. The pictures were the first undisputable evidence of Soviet involvement in the Lao conflict. Later, the Distinguished Flying Cross was awarded to Toland for his bravery and success of that particular reconnaissance mission. But Toland wasn't done, and he went on to fly more missions in the closing days of 1960. On most occasions, the VC-47 would land with numerous bullet holes in its skin.

Meanwhile, on the other side of the world, President Eisenhower was briefed on the deteriorating situation in Laos. Also present for the briefing was Allen Dulles, Director of the CIA, and the Chairman of the Joint Chiefs of Staff, Army General Lyman Lemnitzer. After the briefing, the trio unveiled a tough response to the deteriorating situation in Laos. First, JTF-116, headquartered in Thailand, was to prepare for possible deployment to Laos if required. Second,

Figure 10. North American T-6 Texan
(Photo from the Public Domain)

USAF C-130 transport aircraft were approved to haul emergency supplies to Laos as required. And, third, detailed aerial surveillance was authorized using a variety of aircraft, including Air America C-46s, an RT-33 reconnaissance jet on loan from the Thais, and high-flying CIA U-2 reconnaissance aircraft stationed in the Philippines. Additionally, surplus U.S. T-6 "Texan" trainer aircraft were to be converted to light attack aircraft and provided to the RLAF in the event the Soviets tried to airlift supplies to the enemy.

Washington also realized that continued Soviet airlifts to Vientiane and the Plain of Jars would thwart Phoumi's ability to get Kong Le and the Pathet Lao under control. The introduction of the T-6 attack aircraft could help, but might not be the ultimate answer. An even more potent alternative was then discussed. To that end, several unmarked B-26 bombers were discreetly transferred to Takhli Air Base in Thailand. These bombers could carry bombs both in their internal bays and also mounted under the wings. Each aircraft also had several cannons installed in the nose. The bomber's cruising speed was close to 200 miles per hour, with a range of over one thousand miles, and it could carry about 10,000 pounds of bombs. In December, President Eisenhower authorized use of the B-26 in Laos. And, for good measure, an SC-47 photo reconnaissance aircraft was transferred to Vientiane.[16]

When Ambassador Winthrop Brown received the information regarding the T-6 aircraft, he dispatched telegrams to the Secretary of State on December 28 and December 30. Summarized below is essentially what Brown said in reference to the T-6 aircraft:

> *28 December, Brown to State: We concur with preparatory steps regarding training of pilots for T-6s, and preparing aircraft for transfer to Lao Armed Forces (FAL).*

> *30 December, Brown to State: I told Phoumi that in addition to diplomatic measures against Soviet airlift, we are prepared, if proper political basis were established, to supply him with T-6 armed aircraft, and arrange for pilot training in Thailand.*

On January 1, 1961, the Thai government offered to begin immediate training of four RLAF T-6 pilots. The Thais also offered ten of their own T-6 aircraft equipped with twin gun pods, rocket pods, and racks for loading iron bombs. On January 9, the first four fully-trained RLAF pilots flew the first four T-6 aircraft from Bangkok to Savannakhet Air Base in Laos, and then continued on to Wattay Airport in Vientiane to await their first mission.

The year 1961 literally began with a bang in northern Laos: Kong Le and his men shot their way into Phong Saly and Khang Khay, and took both towns with little opposition. As January 1 wore on, more Soviet transports came and went from airstrips around the Plain of Jars. Each aircraft contained artillery pieces, ammunition and fuel. Fortunately, few people had lost their lives thus far. After taking Khang Khay, Kong Le moved into the PEO compound, which had been vacated a day earlier by the U.S. Army advisors. Meanwhile, Colonel Sourith, MR 2 commander, was fast losing confidence in the FAL and its ability to hold onto northern Laos.

In an attempt to stop Kong Le, Vientiane dispatched several hundred paratroopers, who were dropped into Xieng Khouangville late in the evening on January 1. The paratroopers joined up with Sourith's troops for a combined push against Kong Le's Neutralists, but the government forces panicked when artillery fire rained down on them. The attacking troops quickly became separated and outgunned, so they joined hundreds of other FAL troops walking away from the battlefield in the direction of Vientiane. Meanwhile, the Pathet Lao defeated the RLA garrison at Nong Het, and then attacked and occupied Ban Ban.

On January 7, Prime Minister Boun Oum's government delivered a note to the Soviet embassy in Vientiane protesting the airlift. The Russians refused to accept the note, saying they only recognized Souvanna as the Prime Minister. Meanwhile, Phoumi continued satisfying his own needs, even though the country's defenses were falling apart, among other things promoting himself to major general.

Back in the United States, a new president was sworn in on January 20, 1961. His name was John Fitzgerald Kennedy (JFK). In the days leading up to the inauguration, President Kennedy was thoroughly briefed on the world situation. Cuba had become a Communist country, and there were the Soviet Union, China,

North Vietnam, North Korea, and East Berlin to deal with, all flying Communist flags. He was also concerned about Laos, South Vietnam and Cambodia. Kennedy had been briefed by Eisenhower on the "Domino Theory," and he understood the importance of not allowing the three Southeast Asia countries to join the other fallen dominoes. But Kennedy was not optimistic, based upon events taking place in Laos. He appeared to think that the best alternative for Vientiane would be neutrality.

When JFK took office, the prospect of war with Communist-led nations loomed large on the horizon. World events concerned Kennedy, and a speech made earlier in the month by Soviet leader Nikita Khrushchev especially troubled him. In his speech, Khrushchev endorsed the kind of warfare advocated by the North Vietnamese and Pathet Lao leaders. A part of Kennedy's concern was the Pathet Lao's bold attempt to seize complete control of Laos. He had also been warned by Eisenhower that Laos held the key to control of Southeast Asia. But, Kennedy was skeptical, based upon a recent study that revealed the kingdom was divided, with no strong Communist leadership. He concluded that the best the United States could hope for in Laos was neutrality: in other words, that the Communist and noncommunist factions would offset each other, politically and militarily.

Meanwhile, The North Vietnamese had their own plan to unite all of Vietnam under the complete control of the Communist regime in Hanoi, as led by Ho Chi Minh. As a part of the North Vietnamese plan, overland supply routes had been reestablished in 1959; these routes passed through Laos and reentered Vietnam in the south. This overland supply route had been named the Truong Son Road by the North Vietnamese. The Americans renamed it the Ho Chi Minh Trail. The established route consisted of many trails, footpaths and roads, and for the most part, the trails remained unimproved for many years. But that would soon change.

Figure 11. The Truong Son Road (Ho Chi Minh Trail)
(Photo from the Public Domain)

By 1961, Communist soldiers and supplies were already flowing down the Trail to South Vietnam. The United States Army's counterinsurgency arm, the Special Forces, had built defensive outposts along the troubled border with Laos to harass and disrupt the infiltration of men and supplies using the Ho Chi Minh Trail; and at about this same time, the USAF had increased the number of photographic reconnaissance flights over Laos.

Meanwhile, on January 7, 1961, four B-26 bombers arrived at Takhli Air Base in Thailand, manned by USAF crews. On January 11, four T-6 aircraft took off from Wattay Airport loaded with rockets and flew to Vang Vieng on their first mission to attack one of Kong Le's outposts. They struck again on January 15, posting their first two truck kills. But on January 17, the first T-6 was shot down while on an air combat mission. Another crashed on March 11; the Thais then delivered replacement T-6 aircraft to the RLAF.

To add fuel to the fire, the NVA established a 30-man liaison unit next to Kong Le's Neutralist headquarters in Khang Khay in early January 1961. This liaison unit was to act as advisors to Kong Le and stiffeners for Pathet Lao units in the area. On January 15, the entire 925th Independent Battalion of the NVA crossed the border from North Vietnam into Laos, with more than 50 mortar and machine gun specialists. On entering Laos, the NVA troops took off their uniforms, donned Pathet Lao uniforms, and took up positions with the Pathet Lao's 6th Battalion, along Route 13 near Vang Vieng. Not to be outdone, the Soviet Union quickly provided a total of eighteen transport aircraft to Souvanna in early January to haul war supplies on a daily basis. The aircraft were also used to drop supplies to Pathet Lao and NVA troops on the ground. While all this was taking place, Phoumi announced that he was forming five new battalions of FAL troops. Later, around the end of March, Phoumi announced that he had seven Regiments of the FAL strung out along Route 13 to interdict Pathet Lao and NVA troops heading towards Vientiane or Luang Prabang.

Meanwhile, morale of the RLAF pilots bottomed out when the PEO and some FAL officers criticized their abilities. It appeared on the surface that the criticism was warranted, given the poor showings by the Lao pilots. But the real problem was that PEO was staffed primarily by ground troops, not aviators. They did not understand that it took a great deal of training to turn a transport pilot into a combat strike pilot. And that was the crux of the problem: heretofore, the RLAF pilots had only flown the C-47 transport or smaller liaison aircraft. Only a few had flown the T-6, which really was a trainer, not a fighter. And of course, the T-6 was obsolete.[17]

On the American side, the situation in Laos was exacerbated by a feud that was slowly developing between the U.S. Ambassador to Laos, Winthrop Brown, and Admiral Harry D. Felt, Commander-In-Chief, Pacific (CINCPAC). Admiral Felt was vocal about using bombs and napalm against the Communists, while Ambassador Brown felt strongly that the use of bombs would be viewed as an escalation. Of course, President Kennedy had just taken office and had heard of the feud, but he didn't want to get in the middle of the fight. The President's belief was that a political solution was the right answer for Laos. Later, in his first press conference on January 25, 1961, President Kennedy offered a face-saving view, stating that he was firm on Laos keeping its independence, and that the tiny kingdom did not have to take sides in the Cold War.

During the month of January 1961, Thailand was called upon to provide aerial reconnaissance over Laos using their jet-powered RT-33 reconnaissance aircraft. At first there was hesitation on Thailand's part, for fear the Communists would retaliate; but the United States was determined and the Thais relented, supplying two RT-33s and "volunteer" pilots. Photo reconnaissance results then began to show there were many Communists trucks, ammunition dumps and armor in northern Laos. In fact, there was so much film to process that the photo laboratory in Thailand could not keep up with the workload. The USAF came to the assistance of the Thais by providing lab technicians, better photo processing equipment, and additional photo interpreters.

By this time, Brigadier General Andrew J. Boyle, U.S. Army, had replaced General Heintges as PEO Chief. After reviewing the photo reconnaissance results from the Vientiane-based SC-47 reconnaissance aircraft, Boyle became convinced that the Communist targets could be eliminated with air power. He proposed that the T-6 aircraft, flown by Thai volunteers and loaded with bombs and napalm, be used to take out the Communist targets. Ambassador Brown disagreed with the proposal, but dutifully forwarded the proposal on to the State Department. Back in Washington, the debate continued. Secretary of State Dean Rusk agreed with Ambassador Brown; the new Secretary of Defense, Robert McNamara, however, believed the T-6 aircraft should be used to attack any military targets, using whatever ordnance the military considered appropriate.

Based upon the escalating Communist activities in Laos, President Kennedy realized the need for a strategy meeting with his secretaries of the Department of Defense and the Department of State; it would also be an appropriate venue to discuss the feud between Admiral Felt and Ambassador Brown. In preparation for the meeting, the Joint Chiefs came up with five recommendations:

1. Relocate about a dozen B-26 light bombers to Thailand to be used for interdiction operations against the Communists.
2. Turn over about 16 H-34 helicopters to the CIA for transfer to Air America, along with four C-130s, three DC-4s, and one C-47.
3. Augment the Lao armed forces with four 105mm artillery weapons/crews from Thailand.

4. Increase the Hmong irregulars' strength by 1,000.
5. Increase the PEO office in strength by 100 men and officers.

On March 6, President Kennedy hosted the planned strategy meeting at the White House with representatives from the Department of State, Department of Defense, and the CIA. During the meeting, Kennedy approved sixteen measures to support the RLG. One of the measures would transfer 14 H-34 Sikorsky helicopters to Air America. The CIA Hmong guerrilla program would also expand, and USAF C-130 aircraft would be authorized to transport military supplies to Laos. And, out of an abundance of caution, President Kennedy also placed JTF-116 on the highest state of alert.[18]

Figure 12. H-34 Helicopter
(Photo from the Public Domain)

During the strategy meeting, President Kennedy also approved plans for a B-26 strike against the Plain of Jars. But with only four B-26 aircraft at Takhli, additional bombers would obviously need to be brought in from other bases. The operation was officially named "Mill Pond," and was to include CIA and USAF assets. The purpose of the mission was to inflict as much damage as possible on the enemy forces holding the Plain. The plan called for twelve B-26s to be flown by USAF pilots, while the other four would be flown by Air America pilots. According to the plan, two bombers would attack and crater the runway on the Plain, and then attack targets of opportunity. Another group of B-26s would attack Pathet Lao forces in the Ban Ban Valley, and the last group would attack the southern end of the Plain. Air Force staffers located 18 B-26 qualified pilots, who were placed on temporary duty and directed to report for training at Takhli.

Even though the use of B-26 bombers had been approved, the Department of State was not optimistic about the value of air power. At an earlier meeting in January, Secretary Rusk had expressed his opinion that a handful of light bombers would have little impact or deterrent value on enemy forces operating in mountainous jungle terrain. Rusk also believed that if air power failed, the United States may be forced to bring in U.S. ground troops. But, in the final analysis, it made no difference how many bombers or bombing missions were authorized, because Ambassador Brown had the final call on the use of napalm or bombs—and he wasn't about to authorize their use. In fact, he didn't until 1963.[19]

Later, on March 12, two T-6 aircraft flown by Thai volunteers crashed in mid-air, and yet another was shot down on March 31. Fortunately, the Thai volunteer pilot was able to escape the wreckage and hid nearby, where he was rescued by Air America pilots three days later.

Of all the decisions President Kennedy made on March 6, 1961, the most significant was the proposal to expand the Hmong irregulars from 3,000 to 4,000. The embassy in Vientiane had tried to obtain more support for the Hmong in the past, but Phoumi was dead set against it. He, like many other Lao, considered the Hmong to be little more than savages, primitive and untrustworthy. In fact, Phoumi also insisted that all assistance to the Hmong be funneled through the FAL. Of course, the Americans considered Phoumi's position absurd, because the Lao military pipeline was already a joke, and corrupt to boot.

Regardless of the outcome from the March 6 meeting, the Lao officials, including Phoumi, realized that it was impossible for the FAL to stop Kong Le and the Pathet Lao. The only way to defeat the enemy was via third country intervention, for example through the U.S. But given Phoumi's view of the Hmong and his other recent antics, the PEO and State Department were fed up with his attitude and stubbornness. With his military career in jeopardy and the embassy ready to come down hard on him, Phoumi finally saw the light and became more amenable to the views of his American counterparts. He also reevaluated his position as related to the Hmong, and reluctantly endorsed the increase in troop strength.

With the obstacles now apparently out of the way, military aid started to pour into Laos once again. The United States also began shipments of carbines, rifles, mortars, antipersonnel mines, and uniforms to Laos, as fast as possible. By the end of April, roughly 5,000 Hmong had been armed; these troops became known as Special Guerrilla Units (SGUs).

The day after President Kennedy authorized support to the RLG, Phoumi decided to fly to Phnom Penh and mend fences with Souvanna. Phoumi was anxious for the fighting to stop, and certain that he could persuade Souvanna to join Boun Oum's government and drop his claim as the legitimate Prime Minister. As an incentive, Phoumi dangled both the position of Vice Premier and the Foreign Affairs portfolio. Souvanna was unimpressed and turned Phoumi down. Souvanna and Phoumi did agree, however, to issue a joint declaration endorsing a 14-nation conference to end the civil war.

After returning from Cambodia, Phoumi was discouraged, but threw himself into preparing for war by placing defensive positions south of the Lik River. Later, suddenly energized, Phoumi replaced some of his incompetent commanders, and ordered his staff to prepare to retake lost territory. The U.S. Embassy in Vientiane took notice of Phoumi's sudden burst of energy, and hoped he would pass on some of this new-found determination to his subordinates. As usual, it was wishful thinking; Phoumi had already changed his focus, and was planning to accompany the King on a ten-day political junket abroad.

Once again, it appeared that the Lao government was drifting, and no one was at the helm steering the ship of state. The United States believed it had no choice but to take action to preclude Laos from being taken over by the Communists. President Kennedy was also troubled, and did not want to commit American soldiers; his preference was still to push for a diplomatic solution.

A National Security Council meeting followed these events on March 20. At the meeting, two proposals were submitted to the President. The first called for sending a small U.S. military contingent to Thailand's Mekong Valley. The purpose would be to deter the Pathet Lao and encourage negotiations, out of fear that the U.S. might follow up the action with direct and overwhelming intervention. This proposal was frowned upon by the Joint Chiefs, who recommended a force of 60,000 soldiers, complete with air support and nuclear weapons. The President listened to both proposals, but elected not to make a decision on either. He did issue orders for JTF-116 to once again assemble and activate its staff, consisting of about 15,000 American troops.

Meanwhile, the fighting caused a mass exodus of Lao villagers from their homes. As soon as it started in December, they began to flee to the hills and mountains in northern Laos, just as they had done for decades; in fact, as the opposing forces came upon villages, they often found them completely deserted. But this exodus created a new problem: even though they took all their belongings with them, the villagers' access to food and shelter was limited in the mountains. Soon, they began to run out of rice, salt, and other essentials, and were living outside in makeshift tents and structures. People were getting sick, and many were dying. They were eager to receive assistance from USAID. There was one problem, however: all the USAID people, including Pop Buell, had been evacuated to Thailand as nonessential personnel when the hostilities broke out.

After being evacuated, Pop recuperated for a few weeks in Bangkok and then signed a contract with USAID to provide assistance to the refugees hiding in the mountains of northeastern Laos. But no one was exactly sure where the refugees were located. Pop had a pretty good idea, based upon what he'd learned from conversations with some of the people who had fled; but for the most part, USAID had no idea how to proceed. It was decided that Pop would return to Laos to find VP and others who might know how to locate the refugees.

Also early in 1961, the CIA decided to take the lead in the direct management of what had become known as the Secret War in Laos. Shortly thereafter, an H-34 helicopter landed on the Plain of Jars. The Plain was partially obscured by smoke from fires set by farmers to clear land for the rice planting season. Against that backdrop, the young Hmong Lieutenant Colonel, Vang Pao, waited to greet his visitors. VP was wearing khaki fatigues, a bush hat, and French jungle boots. As the helicopter landed, an American also wearing khakis emerged from the aircraft; followed by a Thai officer. The American introduced himself and also introduced his traveling companion, a Thai colonel. The American was Bill Lair, an Agency employee who specialized in counter insurgency. He has worked with the Thais for years and was well-respected in Southeast Asia.

Lair wasn't sure that Vang Pao was the person he was looking for at first, but after talking for quite awhile, he knew that VP was the person to lead the Hmong in fighting the NVA and Pathet Lao. Of course, VP pledged to fight the Communists at all cost, and naturally he asked for a show of good faith on the part of Lair. He wanted guns, ammunition and training for his Hmong guerrillas. Lair indicated that he was see what he could do, and later departed for Vientiane to talk to his managers at the U.S. Embassy in Vientiane. It didn't take long for the weapons to be approved, and a deal was forged between Vang Pao and Lair.

Lair then left the Plain, returning to the U.S. Embassy in Vientiane; while VP, along with the Thai colonel, set out on foot to talk with the clan leaders and seek their approval. Meanwhile, upon arrival in Vientiane, Lair located his bosses, Gordon Jorgenson and Desmond Fitzgerald, and briefed them on his meeting with Vang Pao. Lair reiterated the Hmong's commitment to fight, and suggested that the Agency could equip the Hmong with surplus U.S. military weapons and equipment, minimizing the cost of the venture.

Figure 13. Vang Pao, circa 1961
(Photo from the Public Domain)

Fitzgerald and Jorgenson both listened, but in typical CIA fashion, they did not make a commitment either way. Lair left the meeting not knowing if he would get approval. The following morning, Fitzgerald informed Lair that the plan had merit, and requested he write up a proposal and transmit it directly to Washington, with a copy to the CIA station in Saigon. Lair then sat down, typed up the proposal, and dispatched it as directed. In a few days, he got his answer: the proposal was indeed considered to have merit. He later received approval to equip and train 1,000 personnel, using the resources required. The project was to be called "Operation Momentum."

While Lair was briefing the CIA station bosses, VP was busy briefing the Hmong clan leaders. The leaders reminded VP that the Hmong had also supported the French, and now many of their people were imprisoned by the Viet Minh. They also reminded VP that the French had done nothing to seek the prisoners' release, as they had exited the country in haste.[20] The clan elders wanted assurance that the Americans would not do the same thing, when and if the going got tough. VP urged the elders to accept the American's proposal. Shortly after the meeting, the clan elders met amongst themselves, and Lair subsequently received word to return to meet again with VP. Lair returned to the village as instructed, met with VP and the elders, and the plan was approved. During these meetings, VP was reportedly assured by Lair that the CIA would help the Hmong relocate to safety in the event they were defeated.

Soon after all the parties approved the plan, a base at Pha Khao was selected as the training site for the Hmong. Lair and his Thai counterparts, who were members of the Thai Police Aerial Reinforcement Unit (PARU), a paramilitary counter insurgency force, conducted a three-day training course. A new White Star team, which had replaced the PEO personnel who had fled the Plain in December 1960, also provided weapons training.[21]

Meanwhile Heinie Aderholt, a USAF career officer recently detailed to the CIA on special assignment, arranged for the delivery of weapons, ammunition and supplies to equip thousands of Hmong guerrillas. When the weapons arrived, training was conducted, and it was successful. After the training session, VP and his men set up an ambush for a Pathet Lao team in the area, killing many. This was the first official victory for the newly trained Hmong guerrillas. Also, at about this same time, Pop Buell returned to northeastern Laos and was able to establish contact with VP.

Lair was reportedly impressed with the Hmong victory, and confident that the Hmong, led by VP, could operate independently, without direct supervision. He then returned to Vientiane. Shortly after he returned, more CIA personnel began arriving to help Lair. The first to arrive was Pat Landry, an experienced CIA hand with a reputation for being cantankerous and hard to get along with. The next CIA advisor to arrive was Tony Poe, a seasoned paramilitary specialist with a reputation as a drunk and malcontent. The third was Jack Shirley, another paramilitary specialist. Later, other Americans kept showing up at the embassy with orders to assist Lair. But Lair wasn't happy—he hadn't asked for all the paramilitary specialists, and he felt he didn't need them. But that's the way things worked in the government.

Now that Operation Momentum had been approved by Washington, Lair established a permanent training facility at Hua Hin, Thailand. At that location, the PARU and White Star personnel began formal training courses for the Hmong SGUs. All of the guerrillas would learn basic weapons and explosives training, and some of the more adept students would also obtain advanced training as radio operators. While training was being conducted, Lair had his subordinates traveling around the country, hacking out landing sites where aircraft could land and take off. These sites were later identified with the Letter "L" (for Laos, of course), and given a number—for example, L-1 or LS-1. Collectively, they were referred to as "Lima Sites." As additional sites were established, they would be added to a list that was subsequently formalized into a pamphlet and used by all U.S. agencies operating aircraft in Laos.[22]

While Vang Pao and Bill Lair were getting to know each other, problems were developing on the Plain of Jars. The U.S. had initiated the use of aerial reconnaissance flights, referred to as "Rose Bowl," using the SC-47 reconnaissance aircraft equipped with a sophisticated camera, the K-17. Photographs from the flights revealed an increasing NVA presence on the Plain, and a small Soviet embassy was discovered at Kang Khay. In addition, the Chinese had established a cultural and economic mission at Xieng Khouangville, and an economic mission at Kang Khay.

On March 23, the SC-47 was on another reconnaissance mission, after having completed about thirty previous successful reconnaissance flights. This time they were searching for a Soviet homing beacon. As the aircraft passed over a small village near the Plain of Jars, antiaircraft guns opened up from below on the slow-moving aircraft. One of the shells ripped through the right wing, causing it to disintegrate; the aircraft began to roll, and immediately pitched down towards the ground. As it spiraled out of control and headed for Earth, it appeared that only one person was able to parachute away from the doomed aircraft. The SC-47 normally carried a crew of six, but on this day there were two additional people on board. One was Major Lawrence Bailey, Jr., a U.S. Army attaché at the Embassy in Vientiane; the other passenger was U.S. Army Warrant Officer Edgar Weitkamp, also from the embassy. Bailey and Weitkamp were not part of the crew that day; they were reportedly onboard because they needed to go to Saigon, and the aircraft was supposed to fly there after the short recon mission over the Plain. Meanwhile, the SC-47 crashed into the ground, and Major Bailey floated over the Plain, with his parachute being carried by the prevailing breezes.

As fate would have it, Bailey was the only survivor of that ill-fated mission. Apparently, he was the only person on the aircraft who put on a parachute before it departed from Vientiane. The rest of the crew may not have had time to put their chutes, or believed that they did not need them. At any rate, all six regular crew members perished in the crash, along with Weitkamp.

A few minutes earlier, as Bailey prepared to jump from the burning aircraft, he had been struck by a piece of the disintegrating wing, and his left arm was broken; he had also sustained other less serious injuries. He was unable to control the direction of his chute, so he drifted lazily over the Plain, finally landing in a grassy field. Upon hitting the ground, Bailey was unable to move, but he could soon hear the voices of what appeared to be excited soldiers as they approached. A dozen or so young Neutralist soldiers then closed in on him, unsure of what they should do. They were not seasoned troops, but finally mustered enough courage to apprehend and restrain Bailey. The troops then fired their rifles into the air and proceeded to search Bailey. They took his shoes, cigarettes, wallet, and a knife that was in his pocket. At that moment, Colonel Bailey became the first U.S. POW in Laos.[23]

Figure 14. EC-47 Aircraft, Very Similar to the SC-47
(Photo from the Public Domain)

Still unsure of what to do, the young Neutralists took Bailey to a NVA hospital in the area and turned him over to the commander. The medical personnel treated Colonel Bailey's wounds, and he was bedridden for a week; most of that time was spent in a medicated state. While he was in the hospital, an NVA intelligence officer would come to Bailey's bed each and every day and ask him questions intended to illicit intelligence information. Bailey, enjoying the game of mental chess, passed the time by giving the officer false information, periodically changing his answers.

Finally, the intelligence officer realized that Bailey wasn't going to cooperate, so he gave up and it was decided that Bailey could be moved. He was then taken to Sam Neua City, where he was confined in a makeshift cell in a house that had once been a French villa. For the next week or so the NVA continued to question Bailey, hoping that he would cooperate, but they finally gave up and left him to the tender mercies of the Pathet Lao.

Major Bailey was then kept in a dark room for about a year. On occasion he would be let out of the room, but was always monitored. Later, he was moved to another cell in a building nearby where he was held for about five more months. While in captivity, Major

Bailey was given only enough food to keep him alive, and he was not allowed contact with any other Americans until just prior to being released, after 17 months in captivity. After his release, Bailey returned to the United States to join his family, went on to achieve the rank of Colonel, and later retired. Years later he wrote a book entitled *Solitary Survivor* (Brassey's Publishing, 1995), in which he shares his story of capture and imprisonment.

On March 23, 1961, President Kennedy was scheduled to hold a televised news conference in Washington, D.C. The location for the event was a new auditorium at the State Department near the Potomac River, in an area called Foggy Bottom. At the front of the room was a stage filled with television cameras. There were also three large easels on the stage, each covered with an opaque material. Moments before the President entered the room, an aide removed the covers from the easels, exposing large maps of Laos on each of the stands. Areas on the maps were shaded in blue, white and red. Red represented the Communist controlled areas; blue represented the government-held areas; and white depicted the Neutralist-held territory. The first map demonstrated how the country had looked prior to Kong Le's coup in 1960; there was only a small area shaded in red. The second map depicted spheres of influence after the coup; the red area was slightly larger, and shaped like an elongated sliver. The third map indicated the current situation. It depicted a large, menacing red blob taking up the entire area of the territory on and around the Plain of Jars. Of course, the third map wasn't an accurate representation of the real situation, but it served the President's purpose.

A few minutes later, President Kennedy walked out onto the stage and began his speech by saying he would like to make a few comments. He opened his remarks by noting that Laos was a "difficult and potentially dangerous problem." His demeanor appeared tough yet balanced as he tried to prepare America for the possibility of war; but he also wanted to send signals to Moscow that peace talks regarding Laos would be welcomed. He then proceeded to make three points: first, he said, "We strongly and unreservedly support the goal of a neutral and independent Laos." Second, "If there's to be peace, there must be a cessation of armed attacks by externally supported Communists". And third, "We are strongly in favor of constructive negotiations among nations concerned, and among the leaders of Laos."

The President concluded his remarks by saying,

> "My fellow Americans, Laos is far away from America, but the world is small. The security of all of Southeast Asia will be endangered if Laos loses its neutral independence. Its safety rests with the safety of all of us. I want to make it clear to the American people and to the entire world that all we want in Laos is peace, not war. A truly neutral government, not a Cold War pawn, with a settlement reached at the conference table and not on the battlefield".

In his speech, the President did not mention Operations Momentum or White Star, and he did not mention Vang Pao, Pop Buell, or the Hmong. Nor did he bring up the CIA's paramilitary efforts. In any case, there was already plenty of other trouble brewing elsewhere in the world: there were Cuba, the Belgian Congo, and Berlin to deal with, to name a few. The President did not want to lose Laos; but he would settle for a draw, and that meant striking a bargain with Kong Le and Souvanna. The British did not want a ground war in Southeast Asia either, and of course the French were still interested in returning to the region. And then there was India, which sympathized with the Laotian Neutralists.

At about this same time, the idea of revitalizing the Geneva talks came to light, so President Kennedy contacted Averell Harriman to go to Geneva to reinitiate those peace talks. Harriman was a well-known and successful businessman who was recognized for his tough negotiating skills; of course he didn't want to disappoint the President, so he agreed to go. As his deputy he selected William Sullivan, a successful government diplomat.

Meanwhile, near the end of March 1961, Phoumi's soldiers back in Laos abandoned Tha Thom and retreated down Route 4, in the direction of Paksane. While trying to provide cover the retreating forces, the RLAF lost another T-6 aircraft. Out of the original ten aircraft provided, five had been lost thus far. Also by April 3, all sixteen Mill Pond B-26 aircraft were at Takhli. General LeMay, the USAF Chief of Staff, asked that the bombers be put into use right away. He believed that it was time for action, not talking. He also wanted to exact revenge for the recent loss of the SC-47 over the Plain of Jars.

While the Lao government troops were retreating, the PEO was undertaking an operation to sever Communist-held Muong Kassy from its supply base on the Plain of Jars. Seven C-47 transports, 14 H-34 helicopters and T-6s flying cover were in the air, shifting more than 600 Lao government troops to positions east of the town. The troop movement came off without a hitch, but once again the Lao troops would not engage the enemy. Needless to say, this was a big embarrassment to the U.S., and one newspaper even carried an article saying, in effect, that the RLA lacked the will to fight.

Meanwhile, on April 13, the State Department sent a telegram to the U.S. Ambassadors in Bangkok and Vientiane entitled, "Laos Situation: April, 1961." The telegram was stamped *Top Secret, Eyes Only, Ambassador Winthrop Brown, Gavin Bruce, Unger, and Creel.* It provided certain information and directed the ambassadors to take certain actions. As related to Laos, the following information was provided:

> *Soviets disturbing delay in executing calls for cease fire faces us with obvious dangers. (1) Build up of enemy supplies and base of operations continues with no indication of abatement; even gradual increase is evident. (2) Overall military situation deteriorates and Communist in position to exploit weakening situation of FAL at will which could place RLG in untenable position while waiting for cease fire to be accomplished. (3) Aura of pre-cease fire atmosphere and current political speculation associated with Souvanna Phouma's travels could tempt King and Phoumi to contemplate concessions inimical to our interests. In view this continuing decay could result in sudden collapse military situation and place us at extreme disadvantage at conference table. President has authorized the carrying out of the following action in order bolster military position FAL and restore morale RLG to appreciable degree:*
>
> *JCS by separate orders tonight authorizing CINCPAC order PEO personnel Laos and LTAG (Lao Training Advisory Group) personnel to (1) lift all restrictions with respect to their participation combat operations; (2) use of rank; (3) wearing of uniforms.*

This will enable US military personnel to provide essential leadership and guidance essential for conduct of operations. They will operate in all essentials comparable to MAAG. Phoumi must understand that in order for LTAG teams to be effective with FAL units there must be no restriction to their participating fully with combat elements at all levels.

We are informing French Ambassador of this action tomorrow morning; also UK Ambassador. French may indeed protest but action will be carried out over such protest if necessary. In informing British and French of this action we are taking to stiffen FAL posture, we are requesting their approval and cooperation and advising them that should overt action of this type within scope of operation indulged in by Communists themselves be used as pretext for Communist retaliation, our next step will be to consider appropriate action in which we would expect their support. FOR BROWN: Request you return to Vientiane at once to inform Prime Minister and Phoumi and if possible King of this decision. In order provide necessary authority for this action you should ask RLG to place appropriate request our hands so that military assistance will be covered by agreement with RLG.

In your discussion this whole situation with Phoumi should be made clear US taking this additional step to ensure integrity of Laos and we urge in all seriousness to put forth every effort achieve tactical advantage on ground as rapidly as possible. In discussion with Phoumi emphasize President's view he must give us something to support.

Rusk (Secretary of State Dean Rusk).[24]

The PEO subsequently assumed their new title as the United States Military Assistance Advisory Group (MAAG). The Special Forces troops removed their civilian attire and donned their uniforms; then they returned to the field, leading the RLA into battle. CIA helicopters delivered two Lao battalions to support the Special Forces north of Vientiane. Two other regiments were also scheduled to arrive to reinforce the Special Forces, but they did not get to the battle in time. By mid-April, Pathet Lao troops had overrun the town of Vang Vieng, and the Americans had no choice but to retreat.

Finally, on April16, the B-26 aircraft at Takhli were loaded with bombs and ammunition for the cannons, and were ready to go. The crews all attended strike briefings and went to bed early for the mission on the next morning. Inside the barracks, the pilots listened to a radio broadcast of another special mission of Kennedy's called the Bay of Pigs invasion, and it appeared to fail miserably. On the following morning, when the pilots and crews arrived at the flight line, they learned the White House had cancelled their mission under Operation Mill Pond.

Also, by the second week of April, the NVA "19" Border Defense Battalion evicted RLG troops from Khamkeut and Lak Sao in the upper panhandle of Laos. Among the fleeing troops were Phoumi's own FAL soldiers. We should also mention that during this same general time frame, Phoumi's troops were only performing marginally throughout northern Laos; in some areas, they made no progress whatsoever, and merely stayed in their heavily defended positions near large towns.

As April 1961 began to wind down, President Kennedy was beginning to have second thoughts about a tough stance in Laos. Still smarting from the Bay of Pigs fiasco, he chose to take a more cautious approach to Laos: he ordered the military to increase its reconnaissance activity over the kingdom, hoping for a more accurate picture of what was actually taking place on the ground.

The Pathet Lao were also growing weary of the level of fighting, and dispatched a representative to meet with the RLG to discuss a ceasefire. The Lao Armed Forces hadn't been doing much fighting, so they had no problem going along with a ceasefire. Finally, on May 5, a team from the ICC arrived and delegates from the RLG, the Pathet Lao, and Kong Le's Neutralists met in the town of Ban Namone to negotiate a lasting truce.

Meanwhile, on April 22, U.S. Army Captain Walter Moon and his Special Forces White Star team were leading one of the RLG regiments when the Communists began to attack. Moon and his team had been slowly making their way up Route 13 near Vang Vieng when the regiment was shelled with artillery rounds and took small arms fire. The Lao regiment panicked and fled into the jungle, leaving

Moon and his team all alone to face the advancing Communists. Ultimately, the Pathet Lao forces overran the team, killing two of its members. And, after intense fighting, Captain Moon and Sergeant Orville Ballenger were captured. Ballenger immediately bolted and ran, but was captured again the following day. Moon and Ballenger were then held in an abandoned International Voluntary Services (IVS) house that was being used as a makeshift confinement facility. Captain Moon tried in vain to escape on two occasions, and the North Vietnamese guards summarily executed him out of anger after the second attempt. Sergeant Ballenger remained a POW, and was subsequently moved around to several prisons until he finally wound up in a prison camp with three Air America personnel and two Thai advisors. Ballenger was later released on August 17, 1962.[25]

By this time, Bill Lair believed that Operation Momentum was going well. The first 1,000 Hmong personnel had been trained, and approval was received to train many others. Thai PARU teams were also operating in northern Laos, and additional Hmong personnel were being trained by the teams. Progress in other areas was also being made. New sites were opened, and reconnaissance teams were being dispatched. Weapons, ammunition, explosives and other equipment were being flown in by Air America from storage warehouses on Okinawa, and Air America was also busy hauling personnel, and performing other air support missions.

On April 19, the NVA decided to test the strength of Project Momentum with an infantry assault at San Tiau (Lima Site 2). Approximately three hundred Hmong fighters, one PARU and two CIA field agents, Jack Shirley and Thomas Ahern, defended the site. Jack Shirley reported on the radio they were in a heavy firefight, and asked that mortar shells be sent to the site right away. The following day, he called again requesting .30-caliber machine gun ammunition. He also reported they were taking casualties. It was obvious that the enemy was close, and they kept advancing. On April 22, it was apparent that Lima Site 2 could not hold, and an evacuation would have to be initiated. The following day, the CIA personnel, the Hmong defenders, and the Thai PARU team left LS-2 on foot, using a predetermined escape route south. They had already mined their escape route and followed the carefully laid path through the minefield to safety. As a precaution, they rigged additional booby traps along the way as they headed south. After they were a safe distance away from LS-2, they heard explosions from the direction of the mine field. The retreating men kept walking, and on the following day, Ahern, Shirley and the PARU team was picked up by Air America H-34 helicopters and taken to safety.

By this time, Pop Buell had spoken at length with Vang Pao about the USAID refugee program. VP was appreciative of the USAID offer for assistance, and expressed great concern for the refugees hiding in the mountains. With VP's help, Pop Buell was able to begin to find the large refugee enclaves; as he did, he coordinated with Air America and the embassy to get relief supplies and medicines to them. From this simple beginning, Pop was able to help feed, clothe and provide shelter for hundreds of thousands of refugees during the war.

Meanwhile, on April 24, Great Britain and the Soviet Union called for an international conference on Laos, to include the three Lao factions, the 1954 Geneva signatories, the three ICC countries, Burma, and Thailand. The conference was slated to begin on May 15, 1961. It was hoped the fighting would stop and, in the interim, that a ceasefire would be observed. The proposal won the support of Hanoi, Peking, and the RLG; but for several days, Kong Le and the Pathet Lao did not respond.

Meanwhile, skirmishing continued along the Lik River. At about this same time the war took a surprising twist: Kong Le and the Pathet Lao did not advance on Vientiane. The MAAG group and the Lao military officers were thankful, because the Lao troops were already demoralized and believed to be near collapse. Later, Kong Le explained that he did not attack Vientiane because he was considering the ceasefire proposal, and was consolidating his recent gains.

Kong Le's explanation was believable, but his decision not to attack could have also had something to do with logistics and terrain. His stronghold was in the mountainous regions around Veng Vieng, and his source of resupply was on the Plain of Jars. Once his troops headed south, they would be vulnerable to attack from the air, and supplies could be interdicted by the Lao military. Also, to take Vientiane, Kong Le would have had to cross the Lik River, which by that time of year would be out of its banks due to recent monsoon rains. And even if they crossed the river, Phoumi's troops were dug in and well-defended. At any rate, Kong Le did not attack; and by May 3, all parties had agreed to a ceasefire.

Back in the United States, it was the spring of 1961, and in Princeton, New Jersey, a young graduating senior, James Vinton (Vint) Lawrence, was approached by a CIA recruiter who offered him employment and the opportunity for adventure in a faraway place called Laos. After thinking it over, Lawrence took the CIA up on their offer, and upon graduation in June, he was off to Camp Perry, Virginia for training in basic CIA tradecraft. Camp Perry was also called "The Farm," though it didn't look like much like a farm at all: it was actually a former military installation with modern buildings and all the facilities required for training. It was here that new employees of the CIA, and other government agencies received training in various subjects. But Camp Perry was not primitive by any stretch of the imagination. It was situated in a tranquil setting, with lots of open spaces, trees, green grass and many of nature's creatures. There was also housing for camp personnel, and it wasn't uncommon to see deer grazing on someone's front lawn, or sharing the roadway with cars at night.

Inasmuch as the facility had plenty of space, training could be performed in all types of settings. Upon arrival at The Farm, all recruits were given a security briefing and told where they could and could not go. During the briefing, they were also told, "Do not assume anything about anyone you see here." Suffice it to say, the point was made. At any rate, young Lawrence soon completed his initial training and was then off to the Panama Canal Zone for paramilitary training.

Meanwhile, back in Laos, the ceasefire was being violated daily by the Pathet Lao and NVA. One of the more flagrant violations took place at Padong, the Hmong stronghold, just a few miles south of the Plain of Jars. As mentioned earlier, the Communist troops had taken San Tiau and decided to go after Vang Pao's new headquarters at Padong.[26] The base sat on a plateau, surrounded by thick vegetation and trees, with a high peak to the south. To the north there was a lower ridgeline, and beyond that was the Plain of Jars, which was currently being held by the Pathet Lao, the Neutralists, and the NVA. Padong was a lively place at this particular juncture in the war: many tribal leaders came to the base to visit and pay respect to VP Many clan leaders also came, bringing fresh recruits who wanted to join VP's cause. The base also attracted pilots, Thais and the Americans, including CIA and White Star personnel. But the base didn't only attract the good guys: the NVA and Pathet Lao had also discovered the base, and were digging in for an attack.

The Pathet Lao had dragged an old 75mm howitzer to the location and set it into place. The NVA also brought their artillery up the steep hills to use in the attack on Padong. Many at the embassy in Vientiane were puzzled and curious as to why VP would pick this place to defend, when it was best to stay mobile and hit the enemy at his convenience, not stand and fight on their terms. After, all that was what they trained for, and they should have stayed mobile and well-hidden. But for some reason, VP decided to make a stand at Padong, and the CIA did not override his decision. Bill Lair was also puzzled by VP's decision, and voiced it to him; but he said nothing more, because it was his nature to let the indigenous leaders make their own decisions. At any rate, Padong had become an awfully large and inviting target.

In early May, a radio operator at Padong was busy listening to the transmissions, or traffic as it was called, when he intercepted conversations indicating an attack on Padong was imminent. Shortly thereafter, shelling began as 75mm and 105mm artillery rounds began to find their marks at Padong. The shelling continued as NVA reinforcements continued to arrive and dig in. As the incoming shells found their targets, they tore into human flesh, tents, makeshift huts and even the old wooden buildings. The Hmong's weapons were all small arms, and their rounds did not have the range to reach the enemy. VP grabbed a mortar and began firing, while shouting words of encouragement and orders to his men. Some of the Green Berets were also able to get a mortar tube set up, and they fired off several rounds that apparently found their marks, because the artillery was silenced—for the time being, anyway. A day later the shelling began again. But many defenders and civilians were already dead, and VP was encouraged by the Americans to abandon Padong. He objected, but did agree to let women and children begin their southward trek away from the base.[27]

For days afterward, the incoming artillery fire would start and stop without warning, and the pattern was unpredictable. One day it could be a dozen rounds, the next day a hundred or more. The tactics of the attackers were effective, because VP and his troops did not know from moment to moment what was going to happen next. This kept the good guys continually stressed, and it was beginning to have the desired effect. Later, on May 15, the Communists launched a full-scale attack on Padong, reinforced by the NVA 148th Independent Regiment. Ironically, this was the day before the peace talks in Geneva were to officially begin.

Meanwhile, on May 13, 1961, eighty miles to the east, the North Vietnamese attacked Muong Ngat. The Hmong and PARU defenders mowed them down with machine gun fire. It didn't matter, however, because the NVA were willing to sacrifice lives for property, so they sent wave after wave of soldiers until the defenders could no longer keep them out. Finally, the NVA overran the site and killed all the Hmong and PARU personnel. When word of this defeat reached Padong, it devastated the Hmong, and they saw it as a very bad omen.

On May 30, two Air America H-34 helicopters winged their way to Padong to deliver much-needed supplies and ammunition. As mentioned earlier, flying conditions in Laos were dangerous at best, given the terrain and weather. This day was no different. There was a heavy mist limiting visibility, and the air was filled with smoke. As the helicopters approached the base, the first aircraft was able to find a hole in the mist, spiral down, and land successfully. The second helicopter could be heard above, trying to find a way down. Unfortunately, the next sound heard by those on the ground was the whopping sound of the rotor blades, then a whine, followed by a screaming transmission racing out of control. The people ran to investigate, and when they were able to climb up the ridgeline they could see the helicopter hanging in the trees. The aircraft was badly damaged, and the two pilots were still buckled in their seats. Both had been killed when the aircraft struck the mountain and fell into the trees. These two pilots were the first Air America personnel to be killed in the war.[28]

After the helicopter crashed, the Hmong were afraid, because they believed the spirits had been angered—again, a bad omen. Later in the day, the radio shack at Padong received a message from the embassy in Vientiane. The message indicated that the NVA were planning an even larger attack, and the coordinates were provided. It was at that moment that the Americans and the Hmong realized they were the target.

To avoid a confrontation that would have meant total devastation, the Americans began a retreat to the south away from Padong, leading the Hmong and other friendly fighters away and into the darkness. They continued walking all night, and occasionally incoming shells would fall on the group. Most of the shells fell harmlessly into the mud and did not explode, but there was smoke and fog everywhere, and it was difficult to see anything at all.

At daybreak the next morning, the sound of helicopters could be heard, and shortly thereafter Air America H-34s began to land in the valley near the retreating troops. Finally, the ordeal was over, and the helicopters took all of them to safety. But Padong and Muong Ngat had been lost, and the morale of the Hmong had been badly shaken.

While the peace talks took place in Geneva, President Kennedy met separately with Soviet Premier Nikita Khrushchev in Vienna to discuss Laos. The two leaders issued a joint communiqué on Laos thereafter, endorsing a neutral and independent kingdom under a government chosen by its people. A month later, on June 19, 1961, the three Lao Princes—Souvanna Phouma, Souphanouvong and Boun Oum—met in Zurich. And, on June 22, the brothers agreed, in principle, to a tripartite government that would rule Laos until new general elections could be held.

After the battle at Padong, VP estimated that several hundred artillery shells had fallen during the battle. The ICC had reportedly tried to visit Padong during the siege, but they were refused access by the Pathet Lao. To disguise the real reason for not allowing the ICC to visit the area, the Communists said they were in the final phase of rounding up bandits, and that the area was just too dangerous to visit. Phoumi had tried to assist the Hmong at Padong also by sending over 200 RLA troops to help, and the RLAF had flown some support missions in the T-6 aircraft (without bombs, of course). But the result was too little, too late.

Many felt that Vang Pao had made a bad tactical decision in trying to defend Padong against a sustained Pathet Lao and NVA attack, but VP did not feel the same way. He was impressed by the results of the fight between the NVA and the Hmong. Even though they had been outnumbered by a large margin, the numbers of dead on the Communist side far outnumbered the casualties among the Hmong. VP saw this as a victory for his people, even though the Hmong strongholds in three locations had fallen. But was it victory, or stubborn pride?

The Hmong had made a conventional defense of Padong because the base was the prestigious headquarters of Vang Pao, and a large Hmong refugee camp was located nearby. The troops felt they owed that much to their leader and their people. And of course, the outcome at Padong might have been much different if the Lao government had possessed a cohesive military structure, including an effective air force.

But they did not. The RLG had no advanced training program for its air force, relying upon agreements with other countries for training. For example, the United States had an agreement with the Lao government to train some Lao pilots, but none were actually trained in 1960 because the applicants did not speak or comprehend English. Aircraft mechanic training was conducted by the French at its bases in Europe and Africa. Additionally, some pilot training was being conducted using the L-19 light observation aircraft at Savannakhet, but it was cancelled by Phoumi when the Thai government agreed to begin pilot training for the T-6. Phoumi also cancelled the mechanic's training program, because he had lost confidence in the French.

Back on March 3, the Joint United States Military Assistance and Advisory Group, Thailand (JUSMAGTHAI), the PEO, the RLG, and Thailand had agreed to continue pilot training for the RLAF. The training would consist of a ten week course in the L-19 aircraft taught by the Thai Army, followed by 45 hours in the T-6, taught by the Thai Air Force. The cost of this program was estimated to be about $300 million. To complement the pilot training, the MAAG (as the PEO was then called) negotiated an aircraft mechanic training program with a private firm in Manila, but this program had little success due to the language barrier and the fact that the Lao students despised the Filipinos.

Fortunately for Laos, however, an energetic USAF maintenance officer by the name of Captain Ron Shaw was assigned to the MAAG group in Vientiane. Recognizing the problems facing the RLAF, Captain Shaw began to translate the maintenance manuals into French. The Eastern Construction Company in Laos (ECCOIL) was also contracted to provide aircraft maintenance, and hopefully to help in the training of the RLAF. Language training equipment, complete with earphones, tape recorders and booths, had arrived earlier in October 1960, but was just sitting in storage awaiting the RLAF Chief's decision on where to locate the training program.

Meanwhile, the ongoing indecisiveness on the part of the Lao government officials had severe repercussions for the RLAF C-47 transport fleet for more than a year. There was little if any aircraft maintenance being accomplished, causing rapid deterioration of the fleet. With the establishment of a MAAG office at Savannakhet, fourteen ECCOIL mechanics were sent to the facility to provide regular maintenance to the already aging aircraft. The Filipino mechanics did their best to keep the C-47s flying, but the facilities were crude, and spare parts were few and far between. Fortunately, in the fall of 1960, as an interim measure, Thai Airways agreed to provide periodic Inspection and Repair as Necessary (IRAN) for the C-47 aircraft.

In addition to the maintenance woes, the attitudes of the RLAF commanders also affected performance. Colonel Sourith headed the Air Force from 1957-1960, and his replacement was Colonel Thao Ma. Sourith was lackluster at best, and his influence came from family connections, not leadership ability. He did little flying and shunned advice from the MAAG. He was also difficult to work with, and his attitude did not go unnoticed by the rest of the American staff at the embassy. After Kong Le's coup in 1960, Sourith threw his support behind Phoumi, and was rewarded with the position as Commander of MR 3.

Despite his young age (32), Thao Ma was highly qualified, with 2,000 flying hours in the C-47. He was well-liked by some American pilots, but he was subject to constant mood swings. In addition, he was like most of the RLAF officers and did not delegate matters to subordinates, considering them incompetent at best. He reluctantly sent candidates to flight training, and resented advice given by the MAAG. He later declined to fly at all, indicating that he was too valuable to be lost in combat. The U.S. Air Attaché truly had his work cut out for him.[29]

In addition to less-than-desirable RLAF leadership at the top, the U.S. had its own problems in the aviation support arena. Some of the USAF technicians lacked the disposition or background to work with the uneducated and unskilled Lao. They didn't speak Lao or French, and they didn't bother to learn. Instead, they spent most of their time complaining about the accommodations and living conditions. Some of the technicians didn't even want to leave the embassy compound, so they simply sat on their backsides and killed time until their assignment was up. Then they left for the U.S. and their next assignment.

Fortunately, there were people like Captain Shaw, and later, USAF Colonel Harry S. Coleman and others, who began to build a support infrastructure in late 1961. Coleman had been sent to Vientiane to set up an Air Operations Center (AOC), but he wound up cleaning house on the USAF side. He fired incompetent workers and sent them home. He was later promoted to commander of the air section. He didn't speak French, but he quickly gained the trust and confidence of the Lao. It took a while, but it worked; and as confidence grew, the performance of the local personnel improved.

But Coleman and Shaw didn't stop there. They next turned their attention to the facilities, or lack thereof, and began to improve the maintenance capabilities by any means necessary, using an age-old military style of getting what they need. That method was called "Midnight Requisitioning," and it simply meant scrounging and commandeering what they needed to get the job done. No stone was left unturned, including the tactic of befriending the French. On Shaw's part, his charm and fluency in their language resulted in obtaining the materials to build new maintenance facilities at Savannakhet.

Later, in September 1961, a new team of U.S. advisors arrived in Vientiane to build upon the work started by Coleman and Shaw. The team consisted of 13 USAF officers and five airmen who quickly picked up where their predecessors had left off; they even brought Thao Ma around to the idea that on-the-job training programs would work using the RLAF subordinates. The team also convinced Thao Ma of the necessity of his students learning English, and within a few months four RLAF pilots had learned enough English to be sent to the United States for T-28 training. Thao Ma was so impressed he increased the time spent in classrooms by the students, and within a few more months, over 120 personnel were enrolled in English training.

On October 6, Souvanna, Souphanouvong and Boun Oum met again. This time it was on a bridge spanning the Lik River, near Vientiane. At the conclusion of the meeting, it was announced that a new cabinet would be formed, and that it would be composed of eight Neutralists, four Pathet Lao, and four Rightists (RLG) members.

Souvanna was later selected by King Savang Vatthana to head the new government.

Figure 15. T-28 Trojan
(Photo from the Public Domain)

Despite these signs of progress, the Lao military officers were still not taking leadership roles in Laos. They just didn't have the will or desire to fight and lead, and they couldn't pass those qualities on to their men. The MAAG predicted that it would take from three to five years to develop any real leaders in Laos. And despite the small gains made in the Lao ranks, they were offset by similar gains in the capabilities of the Pathet Lao. By the end of 1961, the enemy strength was estimated at about 30,000; of that number, over 5,000 were NVA troops serving as advisors, cadre and technicians. In addition to the technical assistance, the Pathet Lao had been well-provisioned by the NVA, allowing them to gain control of Sam Neua, Phong Saly and Xieng Khouang Provinces.

* * *

As 1961 draws to a close, it may serve us well to step back and review recent events. Eisenhower has left the White House;

Kennedy is now in charge. His approach to the situation in Laos is more pragmatic and measured. Ike had believed in swift decisive action to stop Communism in its tracks; Kennedy believed that the best approach for Laos was neutrality, not war. Also, Kennedy was smarting from the Bay of Pigs fiasco, and it affected critical decisions in Laos. The NVA and Pathet Lao had won recent battles at San Tiau and Padong. The Communists were not going away. Ho Chi Minh had activated the Ho Chi Minh Trail to move supplies, equipment and men into Laos and South Vietnam, and U.S. air power was slowly beginning to be introduced, though its future success could not be predicted. The CIA had decided to take the fight to the enemy by kicking off the Secret War in Laos. In the middle of all this is Vang Pao, who thus far hasn't flinched.

Against this backdrop, we enter the next phase of the conflict.

Chapter 4

Air America

Motto: Anything, Anywhere, Anytime, Professionally

Welcome back to the war. We've just finished discussing the beginning of the Secret War in Laos. We've introduced some of the characters, and acquainted you with the terrain. We've also talked a bit about Air America. But at this juncture, we should deviate for just a while and tell you more about this elite group of aviators and support personnel.

In 1990, a motion picture entitled *Air America* opened in theaters, starring two of Hollywood's up-and-coming actors, Mel Gibson and Robert Downey, Jr. The picture was loosely (and we emphasize *loosely*), based on Christopher Robbins's 1979 book by the same name. In the story, a CIA officer arranges for Air America to transport opium from the far-flung provinces of Laos to Vientiane, refine it into pure heroin, and sell it at a handsome profit. A corrupt Laotian general then gives the CIA part of the money from the sale of the opium, and provides Hmong guerrillas to fight the Secret War. Eventually, we learn from the movie that the supposed war between Communist and anti-Communist forces is just a façade for the real war, which is a struggle for the control of opium.

In the film, Air America pilots are represented as less-than-professional soldiers of fortune, taking part in a war they don't believe in. They're resentful of the drug lords getting rich by hooking the U.S. soldiers in Vietnam on heroin. The movie provided many people around the globe with only a brief view into the Secret War, the CIA and Air America; most people who saw the movie probably didn't read Robbins' book or follow the actual events as they unfolded in Laos from 1960-1975. And they didn't know who, or what, the real Air America was all about. In this chapter, we'll explain what the real Air America did in Laos.

By the time the Secret War erupted, the forerunner of Air America (AAM) had been in existence since roughly 1945, though under other names. As early as 1946, the airline flew under the name of Civil Air Transport (CAT). The famous U.S. Army Air Corps General Claire L. Chennault, who had led the famed Flying Tigers during the Chinese Civil War, started the company. CAT had bought some surplus U.S. Government cargo airplanes, and flew under contract to the Chinese Nationalist Government. Their job was to haul food, equipment, people, and just about anything else capable of being placed in the aircraft.

Beginning in 1946, CAT flew supplies and food into China to the war-ravaged citizens. Later, the CIA also contracted CAT to fly war supplies to the U.S. forces fighting the Korean War.

The story of Air America as a governmental entity, however, began in 1950, when the CIA decided it needed an air transport capability to support U.S. government contracts in Southeast Asia. The CIA bought CAT that same year through a holding company called Airdale Corporation. Later, the name was changed to The Pacific Corporation, and it became a holding company for several front companies, including Air Asia, Bird & Sons, CAT, and Thai Pacific Services, to name a few.

George A. Doole, a former military and airlines pilot, started the company amidst allegations that he was also an employee of the CIA. Doole worked out of a small, nondescript office on Connecticut Avenue in Washington, D.C., where he interviewed and hired many new pilots. From that small office he also ran the far-flung organization, juggling airplanes as needed to carry out the requirements placed on the company by the CIA. At its peak, the company employed roughly 20,000 people and owned about 200 airplanes. Doole was the perfect person to run the company, because he himself was an anonymous man. He was a mature, portly gentleman who always dressed well. He didn't advertise what he did for a living, and was content to let people guess or surmise as they would. And, if the truth was known, he probably enjoyed the mystique that went with his job, and with the company.

Despite his anonymity on the job, he was quite a different person away from work. He was a very social person by all accounts, and a regular at some of Washington's best clubs and restaurants. He also lived in one of the most prestigious residential buildings in D.C., but he did not entertain at his home. Actually, he wasn't around enough to entertain, given all his traveling on behalf of the company.

He traveled extensively promoting Air America, and negotiating with important people representing entities that required the type of services offered by the company. He would also show up occasionally in Vientiane, but did not fraternize with the employees of the company. One CIA official was quoted as saying that Doole played bridge, flew airplanes, and handled his business deals in a slow, deliberate fashion.[30]

In 1953, the French, embroiled in a war with the Viet Minh, needed help. They appealed to President Eisenhower for the use of USAF C-119 transports and crews to fly heavy equipment and war supplies to their troops under fire at Dien Bien Phu, North Vietnam. Eisenhower was eager to help the French, but did not want to commit U.S. troops in Indochina. As an alternative, CAT was contracted to airlift supplies in support of the French, using C-119 transports, from March 3-May 7, 1954. During that period CAT flew more than 600 airlift missions in support of the French at Dien Bien Phu. Of course, the French lost the battle on May 7, and withdrew from North Vietnam; but CAT continued to support the French as they slowly departed Southeast Asia.

Fast forward ten years to 1955, when the United States signed an agreement to supply economic and military aid to Laos after implementation of the Geneva Accords. The U.S. was once again in a situation where they needed airlift support, but were unwilling to bring in the military to do the job due to legal entanglements resulting from the Accords. During that same year, CAT airlifted food and medicine to the remote mountainous regions of Laos to feed starving civilians. In July 1957, CAT established facilities at Wattay Airport in Vientiane to provide continuing airlift service and maintenance under a new contract with the U.S. embassy.

On March 26, 1959, CAT officially changed its name to Air America (AAM), even as it increased support to the FAR. Later, in the summer of 1959, Colonel Bull Simons and the U.S. Army Special Forces arrived in Laos to provide training to support the Lao military under the Military Assistance Program (MAP). Coincidentally, their arrival presaged an increase in the fighting between Lao government forces and the Pathet Lao.

In August 1959, AAM began to train some of its pilots in helicopters, in preparation for the subsequent arrival of several H-19A Sikorsky Chickasaws at AAM locations in Southeast Asia. By then, it was obvious that helicopters would see extensive service in Laos, Cambodia and South Vietnam, due to the unique topography of the area. Before long, the H-34 Sikorsky King Bee replaced the underpowered H-19. By 1960, as AAM's business base expanded, it wasn't always possible for George Doole to recruit civilian pilots fast enough; so at times, the U.S. military took the unusual step of releasing pilots from active duty to supplement Air America's ranks. The H-34 aircraft was a good example of that practice, because the best pilots were all active duty U.S. Marine Corps (USMC) aviators. Thus, several USMC H-34 pilots were loaned to AAM for flight duty in Laos. Meanwhile, Air America also received the Helio Courier STOL aircraft, made by the Helio Aircraft Company, for trials in Southeast Asia.

The STOL program got off to a shaky start in Laos, for two reasons: (1) the pilots had not received enough training, and (2) the aircraft proved temperamental. In fact, the effort almost stalled until USAF pilot and aerial resupply specialist Heine Aderholt came to the rescue. Major Aderholt was a proponent of the Helio Courier, and he personally demonstrated the versatility of the aircraft to Air America. After observing Heine put the Helio through its paces, the Air America pilots accepted the aircraft, and it was used extensively throughout Southeast Asia for the duration of the Vietnam War. The aircraft was also used extensively in Laos, though it did need some minor modifications for the harsh environment; but after the adjustments were completed, the Helio was in Southeast Asia to stay. Major Aderholt was also instrumental in the establishment of the Lima Site airfields in Laos during the Secret War.

Also by 1960, Laos had NVA troops massing in the Sam Neua area, and they were beginning to attack the RLA in northern Laos. Meanwhile, the civil war continued to rage: the Neutralists, Pathet Lao and the RLG all fought each other for control of the country, but none of the three entities ever had the upper hand. The Soviets backed Kong Le's Neutralists, the NVA supported the Pathet Lao, and the CIA sponsored the RLG. In the middle of all of this, Air America was flying the unfriendly skies of Laos delivering food, medical supplies and hard rice (ammunition) to the RLA and Vang Pao.

In January 1961, President Kennedy ordered the transfer of fourteen H-34 helicopters to Air America. The war between the Communists and Vang Pao had rapidly expanded, and resupply was critical to support the Hmong guerrillas and the RLA. As the fighting increased, the number of refugees also expanded dramatically; and as usual, the refugees needed airlift to safe areas. Once again, Air America stepped up to the increased demand for air support.

As mentioned in the previous chapter, President Kennedy met with Soviet Premier Nikita Khrushchev in Vienna in June, and releasing a joint statement calling for a "neutral and independent Laos." Meanwhile, in Geneva, the U.S. and more than a dozen other countries, including North Vietnam, met to discuss peace. On July 23, 1962, a formal agreement was reached in Geneva. The so-called "Declaration on the Neutrality of Laos" provided for a coalition government and the withdrawal of all foreign troops from the country. In response, the U.S. withdrew all its military advisors from Laos, and Air America stopped delivering weapons and ammunition to VP. North Vietnam withdrew a few of its civilian engineers and specialists from Laos, but since they refused to admit a troop presence in the country, they didn't remove any NVA soldiers.

For several months after the agreement, Air America's resupply efforts decreased substantially. But U.S. leaders later realized that North Vietnam's presence in Laos had actually increased, as had the level of violence. Since the NVA weren't playing by the rules, the Americans decided to skirt the rules as well; and soon, it was business as usual in Laos. As the fighting increased, the air movement of men and equipment expanded as well. The U.S. was still reluctant, however, to commit U.S. military air support to Laos, and air reconnaissance was desperately needed. Once again, Air America stepped up by providing limited air reconnaissance.

It didn't take long before Air America had a steady stream of good pilots coming to work for the company. The pay was good, bonuses were paid for special missions, and dangerous flying paid an extra ten dollars an hour. In a good year, a pilot could make from $50,000-$75,000, which was very good money in those days. The unique flying conditions required special people, and so the pilots attracted to these dangerous jobs were adventurous, materialistic individuals who didn't want or need much oversight or supervision. These were guys who would fly in any weather, while under fire, complete their missions, and return without complaining. They were all brave men who made the impossible look routine.

On a typical day, the pilot and crew would begin their day at Wattay Airport in Vientiane. They would eat breakfast in the company cafeteria, then go to the Operations shack for their daily briefing. They would be told where they were going and what they would be hauling. Next, they would gather their gear and head outside to inspect their aircraft. After the preflight inspection, they would fly out to their first stop to pick up or drop off cargo and troops. Then they would taxi out again and fly on to the next stop. This routine would continue all day long, with the pilot and crew returning just before sundown.

This type of flying sounds routine, but during every leg of their daily schedule, they were usually under fire—and it wasn't uncommon for them to return with bullet holes in the skin of the aircraft. As if that weren't bad enough, the pilots were never sure if they would be touching down in friendly or unfriendly territory, because the turf changed hands almost daily. On occasion, an unforeseen event would require the airplane to Remain Overnight (RON) at a Lima Site. When this happened, there were seldom reasonable accommodations for the pilot and crew. Often they would sleep in the aircraft; or if they were lucky, they would find shelter in one of the village huts. These overnight stays were never desirable because they were sitting ducks, and the Communists liked nothing better than to open fire on a grounded aircraft and its crew.

It also became clear early on that the USAF would have to begin regular aerial reconnaissance over Laos to overcome the threat presented by the NVA. Once the reconnaissance flights were initiated, limited air strikes soon followed. In order to discourage aerial reconnaissance, North Vietnam responded by moving antiaircraft weapons to northern Laos as a deterrent. As soon as USAF aircraft appeared, the NVA responded with relentless anti-aircraft fire. Soon, the USAF began to lose aircraft to the anti-aircraft weapons, and unfortunately, the U.S. lacked a Search and Rescue (SAR) capacity in Laos. Once again, Air America stepped up to provide the necessary SAR services. As the war continued to intensify, the USAF set up its own SAR capability in Laos. But the Air Force was not familiar with the terrain, and Air America came through once again by providing personnel for a command and control capability.

We could continue our discussion about Air America, but we would be getting ahead of the story. So for now, we'll return to the Secret War in Laos, where the war is expanding and America's involvement is deepening. Thankfully, Air America was also there to help by providing airlift capability and a myriad of other services. Please continue reading to find out what happens to this group of incredibly brave and courageous airmen.

A. Bell 47 Helicopter   B. Hughes 500 Helicopter   C. C-123 Provider Transport

D. C-7 Caribou Transport   E. C-119 Transport   F. C-47 Transport

G. C-46 Transport   H. Helio Courier   I. Dornier DO28

J. Cessna U-17   K. DHC-6 Twin Otter   L. H-34 Helicopter

Figure 16. Aircraft Used by Air America in Southeast Asia
All photos are from the Public Domain. These photos are
representative, and do not include all the types of aircraft
used by AAM.

Chapter 5

The Business of War

As we discussed in Chapter 3, the Hmong had been defeated at Padong and San Tiau by NVA and Pathet Lao troops, and Vang Pao had established a new headquarters at Pha Khao. Earlier, during the 1961 talks in Geneva, a ceasefire had been negotiated; but this meant nothing on the ground in Laos, where the fighting continued. VP was frustrated, because too few of his Hmong fighters had been adequately provided with training and weapons. He wanted more training, he wanted it now, and he insisted upon the right weapons to do the job. Bill Lair tried to appease VP and explained they would have to proceed slowly, because the talks in Geneva were under way; and, depending on the outcome of the talks, the United States might be required to leave Laos. For that reason, Washington had essentially put a halt on weapons shipments and training for the Hmong until the talks in Geneva concluded. In fact, the U.S. deliberately withheld much-needed ammunition and weapons at a time when the Hmong desperately needed it.

Not one to be put off, VP became more persistent, because if the Americans were going to pull out, he wanted to stockpile as many weapons as possible to use in fighting the Communists. His repeated requests for equipment went unanswered, but violations of the ceasefire agreement by the NVA and Pathet Lao continued. Finally, William Colby, the CIA's Far East Division Chief, pleaded with President Kennedy to provide additional assistance to the Hmong. Kennedy relented and approved a plan to increase the Hmong army to 11,000.

While the talks in Geneva continued, it was business as usual in Vientiane for Ambassador Brown and his staff, who held meetings regularly to discuss the situation on the ground. These gatherings were called "Country Team Meetings" and included the ambassador, the CIA station chief, MAAG personnel, and other personnel as necessary from the embassy staff. After one such meeting on January 26, 1962, Ambassador Brown published an estimate of NVA troop strength, concluding that there were approximately 12 battalions of NVA troops in Laos, totaling more than 5,000 personnel. In addition, it was estimated there were approximately 4,000 NVA service units in play, including engineers, cadre, and advisory personnel to the Pathet Lao.

A few days later, on January 31, intelligence officials in Washington, D.C. commented on the capabilities of opposing forces in Laos. Their assessment indicated that in recent weeks, the Royal Armed Forces (FAR) had engaged in several military clashes with antigovernment troops—and had been forced to withdraw each time. It was opined that several problems, including poor morale and leadership, contributed, in part, to the poor performance on the part of the FAR. The Communists, on the other hand, were considered by U.S. intelligence officials to have superiority in artillery and armor, though they were outnumbered by the FAR. Additionally, the Pathet Lao had been supplemented by NVA cadres and combat troops, even though actual numbers could not be provided, given their close proximity to the border of North Vietnam. With continual border crossings, the numbers changed daily in any case. In conclusion, the intelligence officials estimated the Communists could continue to hold certain key positions in northeastern Laos without reinforcements; but with additional reinforcements of NVA troops, the Communists could overrun the entire country of Laos.

Meanwhile, training of Hmong guerrilla units resumed, under the auspices of PEO and White Star personnel. White Star advisors had established a camp at Sam Thong in March 1962 and were busy building a logistics base, complete with warehouses and a communications center. Sam Thong also had an airstrip, so it was officially named Lima Site 20 (LS-20). Not long after ramping up at LS-20, several thousand Hmong troops had been trained, and some were sent on to other locations for specialized training. Many of the newly trained troops were also dispersed around the perimeter of the Plain of Jars as local militia forces.

Even though recruitment and training continued, Washington wanted to keep the pace slow in order not to overshadow the Geneva talks. VP and his men were therefore limited to training, intelligence gathering missions, and defense of the existing camps; they were not allowed to initiate any offensive operations. To make sure the pace remained slow, ammunition shipments were small, in order to keep the field commanders in check.

Later, on January 25, Pathet Lao and NVA troops lobbed several mortar rounds into the town of Nam Tha (L-100). Phoumi reacted quickly by reinforcing the RLA garrison in the town, using RLAF C-47 aircraft. One of the planes was subsequently fired upon during the flights, so Phoumi brought in four 105mm howitzers and approximately twelve 75mm pieces. Having done that, Phoumi next ordered a T-6 Texan fighter to attack a Communist gun position not far from Nam Tha. Of course, the RLAF pilots were not proficient in the T-6 at the time, so nothing was seen or hit by the pilot. Unwavering, Phoumi pushed forward, determined to convince the U.S. that he was, indeed, the man in charge.

Minor skirmishes continued until February 1, at which time the Communist troops stepped up offensive actions. The airstrip at Nam Tha was mortared again, forcing the T-6s to reposition at Luang Prabang. Two days later the shelling intensified even more, with artillery rounds landing closer to the center of town, causing panic among the civilians. Phoumi again reacted quickly, bringing in several hundred paratroopers using RLAF transports. The PEO was against this move, because they perceived it as a potential trap by the Communists to lure government troops into an ambush situation—similar to the slaughter of the French at Dien Bien Phu, but on a smaller scale.

Later, the shelling intensified again, destroying approximately 50 homes in the town and prompting Phoumi to request airlift support from the U.S. to bring in a parachute battalion from Seno Air Base near Vientiane. The PEO balked, because they were now certain the trap at Nam Tha would be sprung by the Communists. Phoumi then decided to use his own C-47 aircraft to bring in the battalion. The PEO Chief, General Boyle, was irritated because Phoumi had gone against his advice, and he voiced his displeasure in a cable to JCS. He reported that he believed Phoumi was intentionally attempting to widen the war, which could lead to a requirement for U.S. ground troops. Phoumi's action also got the attention of the White House, and on February 28, JFK directed Admiral Felt, CINCPAC, to make the U.S. position clear to Phoumi. To accomplish that, Felt was to contact Marshal Sarit, the Thai military chief, who was Phoumi's cousin. Felt was instructed to tell Sarit that the U.S. would not be drawn into war based upon Phoumi's stubbornness. Kennedy also wanted Sarit and Phoumi to understand that he still supported Phoumi, in order to keep a balanced coalition in Laos, but wanted him to understand that he was courting military disaster.

On March 5, Felt met with Sarit as directed, and passed on the President's message. On the next day, Felt sat down with Phoumi in Bangkok, and very carefully repeated the message sent by President Kennedy. The Admiral also emphasized the need for Phoumi to join with Souvanna in a united front against the Pathet Lao and North Vietnamese. After considerable arguing and posturing, Phoumi reluctantly agreed to comply with President Kennedy's guidance. Having completed his mission, Admiral Felt returned to Honolulu, but had the nagging feeling that Phoumi had no intention of following the President's guidance or aligning with Souvanna.

As it turned out, the little voice in Felt's head was correct. Phoumi completely disregarded all the advice from the United States, and in effect ignored all the U.S. officials. To emphasize its position, the U.S. later withheld the monthly payroll for the RLG. In the interim, Phoumi and Boun Oum were left to stew in their own juices for several weeks. At that point, Sarit used his influence to schedule a meeting between himself, Phoumi and Averell Harriman, the U.S. Assistant Secretary of State for Far Eastern Affairs. The meeting was held in Nong Khai, Thailand, a Mekong River town near Vientiane. At the meeting, Sarit warned Phoumi that if he proceeded with the troop build-up at Nam Tha, he could wind up causing Laos to be overrun by the Communists. But, he pointed out, if Phoumi aligned himself with Souvanna, the country had a good chance of remaining independent. Sarit also encouraged Phoumi to invite Souvanna to Vientiane for discussions on the matter. At that point, Harriman spoke up, and said that any such meeting would be meaningless, unless Phoumi was agreeable to relinquishing his control of the defense and interior ministries. Phoumi listened, but was not amenable to the terms set forth by Harriman and Sarit. He did agree, however, to a meeting with Souvanna in Vientiane, and also promised to consult with his government colleagues on future matters. But that was as far as Phoumi would go. With that being said, the meeting ended, and Harriman dutifully reported the results of the meeting to Washington. He didn't stop there, however.

That afternoon, Harriman flew to Vientiane and requested an audience with the King. He was received, and bluntly told the King that Phoumi was an obstruction to peace in Laos. The King listened, but took exception to Harriman's characterization of Phoumi, and countered by stating that Phoumi was a patriotic national leader fighting against Communism locally, and against the North Vietnamese. King Savang Vatthana went on to say that he supported Phoumi's position and that no matter what happened, the Pathet Lao would not have a place in any new government. Later, as the meeting wound down, Harriman cautioned the King about the potential consequences of Phoumi's actions, including the possibility of the Communists taking over Laos. The meeting ended with the King essentially saying that history would take care of itself.

The following day, Harriman held another meeting in Vientiane to reemphasize the comments he had made the previous day to Phoumi and the King. Present at the meeting was the Country Team, Boun Oum, Phoumi, and other Lao Cabinet members. Harriman's comments did not, however, lead to any revelations or commitments by the Lao officials attending the meeting. By this time Harriman was convinced that his attempts to get Phoumi and the Lao to see things his way had been completely unsuccessful. So Harriman called it a day and departed Laos. His assistant, William Sullivan, stayed behind, and later met with Souvanna at Khang Khai. During the meeting, Sullivan assured the Prince the United States was still committed to do everything it could help Laos form a coalition government.

Not long afterwards, on May 6, four Pathet Lao battalions reinforced by NVA troops attacked Nam Tha again, and drove the RLA troops from the city. The retreating government troops fled across the river into Thailand. Also in May, three U.S. T-28 Trojan aircraft were transferred from South Vietnam to the Royal Thai Air Force at Kokotiem. The aircraft were provided to allow the RLAF pilots the ability to upgrade from the antiquated T-6 to the better, newer, faster T-28. Five USAF instructors were also assigned to run the T-28 training facility, and by August, approximately 20 RLAF pilots had received upgrade training in the T-28s. The instruction included formation flying, night operations, gunnery, and instrument flying. They also practiced different types of bombing techniques. But the T-28 was restricted to daytime use, flying due to instrument limitations; and the aircraft had not been modified to carry napalm or rockets. In addition to pilot training, 48 RLAF mechanics received classroom and on-the-job training (OJT) in maintenance and repair of the new T-28. Still, by year's end, no T-28s had seen action in Laos. It appeared that the reason was because Ambassador Brown believed the Lao already had sufficient aircraft available to handle their requirements.

At this juncture, It seemed that the only hope for Laos lay with the talks in Geneva. Nam Tha was lost, and North Vietnam had increased its troop strength yet again in Laos. Sam Neua and Phong Saly were solidly under Pathet Lao control, and President Kennedy's confidence in General Phoumi had been shattered. Also, Phoumi had gone against the advice of the PEO and Admiral Felt. Secretary Rusk believed that Phoumi had rejected any political compromise that would have led to the NVA removing its troops from Laos. But history had already shown that North Vietnam had no intention of leaving Laos; In fact, just the opposite was the case. The NVA had consistently increased the number of troops in Laos since the mid-1950s. At any rate, JFK believed Phoumi should be removed from power, once and for all. And, to that end, Ambassador Brown was told to spread the word that Phoumi was to blame for the current state of affairs in Laos, and that the United States had no confidence in the General.

The new MAAG commander, U.S. Army Major General Reuben H. Tucker, was also directed to tell Phoumi that the defeat at Nam Tha was his fault, and the U.S. would stop paying the salaries of the FAL if American guidance continued to be ignored. Later, a somewhat subdued Phoumi met with Ambassador Brown on May 10 to discuss Nam Tha. Of course, Brown blamed Phoumi for the debacle at Nam Tha, and said that it wouldn't have happened if he had listened to General Boyle. Brown also encouraged Phoumi to give up the Defense and Interior ministries. Phoumi then met with General Tucker on May 13, and Tucker reiterated what Brown had said. Tucker also submitted a list of proposals (demands) to Phoumi designed to restore confidence in him.

Essentially, the proposals called for the removal of all incompetent senior officers, and that Phoumi was to follow MAAG's advice on backfilling those slots. Phoumi was also directed to develop a first-class Non Commissioned Officer (NCO) corps and better utilize existing training facilities. Additionally, the Ministry of Defense was to be reorganized, and a better system of delegation of authority instituted. And, finally, the MAAG was to approve the final rosters of all applicants selected for training.

Most of General Tucker's proposals were designed to correct long-term problems in the Lao Armed Forces. For example, training materials provided by the U.S. had not been utilized; and there was no delegation of authority in the FAL, because the higher ranking officers considered everyone below their level as incompetent. But Phoumi was not completely at fault, because he, personally, had little say in the appointment of senior officers. In Laos, high ranking officials were appointed based upon wealth, status and family lineage. So even if he wanted to replace some members of his senior staff, he didn't have the authority.

Phoumi also believed that when, and if, the Geneva Accords were signed, the MAAG would be required to vacate Laos, taking General Tucker and his staff out of the equation and out of his hair. But what Phoumi failed to take into consideration was that the MAAG wouldn't go far if it was directed to leave Laos: it would just relocate across the Mekong River, in neighboring Thailand. And, obviously, Phoumi didn't stop to realize that the United States would still be paying the salaries of the FAL. So ultimately, Phoumi made the career-limiting decision to smile, pay lip service to the U.S., and wait for the Geneva Accords.

Meanwhile, in early June 1962, the three brothers—Souvanna, Souphanouvong, and Boun Oum—met on the Plain of Jars for a series of talks. On June 11, the three princes agreed on the structure of a new coalition government. Seven cabinet posts would go to Souvanna's Neutralists, four would go to Souphanouvong's Pathet Lao, and four would go to Phoumi's group. Four additional posts would also go to the right-wing neutralists in Vientiane who remained uncommitted to Phoumi. Souvanna was to be the Prime Minster; Soupannavong was to be the Deputy Prime Minister and Minister of Economic Planning. Phoumi would be granted the titles of Deputy Prime Minister and Minister of Finance.

At that time of year, the monsoon season was in full force, and was drenching Southeast Asia with rain. The few roads existing in Laos were rain-soaked and slick, and did not offer a viable way to get supplies to the troops and the refugees. The only effective way was by air, but this alternative wasn't easy either. The monsoons brought heavy cloud cover, making flying in the mountains extremely dangerous. Nonetheless, Air America did an extraordinary job in getting supplies delivered . . . but even they could only do so much. When the clouds did break, Air America was airborne, and after winding their way through narrow valleys and finding small holes in the clouds, down they went to deliver the much-needed supplies. During that monsoon season, approximately 20 Americans were lost while delivering supplies.

Meanwhile, Vang Pao was looking for a new place to establish a headquarters. Pha Khao was getting a lot of attention, and the Communists already knew too much about Sam Thong. But, a few miles away from Pha Khao, and just over a ridgeline from Sam Thong, was a place called Long Tieng (Long Cheng). One of Bill Lair's men had recently taken a ride with an Air America pilot to survey Long Tieng; he reported that the grassy valley and surrounding limestone karsts of Long Tieng would be an excellent place to establish a new base of operations.

Long Tieng was on a five-mile-long plateau south of the Plain of Jars, and about 60 miles northeast of Vientiane. Limestone mountains formed a natural barrier on three sides of the plateau, a fur of dark green moss covered the mountains, and scrubby trees grew in a myriad of shapes and sizes. Pop Buell had also discovered Long Tieng, and had been busy having a dirt airstrip prepared on the valley floor for use in the USAID refugee relocation program.

Pop envisioned Long Tieng as an excellent place to resettle the refugees. He had even commenced construction of living quarters, medical facilities and schools, so the homeless war-torn Hmong could start over in peace. But the valley's strategic value made it a better choice for VP's new headquarters. So Pop reluctantly agreed to relocate the refugee center to Sam Thong. With all the details hashed out, Long Tieng soon became the new Secret War headquarters, and received the designation of Lima Site 20A (LS-20A).

Figure 17. Pop Buell and USAID Nurse
Photo from the Public Domain

Later that summer, Pop settled into the abandoned U.S. Army Special Forces base at Sam Thong, or LS-20 as it was also known. By this time, he had successfully relocated thousands of Hmong refugees out of harm's way to LS-20. With the assistance of USAID, Pop provided the refugees with food, shelter and medical care. Based upon his successful efforts with the refugee program, Pop was also becoming a well-known person in Laos; he could walk into just about anyone's office at the embassy in Vientiane unannounced, and without an appointment. In fact, Pop had been known to walk into a room, interrupt a meeting, say whatever was on his mind, and walk out. On some of these occasions, he had just returned from several days in the field. It didn't bother him any that his clothes were dirty and that he hadn't had a bath in days. You could say that he was a man who was comfortable in his own skin.

Also, by this time he had started many schools, and the Hmong were enrolling their children in record numbers. But for all the good that Pop intended, the bureaucrats at the embassy were not pleased. In their view, the schools had been constructed of substandard building materials, and the teachers weren't college-educated professionals—which was a requirement of USAID. In his simple way, Pop explained to the bureaucrats that the program was working, and the kids were learning, and that was the true measure of success; not the credentials of the teachers. As we mentioned earlier in the book, Pop was a retired farmer from Indiana. He was a simple man of ordinary stock. He didn't mince words, and he spoke very simply and frankly. On occasion, when he would get frustrated with the embassy staff, he would refer to them as being "educated fools" when they did not, or could not, see things from his perspective.

Pop also oversaw the construction of a modern hospital at Sam Thong, and established a medical training program for nurses and medical assistants. He then filled the vacant warehouses at Sam Thong with blankets, cookware, and rice for the refugees, and even went so far as to anticipate and distribute food and other essentials to the refugees on a scheduled basis. For his own comfort, Pop used an empty office in one of the warehouses as his residence and office. It was just a makeshift office in the back corner of the building, with a cot in the corner. That was the extent of his accommodations, and he was perfectly happy with that arrangement.

Earlier in the year, Vint Lawrence had arrived in Bangkok and had spent a few days getting acclimated. He got to know the people at the embassy, and took care of some routine administrative matters. Then he proceeded to Vientiane to meet his employers at the U.S. embassy there. It wasn't a good idea to go around town telling people that he worked for the CIA, so like the other Agency personnel in Vientiane, he needed a cover, an innocuous title that would not draw undue suspicion. But, it had to be something that was at least somewhat believable. He soon learned that his cover would be that he was an Army artillery officer assigned to the joint liaison group working out of the embassy. He was to report directly to Bill Lair, who, up to this point, had no idea who Lawrence was, or why he has been assigned to him. In order to get Lawrence out of his hair, Lair sent Vint to assist Pat Landry, who was running a guerrilla training camp southwest of Bangkok. L,ater after his 60-day probationary period ended, Lawrence traveled back to Vientiane to join Lair and the paramilitary operations in northern Laos.[31]

For the next several months, Lawrence spent his time traveling around to the various Lima Sites in Laos. Along the way he met Vang

Pao, and struck up a friendship with him. VP seemed to take a liking to Lawrence, and more importantly, he could communicate easily with Lawrence because they both were fluent in French. The two new friends spent quite a bit of time in quiet conversation, and a bond of mutual trust soon developed.

Meanwhile, North Vietnam steadily increased the number of their soldiers in Laos. In August, NVA troops attacked the town of Ban Ban in northeastern Laos, home to over 5,000 Lao and Hmong citizens. Having almost no means to defend themselves, the villagers fled southward. After almost 24 hours of flight, they finally stopped to rest in a bowl-shaped valley off the beaten path. Thinking they were safe, the weary villagers quickly went to sleep. But just after midnight, NVA soldiers crept into the camp where the villagers slept, slowly encircling the entire encampment. Then they began shooting, stabbing, and beating the villagers. In panic, the villagers fled again, only to be pursued by the soldiers. One by one, they were overtaken and killed. Some of the older people were shot in the legs and left to die in the jungle. Small children were killed with crushing blows from the butts of AK-47 assault rifles. Women were raped, stabbed, and left to die beside the trails. The slaughter finally ended early the next morning; but by then, over 1,000 unarmed villagers had been murdered, and another 200 had been taken prisoner. Those who managed to escape slowly continued on to the town of Muong Meo, 40 miles away.

It didn't take long for the news to reach the embassy in Vientiane. Pop Buell and other USAID personnel responded quickly, and subsequently arranged to move the survivors by Air America aircraft to Muang Cha, where they could hopefully recuperate and start over. Doctor Charles Weldon, a USAID physician, and his staff attended to the survivors as well as they could.[32] But dysentery had also struck the survivors, and many died. VP visited Muang Cha as often as possible to offer encouragement and assistance to the refugees.

Meanwhile, in Geneva, the talks dragged on. The North Vietnamese were stubborn and tried to intimidate some of the participants; but Averell Harriman, the U.S. representative, refused to be intimidated. When he made a point, he continued to repeat it, over and over, until his opponents finally gave in. Then, when it was the North Vietnamese turn to speak, Harriman would appear totally uninterested as he sat and read *The New York Times*. Thankfully the talks finally ended on July 23, 1962, with all fourteen nations signing the "Declaration on the Neutrality of Laos." The agreement was something of a rehash of the 1954 agreements. Laos was to remain a neutral country; except for military attachés, there were to be no foreign troops on Laotian soil, and any foreign military personnel already there were to leave by October 6. The only arms and military equipment allowed in Laos would be those used by the Lao government for self-defense. In addition, foreign countries could not establish a presence in Laos that could be used to attack, or interfere with, other countries. Finally, the International Control Commission (ICC) was to monitor activities in Laos to ensure the accords were honored.

The Geneva Accords allowed only the French to retain military advisors in the country. The U.S. Air Force Attaché (AIRA) and the Army Attaché (ARMA), who were allowed to remain in Laos, later assumed the duties previously handled by the MAAG. To handle the air portion of the MAAG duties (including the RLAF) and to handle the USAF combat activities, the AIRA was limited to just 100 support personnel. In addition to the above, the AIRA had to also attend to his routine attaché duties and all the other miscellaneous administrative duties assigned to his office.

Even though the Geneva Accords had been reached (again), violence continued to escalate in both northern Laos and along the Ho Chi Minh Trail in southern Laos. Of course, none of the parties at the Geneva talks chose to correctly invest the resources necessary to stop the continued violence. And inasmuch as North Vietnam had previously gone on record as not having military personnel in Laos, they did not have to remove any from the country. So it appeared that except for the U.S. troops leaving the country, it would be business as usual in the Secret War—though no new weapons were being issued to the Hmong, and ammunition drops were temporarily discontinued.

As required by the Geneva Accords of 1962, the United States withdrew all military personnel (numbering about 1,000) from Laos. That number included all the White Star personnel and the MAAG staff; the withdrawal also affected the new logistics center at Sam Thong. Everything was left just where it was. The U.S. military personnel simply walked away—or more accurately, boarded helicopters and flew away. Right after the logistics center at Sam Thong was vacated, looters swarmed over the base, taking all the medical supplies and materials stored in the warehouses.

In the haste to vacate Laos, the Thai PARU personnel were not noticed by the ICC, because they managed to blend in with the Hmong guerrillas; so they didn't leave Laos after the Geneva Accords were implemented. They continued to help the Hmong and the CIA. And of course, the U.S. troops who left Laos didn't go far away. Secretary of Defense Robert McNamara decided to relocate the MAAG to Bangkok, and General Tucker would remain its head under the pseudonym of Deputy Chief, Joint United States Military Advisory Group, Thailand (DEPCHJUSMAGTHAI). The MAAG would still support Laos, but would have no external identification with the kingdom. The total authorized strength of the MAAG would be just about 100 personnel. In order to work closely with the FAL, a Requirements Office (RO) was installed at the U.S. Embassy in Vientiane. Their task was to monitor the defense support budget, and receive, store and distribute all MAP equipment. The RO would be staffed by civilian logistics specialists and retired U.S. military personnel.

At about this same time, a new U.S. Ambassador to Laos was named as a replacement for Winthrop Brown. His name was Leonard Unger; he was a career diplomat, and former Deputy Chief of Mission in Bangkok.

Under the Geneva Accords, the CIA paramilitary officers overseeing the conduct of the Secret War were required to leave Laos, along with the MAAG. And for the most part they did, except for Tony Poe and Vint Lawrence, who (illegally) remained behind at Long Tieng. But the CIA didn't go far away in any case; they also simply moved across the river into Thailand. At first, Bill Lair set up a temporary headquarters for his paramilitary operation at Nong Khai, a village across the river from Vientiane. That way, he would still close to the action. But the location didn't offer much in the way of security, and Lair was quite a ways away from other support functions. In fact, at Nong Khai, just about anyone could literally walk in off the street. So it was decided that Lair would stay in Nong Khai only until he could find a better, more secure operating location. Since the CIA also controlled property at Udorn Royal Thai Air Force Base, Lair went there to take a look. What he discovered was an empty wooden building with a sign above the door that read "AB-1."

Apparently the CIA owned the building, but hadn't used it in quite some time. It resembled a traditional Thai style bungalow, and it was located near the Air America compound, adjacent to the huge concrete runway. It was perfect; Lair knew he had found a new home from which he could run the Secret War over in Laos. The location would work well, because there was already so much activity going on at Udorn in support of the Secret War that a few more Caucasians wandering around in khakis wouldn't draw all that much attention. Therefore, Lair and another CIA officer by the name of Roy Moffit (later replaced by Pat Landry) set up shop in what would always thereafter be referred to simply as "AB-1."

Now that the CIA was active on an installation run by the USAF, they needed some kind of cover story and name. After much discussion, It was decided that their official cover would be as the 4802nd Joint Liaison Detachment (JLD). It sounded good, and since it wasn't officially tied to the CIA, no one could ever trace the name back to the agency. They didn't bother tell anyone who they were; they just chose the name and moved in at AB-1. From then on, many people would come and go from AB-1. It was a busy place, just as the Air America compound nearby was a busy place. In fact, everyone on the base was busy because, in one form or another, they were all supporting the Secret War.

Over the years, many important Congressmen, Senators, and other Washington big shots would visit the little building known simply as AB-1, while on official missions (boondoggles) to Southeast Asia. Some of the government officials wondered how such an important paramilitary war in Laos could be run from this rundown little bungalow. Some even voiced their concerns upon returning to Washington. So after several years of much thought and careful consideration, it was finally decided by some bigwig at CIA Headquarters that AB-1 would be replaced. In 1967, construction began on a new concrete building. The large building was over-designed, overbuilt, and exceeded the budget several times over. In other words, it was another successful project of the Agency's Overseas Buildings Office (OBO). It should be pointed out, however, that Bill Lair wasn't responsible for the new concrete monster; he and his team had been just as happy as clams in the old wooden bungalow. Bill didn't want the concrete behemoth, and he didn't need it.

Another action taken under the accords was to suspend all aid to Laos. President Kennedy was adamant that the United States abide by the agreements reached in Geneva, so even the USAID contracts were terminated. The only aid provided was an occasional emergency delivery of refugee supplies to Pop Buell, and mercy missions to the Hmong. This was pretty much the way it was for the next few months.

Meanwhile, Hanoi put on a public display for the press and announced that it didn't have any combat troops in Laos, but it would withdraw all its military officers, technicians and advisors. Ultimately, Hanoi removed just under 100 personnel, and no mention was made of the 10,000 uniformed troops that North Vietnam had in the country. The Soviet Union also halted its covert airlift in November 1962, and turned over about a dozen of its aircraft (and instructors) to the new coalition government in Vientiane.

Before the ink had dried on the Geneva Accords, North Vietnam began a steady build-up of troops in northeastern Laos. Part of the reason for the increase was to stiffen the Pathet Lao ranks. The NVA had hoped that Kong Le would bring his Neutralist troops to join the Pathet Lao, but that didn't happen; so to hedge their bets, the NVA began sending more of their own troops into the country. Meanwhile, the fighting continued in northern Laos, as Hmong guerrillas continued to die in order to keep Laos free and to perform to the expectations of the CIA. As the fighting continued, VP, now a general, arranged a meeting with Souvanna Phouma, the Prime Minister. VP told the Souvanna that he was happy the talks in Geneva had taken place, but that he was also sad because he knew that North Vietnam had no intention of honoring the accords. Some of those present at the meeting reported that Souvanna listened, but said nothing.

Meanwhile, by the fall of 1962, VP had settled into his new headquarters at Long Tieng. The CIA was also busy constructing its facilities at LS-20A, which were simply referred to as "Sky." Still more CIA officers continued to arrive. A small village sprang up in the valley almost overnight, complete with an outdoor market and dozens of huts that served as residences and businesses. There were no roads into or out of Long Tieng in 1962, but within a few years, a dirt road was constructed between Long Tieng and Sam Thong, a distance of roughly ten miles.

As mentioned earlier, Pop Buell had made arrangements to have a dirt airstrip carved out of the valley floor at Long Tieng. Initially it was about 2,000 feet long, but some years later, it was extended to about 4,000 feet and topped with asphalt. When LS-20A became operational, aircraft began to come and go on a daily basis in support of the Secret War. The positioning of the runway, however, did offer some challenges. For, example all landing aircraft had to approach from the only side of the valley that had no mountains; and after touching down, depending on the size of the aircraft, the pilot needed to apply the brakes right away, because at the end of the short runway was a large limestone rock formation, or karst, as they were called, rising straight up into the sky. The rock formation was affectionately referred to as "the vertical speed brake"—and it did see occasional use when an unfamiliar pilot underestimated the required stopping distance, resulting in an aircraft being reduced to a pile of aluminum scattered about the base of the karst. The old hands who flew there regularly knew the perils well, and didn't hesitate to share their stories with the younger pilots.

A former USAF helicopter pilot was quoted as saying that the runway at Long Tieng was also unusual because

> " . . . All fixed wing aircraft landed west and departed east regardless of the wind direction. The west third of the runway had a hump that prevented aircraft on one end from seeing aircraft on the other end. There was also a well-used road that crossed the runway, near the center. A makeshift tower would display a large piece of plywood, painted green, when it was safe to cross the runway using the street. When it wasn't safe, the tower would display a piece of plywood painted red, indicating not to cross due to aircraft traffic coming or going. And if the red warning panel was ignored, the guy manning the tower would fire a machine gun into the air to discourage villagers from crossing the runway."

This same pilot recalled a personal experience when he was stopped on the side of the runway waiting for the green panel to be displayed.

"While waiting, an RLAF captain on a motorcycle pulled in
front of a waiting truck and stopped. After waiting for a few
minutes and not seeing the green panel, the captain motored
on, ignoring the red panel. The captain's arrogance apparently
irritated the tower operator, who grabbed a machine gun
and began firing it wildly into the air. The RLAF captain then
pulled out his own pistol and likewise fired it wildly into the
air. The activity then emboldened the USAF pilot, who also
proceeded up the runway, disregarding the red panel. When
the shooting stopped, both pilots made it to the briefing
room unharmed, where they attended a weather briefing for
the next leg of their flights that day. The pilots departed later,
and waved to the tower operator as they flew by."

When Long Tieng opened, the only CIA personnel in residence
were Tony Poe and Vint Lawrence, who had illegally remained
behind after the Geneva Accords were reached; but as time passed,
the CIA constructed many buildings at Long Tieng. The CIA personnel
were not the only residents of the new secret base, however; many
Hmong refugees also relocated to the site, as well as the families of
the Hmong guerrillas working for Vang Pao. Soon, Long Tieng was
one of the larger cities in Laos, although it had no running water
or electricity. Long Tieng, or, "The Alternate", as it became known,
was a very busy place. On any given day, Air America aircraft would
begin landing fairly early in the morning. The aircraft would disgorge
supplies, ammunition, guerrilla fighters, and numerous Americans
transiting the base on official business. The activity would continue
throughout the day, with the last aircraft leaving just before sundown.
Generally speaking, aircraft didn't remain on the ground overnight,
unless absolutely necessary, because they could become targets for
snipers or Communist artillery. And early on in the war, there was no
real transient billeting facilities for overnight visitors.

One thing that was really frowned upon at Long Tieng was
night landings, for many good reasons. All landings and take-offs
were uncontrolled; that is, there was no radar or ground-controlled
approach. Instead, arriving and departing aircraft used visual flight
references; in other words, they looked to make sure no other aircraft
were landing or taking off when they needed to land or take off. Also,
there were no runway lights for night landings, so to land at night

would be considered suicidal. Night landings did take place, but only in emergency situations. In the event an aircraft needed to land at night, Long Tieng would be contacted by radio, and a jeep would park on the approach end of the runway with its lights on. As the aircraft approached, the pilot would line up on the jeep's headlights, attempt to find the runway surface, and try to stop in time before coming in contact with the vertical speed brake. To assist the landing aircraft, lighted lanterns would be placed at intervals along the runway edges if time permitted. Suffice it to say, night landings rarely took place.

One such emergency situation reportedly took place in 1970, when USAF Captain John Halliday was forced to make an emergency landing in his C-123 Provider, after flying an illumination flare mission over northern Laos. The crew had tried, unsuccessfully, to alert Long Tieng that they were coming, and they were not sure of their direction. To make matters worse, it was pitch black and no visual references could be seen. The aircraft did finally land from the wrong direction (west to east), which would have been technically improbable. After landing, Halliday applied the brakes, and the aircraft finally stopped at the very east end of the runway. Captain Halliday described the landing and the events that followed in exciting detail in his book *Flying through Midnight*.

But getting back to 1962, and the time period just after the Geneva Accords were signed: the two Americans remaining at LS-20A, Tony Poe and Vint Lawrence, did their best to maintain good relations with Vang Pao. With no

A. LS20A Aircraft Parking Ramp   B. LS20A Aerial View

Figure 18. LS20A Landing Area
(Photos from the Public Domain)

aid coming in, they occupied their time by collecting raw intelligence information. Teams of indigenous personnel in the field would send in daily coded reports to Long Tieng, and people of all descriptions coming and going from Long Tieng would be debriefed. The collected information was then formalized in a daily situation report and transmitted to Bill Lair at Udorn. In addition to his paramilitary duties at Long Tieng, Lawrence would also provide assistance to Pop Buell at Sam Thong by helping Pop prepare the refugee shipments for transport by Air America. In exchange, Pop would provide Lawrence with intelligence information gleaned from the refugees who passed through Sam Thong, or people Pop had otherwise talked to while he was in the field. As mentioned earlier, Vint and Vang Pao became fast friends. VP knew that Vint cared about the Hmong and the cause for which they were fighting. The two also had many interesting conversations about politics, war, and the world.

It was also well-known that VP held big dinners just about every night at Long Tieng. On any given evening, as many as forty people might be invited. VP would also have his visiting field commanders present, on occasion, and any Americans transiting the base may also be invited. The fare was usually simple: chicken, pork if they had it, and any other meat that could be found would be served, along with sticky rice and local vegetables. The local whiskey, Lau Lau, would flow freely at these dinners, and occasionally a bottle of good whiskey would appear, courtesy of Air America or a pilot passing through. In those days it was not uncommon for aviators to carry bottles of liquor in their flight bags. It could be used for trading or given as a gift, and on rare occasions used by the crew (strictly for medicinal purposes, of course) if the need arose. At any rate, the evening meal at VP's house was an event in and of itself. Attendees were free to speak their minds, even if it was on a matter with which VP disagreed. Of course, everyone realized who was ultimately in charge, and that was VP. It had to be that way, at that time.

One pilot, transiting Long Tieng, described his experience after being invited to VP's house for dinner. As he recalled it, he, and his crew were on a special mission to relocate refugees for VP. Normally, they did not Remain Overnight (RON) at LS-20A, because their aircraft made attractive targets, but on this occasion, they were required to stay overnight, and were invited to dinner. As the story goes, they arrived at the residence in the late afternoon and joined numerous other guests who were standing in a large meeting room waiting for the festivities. Suddenly, a Hmong captain, in uniform, was physically dragged into the room for a hearing before VP. Apparently, the captain had been accused of not being aggressive in leading his men in the defense of a hilltop position, and was being held accountable. VP reportedly listened to the testimony offered by all the concerned parties; the officer was found guilty by VP, and sentenced to serve time in an underground tiger pit. The officer was apparently unhappy about the sentence. He legs buckled, and he was physically carried from the room, protesting along the way. Later, VP acknowledged all his guests, and presented them with tokens of his appreciation for assisting the Hmong.

After the ceremony, everyone moved to the dining room next door, where dinner was served. They were each given a water glass filled three-fourths of the way up with brandy, and serving plates were then passed containing rice and a vegetable that appeared to be spinach, two sauces, and meat. The visiting pilots, not wanting to stand out, quickly dug into their rice and vegetable dishes, as did the other guests. Then they suddenly realized that they had both bitten into, and were chewing, some very hot delicacies. The only problem was that there was no water on the table to drink and wash the food down.

By this time, the other guests appeared to be aware of the visiting pilots' dilemma. But, in reality, they knew exactly what was taking place, and were having a good laugh along with the other guests. In fact, this very situation took place countless times over the years, and was a source of great entertainment for the regular attendees who dined at VP's house. The two pilots were able to make it through the evening, however, pretty much unscathed, and returned to their quarters, where they thoroughly enjoyed a few cold beers to finally put out the last of the fires in their mouths.

At this point in time, the Geneva accords were still being implemented in Laos. The new coalition still retained its military forces; the strength of the FAR was at about 50,000 men, and Phoumi's crony, General Bounleut, remained as its Commander in Chief. Under Bounleut was Ouane Rathikoun, his Chief of Staff; and, under Rathikoun in the command structure were the five Military Regions. Following close behind were the Neutralists Armed Forces (FAN), commanded by Kong Le, who spent most of his time at his headquarters in Khong Kai. And last, but certainly not least, were the ever-present Pathet Lao, with over 19,000 men on the roster. The Pathet Lao operated primarily out of the Sam Neua and Xieng Khouang Provinces, and supporting the Pathet Lao were hundreds, if not thousands, of NVA advisors and stiffeners.

Of course, the North Vietnamese didn't officially exist, because they had gone on record as not having any ground troops in Laos. And since many NVA soldiers wore Pathet Lao uniforms, no one knew for sure what the real numbers were. The ICC certainly didn't. In October 1962, Souvanna Phouma sent letters to Ambassador Unger and to the Soviet Ambassador, Sergei Aianasseyev, asking for assistance for his Neutralist forces in northern Laos. The Russians responded by offering Souvanna several Ilyushin transport aircraft that had already been operating in Laos. They also offered pilots and crews to fly the aircraft, until such time as RLAF personnel could be trained. The Americans were unsurprised by Souvanna's request for assistance because it was common knowledge the Pathet Lao had been short-changing Kong Le for some time. The problem arose when the Communists took control of all supply deliveries early on. They would take what they wanted first, and Kong Le would get what was left over—and what he got wasn't enough to supply his troops. When Kong Le complained, he was accused by the Communists of not being a true Neutralist.

After promising support, the Russians were slow to act, and supplies were still not reaching Kong Le's men. This was due, in part, to the continued support of the Pathet Lao by the Soviets. It was something of a balancing act, keeping the Communists well-provisioned and appeasing Souvanna at the same time. Of course, this arrangement didn't work, and tensions increased on the Plain of Jars. In September 1962, Ambassador Unger flew to the Plain for a meeting with Kong Le. By this time, the Neutralist leader had toned down his anti-American rhetoric and had requested U.S. assistance for his troops. Unger approved, and authorized an airlift to Kong Le. Later, on November 27, two C-46 transports and one C-123 aircraft flown by Air America personnel departed Wattay Airport in Vientiane, destined for the Plain of Jars. All three were loaded with supplies for Kong Le's Neutralists.

What happened next isn't completely clear, but it was believed that both C-46 transports landed without incident; but the C-123 was shot down by antiaircraft fire while on final approach. The aircraft was damaged beyond repair and the two Air America pilots, Frederick J. Riley and Donald C. Heritage, were killed in the incident. The flight engineer, who was not named, survived the crash.[33]

Ambassador Unger suspected the Pathet Lao were behind the downing of the Air America C-123, as they had been complaining for several months about Air America's support to the Hmong. Air America aircraft operating in the area had been fired on at least a dozen times in the previous three weeks. Perhaps the addition of the Neutralists to the resupply roster was the last straw for the Pathet Lao—or so it was thought. Later, it was determined that Kong Le's disgruntled deputy, Lieutenant Colonel Deuan Sunnalath, had ordered the aircraft to be shot down. Apparently, Sunnalath had become a Pathet Lao sympathizer. Souvanna then complained to his brother, Souphanouvong, but the Pathet Lao leader downplayed the incident. He related that it had been merely a misunderstanding about the aircraft's authorization to land that day on the Plain. According to Souphanouvong, there was no clearance on file for the aircraft to land, therefore it was deemed a hostile aircraft and fired upon. But, based upon all the other things going on at that particular moment, Souvanna did not press the issue. It would just have to wait until another time.

On November 27, the same day the C-123 was shot down, Souvanna presented Ambassador Unger with an even larger shopping list for war materials. He asked for hundreds of thousands of rounds of small arms ammunition, thousands of artillery shells, and more than 30,000 gallons of gasoline. Unger wasn't completely surprised by the request, but wasn't about to provide everything on the list. He wanted to keep Kong Le in the war, but anything other than small shipments of arms and ammunition would have to be approved by Washington.

The list was forwarded to the State Department in D.C., where it was reviewed by William P. Bundy, Deputy Assistant Secretary for International Security Affairs under the Secretary of the Navy. Bundy was somewhat reluctant to support Souvanna's request, because he was wary of Kong Le's propensity to share supplies with the Pathet Lao. Bundy wanted a pledge from Kong Le agreeing to only distribute the supplies to the 4,000 or so troops under his command. Bundy also questioned the munitions requirements. Later, on December 4,

Bundy approved Souvanna's request with stipulations. First, Kong Le would have to promise the supplies would go to his men only; and Bundy wanted the ammunition to be doled out in small portions, to hopefully keep it out of Pathet Lao hands.

While all this activity was taking place, the Soviets delivered six of their older model IL-14 transports, two AN-2 Colt Biplanes, and one Mi-4 Hound helicopter to Wattay Airport. This event took place ahead of schedule, and the Soviets vowed not to exercise any operational control over the aircraft. They also pledged to follow-through with the pilot training programs, and not to operate the aircraft until the RLAF pilots were trained. But the Soviets were a little more generous to the North Vietnamese, giving them newer long-range IL-14s to fly supplies to the Pathet Lao forces in Laos.

By this time, it was apparent the fragile Geneva Accords were unlikely to deter violence in Laos. Likewise, the relations between the Neutralists and Pathet Lao were deteriorating rapidly, not that they had ever been that strong from the beginning. The NVA had always kept the Pathet Lao well-provisioned, but supplies to the Neutralists were sporadic at best. Recognizing an opportunity, the Royalists, Neutralists and the United States soon developed an alliance.

Late in 1962, it was apparent that North Vietnam was prepared to stay the course in Laos. More NVA troops kept pouring into the country, and traffic on the Ho Chi Minh trail increased daily with the movement of war supplies and troops into South Vietnam. Given his small budget, Bill Lair did his best to keep the Hmong operating, and was even able to slowly expand the guerrilla forces. At this juncture, the U.S. finally realized they could do the same thing that North Vietnam was doing—that is, they could project the *appearance* of supporting the neutrality of Laos in public, while quietly increasing their troop strength and activity in Laos. That realization then became the new plan, and slowly, the CIA paramilitary officers quietly and illegally returned to Laos.

Meanwhile, the resupply orders from Laos continued to arrive in Washington, requesting more and more supplies for the war effort in Laos—so much so, in fact, that they prompted a fact-finding trip to the Plain of Jars. Among the visitors were Roger Hillsman from the State Department, Special Presidential Advisor Michael V. Forrestal, Ambassador Unger, and other members of the Country Team. As fate would have it, the entourage was flown to the Plain in January 1963 in one of the donated Russian IL-14s. Kong Le met with the group on January 11, and gave his assurance that supplies and ammunition would only be used to further Souvanna's goals. He also pledged his continuing support to Souvanna. During the meeting, Kong Le also took the opportunity to request additional war supplies, including a better radio base station to communicate with his troops.

After the visit, Hillsman, Forrestal and the rest of the group were convinced that it was in the best interests of the United States to support Kong Le's requests. Admiral Felt also supported the requests, but had some reservations which he later expressed to Washington. Notwithstanding, President Kennedy approved, and directed Admiral Felt to give Kong Le what he needed when he needed it. By the end of February 1963, the supplies were again being delivered to the Plain.[34]

Coincidentally, by January 1963 things were going well for Vang Pao, but he wasn't getting the supplies he needed from the CIA. He told Vint Lawrence and Tony Poe that he was considering pulling out of Operation Momentum altogether. He explained that he needed guns and ammunition, not just rice, and related that his people were sitting around and waiting without the equipment they needed to fight the war. With Lair's new authorization, VP's timing couldn't have been better. The arms and supplies began to flow.

Slowly, VP became even more convinced that Vint Lawrence was a good guy who was doing what he could to support him. So he began to open up to Lawrence, revealing his different personalities. He could be amiable and outgoing, at times, but he could also be emotional and moody on occasion—and he could be brutal when he had to be. Regarding politics, VP was very opinionated; for example, he would say that capitalism was good, and that Communism was bad. He considered himself a good guy, and was blunt in his opinion that the world was populated only by two types of people: good and bad. His money was on the good guys.

At this juncture, Souvanna's government was stumbling; but it hadn't gotten off to a good start in the first place. The Pathet Lao, of course, had no intention of supporting Souvanna; they had merely paid lip service to the coalition in order to buy time to strengthen their Communist ranks. And, by early 1963, the Pathet Lao had been further stiffened by the NVA and had solidified their power bases in Phong Saly, Xieng Khouang and Sam Neua. Their near-term objective was to weaken, divide and destroy Kong Le's troops on the Plain, while building up support for their new convert, Deuan Sunnalath. There was one obstacle, however, to the Pathet Lao's plan, and that was Colonel Ketsana—the Neutralist commander on the Plain, and one of Kong Le's deputies. Ketsana was very outspoken against Communism, and even used his connections in the newspaper business to print articles against the Pathet Lao.

While conditions deteriorated In Laos, King Savang Vatthana and Souvanna departed Laos in February for a visit to the countries that had participated in the Geneva talks. On February 12, Ketsana was assassinated. There was no clue as to the identities of the assassins, but it was suspected that the Leftist foreign minister, Colonel Quinim Pholsena, had financed the killing. The main suspect in the killing itself was Colonel Deuan Sunnalath. Deuan had been openly sympathetic to the Pathet Lao; he had also reportedly encouraged the shoot-down of the Air America C-123 back in November 1962. Kong Le and Ketsana's supporters promised retaliation.

At this point, it was obvious to everyone that the Geneva Accords would not hold, and that Laos was edging closer to all-out civil war. Upon hearing the news, President Kennedy authorized the covert delivery of supplies to the Neutralists, and directed the CIA to do what it could to save them from annihilation. Bill Lair used Kennedy's directive as an avenue to reopen the weapons pipeline to VP's guerrillas.

Shortly thereafter, in March 1963, Kong Le and his Neutralist forces on the Plain staged a rebellion. He was tired of trying to appease the NVA and others who kept offering him deals in exchange for his cooperation. Fighting soon erupted between Kong Le and the North Vietnamese, who initiated an attempted coup against Kong Le. Meanwhile, VP's scouts reported that Pathet Lao troops were moving out of Xieng Khouang to mount an attack against Kong Le. VP then planned a counterattack against the Pathet Lao to get them to retreat. He later reviewed the plan with Vint Lawrence; Lawrence liked the plan, and enhanced it by having some surplus rockets brought to the area. It would be Tony Poe's job to train the Hmong on how to use the rockets, while Lawrence and VP departed to find a site above the Plain and prepare to attack the Pathet Lao. A nearby Hmong village would also join the fight as a diversionary force.

A few days later, after Poe had finished his training and the other plans were rehearsed, the attack commenced. The Hmong guerrillas used the rockets as instructed, and the plan worked; the Pathet Lao retreated. Even though this was no great defeat for the Pathet Lao and no territory was taken, the psychological value of the win was enormous, and Washington was impressed.

On April 1, the King and Souvanna returned from their junket abroad. To celebrate their successful trip, they had planned a diplomatic reception; however, after returning from the reception, Quinim Pholsena was killed as he arrived at his home. Quinim's death infuriated the NVA and Pathet Lao, who stepped up their attacks against Kong Le. In retaliation for Quinim's killing, they attacked all Neutralist positions on the Plain. Their objectives were to cut off the delivery of supplies to Kong Le and destroy all his soldiers. Believing that Kong Le's army might be destroyed without help, Washington authorized the CIA to assist in any way necessary to avoid annihilation. Having received the green light from Washington, Lair increased VP's weapons and ammunition deliveries. In exchange, Lair expected VP and his troops to conduct a series of diversionary attacks on the Plain to draw the Communists away from the Neutralists.

By April 8, Kong Le's troops were forced to withdraw from Xieng Khouangville, Khang Khai, and Ban Ban. Souvanna then went to the ICC and requested they send a team to the Plain in order to preserve the ceasefire, but Souphanouvong protested, insisting the fighting was just an internal dispute among Kong Le's followers. Souphanouvong then quietly slipped out of Vientiane and made his way to Khang Khai, proving that security in Vientiane was inadequate. The other Pathet Lao personnel in the capital also departed for Khang Khai, signaling an end of their support to the coalition government. Meanwhile, Phoumi, who had been cooling his heels and enlarging his forces at Savannakhet, suddenly sprang into action and airlifted supplies to Kong Le's troops. His hope was that Kong Le would throw his support behind the Rightists.

Souvanna, on the other hand, preferred going to the Americans for help, so he submitted another long list of equipment and supplies to Ambassador Unger. With the war broadening, Admiral Felt directed General Tucker to fill Souvanna' s wish list immediately from existing MAP supplies. In late April, the supplies were airlifted to the Plain using RLAF C-47 transports.

With all the activity taking place in the summer of 1963, VP saw an opportunity to retake the city of Sam Neua from the Pathet Lao. His plan was to begin the operation with a diversion, using three of his four battalions of guerrillas; and that's exactly what he did. They overran a Pathet Lao garrison north of Sam Neua, and circled around it towards the east. Other Pathet Lao troops in Sam Neua fell for the trap and rushed out of the city to engage the guerrillas. Then, with San Neua only lightly defended, the fourth Hmong guerrilla battalion easily captured the city. VP's plan had worked, and the operation was a complete success. VP was suddenly an instant hero.

Meanwhile, U.S. Secretary of State Rusk received the news of the increased level of fighting in Laos, and directed Admiral Felt to prepare for stepped up action against North Vietnam. For starters, JTF-116 was notified to prepare for deployment. The USAF was told to prepare F-100 fighters for deployment to Thailand, and Admiral Felt instructed U.S. Navy ships to head for positions off South Vietnam. After this was done, the JCS began the development of a contingency plan against North Vietnam.

On April 25, the JCS forwarded several alternative plans of action to Secretary of Defense McNamara for review and presentation to Secretary Rusk and President Kennedy. The first scenario would include possible actions, such as troop buildups and demonstrations of capability, that would not violate North Vietnam's sovereignty but which *would* indicate America's intent. The second scenario included possible actions that would violate North Vietnam's sovereignty, but without physical hostile intent, such as increased aerial reconnaissance over-flights and psychological operations (leaflet drops). The final scenario included actions with hostile intent, such as blockading Haiphong Harbor and interdicting shipping

Meanwhile, Secretary Rusk dispatched Averell Harriman to Russia to solicit Soviet help in convincing North Vietnam to withdraw its troops from Laos. Andrei Gromyko, the Foreign Minister of the Soviet Union, listened to Harriman's request and then characterized the assertions of the United States as absurd. Gromyko considered the claim that North Vietnamese had troops in Laos as being unfounded. He countered that it was the United States who violated the Geneva Accords by having scores of American military personnel in Laos disguised as civilians. Harriman rebutted the allegation, stating the United States had no military personnel in Laos except as provided for in the Accords. Harriman then met with Russian Premier, Nikita Khrushchev, who was no more sympathetic to his request than was Gromyko.

Meanwhile, back in Laos, Kong Le was preparing for a counterattack against the Pathet Lao on May 16. His plan was to retake positions lost during the assaults of April. Actually, it would be more of a coordinated plan between Kong Le, Vang Pao and Phoumi, calling for simultaneous attacks by the FAR, Meo, and Neutralists in Xieng Khouangville, Nong Pet, Khang Khai and Ban Ban. The Country Team, of course, was aware of the plan, but didn't think it would succeed, because the Lao had a poor track record of coordinating and executing operations in a collective and cohesive manner. As a matter of fact, the embassy believed that if the North Vietnamese and Pathet Lao counterattacked, they could conceivably drive the government troops right off the Plain of Jars.

When Harriman got wind of the plan, he immediately cabled Unger in an attempt to squash Kong Le's reckless and foolish intentions. But at the same time, Harriman advised Unger to keep supporting the Neutralist in strong defensive positions. In that way, the Pathet Lao would show flagrant disregard for the Geneva Accords if they openly attacked the Neutralist. In other words, Harriman wanted the U.S. on firm footing if the Accords were violated. He believed that other nations in the region would stand solidly behind the US. in the event of a violation, and possibly endorse sanctions against the Communists.

There wasn't much to worry about regarding an all-out assault by Kong Le and the Neutralists, or even a large retaliation by the North Vietnamese, because the monsoon season was due to arrive in Southeast Asia. There would be no large operations during the rainy season, because the North Vietnamese always took the opportunity to withdraw most of its troops during the rainy season to rest, refit and rearm. But as a show of force, they took the opportunity to shell Kong Le's positions on the Plain before they departed for North Vietnam.

The monsoon rains did arrive shortly thereafter, and Ambassador Unger took this opportunity to reevaluate U.S. strategy. He recalled that in 1961, the U.S. had provided extensive funding and military aid to Phoumi for the establishment of a strong military to put down any Communist threat. The U.S. had also attempted to unify the country under a pro-Western style government. Inasmuch as none of this had worked, the United States decided to withdraw its support from Phoumi and put their put their support behind Souvanna Phouma. The hope was, of course, that political infighting might subside, even though Laos would remain weak from a military standpoint. It had also become clear the North Vietnamese were not going to leave, and the Pathet Lao weren't going to participate in any Lao government coalition. Unger also knew that an all-out Communist attack could come at any time, but believed that North Vietnam would be content to continue their harassment raids against the RLG positions.

Another matter that had to be considered was the type and size of the military force necessary to defend Laos. Should it be a large force capable of dealing with the Pathet Lao, or should it be a smaller force that would simply serve to sound the alarm when attacks were coming? Based upon history, and the fact that the U.S. military wasn't officially allowed to assist Laos, Washington opted for the latter. In other words, what the Lao had now would remain, without any increase in size or scope, and the status quo would be maintained.

Earlier in 1963, the United States had opted not to send U.S. ground troops into Laos; and by May, the U.S. had firmly decided to maintain the status quo, only providing support and equipment when absolutely necessary. Then June rolled around, and the White House asked the JCS to propose alternatives to sending in U.S. ground troops. On June 19, the JCS responded with a three-phase plan of gradually escalating measures. The first recommendation was to increase military assistance, intelligence collections, and air resupply to FAR, Neutralists and Hmong forces conducting operations against the Pathet Lao and North Vietnamese. This recommendation was approved immediately, and was published in what became known as National Security Action Memorandum (NSAM) 256. The second recommendation contained more aggressive measures, including aerial reconnaissance, expansion of U.S. military advisors in Laos, commencement of pilot training programs, and harassment of North Vietnam from the air. This recommendation was approved from a planning perspective only, but not for implementation. The third recommendation called for direct intervention in the conflict by U.S. ground forces.

While the discussions concerning the recommendations continued, steps were taken to enhance the posture of the Lao Armed Forces. That enhancement was in the form of better attack aircraft to deter the Communists. The T-6 was obsolete, limited in capability and, from a practical standpoint, not really airworthy. The newer, faster and more lethal T-28s had become available and ready for deployment to Southeast Asia.

Meanwhile, the State Department vacillated in making a decision regarding replacement of the T-6 aircraft. Therefore General Phoumi sought, and reportedly obtained, a commitment from Thailand to transfer eight T-28s. The T-28 had been developed by North American Aviation and named the "Trojan." It was first used by the U.S. in about 1950, and over the years more than 2,000 were produced. It was first used as a trainer, but later, with a larger engine, it began to replace the P-51 Mustang. The T-28 was well-known for its toughness and reliability. Also, very little maintenance was required, other than oil changes and an annual inspection. During any given year, it was estimated that only 55-60 hours of maintenance was required on the average T-28. The Trojan also had two in-line seats, tricycle landing gear, huge flaps, and superb flying characteristics. In fact, trainees found the aircraft quite easy to fly.

Phoumi hoped that the U.S. Ambassador would support the transfer of the T-28 aircraft, but in actuality, Unger lacked the authority to approve the transfer; that decision would have to be made in Washington. As a show of good faith, however, Unger forwarded Phoumi's request to Washington, and talked to Souvanna about the T-28 transfer the following week, on May 6. When asked, Souvanna had no problem with the transfer, but suggested the T-28s be housed at the RLAF base in Savannakhet.

When the State Department received the news about Souvanna's endorsement of the T-28 transfer, they approved the transfer with stipulations. First, it would have to be a one-for-one switch with the T-6s, and the T-28s would have to remain in Thailand until actually required for duty. Only then could the T-28s be flown into Laos, and, in order for a Trojan to be used in combat, it had to be under extraordinary emergency conditions—but use of the T-28 to interdict North Vietnamese airlifts to the Pathet Lao was authorized. The State Department also implied that, in view of the change from the T-6 to the T-28, the issue of using iron bombs could be relaxed, but napalm would still be prohibited.

Secretary Rusk still was not confident of the RLAF's ability to fully utilize the T-28s, but he hoped the threat of using them might cause the Communists to think twice before initiating future attacks. Rusk also believed that the morale of the Lao military would be bolstered by the use of the T-28s; and if nothing else, it would serve notice that the United States and Thailand were solidly behind Laos. Later, on July 2, the USAF began refresher T-28 training at Kokotiem, Thailand for six RLAF pilots and mechanics. The program lasted two weeks, and eventually qualified 12 pilots and over 15 technicians. The training covered skip bombing, dive bombing, gunnery, and rocket attacks.

All trainees were provided with live ammunition, bombs, and rockets for the exercises, and while the training was taking place, four more RLAF T-28 qualified pilots returned from a year-long T-28 training program in the United States. Meanwhile, the British and French ambassadors expressed concern about replacing the T-6 Texan with the T-28 Trojan. Both felt the Pathet Lao would consider the move an escalation of the war. Secretary Rusk also received information indicating the T-28 would be viewed as an escalation of the war in Laos. Ultimately, it was decided the T-6s would be slowly replaced with the T-28s over an extended period of time, so as not to draw attention to the introduction of the T-28 into the Secret War. A decision was also made to keep the T-28s in Thailand until an emergency situation required its use in Laos.

Coincidentally, on that same day, July 18, Phoumi reported that a large-scale raid by the Pathet Lao was taking place on the Plain of Jars. He quickly developed a plan to combine the Hmong, Neutralist and FAR troops into one big task force to sweep the Pathet Lao from the Plain. In order to accomplish that task, Phoumi desperately needed the T-28. His timing couldn't have been worse. Unger was in Washington, the T-28 pilots were just completing their upgrade training, and the Pathet Lao were causing trouble on the Plain. It just didn't seem right, so Deputy Chief of Mission Phil Chadbourn, the man in charge at the U.S. Embassy in Vientiane, decided to talk to the French, to get their opinion on this sudden move by the Pathet Lao. The French, who had their own spies on the Plain, reported back to Chadbourn that Phoumi had exaggerated the reports, and that things had calmed down.

Meanwhile, throughout the summer, Souvanna continued talks with Souphanouvong, but little if any progress was made. Meanwhile, the Pathet Lao stepped up their attacks against the Hmong, Neutralist and FAR troops in the areas where they were the weakest. They looked for small units far away from their bases, and relentlessly punished the troops. The U.S. embassy called these attacks "nibbling". The Ambassador then came to the conclusion that it was time to use the T-28s against these nibbling attacks in order to deliver a clear message to the Pathet Lao.

The village of Ban Pha Tang was to serve as an example. The Pathet Lao had harassed the village with artillery shelling on a regular basis, and ultimately the defenders and villagers had abandoned the town. Unger wanted to retake it using the T-28s; he subsequently briefed Secretary Rusk on August 19, and the plan was approved. The guidelines set forth by Rusk were that the T-28s could be used to punish the Pathet Lao if they attacked a government position, and they could also be used against enemy troop concentrations in critical areas. Additionally, the aircraft could be used against Communist vehicles and fuel storage areas, but deep penetrations were not to be flown. Rusk also approved rockets, bombs, machine guns, and napalm for the T-28s.

Also in August 1963, Bill Lair received additional orders from CIA headquarters: specifically, he was to disrupt the North Vietnamese truck traffic on Route 7, which ran from North Vietnam into Laos and the Plain of Jars. The road had been built many years before and was in good repair, and served as one of the main NVA routes for transporting supplies and war materials. Lair's new undertaking was to be much larger than the harassment raids the Hmong had been conducting heretofore, and it would require special training. The plan called for explosive charges to be placed at strategic locations along Route 7 and detonated, rendering the road unusable for transporting war supplies. For this particular mission, Lair would rely on his Thai PARU explosives specialists. After first carefully thinking it through, Lair traveled to Long Tieng and went over the details with Vang Pao, Vint Lawrence and Tony Poe.

VP was excited at the opportunity to retaliate against the NVA, and pledged his complete support. For the actual mission, about 10 platoons of Hmong guerrillas were selected. They were relieved of their normal duties, and training soon began. The PARU explosives specialists went over all aspects of the mission with the Hmong volunteers, from the type of explosives to be used to how to handle the dangerous materials and how to rig the fuses. They had the Hmong troops practice the scenario over and over until they got it right. Standard cratering charges were to be employed for this particular operation. Cratering charges were not a new technology; in fact, there were several types readily available for a variety of different applications.

The guerrillas and PARU then rehearsed the process many times, and the trainee had to demonstrate what they had learned. Next, the PARU specialists conducted dry runs at Long Tieng in which real explosives were used. Later, when the date of the mission arrived, the guerrillas and PARU personnel covertly traveled to the hills above Route 7. There the troops were dispersed to specific locations above Route 7, late at night, where they dug many holes for the cratering charges. When the charges had all been placed, the guerrillas and PARU personnel retreated to a safe distance and waited. At the appointed time, the explosives were then detonated, literally taking off the tops and hills and blowing very large holes in the roadway.

At first light on the following morning, an Air America aircraft flew over the target area of Route 7 and took pictures of the damaged roadway. After a subsequent review of the photos, the mission was considered to be a complete success. Everyone knew the road would eventually be repaired, but at least it bought the Hmong, Neutralist and RLG troops a little more time to deal with the Communist troops. Everybody involved with the mission was very impressed with its success, and there was a big celebration that night at Long Tieng. Pop Buell even came over from Sam Thong to join the celebration. Needless to say, by the end of the night, a lot of Lao whiskey had been consumed, and a good time was had by all. And of course, the next morning there were a lot of people walking around nursing bad hangovers.

Another version of this event is recounted in the book *Mr. Pop: The Adventures of a Peaceful Man in a Small War* by Don A. Schanche. Schanche wrote that VP asked Pop Buell if he could blow up the road. According to Schanche, Pop then took 30 Hmong guerrillas and personally trained them to dig the holes, plant the explosives, and rig the charges for firing. At 3:00 A.M. on the following morning, the explosives were detonated, destroying six bridges and twelve mountain passes along a fifteen-mile stretch of Route 7.

It's doubtful that events described by Schanche actually took place as reported, though he did travel to northern Laos and did meet with Pop and others in 1970 while writing the book. Pop was undisputedly a giant of a man in the refugee resettlement endeavor, and he did everything humanly possible for more than fifteen years to help the Hmong. He was a humanitarian—but an explosives expert he was not. In any case, it was highly unlikely that Pop's boss, Charles Mann of USAID, Laos, would allow Pop to participate in an assignment outside his normal duties of refugee relief.[35]

In any case, it didn't take long for the NVA to send several battalions of laborers to the section of Route 7 that had been cratered. The laborers immediately went to work, clearing away the debris and reconstructing the road. But,it took several months for the crews to complete the repairs to the roadway, temporarily suspending resupply runs along Route 7 by the NVA. Vang Pao used the respite to deal with other Communist troops farther north.

At this point in time, the complexion of the Vietnam War and the Secret War in Laos were about to change. In November 1963, John F. Kennedy was assassinated in Dallas, and Vice President Lyndon B. Johnson was sworn in as President of the United States. Meanwhile, the fighting in Laos continued. The guidelines for use of the T-28 had been established, and bombs and napalm had been approved. But the RLAF pilots had not been trained in the use napalm—and not surprisingly, napalm was very unpopular. Its use wasn't viewed as an acceptable part of conventional warfare; it was nasty, and it contained a lot of toxic chemicals. Meanwhile, Ambassador Unger had to contact Washington for approval before issuing any bomb fuses, a process he considered unacceptable. How could he effectively run the war if he had to ask Washington for approval of everything? The process was obviously time-consuming and self-defeating.

While the dialogue continued between Washington and Vientiane, one of the original Momentum sites under Bill Lair's cognizance, Tha Lin Noi, fell to the Communists. And, to make matters worse, the RLAF was having problems maintaining the T-28s. The RLAF mechanics just weren't proficient about providing periodic maintenance, and on several occasions, USAF maintenance personnel had to travel to Savannakhet to perform the maintenance themselves. Of course, the use of American military troops in Laos was a violation of the Geneva Accords, and Ambassador Unger was troubled. Later, in mid-November, two RLAF T-28s were crashed by new pilots attempting unauthorized low-level aerobatics. Two of the four remaining T-28s were then relocated from Savannakhet to Vientiane for use over northern Laos, leaving the rest of the country short of resources. With only two T-28s left in Savannakhet, it would not be long before RLAF pilots would lose their proficiency rating due to non-availability of aircraft to fly. To help, the USAF Air Attaché, Colonel Tyrell, suggested that Thailand be approached to provide additional T-28s. Tyrell's counterpart in Thailand, Colonel Roland McCoskrie, doubted that Thailand would go for the proposal, because they had already provided aircraft once, and they didn't want to be looked upon as a replacement pool for air assets.

The only other possible solution was to see if the USAF Special Air Warfare Center at Eglin Air Force Base, Florida could send a dozen or so T-28 aircraft to Udorn Air Force Base in Thailand. The logic behind this proposal would be that USAF personnel could train RLAF and Thai pilots and mechanics. The USAF could also provide spare T-28s for combat missions when they were not being utilized for training. Finally, somebody had come up with a good idea! It didn't take long for the idea to become a recommendation, and it would later end up on Admiral Felt's desk for consideration. Felt liked the idea and thought it had merit, so he forwarded it on to Secretary of Defense McNamara.

Even as the T-28 situation continued to plague the planners in Vientiane, VP had been getting a lot of recognition for the successful cratering of Route 7. Phoumi, not wanting to be left out, was also looking for ways to make himself look good. In early November, he launched a multi-battalion offensive in the upper panhandle of central Laos, utilizing FAR and Neutralist troops. General Sang, the Ground Forces Commander of the FAR, was placed in charge. The CIA had complained that Phoumi's initiative was ill-advised, but Phoumi, in typical fashion, pressed forward.

At first, things went as planned. Near the border with North Vietnam, Phoumi's troops were able to gain the upper hand on the Pathet Lao defenders in the area of Lak Sao, and he pushed the Pathet Lao to the edge of the border. But instead of continuing to fight, the Pathet Lao simply retreated. Phoumi, assuming victory, made the mistake of flaunting his temporary gain. On December 15, without warning, three battle-hardened NVA battalions attacked by way of Route 8 in the north and Route 12 farther south. They mauled Phoumi's troops; he called for reinforcements, and when they arrived, the NVA mauled them as well. Watching and sensing victory, the Pathet Lao rejoined the fight and attacked the retreating FAR troops.

The FAR troops took a severe beating, and the entire fiasco was just one more example of Phuomi's poor leadership skills. Instead of the accolades he had hoped for, he received only criticism, in large doses.

In December, Souvanna Phouma and the Pathet Lao signed a preliminary agreement on the neutralization and demilitarization of the royal capital at Luang Prabang. Phoumi objected, and demanded that similar concessions be made with Pathet Lao-held territory. But, the Pathet Lao refused, and immediately resumed military operations. Meanwhile, the United States continued to transfer aircraft to the Lao government. These transfers did not affect the T-28 effort, but did have a lot to do with the RLAF. In 1963, two transports—one a C-46, the other a C-47—were transferred to the RLAF, along with three U-17 light observation aircraft and three additional H-34 helicopters. As usual, the RLAF wasn't very effective at managing the resources, because they didn't have any trained air operations specialists, and also didn't have an organization dedicated to managing the transport resources.

Ambassador Unger decided to seize this opportunity to suggest the creation of an RLAF air transport operations board composed of cargo aircraft owners and users. He believed that once it became operational, the board could screen flight requests, and manage priorities and space. Unger's suggestion appeared to have merit, but the problem was that Air America had been contracted to handle most of the airlift in Laos, especially to the CIAsupported Hmong guerrilla units. When Souvanna learned of Unger's proposal, he also endorsed it. The prince had worried for some time about Air America's expanding role and the negative feelings that it created among the Pathet Lao, knowing that bullets transported by Air America to the Hmong would be used against them.

Souvanna also believed that the Pathet Lao would be more willing to participate in the new coalition government if Air America didn't have such a large charter. Unger then suggested that the contract with Air America could be withdrawn, and its 20+ transports could be turned over to a new contractor without pre-Geneva connections in Laos. Unger even went so far as to recommend using non-Americans as pilots, in order to reduce U.S. visibility. Eventually, the U.S. State Department became aware of Unger's plan and endorsed the creation of an air transport board. But they weren't keen on the part about dissolving Air America, so nothing more was said about the proposal, and it was quietly, and permanently, filed away.

As mentioned earlier, President Kennedy had been assassinated in Dallas in November 1963, and Vice President Lyndon Johnson (LBJ) had been sworn in as president. By January 1964, the Johnson Administration had settled in at 1600 Pennsylvania Avenue, and they were asking a lot of questions about Laos. LBJ had become convinced the coalition government formed after the Geneva Accords was the right way to go; but it had also become clear to him that it wasn't going to work, because the Pathet Lao wouldn't participate. They talked a lot, but all the while continued fighting against both the Neutralists and the Hmong. "Talk While Fighting," it was called. It had been used by the North Koreans in the Korean War, and had also been used in North Vietnam by the NVA. The White House believed the only purpose of the actions now taking place in Laos was to discredit Souvanna Phouma and his government.

On February 26, Secretary Rusk asked Ambassador Unger to review a memorandum he had written to President Johnson. Unger perused the memo, wherein Rusk recommended expanded use of T-28 Trojans in Laos. Rusk also recommended sabotage and psychological operations against the North Vietnamese, as well as high-level aerial reconnaissance, and South Vietnamese border patrols into Laos. After reading the memo, Unger reportedly told Rusk that Phoumi would endorse all the recommended actions, because it would further obligate the United States from both a manpower and a monetary standpoint. Unger also opined that the recommended actions might tend to discredit Souvanna's government, because it would appear that neutrality had been abandoned. Additionally, the recommendations would do nothing to stop the constant harassment raids by the Pathet Lao that were slowing eroding RLG control of the Plain of Jars and northern Laos.

Unger endorsed the use of T-28 aircraft, and added that he should have the authority to send the T-28s on missions without even consulting Washington. He believed the RLA could hold its own against the Pathet Lao under normal circumstances, but with NVA stiffeners in the Pathet Lao ranks it was a different proposition. Unger didn't believe the FAR was capable of taking on the NVA, and stressed there would be no improvement in the RLAF until bombing restrictions were lifted.

Not only was the FAR weak, but the military and government infrastructure in Laos remained almost nonexistent. Also, the abilities of the RLAF pilots varied. Some were fairly good, and others had only recently completed pilot training—and none had been really tested in combat. Most could fly the aircraft, but they didn't know the first thing about directing air strikes. Prior to the arrival of the Americans, the Lao military was controlled by the French—so they were taught tactics and skills practiced by France, and the French were simply not a potent opponent in the air. As mentioned earlier, most of their fighting took place on the ground in classic "set-piece" warfare. They didn't use Forward Air Controllers (FAC), and that was a major deficit, because without information about location, priority, troop disposition, or enemy antiaircraft capability, the ground commanders could not effectively manage their troops.

Ambassador Unger reasoned that consulting Washington before issuing bomb fuses both delayed the opportunity to strike the enemy and affected the morale of the Lao troops. He recommended the fuses be turned over to the Lao themselves, with the understanding they would only be used as a defensive measure—and only after consulting with the U.S. Embassy and receiving approval from Souvanna. Meanwhile, USAF Chief of Staff Curtis E. Le May was following the dialogue, and believed that Unger's approach didn't go far enough. General Le May believed the RLAF pilots should be hitting the supply lines from North Vietnam. He also believed that Thai, Vietnamese and United States pilots should also be used to augment the RLAF. Le May communicated this information to the JCS, who then rewrote the memorandum and sent it to Secretary of Defense Robert McNamara. The memo recommended defensive and offensive actions, and included giving the RLAF napalm once they had been taught how to use it. The JCS felt the first priority should be interdiction of North Vietnamese convoys, cratering of roads, and bridge destruction. They also believed the RLAF didn't need to be involved in aerial reconnaissance, because that task could be adequately handled by the USAF.

As this part of the story ends, let's assess the situation in Laos. Frankly, the tiny kingdom is no better off than it was before the United States stepped in to help. The fragile government is splintered. Souvanna is a Rightist, but he also supports the Neutralists. To his credit, he does want his country to be free, and to thrive. Souphanouvong is in northern Laos. He has thrown his support behind the Pathet Lao. Boum Oum doesn't really want to be involved in any of the important matters affecting Laos; he just wants out.

President Kennedy had pushed for the Geneva Accords because he believed that neutralism was the best alternative for Laos. But Kennedy has been assassinated, and Lyndon Johnson has become the new President of the United States. Johnson isn't happy, because he's inherited a mess not of his own making—and he hasn't yet announced a clear direction for American involvement in Laos. The Geneva Accords afforded Laos neutralism and directed all foreign troops to leave, but the fighting continues. In fact, the NVA strength is increasing in Laos. The Hmong guerrillas under Vang Pao are trying to do the right thing and defend their country, but the U.S. isn't giving them the backing they need when they need it. The CIA is putting a Secret War infrastructure in place, but will it be effective? And can the Americans in Laos take the country in the right direction? Also, is Laos really capable of fielding an army and defending itself? More importantly, can they succeed as a democracy?

We'll have to wait for the answers to all those questions. Please keep reading to find out how things turn out for this tiny kingdom.

Chapter 6

The Seasonal War

By late November 1963, the North Vietnamese had repaired Route 7, and were trucking a steady stream of war supplies into northern Laos. When the information reached Vint Lawrence at Long Tieng, he caught a ride on one of Air America's aircraft to a village near Route 7. Upon arrival, he talked to local sources. While he was at the village, he recruited a small team of villagers for training as a Road Watch Team. After the team completed their training, they would be able to provide regular reports on NVA truck traffic transiting the area, and ideally on the cargo being transported. While visiting the village, Vint learned of President Kennedy's murder; he was asleep when one of the soldiers woke him with the news. Bill Lair, who was working at Long Tieng, was also asleep when notified of Kennedy's death by a shocked Tony Poe.

Both Lair and Lawrence wondered how effectively Lyndon Johnson would lead the United States, but more importantly, they were unsure about the future of the Secret War. President Johnson wasn't in favor of the operation, and he believed that the U.S. shouldn't take part in the Vietnam mess, either. In fact, he had spoken out more than once to denounce U.S. actions in Vietnam. Whatever happened as a result of Johnson being President was beyond Lawrence and Lair's control. But, for the present, everyone involved in the Secret War had to concentrate on their job in Laos. That was their priority and focus.

Meanwhile, up north in Sam Neua City, Vang Pao's guerrilla units were ready to fight. Tony Poe had arranged for airdrops of ammunition and supplies to the guerrillas, and their training had been completed.

Meanwhile, on December 10, King Savang Vatthana arrived at Long Tieng for a visit. The entire base had been cleaned up and made presentable for the King and his party. They even had little children, dressed in their best clothing, lining the runway holding Laotian flags out of respect. As the aircraft landed and taxied to the reviewing stand, the king deplaned to a waiting throng of Hmong villagers, all holding flowers and singing. The king was an impressive figure, lean and sharp in his white Royal summer uniform. The villagers had planned a parade for him, along with a local ceremony called bacci.[36] A little later, when the ceremonies ended, everyone had lunch, and the king and his entourage then left. It was a good day for VP, because it showed that he had the king's respect—and so did the Hmong guerrillas.

At this point in time, there was already a great deal of dissension in the RLG ranks. Phoumi had demonstrated that he was a poor leader, and on top of that, he was corrupt. Even his underlings, Generals Ouane Rathikone and Kouprasith Abhay, had turned against him. Despite the fact that they had been overseeing Phoumi's criminal enterprises, Phoumi had even tried to take advantage of *them*. But, in the past, Phoumi had had an ace in the hole that kept his would-be opponents in check: his cousin, Sarit Thanarat, was commander of the armed forces in Thailand. It was common knowledge that, if necessary, Sarit would use his troops to protect Phoumi. But Phoumi could no longer play that card, as Sarit had recently died. Now he stood alone.

Sensing a power vacuum, General Abhay tried to take over Laos' fragile government in a coup on April 18, 1964. His partner in crime was General Siho Lamphouthacoul, head of the Directorate of National Coordination (DNC), or the national police, as they were called. But Siho's men were no ordinary police officers; they were also well-trained paramilitary troops, although some insiders considered them to be little more than a bunch of thugs. Using standard takeover protocols, Siho, who orchestrated the coup, sent two of his battalions into Vientiane at 10:00 PM to take over the airport, radio station, and national bank. In the early morning hours of April 19, Souvanna and many other diplomats were arrested. Next, Siho's men riddled the home of RLG General Bounleut with automatic weapons fire; then the group moved to the home of the Minister of Interior, Neutralist Pheng Phongsavan. At Phongsavan's house a firefight ensued, resulting in the deaths of a DNC major and a Neutralist guard. For good measure, Siho's men looted Kong Le's Vientiane home.

After seizing the city, General Abhay called a special session of the National Assembly. There he forced a vote that filled the cabinet with Rightists, removing Phoumi, who had not received an invitation to the session. There was no place for him in the new government in any case. When the coup took place, Ambassador Unger was in Saigon, attending a meeting with Secretary Rusk, Henry Cabot Lodge (the ambassador to South Vietnam), and William Bundy, Assistant Secretary of State. When Unger heard the news, he rushed back to Vientiane. Upon arrival, he first checked on Souvanna to make sure he was all right, and then he confronted Abhay with an ultimatum: either restore Souvanna as Prime Minister immediately, or the United States would cut off all aid to Laos.

Abhay agreed, with the stipulation that all his Rightist appointees remain in their positions. Souvanna agreed in turn, and resumed his post as Prime Minister with the goal of asserting his political independence. But daily exposure to Abhay's appointees proved more than he could take. Within a month in the new regime, Souvanna announced that he was merging the Neutralist and Rightist armies. As expected, Kong Le did not get an appointment to fill any office in the new government. Everyone waited for a reaction by Kong Le, but he did not oppose the new government. The Neutralists widely viewed his inaction as a sell-out, and hundreds shifted their allegiance to the Pathet Lao.

Before this latest coup, the NVA and Pathet Lao had tolerated Kong Le's presence on the Plain of Jars only because he had acted as a buffer between the Communists and the Rightists. But now that he was considered a Rightist, Kong Le was viewed as a threat. To remove that threat, the NVA and Pathet Lao moved together against all the Neutralist positions on the Plain, whereupon Kong Le and his remaining forces retreated to the western edge of the Plain of Jars.

When the news of Kong Le's predicament reached Washington, the White House initiated action to support both the RLG and the Neutralists. For the RLG, Washington drew up plans for a 13,000-man SEATO emergency intervention force in Laos if needed. Ammunition and fuel were sent to the Plain for the Neutralists, in sufficient quantities to last about two months. The U.S. also staged an additional thirty-day supply of ammunition and fuel in case it became needed, and airdropped hundreds of weapons to Kong Le's men.

In February 1964, after coordinating with the U.S. Ambassadors in Vientiane and Bangkok, the JCS had directed the USAF to send a Special

Air Warfare (SAW) unit to Udorn, Thailand on a temporary basis. For at least six months, the unit—officially designated Detachment 6, 1st Air Commando Wing—would participate in a project codenamed "Waterpump." The USAF also sent four T-28s to Udorn, along with more than 40 active duty USAF personnel commanded by Major Barney Cochran. By April 1, all personnel had arrived and were ready to begin work. Detachment 6 would report to U.S. Army Colonel Jack Cornett, Deputy Chief of JUSCHMAGTHAI, with dotted-line oversight to the U.S. Ambassador in Laos.

Waterpump initially consisted of 38 pilots, four crew chiefs, one propeller mechanic, one engine mechanic, and four armament specialists. The purpose of Waterpump was to train RLAF and Thai pilots in counterinsurgency tactics and techniques. The unit was later renamed Detachment 1, 56th Special Operations Wing, with organizational control out of Nakhon Phanom Air Base, Thailand (NKP). In addition to providing counterinsurgency training, the detachment would also provide material support, sponsor Lao-Thai cooperation, and, as necessary, supplement the RLAF.

While the Waterpump personnel were settling in and updating their airfield charts, information was received indicating that the town of Nong Boua had fallen to the Pathet Lao. Apparently, Nong Boua had been harassed for weeks by Communist troops, and all the residents of the town had finally left, rather than remain behind to be killed outright by the Communists. Ambassador Unger used the incident to illustrate his theory of the "nibbling" effect of the Communists, and again requested that Washington delegate the authority to release bomb fuses to the RLG, so they could quickly respond to Communist attacks using their T-28s.

Surprisingly, Washington approved the request, but before the RLAF could retaliate, another ceasefire was called in Laos, and talks by the Pathet Lao, Neutralist and RLA were scheduled to take place on the Plain of Jars. The fuses hadn't been used, but with the approval, a turning point in U.S. policy was reached on fighting the Secret War. First, it signaled that the United States would no longer tolerate the Pathet Lao's nibbling. Second, bomb fuses would be released to allow bombing to regain control of territory lost; and third, use of the T-28 aircraft was no longer viewed as escalation.

In April 1964, the USAF set up an Air Operations Center (AOC) in an empty warehouse at Wattay Airport in Vientiane. It was staffed by a half-dozen USAF personnel under the Air Attaché's office. The AOC provided ordnance and crew briefings to the Air America, Thai and RLAF pilots conducting interdiction missions in northern Laos. Later, in May 1964, Waterpump also provided two USAF air commandos to the AOC at Wattay. The two airmen would provide targeting information to the T-28 pilots flying interdiction missions. By this time, five Air America pilots had received checkout training in the T-28 and were ready to fly the Trojans into combat against the Communists. By then, Kong Le's position at Muong Soui had become tenuous, and USAF reconnaissance flights had been scheduled over Kong Le's position.

By this time, a pattern of fighting had evolved that could be compared to a seesaw. The opposing forces consisted of Pathet Lao and NVA troops on one side, with the RLG and the Hmong guerrillas on the other. Essentially, it was the Communists fighting the non-Communists. Each group chose to start their offensive operations when the weather best suited them. The seesaw pattern began that year with Communist offensives in progress on the Plain of Jars, in May, at the end of the dry season (which stretched from October to May). During this period, the ground was hard and the roads were good, allowing resupply to the troops in contact. Conversely, RLG and Hmong troops preferred to launch their operations in the rainy season (June to September) because they traveled on foot, were lightly armed, and everything they needed was airdropped to them. This seesaw type of combat which had evolved was also referred to as "Seasonal War."

On May 19, the United States, with the concurrence of Souvanna Phouma, authorized air reconnaissance flights over the Plain of Jars, using the USAF RF-101 Voodoo aircraft under a program code-named "Yankee Team." The reconnaissance flights also opened a new debate among U.S. military leaders in Southeast Asia, Hawaii and Washington regarding command and control of air assets over northern Laos. The 2nd Air Division, Air Force Component Commander (AFCC) under the 13th Air Force had established a command post in May at Udorn Air Force Base, Thailand, and began to oversee the air operations. As the AFCC, General Moore was responsible for conducting the reconnaissance flights and the retaliatory strikes on Pathet Lao gun positions in June, following the shooting down of two American aircraft in May by North Vietnamese artillery units.

By early May, Pathet Lao forces had also seized the hills around Phou San overlooking Route 7. From this vantage point, the Communists could use their artillery to restrict resupply missions to Kong Le and his Neutralist forces. Later, the Pathet Lao also moved against Tha Thom, the southern anchor of Kong Le's defensive line. To make matters worse, the Neutralist commander at Tha Thom, Lieutenant Colonel Cheng Saignavong, had become disillusioned, and was getting cozy with the Communists. He became more rebellious on May 14, when he received news of Souvanna's intent to reorganize the Neutralist and Royalist forces into one command. With turmoil running rampant among the Neutralists, the Pathet Lao had decided to attack Tha Thom, and Cheng was killed in the ensuing fight. His fellow collaborator, Lt. Col. Soulideth Rattanakone, the Armor commander, should have used his tanks to counterattack the Pathet Lao when they were attacking Cheng, but instead Rattanakone lobbed several rounds in the general direction of oncoming Communist forces. As a result, most of the Neutralists then fled, leaving behind huge stores of supplies and ammunition that had been stockpiled for the rainy season offensive. Later, the Pathet Lao walked unopposed into Tha Thom and took possession of all the war materials. Meanwhile, the fleeing Neutralists regrouped at Muong Soui, a small village on Route 7 at the western edge of the Plain of Jars.

Meanwhile, on May 19, Yankee Team reconnaissance flights resumed. Based on the vulnerability of Yankee Team reconnaissance aircraft, a professional SAR force would become necessary, since the capture of an American pilot in Laos could create an international incident—not to mention unwanted publicity. The JCS had already approved sending USAF Air Rescue and Recovery Service (ARRS) aircraft and personnel to South Vietnam, but this force had not yet arrived—and even if they were in place, their HH-43 helicopters would be of no use in Laos, because they didn't have the range to fly from South Vietnam to Laos.

By May 21, Kong Le's situation at Muong Soui was so critical that aerial reconnaissance was ordered. It clearly showed the Pathet Lao slowly moving towards Kong Le's position. On May 24, sure enough, the Pathet Lao began probing Kong Le's position at Muong Soui. At this point the situation was critical and something had to done, and quickly, because Kong Le was ready to abandon his compound and take up positions in the surrounding hills.

Fortunately, the USAF Waterpump personnel at Udorn had trained the five Air America pilots for use in the T-28, and on May 25, Air America pilots flew their first air combat missions, completing ten sorties along Route 7 on the Plain of Jars. They cratered the road in several spots, and tried to create rock slides to destroy bridges, but were unsuccessful.

As the pilots touched down at Wattay after completing their sorties, Ambassador Unger was waiting to greet them. The flights were considered a success, but the T-28s were riddled with bullet holes. The crews were unfazed, however, because they were unaware that they had been fired upon. But Unger was distressed over the prospect of possibly losing an American crew member, for fear the press and the ICC would have a field day with that information. To avoid trouble, he temporarily closed down the AOC at Vientiane, and suspended further flights by American pilots. Furthermore, on May 30, Unger informed the Department of State that he believed Yankee Team reconnaissance flights should not be undertaken at that time, as they might agitate the Communists, who could retaliate with antiaircraft weapons. As an alternative, he suggested aerial reconnaissance using the RT-28, a reconnaissance version of the trusty Trojan.

At any rate, things temporarily quieted down on the Plain, but Unger knew he needed to put an end to the Pathet Lao attacks, once and for all. For help, he turned to the U.S. Army, submitting a request for assistance in restoring conditions on the Plain to the way they were prior to May 1964. Once that was accomplished, the U.S. troops would withdraw. He believed that this would give him breathing room until he could find a better alternative. However, to say that the Army generals weren't fond of Unger's plan would be an understatement. In fact, they flatly refused to get involved. Colonel Law, the Army Attaché in Vientiane, also disagreed with Unger's plan, and said so in writing. Later, when all the documentation worked its way up the chain of command and to Washington, the plan to use Army ground troops in Laos was shelved.

Soon, the AOC in Vientiane reopened, the RLAF pilots were given more training in the T-28, and air operations resumed. By June 1, the RLAF pilots were each flying two sorties a day for about a week at a time. Their success level was commendable: they had cratered numerous roads, making them impassable, and destroyed one wooden bridge. Meanwhile, fighting on the Plain began to slowly subside as the rain began to fall every day, for most of the day.

Up to this point, Air America had been providing SAR support, but their capability was limited and didn't include trained life-saving professionals. Also, the H-34 helicopters used by Air America were not equipped for rescues; they were designed primarily for hauling people and equipment. Major General Joseph H. Moore (USAF), Commander, 2nd Air Division, was cognizant of the inadequate search and rescue capability, and took action to correct the problem. On May 29, he asked Pacific Air Force (PACAF) for permission to use USAF aircraft for search and rescue in Laos.

During the first week of June, General Moore traveled to Udorn to meet with the Deputy of the 2nd Air Division, Colonel Jack Catlin. The subject of the meeting was search and rescue. As fate would have it, while Moore and Catlin were meeting, the inadequate SAR capability in Laos was vividly and tragically illustrated: on June 6, a mayday call from Cork Tip 920 was picked up by a RLAF T-28 pilot. The call came from U.S. Navy Lt. Charles Klusmann, who was on a reconnaissance mission over Laos in his RF-8A from the *U.S.S. Kitty Hawk*. While flying at 1,200 feet near Xieng Khouang, Klusmann's wingman reported him down inside Communist-controlled territory near the border between Laos and North Vietnam. An Air America C-123 Provider and a C-7 Caribou happened to be working in the area, and picked up the call for help. They jettisoned their cargo and diverted to the location to assist in the SAR mission. Meanwhile, two Air America Helio Couriers and Hmong guerrillas working nearby were alerted to stand by, in the event their assistance was needed.

General Moore heard the news and immediately proceeded to the Air America Operations Center to monitor the SAR. He then placed a telephone call to General Jacob E. Smart, Commander In Chief, Pacific Air Forces (CINCPACAF), and Admiral Felt. With their approval, Moore launched three T-28s manned by USAF Waterpump pilots and five F-100 Super Sabres from Takhli Air Base in Thailand to assist in the SAR effort.

Within an hour, Lt. Klusmann was located. Two hours later, two Air America H-34 helicopters had reached the location to attempt the rescue. Upon their arrival, the entire area erupted in gunfire. The rescuers didn't know it at the time, but the Communists had employed a tactic that would be used many times in the future: the "flak trap." The enemy would surround the downed airman and hide in the rocks, trees and brush, let the airman activate his emergency radio, and then wait patiently and quietly until the rescuers came. Then, when the pick-up attempt was made, the enemy would open fire with all the weapons they had in an attempt to shoot down the rescue aircraft. When time permitted, the Communist would bring anti-aircraft artillery to the location to also assist in destroying the rescue aircraft.

In this case, both Air America aircraft were hit, and two crew members were critically injured. The pilots then broke off the rescue attempt and headed for the nearest Lima Site. When General Moore learned of the flak trap, he notified General Smart. Meanwhile, the AOC in Vientiane dispatched four more T-28s to assist in a second attempt to rescue Lt. Klusmann; but this time, they could not locate him. Three additional T-28s, piloted by Americans, were also dispatched, but by that time the Communists had already captured Klusmann and departed the area. With the weather deteriorating, the rescue effort was terminated.

The news of Klusmann's downing and capture by the Pathet Lao quickly reached Washington, and President Johnson was not pleased. He called his advisors together that same morning, and made it clear that he wanted a retaliatory strike conducted in order to serve notice on North Vietnam that the United States would not accept such losses. In the meeting, it was decided that two reconnaissance flights with heavy fighter escort would be launched—and if the reconnaissance aircraft were fired upon, the escorts would return fire. Two US Navy reconnaissance jets later took off on the morning of June 7, escorted by heavily-armed Navy F-8 fighters.

As soon as they arrived on station in the skies above Northern Laos, the reconnaissance jets were fired upon by Communist artillery. The F-8s retaliated. One, "Old Nick 110," piloted by Navy Commander D.W. Lynn, was shot down by enemy gunners while he was making his second pass in the same general area where Lt. Klusmann had been shot down. Lynn ejected safely, and his wingman called in the coordinates to the command center at Udorn. They, in turn, notified the AOC in Vientiane and the Pacific Air Rescue Center in Saigon. Air America H-34 helicopters and T-28 aircraft were dispatched to the location; five F-100 fighters were also launched from Takhli, and two A-1 Skyraiders were sent from Da Nang to assist. But when rescue forces arrived, Commander Lynn could not be found, and the rescue attempt was terminated.

Immediately after the failed rescue, the Waterpump Commander, Major Cochran, called all the rescue crews together for a debriefing. During the meeting, Cochran discovered that the USAF pilots participating in the rescue did not have the correct radio equipment to pick up Lynn's rescue beacon signal. They had been looking in the area described by Lynn's wingman, but could not visually spot Lynn. The Air America participants involved in the rescue attempt, however, *did* have the correct radio equipment, and had triangulated Lynn's position—and had no idea, at the time, that the Air Force was searching in the wrong area. Cochran then reviewed the triangulation fix and realized the USAF rescuers had been searching 40 miles from Lynn's actual location.

On June 8, a second SAR was initiated using the correct information. Upon arrival over the area, it was overcast and visibility was limited, and the crews could not see Lynn on the ground. But Lynn could hear them above, and he fired a rescue flare through the clouds. An Air America helicopter was then able to get down below the cloud deck and rescue Lynn. When briefed a short time later, President Johnson was relieved to learn that Lynn was rescued, but still ordered a retaliatory strike for June 9. The target was to be a star-shaped Communist artillery position about a mile from the town of Xieng Khouang; it was believed that this was the gun that had taken Lynn's aircraft down.

Prior to executing the raid, President Johnson wanted to get Ambassador Unger's thoughts on the planned attack. Unger later made it clear that he was against the strike, and voiced his concern that it would signal an escalation of the conflict on the part of the U.S. Souvanna Phouma was already on record as saying he would not publicly acknowledge giving the U.S. permission to escort its reconnaissance aircraft with armed fighters, and Unger believed the retaliatory strike would jeopardize future reconnaissance flights. But by the time the ambassador's comments reached LBJ, Eight F-100 Super Sabres were already in the air headed for northern Laos, laden with iron bombs.

A short time later, the aircraft assembled above the target area in the skies over northern Laos. An air tanker showed up right behind them, and the planes were rapidly refueled. During the process, however, clouds began to close in, and the Super Sabres lost visual contact with each other. In addition, while refueling, some of the planes received less fuel than they actually needed. The first flight of four f-100 aircraft then lined up, soon found the target, and prepared to strike. By this time, enemy ground fire was extremely heavy, but four of the aircraft rolled in for the attack anyway. Ultimately, only about six of the twenty-eight bombs dropped found the target, resulting in a success rate of about 20%. Meanwhile, the four other Super Sabres were not yet over the target area, and the weather still wasn't cooperating. Lacking proper navigational aids, they were preparing to jettison their bombs and return to base when the clouds parted somewhat, and they spotted a star-shaped artillery position through the clouds. The bombers then lined up and made their bomb runs on the gun's position, destroying about 50% of the target area. But as it turned out, this second flight was actually hit a Communist artillery position near the town of Phong Savan, an old opium trading center with an airport. Phong Savan had previously been taken over by the Communists and the star-shaped gun position had been installed next to the airstrip.

After the strikes, all eight aircraft headed for the tankers for more fuel. Six of the birds made it, and took on fuel before returning to South Vietnam. The other two, however, were not able to get back to the tankers because they were too low on fuel, and instead diverted to Ubon Air Base in Thailand.

Meanwhile, in the diplomatic arena, Secretary Rusk encouraged Unger to abandon the notion that the air strikes violated the Geneva Accords. According to Rusk, when one side grossly disregarded the provisions of the Accords, the other side had the authority to retaliate. Rusk added that the United States would vigorously uphold the provisions of the Accords, but would take action in kind, when attacked. For the meantime, however, all reconnaissance flights were temporarily suspended after Lt. Lynn was shot down.

Also on June 8, the Neutralist position at the town of Phou Kout (Iron Mountain) was lost to the Pathet Lao. Eight tanks and many smaller weapons were also lost with the position. After Phou Kout, the next logical target for the Communists would be Kong Le's headquarters at Muong Soui. Souvanna, realizing the danger, went to the French Ambassador to Laos, Pierre L. M. Millet, and asked for tanks and weapons to replace those lost to the Pathet Lao. The French ambassador flatly refused, stating that his country no longer issued weapons to Southeast Asian countries, because the weapons only encouraged hostilities. Not one to be overruled, Souvanna appealed to the King, who merely changed the subject when Souvanna brought up the issue of the French ambassador. The King also told Souvanna during the meeting that the Yankee Team reconnaissance flights, recently suspended, must be resumed.

On June 10, Hanoi and Peking announced to the world that American jets had strafed Khang Khai and the old Neutralist capital. Souphanouvong's headquarters had also reportedly been hit, resulting in several casualties—and a colonel assigned to the Chinese economic and cultural mission in Khang Khai had been killed. In an attempt to verify the Communist claim, a CIA Lucky Dragon U-2 reconnaissance mission was authorized to photograph the site. The U-2 mission was undertaken, but failed to substantiate the Communist claim, because clouds had obscured most of the towns on the Plain of Jars. Meanwhile, extensive debriefings of the F-100 pilots continued regarding the June 9 mission. At that time, it was realized that Phong Savan had been hit by one flight of Super Sabres, but that still didn't explain the claimed strafing of Khang Khai.

The ICC subsequently investigated, and was reportedly shown the strafing and bomb damage at the town. The Pathet Lao also showed them a piece of aircraft wreckage they described as being from an F-100 shot down on the day of the strike. The problem, however, was that the piece of wreckage was clearly identifiable as being a piece of a Navy RF-8A, not an F-100, and so the ICC dismissed the matter completely. The United States was later vindicated of any wrongdoing—but the question regarding who had bombed and strafed Khang Khai still had not been answered. For that answer, the spotlight turned to the RLAF pilots who had been flying the T-28s on June 8 during Lynn's rescue. But additional inquiry failed to disclose the pilot, or pilots, responsible for strafing Khang Khai; and so the matter soon slipped through the cracks, and was subsequently overcome by other events.

On June 11, Ambassador Unger met with Souvanna to discuss several issues of mutual interest. Unger was surprised that the Prime Minister did not mention the American raids on Xieng Khouang and Phong Savan. In fact, Souvanna didn't even mention the raids, while giving Unger permission to restart the Yankee Team reconnaissance missions, acknowledging they would be accompanied by armed fighters that could respond to any ground fire. "Act, but don't talk about it," was the Prime Minister's advice to Unger. In other words, Souvanna was telling the Americans to do what they need to do, and to keep their mouths shut. Meanwhile, back in Washington, news of the American strike over northern Laos was leaked to the press, and the State Department was compelled to brief the media. The media was told only that on June 8, U.S. forces did reconnoiter the Plain, and did return fire after being fired upon.

This event led to a new official U.S. policy of admitting that reconnaissance was being conducted in Laos out of necessity, without addressing any specific mission information. When asked about escorts retaliating to defend unarmed reconnaissance aircraft, the official response was to simply state that the question could not be answered for operational security reasons—and if an aircraft was shot down, only some details would be provided unless there were overriding reasons not to disclose any information at all. Finally, it was also stated that only those military, political and government personnel with a specific need to know would be briefed as required on a one-on-one basis regarding details of Yankee Team operations.

Later, on June 13, 1964, the RLAF flew more than a dozen strikes against enemy antiaircraft and artillery positions east of Muong Soui near Phou Kout, but their success couldn't be determined due to deteriorating weather. During the wet season (June-September), the monsoons made their annual return to Southeast Asia, and it was the RLG's turn to strike back. In these rainy months, the roads, trails and paths became slippery and sticky from the moisture held by the clay-like soil, making it difficult for the NVA to use their heavy artillery weapons. It was also difficult for the NVA to resupply their troops, because the roads were usually impassable by vehicle. The Lao forces, however, traveled light, and had the advantage of air support in the form of resupply helicopters, not to mention fighter support. The Lao rainy season offensive in 1964 was named "Operation Triangle." Triangle had been personally approved by President Johnson, complete with micromanagement from the White House.

Operation Triangle called for a three-pronged attack to secure Route 13 between Vientiane and Luang Prabang, near Kong Le's stronghold at Muong Soui. The plan included a combined attack by FAR, Neutralist and Hmong troops on an enemy pocket at Sala

Phou Khoun that threatened Route 13 and the rear of Kong Le's headquarters. Another Communist contingent near Sala Phou Khoun was also holed up on nearby Phou Kout, the strategic ridgeline overlooking the western Plain of Jars. The importance of the mountain was in its elevation, which provided a commanding view of Route 13, Muong Soui and Sala Phou Khoun alike; from this location, the Communists could call in artillery strikes with great accuracy. The mountain was reportedly held by the Pathet Lao and a battalion from the NVA 148 Regiment. Therefore, to take Sala Phou Khoun, Phou Kout had to be neutralized.

Colonels Tyrrell and Cochran both realized Triangle would require good coordination between the air and ground units in order to be successful. To that end, two USAF Forward Air Controller (FAC) pilots were dispatched to Muong Soui and Vang Vieng to work with the Neutralists and provide training. They both flew the Cessna O-1 Bird Dog observation aircraft, and planned to also use Hmong Forward Air Guides (FAG) to assist in locating enemy targets, verbally relaying information to indigenous forces on the ground. [37]

Meanwhile, Kong Le and VP visited the AOC in Vientiane to arrange details of air support for their forces. Kong Le agreed to provide observers to fly in the rear seat of the T-28s to support his operations; these airborne observers would coordinate with ground forces by radio to coordinate interdiction efforts. Additionally, the ground and air controllers would coordinate with U.S. military advisors by radio, who would, in turn, coordinate by telephone with the AOC in Vientiane.

The U.S. State Department was not optimistic that Operation Triangle would be successful, and thought the Lao troops could be better utilized by holding the line at Muong Soui and Attopeu. They were also reluctant to use U.S. airmen in direct action. Another concern was that heretofore the Lao troops had been reluctant to take the fight to the enemy, and it was not certain that the upcoming fight would be any different. Ambassador Unger also realized the FAR could no longer afford to hold the line and stay on the defensive. And if America didn't get behind Operation Triangle, Souvanna would take it as a signal that the U.S. was not prepared to back up its strong statements of support against Communism.

While the debates continued about the Yankee Team reconnaissance flights, the North Vietnamese were quietly increasing the number of antiaircraft artillery positions in northern Laos. They were also increasing their firepower in the southern panhandle to protect the Ho Chi Minh Trail. Aerial reconnaissance photos of these gun positions were turned over to the Lao Armed Forces, but little, if any, action was taken.

On June 26, an evaluation of the effectiveness of the RLAF T-28 aircraft was compiled by the United States. According to the assessment, the RLAF was authorized to use the T-28 for bombing missions after the outbreak of fighting on the Plain of Jars on May 16 and May 17, and the number of aircraft provided by the United States increased from six to more than 20. Of those, more than a dozen were configured for strike missions, and the remainder was used for reconnaissance.

It was also estimated that in a three week period since May 16, over 400 sorties had been flown around the Plain by the RLAF, and several times U.S. pilots had flown with the T-28 missions in support of the RLAF. The assessment indicated that the RLAF strikes were little more than harassment to the Pathet Lao, and it did not appear that their supply movements had been seriously hampered. The report also stated that the effectiveness of individual sorties was limited, due to increasing levels of ground fire and target identification problems.

On June 26, Unger met with Souvanna and asked him if it would be acceptable to expand the Yankee Team reconnaissance flights beyond the scope of backing up Kong Le at Muong Soui. The Prime Minister generally approved the expansion, but suggested that retaliation should take place in areas where the Pathet Lao presence was less significant. In other words, he suggested that they be discreet, to minimize the likelihood of the ICC getting involved.

As the internal bickering within the Lao military continued, it became apparent to the United States that a peaceful settlement probably wasn't going to be the outcome of the Secret War in Laos. For one thing, the Communists had stepped up their offensive operations, another American pilot had become a POW, and a reconnaissance aircraft had also been lost. After subsequent discussions with CIA headquarters, Bill Lair was given the green light to expand the Hmong guerrilla units on an even larger scale. Additionally, a contingent of CIA officers sufficient to manage a larger force was also sent to Laos. Activity at Long Tieng was about to get kicked into high gear.

Meanwhile, General Moore took the initial steps that would eventually lead to the creation of the first USAF SAR organization outside of South Vietnam. Conceptually, SAR operations would be initially controlled by the Alternate Special Operations Center (ASOC) at Udorn. The next step took place on June 19, when the General Moore placed a small detachment of the USAF 1st Air Rescue Squadron at NKP. The unit consisted of two HH-43 Huskie helicopters and 36 airmen. The helicopters were equipped with single-sideband and UHF radios with a range of 100 miles. To support the Huskies, U.S. Navy A-1 Skyraiders were assigned to stand ramp alert at NKP. In the event a SAR was required, the launch order could come from the ASOC at Udorn, Tan Son Nhut Air Base in Saigon, or the SAR commander. On June 20, the Royal Thai Government (RTG) approved SAR activity from Thailand, paving the way for the Huskies to begin rescues.[38]

Meanwhile, at Long Tieng, Vang Pao unveiled big plans for expanding his guerrilla forces to meet the challenges in Laos. He estimated that he would need approximately 15,000 troops, organized into battalion-sized units of several hundred soldiers each. He requested mortars, recoilless guns, machine guns, and the modern M-16 rifles. VP's idea was for the guerrilla units to be highly mobile "hit and run" units, able to move into and out of an area quickly. VP believed that if he could recruit the right numbers of Hmong guerrillas, giving them modern weapons and the training they needed, he would be victorious over the NVA and the Pathet Lao.

Meanwhile, on June 29, Washington formally approved Operation Triangle, and Yankee Team armed reconnaissance flights resumed over northern Laos. During the flights, their armed escorts were permitted to strike other targets of opportunity, as the need arose. The edict from Washington also gave permission for American advisors to support Lao troops in the field. After the approval was received, several U.S. military advisors were dispatched to Muong Soui to assist in air operations and artillery targeting. Operation Triangle was scheduled to begin during the first week of July. But as July arrived, the weather deteriorated, and the monsoon rains came on with a vengeance.

By July 11, the rain began to subside, and on July 15, the Lao forces were positioned at Muong Soui. The following day, a Pathet

Lao regiment supported by artillery attacked Kong Le's headquarters, but were beaten back with support from the T-28 fighters. On July 19, the Lao troops counterattacked, using artillery and T-28s. Realizing their position was about to be overrun, the Pathet Lao fled in the direction on Phou Kout, the mountain that stood vigil 1,300 feet above the Muong Soui valley.

Phou Kout (Iron Mountain) was covered with dense growths of bushes and scrubby pine trees, and was reportedly defended by several companies of heavily-fortified Communist infantry troops, who had seeded the approaches to the mountain with antipersonnel mines. During the following week, Neutralist troops initiated two assaults on the mountain, but were thrown back. A third assault was later attempted after considerable softening up by RLAF T-28s; this time Kong Le's troops were able to penetrate the defenses, and made it almost to the top of the mountain before they stopped to regroup.

But at that moment they sensed they had been lured into a trap, and hastily retreated back down the mountain to safety. Of course, this didn't sit well with the Lao commanders, and they planned a fourth assault for the next day. The U.S. military attachés, Law and Tyrrell, were not sure that a fourth attack would accomplish the task, and believed that if the mountain was taken, the rest of the operation would be in jeopardy. To increase the odds of victory, the attachés recommended the area be softened up with napalm dropped by the T-28s prior to the fourth attack.

The ambassador had no objection to using napalm, which had recently been approved for general defensive use, but he privately worried whether using it once would open the door to its use on a regular basis. For a second opinion, Unger spoke with the British Ambassador to Laos, Donald C. Hobson, who didn't think it was a good idea to use napalm at all, given the stigma attached to something akin to a chemical weapon. As discussions continued in Vientiane and Washington about what to do at Phou Kout, the Neutralists, Royalists and Hmong troops were slowly and carefully advancing on Sala Phou Koun. The troops were secretly augmented by Green Berets and USAF air liaison officers, who provided leadership and technical advice to the Lao troops.

By July 25, the weather had turned bad and then cleared again, so RLAF T-28 fighters subsequently flew more than 50 sorties against Communist targets along Route 13. Little ground fire was encountered, and on July 30, Lao troops literally walked in to the town of Muong Kassy without firing a single shot. On that same day, Hmong guerrillas captured Sala Phou Koun after only light resistance. Other towns also taken by the Lao included Tan Thieng, Nam Tiat and Phou Suong. The only obstacle remaining was Phou Kout.

In a strange turn of events that same evening, Unger, his deputy Chadbourn, and other Western diplomats were invited to dinner party with Souvanna. During the meal, Souvanna began speaking in heated tones about the Pathet Lao betrayal and the recent losses of Tha Thom and Phou San. Apparently, he had spoken with Souphanouvong, who denied any Pathet Lao involvement in the attacks. Souvanna also related that he had spoken with the Soviet ambassador earlier in the day, and the Russians were washing their hands of the whole Laos mess—and would not exert any pressure whatsoever on the Pathet Lao to vacate Tha Thom and Phou San. Souvanna then pointedly asked Ambassador Unger why the U.S. didn't bomb North Vietnam and China. Unger didn't answer the question directly, but did seize the opportunity to once again broach the subject of American pilots flying the RLAF T-28s. Souvanna listened, and without hesitation approved Unger's request, right then and there.

Meanwhile, the Department of Defense was investigating ways to interdict Communist infiltration routes and facilities in the southern panhandle of Laos. Their hope was to improve the morale of the South Vietnamese troops, and have them focus on something other than U.S. bombing of North Vietnam. On July 26, the DOD recommended using the Vietnamese Air Force (VNAF) Douglas A-1Hs or two-seat USAF A1E Skyraiders in southern Laos, with a combination of VNAF and USAF pilots. The plan was to attack North Vietnamese storage dumps, barracks and artillery positions along the Ho Chi Minh Trail, using conventional ordnance with a projected sortie rate of about 20 a day beginning in August 1964. But Ambassador Unger didn't like the plan, and Souvanna was somewhat ambivalent himself. He didn't see the Trail as his problem. Unger believed the DOD would be better off stepping up the activity in northern Laos, to include interdiction of Route 7, along with increased support for Operation Triangle.

While the Neutralists continued to plan their fourth attack on Phou Kout, other events were taking place in the Gulf of Tonkin that would signal a permanent change in the war against Communism in Southeast Asia (SEA). For some time, the United States had demonstrated its support for anti-Communist forces in SEA by conducting armed patrols off the coast of Vietnam using U.S. Navy destroyers. These patrols were under constant surveillance by the North Vietnamese, who would periodically harass one of the U.S. Navy ships by buzzing it with one of their aircraft; in other cases, high-speed patrol boats would make overt gestures mimicking intent to attack. Not too much was made of these gestures, but the crews on the U.S. destroyers were nonetheless alert and at their battle stations in the event of an actual provocation.

On August 2, the destroyer *U.S.S. Maddox* picked up radar signals indicating hostile intent by three high-speed North Vietnamese patrol boats. The *Maddox* fired several warning shots, but the patrol boats continued to close on the destroyer. The *Maddox* then opened fire directly on the patrol boats, disabling one, but not before it released two torpedoes that narrowly missed the destroyer. A second patrol boat lost power, and a third patrol boat passed close to the *Maddox*, spraying it with machine gun fire.

U.S. Navy fighters from the *U.S.S. Ticonderoga* soon appeared in the sky over the *Maddox*, and the attack by the North Vietnamese ended. Washington learned of the incident as soon as it started, but did not take any overt action immediately. The White House did make it clear, however, that any further provocation would be dealt with swiftly and with great force. As a show of force, the destroyer *U.S.S. Turner Joy* steamed alongside the *Maddox*. When the *Turner Joy* arrived, however, both ships were notified they were being tracked by North Vietnamese radar.

Everything remained quiet until late that night, when enemy patrol boats were observed shadowing the destroyers, positioning for possible attack. The *Turner Joy* fired its guns into the darkness, and the patrol boats withdrew from the area temporarily. Neither of the ships sustained any damage, but Admiral Ulysses Grant Sharp, Jr., who had recently replaced Admiral Felt as CINCPAC, immediately asked Washington to authorize punitive air strikes against North Vietnam.

On the following day, August 5, U.S. Navy fighters took to the air from aircraft carriers in the region and turned in the direction of North Vietnam. On that same morning, President Johnson announced to the world that the United States was responding, in kind, to North Vietnam's aggression. The strike, which was named "Pierce Arrow," targeted the North Vietnamese navy bases Hon Gai, Loc Chao, Quang Khe and Ben Thuy, and petroleum storage depots at Vinh. In the subsequent air attack by the U.S. Navy, 25 P-4 torpedo boats and the oil depots were destroyed, but two Navy fighters and two pilots were lost. One pilot was killed, and the other, Ensign Everett Alvarez, became the first U.S. POW in North Vietnam. A few days later, on August 10, Congress passed a bill known as the

Figure 19. U.S.S. Maddox
(Photo from the Public Domain)

Gulf of Tonkin Resolution, giving President Johnson authorization for the use of military force in Southeast Asia. This resolution became the basis for expanding the war in Vietnam, Laos, and Cambodia.[39]

Meanwhile, on August 5, 23 RLAF T-28 aircraft pounded the Communist troops on Phou Kout. After the mountain was softened up, Lao troops rushed up the hill. When they reached the minefield near the top of the mountain, however, they stopped, unwilling to face the mines. They also heard that heavy Communist reinforcements were on the way—so they hurried back down the mountain. On August 9, Colonel Law, the U.S. Army Attaché to Vientiane, made a trip to

Phou Kout to personally investigate why the Lao troops were unable to take the mountain's summit. After observing the minefield, and knowing that the Lao troops had already suffered more than 100 casualties in the attacks, Law decided the mountain would remain in Communist hands.

Meanwhile, the DOD continued their planning for interdiction missions along the Ho Chi Minh Trail, convening a conference to discuss the matter on August 18 at Udorn. By this time, the plan had changed somewhat, with RLAF T-28s to be used rather than A-1 Skyraiders. It seemed that RLAF Brigadier General Thao Ma had privately assured U.S. Army General William C. Westmoreland, the new MACV commander, that he (Thao Ma) could handle the 20 targets a day and that the mission could be accomplished in ten days. But some of the attendees at the meeting were not optimistic, because the targets were so well defended that the T-28s might not be able to do the job. Colonel Tyrell then offered to review the list and select the targets he thought most feasible for the RLAF pilots.

Also on August 18, during a withdrawal of Lao Neutralist forces from the northwestern corner of the Plain of Jars, NVA gunners brought down an RLAF T-28 that was providing cover for the withdrawing forces. His wingman notified the AFCC in Udorn of the downed airman. Udorn, in turn, notified the AOC in Vientiane, and they dispatched an Air America H-34 helicopter to attempt a rescue. The USAF also sent F-100 Super Sabre fighters from Takhli Air Base to assist in the rescue.

When the H-34 reached the location, it was shot out of the sky by Pathet Lao gunners. Then the USAF F-100s strafed the gunners, but one of them was also hit by antiaircraft fire; the crippled F-100 was able to break off and gain altitude in an attempt to return to Thailand. The pilot made it to the Mekong River, where he safely ejected. Fortunately, he was rescued by Air America and was returned to Takhli. The AOC in Vientiane then launched another Air America H-34 and six RLAF T-28 aircraft to initiate a second rescue attempt.

Meanwhile, at the crash site, U.S. aircraft continued to strafe the enemy positions. After the Pathet Lao guns quit firing, the H-34 helicopter was able to approach the area, land, and pick-up the downed pilot from the first H-34. Unfortunately, the Filipino aircraft mechanic on the downed H-34 had perished. The two airmen from the original downed T-28 were spotted, and observed running into the jungle to escape the Pathet Lao.

Later, on August 20, American officials reevaluated the need for SAR capability to support air operations. They concluded in writing that SAR was a crucial factor in maintaining the morale of pilots, and opined that a combination of Air America and U.S. military assets would be required to maintain the SAR operations in Laos. Recognizing the need for effective SAR capability, it was stressed that use of the T-28 must continue in order to support Souvanna. According to information provided, there had been approximately 40 ground attacks against U.S. transport, passenger and helicopter aircraft. The information also indicated that three T-28s had been lost in the past few days alone. The loss rate was considered acceptable, however, when consideration was given to the fact that over 1,543 combat sorties had been flown during that time.

Other good news came on August 31, when word reached Vientiane that Lieutenant Klusmann had escaped from the Pathet Lao along with several Lao troops and, after hiding for two days in the jungle, had been able to reach an encampment of friendly forces near Bouam Long. Needless to say, the Hmong guerrillas at the camp were somewhat startled and wary of these strangers, who had come from nowhere out of the jungle. But after talking with Klusmann, their commander notified his headquarters at Long Tieng by radio, and in short order a helicopter arrived to pick Klusmann up and take him to Udorn. During his subsequent debriefing, Klusmann told U.S. personnel that he had been treated well by his captors, and was even provided with medical care.

On September 29, Ambassador Unger met with Souvanna to again discuss proposed DOD strikes of the infiltration routes. The Prime Minister was not enthusiastic, and recommended instead that strikes against Route 7 continue; he was convinced that once the roads dried, the Pathet Lao would attack Kong Le at Muong Soui. As a compromise, Unger pledged to provide resources to interdict the Communist troops along Route 7, concurrent with interdiction missions taking place in southern Laos along the Trail. Souvanna agreed to the proposal, but stipulated that all targets had to be approved in advance by the FAR General Staff.

Meanwhile, President Johnson directed that additional T-28s be provided to the RLAF, but the T-28s weren't Unger's primary concern. He didn't want to disappoint Souvanna, so he pressed Washington to use fast-moving jet fighters to bomb targets along Route 7. He believed that the best place to hit the Communists and slow their resupply capability was the Ban Ken Bridge, where Route 7 crossed the Mat River at the eastern end of the Ban Ban Valley. Unger also knew the political ramifications were great, but he felt the risk was worth it, inasmuch as Souvanna had also approved the strikes along the Ho Chi Minh Trail. But unfortunately, the strike on the Ban Ken Bridge would not happen right away because President Johnson disapproved the plan on October 7, arguing that there was no evidence Hanoi was planning an attack on Kong Le.

Later, on October 6, 1964, Secretary of State Rusk dispatched a cable to the U.S. Embassy in Vientiane to explain Johnson's disapproval of the plan to attack the Communist along Route 7 in northern Laos. His orders boiled down to the following:

1. *You are authorized to urge the RLG to begin air attacks against Viet Cong infiltration routes and facilities in the Laos panhandle by RLAF T-28 aircraft.*
2. *You are further authorized to inform the Lao that Yankee Team suppressive fire strikes against certain difficult targets in panhandle, interspersed with additional T-28 strikes, are part of the overall concept and are to be anticipated later, but that such strikes are not authorized at this time.*
3. *Highest levels have not authorized Yankee Team strikes at this time against Route 7 targets.*
4. *You may inform RLG, however, that the U.S. will fly additional reconnaissance over Route 7 to keep current on use being made by the Pathet Lao, and to identify targets and air defenses.*

On October 8, the Coordinating Committee for United States Missions, Southeast Asia (SEACOORD) held its first meeting. The group was the brainchild of General Maxwell D. Taylor, the former U.S. Army Chief of Staff, and more recently the new U.S. Ambassador to Vietnam. Ambassador Taylor believed that the wars in Vietnam and Laos could no longer be separated, and he also believed that SEACOORD would be an excellent way to bring the key military and civilian leaders together periodically to discuss strategy. Its membership would consist of the U.S. missions in Saigon, Vientiane, and Bangkok. The objectives of the committee would be to coordinate policy recommendations and military operational matters affecting more than one geographical area. In other words, they were adding another level of review to further complicate an already cumbersome process.

After the initial meeting, the consensus of the SEACOORD members was that corridor strikes would achieve the desired psychological and political effect *only* if the U.S. directly supported the Lao government. They also believed the Yankee Team reconnaissance flights would be a necessary ingredient in that effort. SEACOORD later asked President Johnson to lift the restrictions he had imposed on American involvement, but he would not yield, even though the JCS, Admiral Sharp, and General Westmoreland were in favor of bombing the Ban Ken Bridge.

On October 13, the RLAF flew approximately 18 sorties in northern Laos, primarily in support of FAR and Hmong guerrillas near Tha Thom. Things remained fairly quiet at Muong Soui, but the Communists were rapidly delivering supplies and ammunition to the Pathet Lao and NVA forces in the region. In fact, during a 10-day period from October 13 to October 23, over 200 trucks hauling war-fighting materials from North Vietnam to northern Laos were counted along Route 7. In order to stem the flow of supplies, the Country Team again asked for a strike on the Ban Ken Bridge—but permission was not forthcoming.

On October 27, the General Staff announced that FAR and Hmong troops led by Vang Pao planned to retake several Pathet Lao positions east and south of Xieng Khouangville, relieving pressure on Tha Thom. On the following day, an operation called "Anniversary Victory" got underway, using the RLAF T-28s to soften up the enemy. But of the 31 T-28s available, only five or six were ready for strike duty. As the days passed, the strikes did take place, and continued allowing the FAR and Hmong ground forces to advance on the Communists. Meanwhile, the NVA hastily sent three battalions to reinforce the Pathet Lao

As fighting continued, the NVA reinforcements began to flank the Hmong guerrillas, and T-28s were brought in to blunt the NVA attacks. But problems with Lao FACs and communications equipment were encountered, so the U.S. provided American controllers to assist the ground effort. Slowly, the ground situation stabilized, thanks to VP's uncanny ability to perceive the enemy's next move. But in early November, Operation Anniversary Victory began to stall; VP was unable to take his objectives, but he was able to blunt the NVA counterattacks. It was also reported that the NVA had suffered heavy casualties, and thanks to the venerable T-28s, Tha Thom did not fall.

After Operation Anniversary Victory was concluded, an embassy assessment concluded that the FAR and Hmong officers placed too much reliance on air support. Essentially, they depended on the fighters to kill the enemy. Instead of closing on the enemy after the T-28s softened them up, the officers held their men back and waited for the smoke to clear before literally walking in to count the dead bodies. In most cases, however, the air strikes didn't kill all the Communist troops. After the fighters departed, the enemy would regroup and engage the Lao forces, who would inevitably cut and run without finishing off the Communists. The U.S. military leaders in Laos believed that this practice of not engaging the enemy on the part of the Lao military would, in time, hamper the proper development of the Laotian armed forces.

Meanwhile, back in the United States, as expected, LBJ was reelected as President of the United States in November—and he was about to take the gloves off in Vietnam. But there was still Laos to deal with. As mentioned earlier, President Johnson refused to approve the bombing of the Ban Ken Bridge—and the American military didn't agree with him on this issue. On November 14, JCS Chairman Earle G. Wheeler signed a memorandum (JCSM 955-64, available in the public domain) wherein he stated that the JCS did not concur with the concept of "tit-for-tat" reprisals espoused by Ambassador Taylor. General Wheeler went on to say the tit-for-tat reprisals were unduly restrictive, inhibiting U.S. initiative and implying a lack of flexibility as to the nature and level of response. The memorandum continued by recommending attacks against specific targets in Laos, including the Ban Ken Bridge, as well as low-level reconnaissance in the southern DRV. The JCS memorandum concluded by stating that it was their belief that a major decision point had been reached in SEA, and the U.S. should continue to aggressively pursue its stated objective of keeping Laos, Thailand and South Vietnam free of Communist domination.

Shortly thereafter, on November 18 and 19, the first large-scale USAF/Air America SAR mission in Southeast Asia took place in northern Laos. It all began during a routine reconnaissance mission, when two F-100 Super Sabres were flying cover for the reconnaissance aircraft. One of the two F-100s, "Ball 03," was shot down while firing on Communist antiaircraft gun positions. Ball 03's wingman contacted the AOC in Vientiane with their last known location: just south of Ban Sen Phan in central Laos, near the border with North Vietnam.

Air America diverted one of their C-123 cargo planes in the area to act as an airborne controller until a USAF HU-16 Albatross rescue aircraft could arrive from Thailand. When the HU-16 did arrive, the control aircraft, call sign "Tacky 44," requested that A-1 Skyraiders join the SAR effort. Meanwhile, HH-43 Huskie helicopters at NKP were placed on alert. Later, as the Skyraiders arrived on station, they began taking fire from Pathet Lao gun emplacements located nearby. The A-1s then went to work on the gun emplacements. They took some flak and small arms fire, but managed to escape serious damage.

Figure 20. HU-16 Albatross
(Photo from the Public Domain)

During the strafing runs on the gun emplacements, one of the A-1 pilots thought that he had found the actual site where the F-100 had crashed earlier, and relayed the information to the AOC. The HH-43s were then launched, and the Skyraiders flew to meet the Huskies in order to guide them to the crash site. Upon arrival at the site, the Huskies carefully combed the area, but could find no wreckage and no parachute, so they departed.[40] The search was terminated without locating the downed airman, but the event was important because it represented the first official USAF rescue mission over northern Laos. On the following day, USAF rescuers returned to the area and were able to find the downed airman and the crashed F-100. Unfortunately, the pilot had died from injuries sustained upon landing on a limestone rock formation.

Later, on November 21, USAF Captain Burton Walz was flying over the village of Ban Phan Nop in northern Laos, photographing the gun positions that had downed the F-100 three days earlier, when ground fire struck his RF-101, causing it to burst into flames and tumble out of control. Captain Walz ejected, but his parachute caught in one of the tall jungle trees, suspending him high above the jungle floor. As he tried to secure himself, the canopy tore loose and he fell to the ground, breaking a leg and an arm and suffering other injuries. Fortunately, an Air America helicopter was in the area and quickly recovered Walz and flew him to Korat Air Base in Thailand for medical treatment.

Also in November 1964, while visiting Kong Le at Muong Soui, Colonel Law was shown a new plan to retake Phou Kout. Based upon recent intelligence information, Kong Le was confident the mountain could be taken, because the NVA had reportedly reduced their troop strength to only two companies. Law didn't think the plan would succeed, however, because it appeared that insufficient air support was planned—and its success would depend on that all-important push at the end that had been lacking in past engagements. At any rate, Kong Le agreed to postpone the attack temporarily, but only for a few days.

The Country Team in Vientiane was in favor of another attack on Phou Kout. They reworked Kong Le's plan, adding sufficient air support and artillery spotters. The attack finally got under way on December 1, with RLAF T-28 aircraft softening up the base of the mountain. On the following day, the T-28s attacked again and five Neutralist battalions moved out, meeting only light resistance. The Lao troops then began working their way up the mountain as the T-28s continued to lay on the fragmentation bombs. By late afternoon, one of the minor peaks had been taken by the Neutralists. At this point, however, the Lao troops stopped, as they usually did, and essentially began to just mill around waiting for something to happen, rather than pressing the attack to the summit. In addition to stopping before reaching the summit, they failed to station patrols at the base of the mountain to protect their rear, leaving themselves open to counterattack.

Sure enough, on December 4, the Pathet Lao and NVA counterattacked using artillery, and the Neutralist troops were forced back down the slope. On the following day, Communist tanks showed up and began pounding the Neutralists. The T-28s tried to take out the tanks, but they were concealed in the trees and could not be spotted. On December 6, the T-28s were finally able to find the tanks and managed to take out four of them, reportedly killing a Pathet Lao commander and several members of his staff. For the next three days, there was sporadic fighting, but no significant headway was made. Finally, on December 10, a fresh NVA battalion showed up and attacked the weary Neutralists, forcing them to retreat from Phou Kout to the safety of Muong Soui.

At about this same time, Ambassador Unger left Vientiane after completing his tour of duty. His replacement was William H. Sullivan, an Asia expert who had served as a special assistant to Secretary Rusk, chairing the Vietnam Working Group. Sullivan also participated in the talks at Geneva in 1961-62. Meanwhile, President Johnson launched "Operation Barrel Roll," which included air operations in northern Laos to support Vang Pao. Barrel Roll was conceived to provide interdiction and close air support to anti-Communist troops. The primary sources of the fighter jets participating in Barrel Roll were U.S. bases in nearby Thailand, but the day-to-day execution of the Secret War remained the responsibility of the U.S. Ambassador in Vientiane. And since the U.S. was not officially in Laos, there was no need for a military hierarchy like the one that oversaw the war in South Vietnam.

As the war in South Vietnam expanded, enemy supply lines through Communist-controlled portions of Laos, via the Ho Chi Minh Trail, increased in number and importance. As a result, Laos became even more significant. While stopping short of committing ground forces to Laos, the United States recognized that the Lao government needed to be supported and maintained, and it was believed that Souvanna provided the best and most stable leadership for the many diverse factions in the country. In addition, if American aircraft were to continue to enjoy the authority to strike enemy supply lines in Laos, support for Souvanna's government and the Lao military forces was necessary. So there were, in essence, two air campaigns being waged simultaneously in Laos. One was directed against the NVA supply lines to South Vietnam; the other was to support the RLG against the encroachment of the Pathet Lao and NVA forces in northern Laos.

It was also necessary to keep in mind the dual nature of the war in Laos, in order to understand the associated problems. This duality, however, did not mean that one was excluded from the other. True, the conflicts were each unique, yet they were connected by their association with the U.S. Ambassador to Vientiane.[41] To support this parallel effort, the CINCPAC directed the U.S. MACV to launch strikes against confirmed RLAF targets, and to conduct armed reconnaissance in authorized areas to interdict enemy supply lines to South Vietnam and Laos.

The Communists had enjoyed a good year in 1964. Kong Le was surrounded at Muong Soui, and the Plain of Jars was controlled by the NVA and Pathet Lao. The Communists also retook most of the real estate lost to VP in 1963, and Phou Kout was still in enemy hands. But in Vientiane, it was business as usual, with the Lao military brass feathering their own nests and fighting with each other.

On December 12, Cyrus R. Vance, Deputy Secretary of Defense, briefed the Operation Barrel Roll program to the National Security Council. McGeorge Bundy, a White House staff member, was quoted as saying the program depicted exactly what President Johnson desired, and that barring any notice to the contrary, the effort should commence immediately. On that same day, Souvanna Phouma was also briefed, and he also approved the operation.

Two days later, on December 14, Operation Barrel Roll commenced. The original purpose of the operation was to signal the DRV to end its support of the insurgency taking place in South Vietnam. The action centered on the Ho Chi Minh Trail, which ran along southeastern Laos near its border with Vietnam, and focused on the interdiction of war supplies as they transited Laos. Later, the operation was expanded to provide close air support to the FAR and the CIA-sponsored Hmong guerrillas under Vang Pao. It also authorized armed reconnaissance patrols for the Yankee Team/Able Mable program.

On December 19, a meeting attended by U.S. embassy personnel and representatives from the USAF and the USN was held to discuss the operational aspects of Barrel Roll. At the meeting, it was agreed that a 40-mile stretch of Route 7, running west-to-east between Nong Pet and Nong Het, should become a priority target—inasmuch as this was one of the NVA's main entry points into Laos. It was also agreed that the next round of missions would include interdiction along this road, but the bridge at Ban Ken would not be bombed. Nong Het was the main enemy resupply and transshipment point, and contained approximately a dozen NVA warehouses. In order to eliminate the warehouses, a mission was subsequently scheduled for the last week of December.

An armed reconnaissance mission followed on December 21, utilizing four F-100s from Da Nang, South Vietnam, and two F-105s from Korat Air Base, Thailand. Route 7 was clear that day and no traffic was observed, but when the jets flew over the Ban Ken Bridge, the sky suddenly filled with antiaircraft fire from artillery emplacements around the bridge. The fighters fought back using 20mm cannon fire and cluster bomb units (CBU). Several of the fighters were hit, but all aircraft managed to return safely to their bases.

Shortly thereafter, as 1965 began, the rainy season ended; traditionally, that meant that the NVA's 316th Division, using the 174th Regiment, would resume its offensive combat operations in Laos. During the rainy season, North Vietnam had quietly increased its troop strength in Laos to approximately 10,000 personnel. Aerial reconnaissance photos verified the build-up. Meanwhile, large NVA convoys hauling war supplies began flowing into Laos via Route 7, and the NVA and Pathet Lao ground forces once again began their annual dry season offensive in northern Laos. Their favorite target, of course, was Sam Neua Province. The Air Force planners quickly scheduled an armed reconnaissance mission to be undertaken by January 10, at night, using F-100 fighters and C-130 flare ships along Route 7 between Nong Pet and Nong Het. The mission did not take place, however, because the weather deteriorated and the entire area was socked in with heavy clouds, precluding the flights.

Later, after three months of debate and briefings depicting several different strike scenarios, a date was finally set to strike the Ban Ken Bridge. That date was January 13, 1965, and the mission would call for 16 F-105 Thunderchiefs. Ten of the aircraft were loaded with iron bombs, and the other six carried AGM-12 "Bullpup" air-to-ground missiles.[42] There were also 12 F-100 Super Sabres planned to support the mission by flying MiG patrol and performing flak suppression. This mission did go on schedule, and the bridge was dropped on the first pass by the F-105s. The rest of the aircraft used their munitions for mopping up and attacking the many gun emplacements protecting the bridge. Unfortunately, one F-100 and one F-105 were shot down during the attack on the bridge, but both pilots were successfully rescued by Air America and taken to Udorn.

Military authorities were pleased, and considered the strike a complete success, even though two aircraft were lost. It was later determined that the AGM-12 wasn't the ideal weapon for use against bridges, but the iron bombs worked perfectly. The strike also brought into the open for the first time the fact that U.S. aircraft were doing more than merely flying reconnaissance in Laos. There was some basis for concern with flak-scarred aircraft returning to Thailand after conducting air strikes in Laos, because it was feared the media might start asking penetrating questions regarding how the damage occurred. But Ambassador Sullivan was not concerned, advising the Country Team to answer any such questions only with the standard line of not being able to discuss operational matters.

Even though the strike on the bridge was a success, other events early in 1965 weren't quite as successful. The enemy's dry season offensive was off to a decent start, with several Hmong positions in the Sam Neua area lost to the Communists, and on January 20, misfortune struck at Wattay Airport in Vientiane: an electrical problem caused a machine gun on an RLAF T-28 to fire into another T-28 in front of it, causing the bomb load to detonate. The detonation then set off a chain reaction among other armed aircraft, and before it could be stopped, several T-28s and one Cessna were destroyed. Two C-47s were also slightly damaged, and numerous buildings were ripped apart by the shrapnel from the exploding bombs.

Naturally, Phoumi took this opportunity to stage yet another unsuccessful coup, and subsequently fled to Thailand, leaving a temporary leadership void in the FAR ranks. The void was later filled by Generals Ouane Rathikone, Kouprasith Abhay, and Bounpone Makthepharak. Ouane remained Chief of Staff, maintaining control over most of northwestern Laos. Bounpone took over Phoumi's area in the south, and Kouprasith solidified his control over Vientiane and the remainder of MR 5. Each maintained their clan ties and business interests, which immediately aroused the suspicions of the other generals.

While all this chaos was taking place, the Pathet Lao and NVA stepped up their attacks in northeastern Laos, with the Hmong losing a key position at Ban Hong Non. VP was concerned, believing that Hua Muong, one of his strongholds in the region, would be the next target of the Communist forces. Meanwhile, the RLAF T-28s continued their strikes in the northeast on a daily basis, temporarily slowing the enemy advance.

VP's suspicions were confirmed when enemy troops began to build up their forces and supplies north of Ban Ban along Route 7. By the end of January, the Communists were edging south in the direction of Hua Muong. To counter this move, VP and his guerrillas attacked the enemy at Ban Hong Non, recapturing some positions. But the Communists did not yield; and by early February, Muong Khao, Pha Thom and Van Na Lieu had fallen to the enemy. Slowly, the Communists tightened the noose around Hua Muong, throwing several more NVA battalions into the fight.

On February 4, U.S. Intelligence sources predicted that recent troop reinforcements from North Vietnam had increased enemy capabilities in Laos. More specifically, a likely Communist move would be an attempt to recapture the junction of Routes 7 and 13, without risking serious escalation of the war. Another probable scenario was a move against Kong Le's position near Muong Soui. The sources also suggested the Soviet Union might provide updated air defense capability to North Vietnam, to include Surface to Air Missiles (SAMs).

Near the Plain of Jars, the Communist troops advanced and easily took Phou Kout. Then they kept moving south. The Hmong guerrillas were doing a fairly good job of hitting the NVA and then retreating, to reform and strike again. Meanwhile, Tony Poe was sent by Bill Lair to Hong Non to assess the situation up north. Poe offered assistance to the Hmong by directing mortar rounds on the advancing NVA. As the fighting intensified, the Hmong women and children began an orderly retreat to the south. Meanwhile, Poe kept leading the guerrillas, and directing sniper fire and mortar rounds. Not surprisingly, the NVA advance slowly began to lose its momentum.

Even though Poe received orders from Lair directing him not to personally participate in the fighting, he felt that he should help, or his position would be overrun. So Poe ignored Lair's orders, picked up an M-1 carbine, and began firing, eventually taking out almost a dozen NVA soldiers. Shortly thereafter, he took an AK-47 round in the gut, just above his groin, and his Thai PARU team leaders were killed by the same bursts of fire. By this time, the fight was too intense for Poe and the surviving PARU team members, who were forced to retreat on foot. They managed to walk several kilometers, dragging the injured Poe along, before being picked up by an Air America H-34 helicopter. Poe was quickly taken to Hua Moung, where he was transferred to a waiting Air America fixed-wing aircraft. He ultimately wound up at Korat Air Force Base in Thailand, where he received treatment for his wound. He remained in the hospital there for several weeks before he was ready to rejoin the other CIA advisors in Laos.

Meanwhile, the NVA 174th attacked Houei Sa An and Hua Moung. Rather than see his troops wiped out, Poe ordered the Hmong guerrillas to fall back. About the same time, the Hmong commander at Hua Moung deserted, taking some of the other officers with him. Without leaders, VP's guerrillas also fell back, leaving Hua Moung to the NVA. Before the NVA took Hua Moung, however, VP called in Air America to evacuate thousands of civilians in the region and take them to safer locations like Sam Thong. Watching the evacuation and the troops falling back from the two sites, VPs confidence was shaken. The NVA had swept right over his soldiers, and he could do nothing to help them. Meanwhile, many other Hmong fighters left with their families, simply walking away. The remaining guerrillas fell back to Na Khang (Lima Site 36).

Na Khang was of strategic importance to the United States for several reasons. For one thing, it was a good place for pilots returning from raids over North Vietnam to eject and be rescued, in the event their aircraft were damaged. Also, the USAF maintained two rescue helicopters there that arrived early each morning, and remained until just about dark. LS-36 also maintained a good airstrip, and could refuel both helicopters and fixed-wing aircraft, except for aircraft with jet engines. The site used U.S. Tactical Navigation (TACAN) equipment to guide aircraft, and a USAF Air Combat Weatherman was usually present to assist with weather updates. And, finally, the site was located near primary transportation routes used by the NVA to bring troops and equipment into Laos. In other words, it was very important to the United States, and therefore it was always an extremely large target of the NVA.

After the evacuation from Hua Moung, VP called a meeting at his residence in Long Tieng. All his top aides were there, as was Vint Lawrence. VP began by talking about all the Hmong soldiers and civilians who had been killed. He questioned whether it was all worth it; he also talked about how the war could eventually lead to all the Hmong being killed. He even talked of quitting the war.

Shortly thereafter, VP was promoted to the rank of Major General and placed in command of MR 2, which included the northernmost provinces in Laos. Despite the promotion, he still wasn't happy. Hmong losses in the north totaled about 1,000 casualties, and the outlook was grim. VP's man in the north, Colonel Thong, held on the best he could as the NVA continued their assault. Colonel Thong and VP had already asked for air support in the north, but no airplanes came. VP then went to the Sam Neua area to personally evaluate the situation. What he saw convinced him that it was going to be a long dry season, and many more Hmong would shed their blood before the rains finally came again.

After returning to Long Tieng, VP met with Vint Lawrence and expressed his concerns. Lawrence and two of his aides listened, but offered no suggestions. Lawrence did tell VP that he would meet with him again in a day or so. VP agreed, and the meeting ended. But on the very next day, VP was somehow his old self again, planning his next move against the Communists. He was tracking the movements of the 174th Regiment, and believed that Na Khang would be their next target. VP then coordinated with Pop Buell, and thousands of civilians at Na Khang were relocated to Sam Thong by Air America.

With the civilians out of the way, VP set up his defense of Na Khang. One Hmong guerrilla unit was already in place, but more troops were needed. Major Douangtha Norasing, an RLG officer from Sam Neua, was in the area with his troops and came to aid VP, and the RLA also sent two battalions. VP placed them on the north side of the town—but the 174th didn't show up.

With the Communists solidifying their presence in northeastern Laos, the bigger question was whether or not Vang Pao could hold Na Khang in any case. If not, could the Hmong fall back and regroup at Kong Le's headquarters near Muong Soui? In order to personally evaluate the situation, Colonel Law flew to Kong Le's headquarters to see if preparations were being made for such an eventuality. Upon arrival, Law's worst fears were confirmed: nothing at all was being done to fortify the base. He discovered that Kong Le was consumed by internal bickering among the troops, and he was trying to find someone to blame for the rout at Phou Kout.

In order to slow the Communists down, Law suggested to Ambassador Sullivan that the U.S. step up their attacks on the Pathet Lao and NVA supply bases along Routes 6 and 7. Sullivan agreed, and called on Washington to give northeastern Laos top priority when assigning Barrel Roll missions, based upon events unfolding on the ground hour by hour. Colonel Tyrrell, the Air Attaché, consulted with intelligence sources from the FAR and came up with two good targets in the Sam Neua area, asking for immediate air support. The first target consisted of four 105mm artillery pieces on Route 6 near the town; the second target included supply and bivouac areas near Hua Xieng (a border town). A third target was also being evaluated, after Hmong Road Watch Teams discovered 20 Russian tanks on a road near the village of Ban Houa Xieng, about twenty miles from Sam Neua. Also traveling with the tanks were self-propelled 37mm and 57mm guns, and several 105mm artillery pieces. In addition, there were other assorted antiaircraft artillery pieces in place near the village. As it turned out, this was the largest weapons cache thus far discovered in northeastern Laos. If this target wasn't taken out, it could spell disaster to the FAR and Hmong in future engagements.

Unfortunately, there was no established procedure or process in place to address targets that required quick reaction. The existing process was cumbersome, consisting of several levels of review, verification and approval. Also, there were no Yankee Team reconnaissance photos verifying the existence of the weapons cache. Ambassador Sullivan briefed Souvanna on the information, and the Prime Minister wanted the target eliminated right away. This information was relayed to the State Department in Washington, and the target was approved for immediate strike. On February 17, the JCS ordered the target to be hit as Barrel Roll mission #30. By February 20, all the pieces were finally in place. Eight F-105 Thunderchiefs from Da Nang, armed with Bullpup missiles and rockets, and eight F-100 Super Sabres armed with CBUs were sent to carry out the mission. But instead of proceeding directly to Ban Soua Xieng, the flight diverted to Sam Neua, where they reportedly struck buildings and trucks. Six trucks were demolished and left in flames, and several buildings were either destroyed or heavily damaged. Unfortunately, this was not the intended target, which was some twenty miles away at Ban Soua Xieng. It wasn't even touched.

The strike at Sam Neua immediately set off a political firestorm. Sam Neua was off-limits to bombing; that fact was well-known. But what had happened, and why was the primary target overlooked? These questions and many more would have to be answered before any more strike missions could be carried out, so Ambassador Sullivan suspended all bombing until the facts could be gathered. Shortly thereafter, the Air Force looked into the matter and discovered that the weapons cache at Ban Houa Xieng was not designated as the priority target because Colonel Tyrrell indicated the weapons were mobile and could start moving at any time. And when the flight leader and his wingmen were lining up over Sam Neua on Route 6 for the three-minute flight to Ban Houa Xieng, they observed vehicles on the road, leading them to believe that it was the motorized weapons on the move. With that information, they struck the trucks on the road. As it turned out, no occupied structures were hit, as had first been reported. What actually happened was that when a Bullpup missile struck a truck, setting it on fire, the flames spread to a small shack, which went up in flames.

Sullivan understood the confusion on the part of the flight leader, and all was forgiven—though he also wondered how he was going to explain to Souvanna that none of the motorized weapons at the priority target area had been eliminated. Sullivan then began to reconsider instituting a process and procedure for quick reaction targets in light of what happened at Sam Neua. In fact, he began to believe that more thought and planning should go into each strike, with fixed areas of responsibility.

Meanwhile, on February 13, a decision was made in Washington to initiate a program to provide regular air strikes to punish the North Vietnamese. The operation was called "Rolling Thunder"—or "Rolling Blunder," as some pilots called it. It was designed to gradually escalate the bombing of North Vietnam until Ho Chi Minh saw the light and agreed to negotiations.[43] Rolling Thunder began in earnest shortly thereafter, as aircraft from the USN and USAF pounded North Vietnam. The operation lasted several years, with intermittent pauses between poundings. Additional fighters soon arrived in SEA to participate in the campaign, providing more assets than were needed. The excess fighters were often reassigned to help Barrel Roll in northern Laos. Finally, the air support VP needed appeared to be available.

Given the increase in air strikes in northeastern Laos and North Vietnam, Air America knew that additional H-34 helicopters would be required; so they requested four additional choppers, increasing their fleet to 16. The increase was necessary due to a general shortage of helicopters for airlift and rescue. H-34s were in short supply worldwide, so Admiral Sharp promised to see what he could do. But General John P. McConnell, the new USAF Chief of Staff, objected to giving Air America additional choppers for SAR activity. He believed that it was time for the U.S. military to step up and assume full responsibility for SAR activity, once and for all.

Ambassador Sullivan objected to McConnell's recommendations, for two obvious reasons. First of all, the USAF personnel assigned to SAR were unfamiliar with the geography of Laos, and therefore, operations could be hindered due to the necessary learning curve. In Sullivan's opinion, the Air America pilots knew the country like the backs of their hands. Secondly, and more importantly, the Geneva Accords of 1962 did not contain provisions that would authorize SAR activity using U.S. military personnel. It was true that the USAF had positioned a few HH-43 Huskie rescue helicopters at NKP, and had assisted in SAR operations in the panhandle; but taking on SAR responsibility for the entire country was a completely different proposition, and one that might invite scrutiny by the ICC.

Later, at a SEACOORD meeting on February 22-23, General Westmoreland stated that he was going to ask Washington to consolidate Rolling Thunder, Barrel Roll and Yankee Team into one program. Upon hearing the news, Ambassador Sullivan objected vigorously, pointing out that such a program would be unacceptable to Souvanna. The Prime Minister still enjoyed warm relations with the Soviet Union, and did receive some support from the Russians. And if the USAF programs were consolidated, it would mean the aircraft departing Thailand would have to fly over Laos in order to reach their targets in North Vietnam. Should that occur, Sullivan was sure the Russians would most likely cut off support to Souvanna.

Sullivan also reminded the group that Yankee Team and Barrel Roll were designed for the environment in Laos, to deal with the insurgency and the NVA—and he believed that it should stay that way. In addition, Sullivan was concerned that once Rolling Thunder got underway, sorties needed for Laos might be reallocated to North Vietnam. Continuing on this line of thought, Sullivan wondered if a specific USAF unit or wing could be dedicated to the Barrel Roll and Yankee Team programs in Laos. As he thought more about the idea, he considered using the A-1 Skyraider in Laos, based upon its ability to sustain significant battle damage and still fly home at the end of the day. But he didn't want to dictate specific aircraft requirements to the U.S. military, because it wasn't his place to suggest equipment for tasking placed on the USAF.

After the SEACOORD meeting, Sullivan shared his views with General Harris, who appeared agreeable; but Harris suggested using jets instead of the prop-driven Skyraiders. The ambassador dropped the subject, but continued to beat the drum for a dedicated air unit to handle Barrel Roll and Yankee Team missions in Laos. The discussions continued into March, and ultimately General Westmoreland backed away from combining the three programs into one. He also stopped short of dedicating a specific air unit/wing to Laos. But Sullivan still wouldn't give up on the idea of a specific unit dedicated to interdiction and ground support for the Lao troops at war with the Pathet Lao and NVA.

Also in March, MACV and the U.S. Embassy in Vientiane put the finishing touches on a concept called "chokepoint," which was designed to frustrate and slow the enemy down. Chokepoints were locations along roads and trails that were easy to cut and hard to bypass. Admiral Sharp was amenable to the concept of chokepoints, but favored the existing practice of bombing the enemy's logistics bases. He believed that destroying the supplies would make it difficult for the enemy to wage war during the rainy season, when the supply lines were interrupted. Sharp especially didn't value the chokepoint concept because of the 48-hour rule, as invoked by the Johnson administration: once an area was bombed, it couldn't be bombed again for 48 hours; the idea was to give the Communists time to think about the consequences and hopefully change their ways. In reality, the 48 hours usually gave the enemy time to clear the bombs, repair the roads, and restart their supply line without fear of reprisal. In other words, the rule didn't work. It was laughable at best.

Finally, CINCPAC started to come around to Sullivan's way of thinking and gave the chokepoint program some consideration. Using topographical maps, current Yankee Team photography, and reports from Road Watch Teams in the Sam Neua area, they identified several potential chokepoints. The plan would be to use 750-pound iron bombs with delay fuses that detonated at varying intervals, hopefully triggering earth slides and harassing road crews for days after the bombing. Then the area could be seeded with antipersonnel mines to deter bypassing of the bombed chokepoints. Subsequent evaluation of the selected chokepoints revealed that no friendly forces were operating in these areas, and the chokepoints were validated by intelligence personnel as good targets.

Admiral Sharp's idea was to hit all the targets at once for maximum psychological value, but that level of effort would require more than 100 aircraft—and an undertaking on that scale would certainly get considerable publicity from the media, a situation that Souvanna probably wouldn't like. When Sharp briefed his plan to Sullivan and others, the ambassador liked the plan, but wanted the strikes carried out over a number of consecutive days rather than all at once. He also wanted the 48-hour rule permanently reduced to 24 hours. State Department officials back in Washington were somewhat wary of the plan, viewing it as widening the war rather than limiting it. Later, on March 18, Sullivan approved General Westmoreland's suggestion for Barrel Roll missions numbering 32-40 to be flown on consecutive days, and the 48-hour rule was permanently changed to 24 hours. By April 3, two armed reconnaissance areas had been established in Laos. The northern area of the country was referred to as Barrel Roll, and the southern portion became Steel Tiger.

After Rolling Thunder began, VP's soldiers became key players in the rescue of downed airmen. From their positions on the top of the mountains, they waited while monitoring their radios. When alerted that a pilot had bailed out or was shot down, they stood by waiting for orders to move out. In a bail-out situation, the NVA and the Pathet Lao were also waiting and watching for downed airmen. Speed was the key in a successful rescue, and usually the good guys and the bad guys were both vying for the prize. As mentioned earlier, the USAF had recognized the importance of Na Khang, and almost every day two HH-43 Huskies and, later, HH-3 "Jolly Green Giant" rescue helicopters would arrive early in the morning and stand by all day in the event a rescue was required.

On April 3, the kick-off date for Steel Tiger, an Air America control aircraft conducting a SAR in the panhandle directed suppressive fire on what they thought were Communist troops—but as it turned out, the troops were friendly. Four were killed and five others were wounded. After the incident, General Thao Ma, the RLAF commander, insisted that one of his officers must always be on board the control ship during any SAR operations in the Steel Tiger area in order to validate targets. He also mandated that the crews had to be briefed at Savannakhet Air Base prior to any rescue mission. And, since most of these crews were USAF personnel, Sullivan felt compelled to sheep-dip the crews (that is, provide them with artificial identities) under Air America cover to conceal their real identities.

To add one more dynamic to the rescue discussion, it was important to consider potential rescues in the northwestern part of North Vietnam, near the Laotian border. As a general rule, USAF units from South Vietnam or the Gulf of Tonkin provided the aircraft and troops for these rescues, but Air America was closer. Sullivan knew that his assets could perform the rescues quicker and more cleanly, but he also knew Souvanna would have a problem with Air America operating in North Vietnam, even though they pulled off just such a successful SAR mission on April 5.

To bolster the Ambassador's position, he pointed out that SEACOORD had recently recommended positioning the NKP HH-43 rescue choppers at remote Lima Sites in northern Laos for potential rescues in North Vietnam and Laos both. And to take it one step further, Sullivan recommended using RLAF T-28s with USAF Waterpump pilots to fly escort for the USAF rescue aircraft. It didn't take long for General Moore to get wind of the SAR recommendations, and he objected to them all, reminding everyone that current regulations prohibited any SAR control ship from directing air strikes. He cited the recent mistake made by Air America that had resulted in the friendly fire incident, but didn't think it would happen again using the USAF HU-16 control aircraft. The long and the short of the whole discussion was that General Moore wanted the rescues to be conducted and controlled by the USAF.

General Moore also stated that if Thao Ma wanted one of his RLAF officers involved in SAR operations, Air America could land a C-123 at Savannakhet and pick up the officer, whereupon the C-123 could take off and join the SAR in progress. That would allow the HU-16 to continue the rescue uninterrupted. But Moore wasn't done: he also expressed his disapproval of any Waterpump pilots being involved in the SAR operations, and aired his concerns about HH-43s being staged in northern Laos, based upon a lack of logistics support and the fact that the Huskies were slow in the air.[44]

Ambassador Sullivan then weighed in, offering his own version of how the SAR should work. He suggested that one of the two SAR HU-16 control aircraft should operate in concert with Air America in northern Laos, and should be the only aircraft to initially respond if a U.S. aircraft went down in North Vietnam. Also, upon initiating a SAR in the panhandle of Laos, the same HU-16 would respond initially, but not conduct the SAR; the control aircraft would actually be the second HU-16 out of NKP. The NKP HU-16 would stage through Savannakhet and be flown by sheep-dipped[45] USAF crews, with an RLAF officer on board.

Later, General Harris added his two cents worth by disagreeing with Thao Ma and Sullivan. The general pointed out that whenever the USAF and USN flew in northern Laos and North Vietnam, the two HU-16s were in orbit over the Laos-Thailand border, and were in constant communication with rescue personnel. Harris also said that in order to be successful, speed was crucial, and to add an RLAF officer to the process would only complicate the process. General Harris also objected to rescue personnel being sheep-dipped, because it would deny them protection under the Geneva Convention.

Meanwhile, on April 7, USAF Captains Arthur D. Baker and James W. Lewis took off from Bien Hoa Air Base, South Vietnam on an interdiction mission in their B-57B Canberra aircraft. The aircraft flew from Vietnam to Laos and was last seen over Route 7 in Xieng Khouang Province, as they descended through a thin layer of clouds in the target area. At that moment, the aircraft disappeared from radar and was not seen again. Extensive SAR efforts in the area through April 12 failed to disclose any trace of the crewmen or the aircraft. Two days later, on April 14, the New China News Agency reported that a B-57 had been recently shot down near Phou Pha Niem in northeastern Laos. According to the news report, it was the first B-57 shot down over northern Laos. Baker and Lewis were not mentioned in the report, and were never heard from again.[46]

While the debates over conduct of SARs continued, the Lao government nervously watched as the Pathet Lao began to build up forces near Muong Phalane. Finally, on April 13, Thao Ma requested that U.S. jets strike the enemy concentrations north of the town. He suggested the T-28s should be used as FACs, and would mark the targets for the fast-moving U.S. fighters. He also wanted an Air America C-123 "Victor" command aircraft to relay messages between the FACs and the fighters. And, as a precaution, Thao Ma wanted all government units to mark their positions with white panels. The mission was subsequently approved and on April 14, more than a dozen F-105 Thunderchiefs from Korat struck the target using 750-pound iron bombs and CBU ordnance.

The operation was executed without a hitch, but a Bomb Damage Assessment (BDA) could not be conducted due to the dense jungle growth around the target area. Even though this particular mission wasn't all that successful, the method of operation using T-28s, an Air America control ship, and fighters from Thailand did prove effective and would later become standard procedure. In fact, the USAF dedicated alert fighter aircraft called "Bango/Whiplash,"[47] which were able to respond instantly to emergency requests for air strikes from the embassy in Vientiane. The USAF then announced that on October 1, the HH-43 rescue aircraft would be replaced with the new HH-3 "Jolly Green Giant" helicopters. Until then, however, Air America would need to shoulder the SAR workload.

On April 14, 1965, the JCS gave approval for Admiral Sharp (CINCPAC) to authorize all Yankee Team reconnaissance missions over Laos, except in the extreme north, where the Chinese were building a road.[48] Additionally, all Yankee Team missions were to be coordinated with the U.S. Embassy in Vientiane. On April 17, Washington also gave CINCPAC and the embassy in Vientiane the authority to approve, plan, and execute Barrel Roll and Steel Tiger missions without the usual restrictions—e.g., sterile periods, day strikes versus night strikes, and type and number of aircraft specified.

While all of this was taking place, on April 29 USAF Captain Charles Shelton's RF-101 Voodoo reconnaissance aircraft departed Udorn as the lead aircraft in a flight of two, headed for a Yankee Team photo reconnaissance mission over northern Laos. Shelton was serving his second tour of duty in SEA, and he was scheduled to return to Kadena Air Base in Okinawa after the mission to celebrate his thirty-third birthday with his family. Meanwhile, Shelton and the other aircraft proceeded to the first target, which was aborted due to weather, so they continued on to the second target near Sam Neua. Shelton and his wingman descended to 3,000 feet as they neared the target, and he was lining up for his first bomb run when he was hit by antiaircraft rounds and fire erupted from the center of his aircraft.

He asked his wingman to fly next to him and check the aircraft for damage. The wingman passed Shelton's aircraft and looked for damage, and noticed the canopy of Shelton's plane separate from the fuselage; he also saw Shelton eject from the disabled aircraft. He watched as the parachute opened and Shelton floated to the ground, then immediately called for a SAR. Two hours later, rescue aircraft were on the scene, and spotted Shelton's parachute and talked to him on the survival radio. He indicated that he was okay, and the rescue aircraft advised that a helicopter would arrive in about thirty minutes to pick him up. Shortly thereafter, rescue helicopters arrived over Shelton's location, but bad weather precluded a rescue. Radio contact was made with Shelton again and he indicated again that he was fine. The rescue aircraft told Shelton that they had to leave, but vowed to return at first light the following day, April 30.

As promised, the rescue helicopters returned at first light, but again bad weather precluded a rescue. Finally, the weather cleared on May 5, and the helicopters returned to attempt rescue—but by then there was no sign of Shelton, and radio contact could not be made. The search was called off, and Shelton was listed as Missing in Action (MIA). Information obtained later indicated that Shelton evaded capture for several days before being taken prisoner by Pathet Lao soldiers. After his imprisonment, there were many stories of escape attempts on Shelton's part, but he was never officially accounted-for in any documentation. It was also reported that while in captivity, Shelton made repeated attempts to escape and even killed three North Vietnamese soldiers who attempted to interrogate him.

Shelton is still officially listed as MIA, and his family waits for him to return.

On May 5, shortly after the Bango/Whiplash fighters began standing alert, Vientiane received information indicating that a group of approximately 12 Russian tanks had been spotted on the Plain of Jars. RLAF T-28s were sent to hunt for the tanks, but could not find them. Later, on May 9, the iron machines were spotted again near Muong Kheung. Eleven RLAF T-28s were scrambled, followed by a flight of Bango F-4 Phantoms. The T-28s soon spotted the tanks, rolled in on them, and expended their ordnance. Then they acted as FACs, marking the targets for the Bango fighters. The F-4s also rolled in and made their runs. After all was said and done, four tanks were destroyed, and approximately seven more were heavily damaged.

On May 14, Air America assembled an extraction team consisting of one C-123 (which was to be the airborne command post), two H-34 helicopters, and six RLAF T-28s for escort. The purpose of the mission was to retrieve an intelligence team of Lao agents who were operating deep inside a Pathet Lao stronghold in northeast Laos. While awaiting pick-up, the intelligence team sent a radio report indicating they had observed Pathet Lao troops escorting a shackled American airman to a cave complex near the city of Sam Neua. When the extraction team arrived at the location of the waiting intelligence team, the H-34 moved in to pick them up. Several members of the team quickly scrambled aboard and reported they had left three team members behind to keep an eye on the cave complex where the American was being held.

Before the H-34 could take off, however, enemy forces opened up on the helicopter with antiaircraft fire. The helicopter was hit, but was barely able to get airborne and limp off to Lima Site 36. The T-28s then went to work on the gun emplacements that had fired on the helicopter. One of the T-28s was subsequently hit, but managed to also make it back to LS-36, where the pilot was forced to perform a dead-stick landing. The T-28 slid off the runway and flipped over, but the pilot was able to climb out of the inverted aircraft. The extraction team regrouped and returned to Sam Neua the following day, but the remaining intelligence team members left behind to keep an eye on the cave weren't at the pick-up point. The extraction was called off due to a heavy concentration of Pathet Lao troops in the area. Based upon all the available information and other accounts, a rescue attempt could have been initiated immediately, to locate and extricate the airman being held at the cave (perhaps it was Shelton), when the intelligence team first spotted the shackled airman. But, that didn't happen, and no additional information was ever obtained about that specific sighting. It *is* known that Air America made repeated attempts to rescue Shelton, and the Hmong irregulars under Vang Pao's guerrillas also made repeated attempts to locate and rescue Shelton. But all their efforts were in vain.

Later that same month, on May 18, USAF Captain David L. Hrdlicka was serving as the lead pilot in a flight of four aircraft over Houa Phan Province when his plane was hit by ground fire. He safely ejected, and was later spotted on the ground, apparently being led away from the area by indigenous personnel. Much later, on July 22, 1966, a Vietnamese newspaper reportedly ran an article on Hrdlicka's capture. Still later, on July 26, it was reported that Radio Peking had aired an audio tape supposedly of Captain Hrdlicka reading a personal letter. In August 1966, the Russian news service *Pravda* published a photo of Hrdlicka, reportedly taken just after he was captured by Pathet Lao soldiers. The picture shows him walking, still in his USAF flight suit. The photograph also shows a uniformed person walking behind him carrying a parachute.

No additional information was reported on Captain Hrdlicka, and he was not among the prisoners of war released in 1973. His fate could not be ascertained, and he is still officially listed as MIA, remains not recovered. In 1982, however, information was received indicating Captain Hrdlicka had died in captivity of natural causes, exacerbated by malnutrition. His remains were supposedly buried near the caves where he was reportedly held; but according to local villagers, the grave site was later destroyed by a bomb dropped from a U.S. aircraft. Subsequent attempts by the DOD to locate Captain Hrdlicka's remains by excavating the site were unsuccessful.

Figure 21. Captain David Hrdlicka in Captivity
(Photo from the Public Domain)

Meanwhile, on May 22, three F-4 Phantoms from Ubon flew close air support for FAR troops trying to hold Muong Nga. During the fight, a liaison aircraft was shot down. A SAR was initiated the following day, and four F-105 Thunderchiefs from Takhli Air Base were dispatched to assist the Air America Victor rescue control aircraft. The Thunderchiefs were there to fly high cover and to protect the H-34 helicopters and T-28s involved in the rescue attempt.

During the rescue, however, the control aircraft called on the F-105s to destroy a cluster of shacks on the ground to scare what they thought were enemy soldiers. The Thunderchiefs rolled in as instructed and leveled the structures using 20 mm cannon fire and rockets. Unfortunately, the troops in the shacks were actually Lao soldiers, and when the strafing was over, 13 personnel were dead and 19 were wounded. Later, Ambassador Sullivan took full responsibility for the error.

During most of May 1965, Ground Control Intercept (GCI) radar facilities at NKP and Udorn monitored Soviet aircraft arriving and departing from northeastern Laos in the vicinity of Sam Neua and the Plain of Jars. Later, on June 2, Souvanna Phouma was briefed, and authorized U.S. personnel to intercept and destroy Soviet transport aircraft flying resupply missions to the Communists in northern Laos. The code name for the activity was "Duck Soup," and in order to fire on the Soviet resupply aircraft, they had to be caught actually unloading supplies and equipment.

In early June, Ambassador Sullivan sent a message to U.S. Army Colonel Jack G. Cornett, Deputy Chief, Joint U.S. Military Assistance Group, Thailand (DEPCHJUSMAGTHAI), requesting approximately ten additional H-34 helicopters due to SAR requirements. On the surface the request seemed appropriate, but numerous factors made it extremely difficult to fill the request. As mentioned earlier, there was a worldwide shortage of H-34s, and those that were available would require significant maintenance and upgrades. In addition, the Air America maintenance facility at Udorn was operating at maximum capacity; if additional H-34s were received, the facilities would have to be expanded. This would require more maintenance personnel and more pilots as well. That wasn't going to happen, so some other method to conduct SARs would be required.

To make matters worse, on June 20 and 21, two Air America H-34 helicopters were heavily damaged while participating in a rescue of a downed F-4 pilot over North Vietnam, east of Sam Neua. Fortunately both aircraft managed to return safely, but Ambassador Sullivan again sounded the alarm about a lack of adequate SAR assets. If either or both aircraft had been lost over North Vietnam, it would have been very embarrassing to the United States. Sullivan knew that help was on the way, with the HH-3s coming in October, but he asked again for HH-43s to be kept at Na Khang with adequate fuel supplies in order to respond to SARs in the area.

Admiral Sharp agreed with the ambassador, and went up the chain of command to General McConnell in Washington. In his message, Sharp pointed out that this would be an opportune time for the USAF to move into the SAR arena and take control, replacing Air America as the lead component. McConnell agreed, and contacted the other Joint Chiefs of Staff for their thoughts on the matter. The Chiefs agreed, authorizing two CH-3 helicopters to be sent to NKP immediately for temporary duty, pending receipt of the HH-3s already approved and scheduled for delivery in October. These two loaned helicopters, however, were lacking armor and single side band (SSB) radios, but they would be better than the HH-43s. At least they could fill the gap until the new choppers arrived. Pending arrival of the

CH-3s and HH-3s, HH-43 Huskies were flown to LS-36, along with extra fuel in the event they were needed to conduct a SAR.[49]

In addition to the issue of SAR responsibility being permanently transferred to the USAF, it stood to reason that the way would also be cleared for the USAF Waterpump pilots to fly the T-28 aircraft in support of the SAR activity. After all, Ambassador Sullivan was already utilizing the USAF pilots to fly low cover in the T-28s, so it was not an issue with him. The next logical step, however, would be to get the Thai Government to also formally approve the use of the USAF pilots to fly cover for the SAR missions. A formal request was communicated to the Thais, and it was approved on June 4. At about this same time, in early June, the Chinese Premier, Chou En-lai, had dinner with Egyptian President Nasser in Egypt. During dinner, the conversation reportedly turned to America and Vietnam. When asked for his reaction to America's presence in Vietnam, Chou essentially had the following to say:

- He didn't think that America would exercise the nuclear option, due to the close proximity of U.S. forces operating in South Vietnam.
- The more troops America sent to Vietnam, the happier he would be, because they would be in China's power, and China could have their blood.
- The closer the Americans were to China, the easier it would be to hold them hostage.
- Chou went on to say that some American soldiers were trying opium, and that China was helping them by supplying the best kinds of the drug. He likened it to the time the West imposed opium on China, pointing out that now China was fighting America with its own weapon.
- Chou closed by saying that China's objective was to demoralize the U.S. soldiers, and have the troops take the addiction home to affect the entire U.S.

Meanwhile, getting back to the war in Laos, on July 5, the two loaned USAF CH-3 helicopters finally arrived in Thailand from the USAF Special Air Warfare Center at Eglin AFB, Florida.[50] Colonel Cornett suggested the new choppers be used for SAR activity in northern Laos, relieving the pressure on the H-34s. He reasoned that the CH-3 was already approved for SAR activity over North Vietnam, and it would be a natural follow-on for them to also conduct rescues in northern Laos. And, by using the CH-3s, it would not be necessary to purchase additional H-34s for Air America. Also, with the range of the CH-3s, it would not be absolutely necessary to stage one in Laos each day at LS-36, even though rescue helicopters would continue to be staged in Laos. Of course, everyone was aware that Sullivan wasn't in favor of using the USAF as the lead entity to conduct rescues. He believed the Air America pilots knew the terrain better than anyone, and that the use of U.S. military personnel in the war violated the Geneva Accord—which did not authorize U.S. troops in Laos.

At any rate, Colonel Cornett pushed forward, convinced that adequate training of the USAF pilots would bridge the experience gap rather rapidly. Later, at a subsequent meeting of U.S. military and State Department personnel, the matter was again discussed, and the consensus was that USAF pilots should be trained to take over the SAR responsibility. This was exactly the result that Admiral Sharp wanted, so he threw his weight squarely behind Cornett.

Figure 22. USAF CH-3 Helicopter
(Photo from the Public Domain)

But the ambassador still wasn't ready to throw in the towel. He scheduled another meeting with Cornett and Lieutenant General Paul S. Emrick, Chief of Staff, Pacific Command. After the meeting, it was agreed that Sullivan would seek guidance from his bosses in Washington; but in the interim, he would accept the plan for the USAF to assume the primary responsibility for SAR activity, with Air America as a backup. He also agreed to maintain the H-34 fleet at 21 aircraft.

As things stood in July 1965, the USAF SAR capability consisted of two HH-43s, two CH-3s at NKP, and two HH-43s at Udorn, with six armor-plated HH-3s scheduled for delivery in October. Upon arrival of the HH-3s, and after crews were adequately trained in the environment, they would be available for SAR activity. At that time, the HH-43s and loaned CH-3s would be withdrawn from Thailand and redistributed. It appeared that, finally, everything was on track in the SAR arena—but, at this juncture, in typical fashion, Washington asked for more information. The CH-3s were capable of operating from Thailand with their existing fuel range, but Washington wanted to know if they were going to remain in Thailand, or if they would be staged on the ground at Lima Sites in Laos. If the birds were going to stage in Laos, the brass wanted to know the identity of the sites, the security posture of each, and the potential for injury or worse to the USAF crews. And of course they wanted to know if Souvanna was on board with the arrangement everybody had agreed upon.

At this point in time, Sullivan's deputy, Emory C. Swank, entered the discussion and said the embassy wanted the CH-3s to stand ground alert in Laos, and to rotate back to NKP once a week for crew and aircraft swap. He pointed out that fuel was already staged, and the facilities (though primitive) already existed to house the USAF personnel at the Lima Sites. He also stated that sites LS-36, 46, and 107 were secure, and that prying eyes would not be able to see the aircraft while at the sites. After mulling the situation over, Washington finally decided on August 5 that Air America would continue the rescues in Laos, and the USAF CH-3s would conduct the SAR activity in North Vietnam, staging from LS-36. And of course, a clause for exigent circumstances was provided, essentially stating that under extraordinary circumstances, either Air America or USAF SAR assets could be used in rescues, in order to keep a downed airman from becoming a POW.[51]

In mid-July, as the SAR discussions continued, the Bango/ Whiplash alert force was expanded. Up to four F-105s and F-4s would be on 15-minute alert from daylight to dusk every day. They could be utilized in Barrel Roll and Steel Tiger areas, and could also support SAR operations. The alert force was primarily at the Ambassador's disposal, but could also be scrambled by the Airborne Battlefield Command and Control Center (ABCCC) to attack targets from an approved list, if required. The alert force expansion took place just in time to support the RLG/Hmong wet-season offensive in MR 2 to retake positions around Sam Neua that were lost during the Communist dry-season offensive earlier in the year. The RLG offensive was initiated from VP's command post at Na Khang.

Between Na Khang and Hua Muong (LS-58) stood a 6,000-foot high mountain called Keo Fa Mut. The Communists had already realized the strategic importance of the peak, and had set up formidable defenses, including two NVA companies. On July 21, Hmong guerrillas moved against Keo Fa Mut and met stiff resistance. RLAF T-28s were called in and flew more than 30 sorties against the site, using white phosphorous bombs and other ordnance. Bango/Whiplash fighters were also called in to hit the mountain's summit with 750-pound iron bombs. The Hmong began to make steady progress, and captured one of the near slopes on July 22. Meanwhile, USAF and RLAF fighter aircraft continued to pound the peak, and the resistance was finally overcome on July 28. After the fighting ended, approximately 120 dead enemy soldiers were counted, with the possibility of more bodies still underground in spider holes and trenches. Losses to the Hmong guerrillas as a result of this action were four dead and 33 wounded.

VP's troops then continued their march in the direction of Hua Muong, accompanied by USAF ground controllers, who directed air strikes along the hilltops and ridges near LS-58. By September 21, the NVA and Pathet Lao were mopped up after two months of heavy fighting around Hua Muong, resulting in renewed spirit and soaring morale among the Lao forces. And thanks to the RLAF T-28s, and the USAF Bango/Whiplash aircraft that flew over 1,000 air support missions, the area was secured with minimal losses.

During the summer of 1965, Operation Duck Soup continued, although its existence wasn't common knowledge. As mentioned earlier, Duck Soup involved an effort to stop Communist resupply flights into northeastern Laos at Sam Neua. Reports were initially received indicating that a pair of Soviet IL-14 Ilyushin transport aircraft was making occasional night resupply flights from North Vietnam. Since the initial intelligence information was sketchy, it was possible that other covert U.S. military aircraft operating in the area could have been mistaken for Communist resupply missions. If that was the case, it would explain the flares and covert night landings. But one other possible explanation could be simply that Hanoi was transporting Pathet Lao officers back and forth from training in Hanoi and/or Son Tay, North Vietnam.

No one knew for sure, however, and it would not be easy to verify. The U.S. had only limited access to the activities or information in Sam Neua, except for a few human assets and Hmong guerrillas working in the area. In the meantime, President Johnson authorized the use of U.S. aircraft to intercept these flights, even though Ambassador Sullivan hadn't even asked for it. Additional verification of the Communist flights into Sam Neua was later provided by Yankee Team reconnaissance missions, including photographs clearly showing two IL-14s parked on the airfield at Sam Neua. With verification in hand, the planning for taking out these resupply flights began in earnest. But there were some questions as to what the best method for accomplishing that was. It seemed that the best-case scenario would be to attack the resupply aircraft while they were on the ground, but existing rules prohibited strikes against the town or the airfield in Sam Neua. Attacks on aircraft carrying passengers into and out of Sam Neua were also prohibited under any circumstances.

So, it appeared that the best alternative was to strike the IL-14s while they were actually dropping supplies by parachute. GCI radar at Udorn and "Skyspot," the Bomb Directing Central Radar Unit at NKP, were monitoring these IL-14 resupply flights, and verified time of day and actual landing sites. It seemed the pattern had shifted from night drops to day drops. With the routes pinpointed, it would be possible for the Bango F-4 Phantoms standing alert to scramble and take out the Communist resupply aircraft. Souvanna subsequently approved the daylight intercepts of the Il-14s, but USAF 2nd Air Division officials stipulated that the NVA transports had to be engaged in aerial resupply before being intercepted. Additional Whiplash F-105s were also placed on alert to assist in Operation Duck Soup.

The actual plan would entail scrambling the fighters from Korat Air Base and having them fly low, staying below Communist radar and clear of Sam Neua and any known antiaircraft batteries. The AFCC at Udorn would monitor other civilian aircraft in the area, as well as any OPPLAN-34A (MACV-SOG) activity that might interfere with the operation.[52] All information would then be fed to the fighters as they winged their way northward toward the target, and it would also be relayed to the USAF ground controllers at Na Khang. They, in turn, would then relay the information to the Air America Victor control ship, which would relay information from the ground to the approaching fighters.

Meanwhile, problems began to arise with Operation Duck Soup. Vang Pao and his troops were heavily engaged fighting the Communist around Hua Muong, and most of the Air America assets were tied up supporting the Hmong general. In early June, a USAF F-105 and a Navy F-4 were shot down over northern Laos, placing an additional drain on the available air support resources. At about this same time, the USAF HU-16 was being replaced by a newer HC-54, and of course that crew would have to learn the terrain and operational environment prior to being utilized to conduct SAR activity. With all this activity underway, 2nd Air Division recommended that Duck Soup be cancelled. But Ambassador Sullivan wanted the operation to continue.

Sullivan recommended that as an alternative, two RLAF T-28s could be positioned at Long Tieng and flown by Air America pilots. The pilots would stand alert at Long Tieng each day, and take off at 5:00 P.M. in order to be in the target area in the event the IL-14s showed up. Then, upon verification from the ground controller at Na Khang, the T-28s would attack using their 20mm cannons. If the IL-14s didn't show up, the T-28s would just fly to Udorn at dusk and RON until the next day, at which time the process would start all over again and continue as long as needed. While all this discussion was taking place, human assets, including indigenous Hmong sources, were on the ground in the Sam Neua area, collecting intelligence information on the comings and goings of the IL-14s.

The operation continued until September, with a constantly changing recipe for success—but a good time to strike the IL-14s never presented itself. Worse, in September, an ICC C-46 aircraft was almost mistakenly shot down by USAF F-100s, causing quite a stir. As a result, Duck Soup was permanently shelved.

Also during this period, two RF-101s were lost over northern Laos due to antiaircraft fire: one in the Phu Tho area on July 29, and another one in the same area on August 13. Later, on September 20, an F-105 Thunderchief piloted by USAF Captain Willis Forby was hit by antiaircraft fire while dropping bombs over North Vietnam. Forby turned his F-105 in the direction of Laos, and shortly thereafter ejected from the crippled aircraft. Using his survival radio, Forby activated a homing signal indicating to his wingman that he was okay. The wingman contacted the Airborne Command and Control Center, call sign "Crown," and shortly thereafter two HH-43 Huskies were launched from a nearby Lima Site where they were standing watch.[53] Upon arrival over the rescue location, Forby activated a smoke flare, letting the rescue aircraft know where he was. All seemed normal, so the rescue crew descended to make the pick-up.

Suddenly, several Communist soldiers clad in the traditional black pajamas emerged from the jungle and opened fire with AK-47s. The helicopter took many small rounds and fell to the jungle floor. The second Huskie moved in and also took small arms fire, but was able to ascend and depart the area. The crew of the downed helicopter, consisting of pilot Captain Tom Curtis, copilot Lt. Duane Martin, Airman First Class William A. Robinson, and Airman Third Class Art Black, Para Rescue Specialist, was subsequently captured and taken prisoner. Approximately nine months later, Lt. Martin and several Air America personnel were able to escape from Houay Het prison camp in Central Laos, but unfortunately, Martin was hacked to death by a villager with a machete after evading the enemy for seventeen days.

It became obvious that strike and reconnaissance aircraft flying over northeastern Laos were vulnerable to ground fire when two RF-101 Voodoo aircraft were hit while on a photo recon mission on October 5. The lead aircraft, piloted by Captain Robert Pitt, burst into flames. Pitt shut down the burning engine and the fire went out. He then turned toward the coast of Vietnam, hoping that he could make it to the Gulf of Tonkin before ejecting. Meanwhile, his wingman was able to complete the photo reconnaissance mission, even though his aircraft was also damaged, and he turned to catch up with Captain Pitt. By this time, Pitt was critically short of fuel. He contacted an Air

Force tanker, which came to give him fuel, but the RF-101 was just too shot up to take it on.

By this time, Captain Pitt was about ten miles from the runway at Da Nang. When he was five miles from the runway, Pitt lowered his landing gear manually and was subsequently able to land—but the damaged aircraft began to slide out of control and off the runway. It finally stopped after crashing into a radio shack. After the aircraft finally came to a halt, Captain Pitt climbed out. Later, it was determined that he had sustained only minor injuries, but the aircraft was a total loss. Meanwhile, his wingman flew on to Udorn Air Base, where he landed and turned in his film for processing.

By October, the Secret War in Laos had become overshadowed by the overt war taking place in South Vietnam. The news media was on the ground in South Vietnam, actually reporting in near-real time as events unfolded. The eyes of America were glued on SEA. The U.S. Government personnel responsible for conducting the war in Laos were glad the focus wasn't on their activities . . . but every now and then, well-intentioned politicians in Washington would inevitably say the wrong thing to the press. One Congressman told reporters the U.S. was bombing the Ho Chi Minh Trail and engaging the Communists on the ground in Laos. The *New York Times* even published an article indicating that bombing of the Trail would increase.

Of course, the publicity caused quite a stir in Vientiane, where Souvanna's position was to admit nothing because the Geneva Accords had designated Laos as a neutral country. The Russian embassy in Vientiane knew full well what was going on in Laos, but willingly turned a blind eye to the activity, and Ambassador Sullivan, obviously, did not want any publicity. So at the end of the day, there wasn't all that much being reported on Laos at this point in time anyway. The benefit of being involved in the war in Laos was that there were no mass media in country. There were also few permanent roads and no public transportation to speak of, and therefore many areas under contest were inaccessible by the media. And, as an added precaution, all information was strictly compartmented, as mentioned earlier.

Later, in mid-October, intelligence information was received indicating that several fresh NVA battalions had been spotted in the Ban Ban area. Hmong Road Watch Teams also observed Communist laborers and engineers rapidly repairing road damage on Routes 7,

12 and 23. Later, during the first two weeks of October, it had been reported that almost 20 unidentified aircraft were spotted dropping supplies to the Pathet Lao and NVA troops. All the activity appeared to indicate that the Communists were preparing for their standard dry season offensive, during which they would try to retake all the ground gained by the Hmong and FAR troops during the rainy season.

On November 10, Lieutenant Colonel Sing Chanthakoumane, Neutralist commander at Muong Soui, announced his plans to retake Phou Kout. He asked for and received assurance that the U.S. would do its best to provide the air support he needed—which was surprising, considering the fact that his plan had not been briefed to management, and therefore no preplanning was completed. At any rate, the attack was initiated, and for the next three days, U.S. aircraft pounded the mountain. The BDA was good, even though the jets faced stiff antiaircraft fire from enemy troops on Phou Kout. On November 16, Sing's troops advanced on the northern slope of Phou Kout, where they met stiff resistance—and were beaten back by the entrenched Communist troops.

Sing wanted to try again on November 19. However, by that time most of the air resources were already committed for other missions. At about this same time, Souvanna asked the U.S. to attack an NVA armored vehicle staging area at Khang Khai, the former Neutralist stronghold. General Westmoreland agreed, and 16 F-105 Thunderchiefs were diverted from Steel Tiger in the south to strike the vehicle staging area. But when the fighters arrived over the target area, the weather had deteriorated, and only eight of the aircraft could complete the mission. After the sorties were flown, the BDA could not be determined until November 24, due to bad weather. When the BDA was completed, it revealed that fourteen structures had been destroyed, with no short rounds.

Finally, on December 2, Sing got the fighter support he had asked for. Sixteen F-105s hit Phou Kout repeatedly, and Bango/Whiplash fighters also strafed enemy reinforcements moving towards Phou Kout along Route 7. All seemed to be going well, until it came time to charge the summit. At that point, Sing's troops refused to move out, demanding more air strikes. There were no fighters available, however, because other targets that had been planned for and approved in advance had drained all the available resources. And, it would be the last week of December before air assets would be available. Meanwhile, north of Phou Kout, several NVA battalions were moving towards Hua Muong (LS-58), slowly tightening the noose around the necks of Vang Pao's troops. So, for the time being, any additional attacks on Phou Kout would have to wait. At LS-58, anticipating the NVA attack, V.P.'s troops departed LS-58 and retreated northward to Na Khang.

Later, on December 23, President Johnson suspended all ground operations in South Vietnam, ordering all aircraft there and in Thailand to stand down.[54] His timing could not have been worse for Laos. Hua Muong was lost, and Na Khang was threatened; and then there was the situation on hold at Phou Kout. But Ambassador Sullivan wasn't about to accept LBJ's Christmas bombing halt, and immediately submitted a request for air strikes.

The JCS notified CINCPAC that the only fighters allowed to fly strikes were the Bango/Whiplash alert aircraft, and that Vientiane would have to work with those resources. At about this same time, the USAF ordered 40 sorties for northern Laos—which was considered rather odd, considering there were only four aircraft on alert.

Sullivan then contacted Admiral Sharp (on Christmas Day) to register a complaint, and Sharp directed MACV and PACFLT to lay on the 40 air strikes. The only problem was there were no aircrews available, except for the Bango/Whiplash alert crews. Apparently, what had happened was that when President Johnson ordered a stand down, the bases in Thailand had released all their personnel for some well-deserved time off, and there were no resources available. All the troops had left the bases and headed for Bangkok or other destinations to escape the rigors of war.

On December 26, however, operations in South Vietnam and Laos resumed, though Johnson continued the ceasefire over North Vietnam in hopes that Hanoi would find their way to the table to discuss peace. Three days later, on December 29, Secretary of Defense McNamara directed the JCS to reallocate all of the strikes previously planned for North Vietnam to operations in Laos. The only prohibition was that no aircraft could transit North Vietnam. Finally, Ambassador Sullivan received the air support he needed. But a new problem had arisen, because fighting in Laos had temporarily subsided; so most of the strikes were finally used in Steel Tiger and Tiger Hound (southern Laos).

For the next two weeks, things were fairly quiet in northern Laos. During the lull, the Neutralists took the opportunity to relieve Colonel Sing, and they came up with a new plan for dealing with Phou Kout. Instead of taking the summit, which had failed repeatedly, they would use the U.S. air strikes to reduce the mountain to a pile of rubble. Then it would no longer present a problem. Based upon all the previous bombings, the mountain looked like a wasteland already, so why not just complete the job of eliminating it once and for all? As it turned out, their plan was wishful thinking at best.

A few weeks earlier, on November 5, the newly arrived CH-3 rescue helicopters had been put to the test over North Vietnam, when they responded to a SAR involving a missing pilot from an A1E Skyraider. Upon arrival over the area where the A1E had gone down, the low rescue aircraft was hit by heavy ground fire, and the high aircraft stood off due to mechanical problems. The low bird had sustained significant damage and was on fire, but the pilot was able to keep the aircraft airborne until the crew could bail out. Meanwhile, the high bird was diverted to pick up the crew of a Navy helicopter that had also gone down nearby. The high bird was able to rescue all the people from the Navy helicopter, but by then was too low on fuel to go back to the location where the low bird had gone down. It didn't matter much at that moment, however, because the area was overrun with NVA troops, temporarily curtailing any further rescue attempt. Later it was learned that the crew of the low bird, which did crash, managed to evade the NVA troops for quite a while, but were eventually captured and sat out the remainder of the war in North Vietnamese prisons. This particular incident vividly pointed out the need for armor-plated rescue helicopters.

Also during the summer of 1965, Vang Pao had merged home defense militia units into SGUs and put them through special CIA training at Muong Cha. By October, the troops were ready for battle. With these fresh troops, VP moved into Ban Peung near Route 42 to attack and hopefully take Xieng Khouangville. With the King of Laos scheduled to visit Long Tieng in January 1966, VP wanted to be able to tell him that Xieng Khouangville had been taken from the Communists. But the NVA were having none of it, and countered by realigning their troops, halting VP's advance—and the rains came in earnest as the year drew to a close.

As 1965 ended, Tony Poe recovered from his bullet wound to the hip and became something of a legend in Laos. Vint Lawrence left Laos just as quietly as he had arrived, and was replaced by a man identified only as "John." The bomb-directed radar units at NKP and Udorn had improved accuracy to the degree that bombing mistakes decreased significantly. Meanwhile, General Vang Pao's guerrillas were holding onto some important ground in northern Laos, doing their best to hang onto the positions taken from the Communists during the rainy season, while Kong Le was busy planning another attack on Phou Kout. But all this increased activity would require more air assets to provide close air support. MACV also planned for more air strikes over the Barrel Roll area, using extra ordnance from cancelled Rolling Thunder missions over North Vietnam.

With all the activity in the air, Ambassador Sullivan was concerned about accidents that might result in more civilians on the ground being killed and wounded. Sullivan believed that by placing navigational aids in Laos, pilots could provide more accurate bomb runs by being able to fix their positions with precision. Subsequent discussions with the USAF resulted in a decision to place a Tactical Air Navigation (TACAN) site in the Barrel Roll area. The system was designed to provide the user with a distance and bearing from a ground station, eliminating guesswork on the part of the aircrews.[55]

On November 27, Washington approved the installation of a TACAN station at Na Khang (LS-36). The system would be installed by the USAF, 1st Mobile Communications (1st MOB) Group, out of Clark Air Base in the Philippines. After the equipment was installed, indigenous personnel would be trained to maintain the TACAN. To expedite the process, the 1st MOB recommended using a TRN-17 TACAN unit recently shipped to Udorn and still boxed up. The only drawback was that the TRN-17 was not automatic, requiring two full-time personnel to run and maintain it. In the meantime, about two dozen USAF personnel were quickly trained at JUSMAGTHAI to man five TACAN stations to be installed throughout Thailand.

At about this same time, a requirement for a similar TACAN station surfaced in the Steel Tiger area in southern Laos. A study was then conducted, and Phou Kate Mountain was recommended as the optimum location. So the USAF decided to utilize the 1st MOB to initially get the TACANs up and running; then the operation and maintenance of the TACAN would be turned over to civilian personnel under contract to Air America. By the end of 1965, however, enemy activity in the areas of Na Khang and Phou Kate had escalated to the point where it was too dangerous to consider installation of the TACAN stations. Later, security around Phou Kate improved, and installation of the TACAN was completed. A second TACAN installation was also completed, but not at LS-36; it had been decided the safest location in northern Laos would be Skyline Ridge, just above the base at Long Tieng (LS-20A).

The year 1966 soon arrived, along with the onset of the yearly dry season. Throughout January and February, there was a steady flow of NVA troops into northern Laos. At about this same timeframe, a similar situation was taking place in South Vietnam, where large battles took place against NVA regulars instead of the indigenous Viet Cong. One possible reason for the build-up may have been because President Johnson had halted the Rolling Thunder bombing campaign over North Vietnam during the Christmas season. Also in January, Ambassador Sullivan requested the 7/13th Air Force reallocate approximately six or eight AC—47 gunships to NKP, Thailand for use over Laos.

Meanwhile, NVA troops moved against Tha Thom and Houei Thom. The positions were defended by Hmong SGUs led by Major Douangtha, one of VP's best field commanders. Douangtha and his men were greatly outnumbered, and after sustained fighting they quietly melted into the jungle and began their trek towards Na Khang. The following morning, the area of Tha Thom was surveyed from the air by CIA case officer Jerry Daniels in an Air America light observation aircraft. Daniels reported that the ground was littered with the bodies of dead NVA troops. Apparently, Douangtha and his men had fought valiantly, and the NVA took a severe beating in the fight. After surveying Tha Thom, Daniel turned in the direction of Na Khang, and was soon able to locate Major Douangtha's retreating column. Daniels then called for Air America H-34 helicopters to pick up the weary troops and take them to safety at Na Khang.

Later, on January 16, a flight of five F-105 Thunderchiefs departed Takhli Air Base; their target was artillery positions on the Plain of Jars. USAF Captain Don Wood piloted the Number 5 aircraft, a reconnaissance airplane. His aircraft was equipped with two powerful camera pods, and his assignment was to photograph the damage inflicted by the fighters for a BDA. He followed each of the four fighters as they made their runs over the targets. On one of the runs, Captain Wood's aircraft was observed doing a 360-degree roll and heading off in a northerly direction. Subsequent attempts to make radio contact with Wood were unsuccessful as he disappeared over the horizon.

It was believed that Wood crashed approximately 10 miles north of the target, but no evidence of a crash was observed by other aircraft in the area. Subsequent searches of the area failed to disclose the location of Captain Wood or his aircraft, and he was listed as MIA. On January 18, Beijing Radio announced that a U.S. aircraft had been shot down over Laos on January 16, and the pilot was observed parachuting to the ground. Years later, in 1974, an unidentified Pathet Lao source recalled capturing a U.S. airman who fell from his aircraft after being hit by antiaircraft fire near Phou Kout, which was the same area Captain Wood had been working in. According to the source, the airman was captured and died soon after being incarcerated. In 1980, Captain Wood's status was changed from Missing in Action, to "declared dead, body not recovered."

Also in January 1966, the Neutralist developed a new strategy. Their objective was to establish a north-south perimeter arcing through the Pen River, 10 miles east of Muong Soui. The Americans didn't have much confidence in the plan, given past performances by the Neutralists; simply put, Kong Le and his men just didn't have the guts to take the fight to the enemy, always stopping short in every engagement. At any rate, by January 25, approximately eight Neutralist battalions were deployed to carry out their plan. Embassy officials in Vientiane dutifully requested close air support for Kong Le's troops amounting to approximately 40 sorties a day by U.S. fighter jets, scheduled to begin on or around January 30.

Unfortunately for all concerned, President Johnson decided to announce on February 1, 1966 that he was ending the bombing moratorium over North Vietnam. In effect, this meant that Kong Le probably would not receive the fighter support he had requested, because those aircraft were already allocated to support Rolling Thunder missions. Notwithstanding, the Neutralists began their offensive with some assistance from other U.S. fighter jets around the Na Khang and Plain of Jars areas. He also received additional support from RLAF T-28 Trojans. On February 7, the NVA 148th

Regiment began their initial dry season offensive by probing several areas in the Na Khang area.

By mid-February, other NVA units had reached the area, and joined the 148th as they attacked Na Khang. The battle began around midnight on February 16, when an outpost about a mile south of LS-36 fell to the Communists. Then the enemy troops quietly crept to within mortar range of the airstrip and waited until just before daylight, when they began to shell the runway. The Hmong troops answered back using 105mm and 75mm artillery fire, and the initial Communist assault was repelled. As the enemy regrouped, an AC-47 gunship[56] called "Spooky" arrived overhead and began dropping illumination flares. The gunship began by spraying the Communist troops with 7.62mm mini-gun fire. The enemy troops were completely overwhelmed and retreated to the hills nearby to escape the fire-breathing monster orbiting in the sky above LS-36.

But by the morning of February 17, the NVA troops were back at the gates of LS-36, having been reinforced with additional troops. A USAF FAC at the site managed to get airborne and flew to Houei Thom (LS-27) to direct air strikes there. When he later returned, he found Na Khang under siege. The FAC was able to land his aircraft, and then began acting as a ground FAC to U.S. fighters that had arrived over the site. For the remainder of the day, the FAC, with the help of an airborne FAC in a T-28, guided the Bango/Whiplash fighters as they pounded the Communist positions. The enemy was once again beaten back, and VP's troops held. The U.S. Ambassador in Vientiane then ordered the Americans at the site to leave for the night. They were flown to Moung Hiem, and included Jerry Daniels, Mike Lynch, another CIA case officer, Don Sjostrom, a USAID refugee worker, and Captain Ramon Horinek, a USAF combat controller.

Even though VP's troops were holding up well, he was concerned that they might not have the will to fight a sustained battle. They were guerrillas, trained to hit, inflict damage to the enemy, and then retreat to the jungle. But surprisingly, they did hold their positions through the night.

On the morning of February 18, the four Americans returned to Na Khang, and VP arrived later that morning in an Air America helicopter to take personal charge of the battle. The situation was deteriorating fast, and the CIA advisors contacted the embassy in Vientiane requesting more U.S. air support, including napalm.

Surprisingly, Sullivan approved the request. Meanwhile, the NVA massed in the hills around Na Khang, where they waited until just about first light on February 19 before they began to attack the airstrip.

The NVA attack appeared to be successful at first, because they were able to get within about 100 feet of the airstrip. But Spooky soon returned, and so did a number of F-105 Thunderchiefs. The air strikes began to take their toll on the attackers, so they retreated. Air America helicopter operations soon resumed. In the afternoon, the Communists received fresh troops, and they attacked the airstrip again. As the fighting intensified, with small arms fire and mortars pounding the site, VP huddled with the defenders on the airfield to discuss strategy. At about that time, the small arms fire intensified, and someone noticed that Vang Pao was hit. He was holding his neck, and his shirt was beginning to show blood stains. The defenders quickly put VP onto an H-34 Air America aircraft, and he was taken to another airstrip, where an Air America C-123 was waiting to take him to the USAF hospital at Udorn.

Ambassador Sullivan realized the NVA were determined to take the site at all costs, so he authorized the use of napalm to hopefully repel the Communists. Shortly thereafter, F-105s showed up from Takhli loaded with BLU-1B napalm.[57] The fighters went to work dropping the canisters on the Communist troops hidden in the trees nearby. But the NVA kept advancing, and appeared determined to take the site. Soon LS-36 was almost completely surrounded, so the Americans and Lao troops began to evacuate, using all available aircraft on the airstrip.

The NVA had won this round, but it wasn't much of a victory. The Communists didn't know it yet, but USAF fighters were on their way to level the site and the village nearby. After the fighters showed up and did their dirty work, nothing was left except scorched earth and approximately 1,000 dead NVA troops. It was a shallow victory for the Communists, because it would be months before the NVA could fully occupy the site.

Meanwhile, Ambassador Sullivan departed Vientiane and flew to Udorn to be with Vang Pao during his medical treatment. Arriving at the hospital just after VP, Sullivan rushed to his side. The doctors had already taken the initial X-rays and were ready to brief the ambassador. Apparently, the bullet to VP's side had taken off a piece of bone at the shoulder socket; and, fortunately, the injury to V.P.'s neck was only a flesh wound. The doctors provided a favorable prognosis, but told Sullivan that it would be necessary to place a steel rod in Vang Pao's shoulder to compensate for the missing bone. The ambassador told VP about the required surgery, the little general approved, and the procedure was accomplished.

After their retreat from Na Khang, the Hmong defenders took refuge at Moung Hiem, one of Kong Le's Neutralist sites. Heretofore, the NVA had not attacked Moung Hiem, because the Neutralists were not technically FAR or Hmong; but with the survivors from Na Khang now in residence at Moung Hiem, the site became fair game. Na Khang was under NVA control, but what was next? Logically, the Communists would go after Houie Thom (LS-27). If it fell, then the next target would be Muong Heim (LS-48). And, if Muong Heim fell, the enemy would control Route 6; the only remaining outpost would be the Neutralist headquarters and Muong Soui.

Ambassador Sullivan wasn't sure what the Communists' next move would be, but he needed to find out. He began to talk to others in the diplomatic community, but no one seemed to have the answer. Meanwhile, things settled down on the western plain. There was a lot of NVA movement, but they appeared to be focused on replenishing their depleted ranks at Na Khang. Kong Le decided to temporarily hold off his planned attack on Phou Kout and took up defensive positions at Muong Soui, hunkering down there.

Ordinarily, Souvanna let the Americans run the war, and he only stepped in when he felt it was necessary. But recently he had been consulting with the Lao military leaders about the unstable situation on the western plain. He was convinced that retaking Phou Kout was essential to holding Muong Soui. Later, on March 4, the Communists suddenly lobbed over a dozen mortar rounds at Muong Soui, killing two people. Two days later, they attacked an outlying Lao military unit and retook the position. Souvanna then asked the U.S. to root out the entrenched NVA troops on Phou Kout using napalm. Sullivan looked at the plan, and believed that it could work if the U.S. military used about two dozen sorties to soften up the area first.

Later, on March 6, an Air America light transport aircraft landed at Moung Hiem. On that aircraft were two Americans: USAF Escape and Evasion specialist Captain Cyrus Roberts, and a USAID employee by the name of George Raynor. After a brief visit to the site, the

Americans and a Thai soldier boarded the aircraft and it took off. On climb-out, the aircraft developed mechanical problems and slammed into the ground. Raynor survived the crash, but Roberts, the Thai soldier, and the Air America pilot, Wayne Ensminger, perished in the crash and subsequent explosion.

Two days later, the NVA attacked the site, and the survivors from Na Khang again took to the bush in an effort to escape death. Kong Le's men remained at the site, thinking the NVA wouldn't molest them; but on March 11, 1966, the NVA rushed the site. In the violence that followed, the Lao leaders at the site were executed outright by the NVA for harboring the survivors from Na Khang. The other Neutralists were killed unless they agreed to join the Communists. Afterwards, the NVA razed the camp to the last hut. Nothing was left but smoldering embers. After disposing of Moung Hiem, the NVA moved on and began attacking the smaller FAR garrisons.

At this juncture, there was concern in Vientiane that the NVA might take this opportunity to attack Moung Soui, the headquarters of Kong Le. There were also some discussions about reinforcing the site with FAR troops, but the decision was made to wait and see what happened before deploying additional troops. As it turned out, the NVA were tired, and the rainy season was again approaching.

On March 14, the bombing of Phou Kout finally got underway. The napalm seemed to do the trick, and soon the Neutralists were advancing up the east slope of the mountain, where they secured the near summit. The NVA were still entrenched on the northern slope, however, and began shelling the advancing Lao troops. The United States then authorized an additional eight sorties a day at Phou Kout, but the NVA continued to hold. So the Neutralists decided the best way to root out the Communists was to send a demolition team in at night to blow up the NVA bunkers on the north summit.

The demolition team was soon in place, and after being briefed, they departed and appeared to be making good progress. Unfortunately, they were discovered prior to reaching the north summit, and most of the team was either killed or wounded in a pitched firefight. The mission was called off. Later, on March 20, Pathet Lao reinforcements showed up at Phou Kout and swept the Neutralists off the mountain—and, while they were at it, they also took Phou Douk. Needless to say, Kong Le's troops were completely demoralized.

By this time, Sullivan was concerned that the Neutralists would lose the will to fight. He was determined to do all that he could to get them moving again, so he asked the USAF to bomb the NVA military complex near Khang Khai. He also requested approximately 40 additional sorties for Barrel Roll, along with close air support, and asked that an AC-47 fly night armed reconnaissance along Route 7. At first the USAF balked, claiming the ambassador had underestimated the required number of sorties; but Sullivan persisted, and on the following day USAF F-105 Thunderchiefs flew 70 sorties against NVA targets near Khang Khai, destroying more than 20 buildings. Additional sorties were flown in Barrel Roll, bringing the total to almost 200.

Meanwhile, the situation at Muong Soui continued to deteriorate, and morale did not improve. In fact, the Neutralists abandoned a position near Phou Kout and walked back to Muong Soui, where they demanded air transportation to Vang Vieng. Their request was refused until Souvanna stepped in and ordered transportation for the troops.

On April 2, the Country Team met to discuss strategy. They agreed to request an increase in the number of air strikes in the Barrel Roll area based upon reconnaissance photos, pinpointing close to 100 targets where the Communists were staging war supplies for the upcoming rainy season. They considered it of the utmost importance in order to lift the spirits of the Lao fighters. The USAF also proposed heavy interdiction of NVA road traffic into northern Laos. Their hope was to alleviate pressure on Muong Soui and slow the flow of supplies down the Ho Chi Minh Trail towards South Vietnam. The only problem was that Rolling Thunder was taking up most of the fighter missions available, so there was a shortage of aircraft for Barrel Roll. There was also a shortage of iron bombs. Ambassador Sullivan contacted General Westmoreland in Saigon and pressured him for more air sorties in northeastern Laos; Westmoreland balked, so the ambassador threatened to suspend air strikes in the panhandle of Laos on the Trail. The general thought twice about his decision not to provide Sullivan with more sorties and acquiesced, agreeing to provide over 500 sorties for interdiction.

Meanwhile, on April 1, Souvanna Phouma had called a meeting with the FAR General Staff, Kong Le, and Brigadier General Thao Ma from the RLAF to discuss reorganization. Kong Le took the opportunity to air complaints about a lack of support. The discussion then became heated, and finally Kong Le sat down and remained quiet. The FAR then recommended the Neutralists be rotated off the front lines at Muong Soui one-by-one and replaced with fresh troops. The thought was the Neutralist troops could get some rest and retraining, and then be mainstreamed into FAR vacancies around the country.

Next, the discussion turned to Thao Ma and the General Staff's belief that the RLAF general was running his own little air force without regard for the needs of the FAR. Jumping into the fight, other generals also chimed in that Thao Ma hadn't supported them either. As the discussion continued, the FAR blamed the U.S. for catering to Thao Ma's and VP's whims. The General Staff also blamed Ambassador Sullivan for circumventing protocol by going directly to VP to levy requirements. The General Staff recommended that all of Sullivan's requirements be channeled through the FAR. The meeting adjourned with Souvanna indicating he would elevate the concerns expressed by the FAR General Staff.

On April 3, Souvanna met with Sullivan to discuss the FAR's concerns. The ambassador listened while Souvanna reiterated all the concerns of the General Staff. After the Prime Minister finished, Sullivan reminded Souvanna that the General Staff had not lived up to their commitments either, including their failure to establish a logistics section in the Tactical Headquarters as promised. Until that was accomplished, Sullivan wasn't going to entertain the FAR's concerns. The ambassador also reminded Souvanna that VP's activities were not part of the MAG agreement; rather, it was a separate U.S. Embassy operation, and was therefore not subject to review by the General Staff. The ambassador continued by complementing Thao Ma's performance, saying the general did a good job, and the argument over usage of the C-47 aircraft could be ironed out. With all that said, the Prime Minister and the ambassador ended the meeting without any feathers being ruffled.

Meanwhile, Muong Soui and Phou Kout were quiet, and the NVA began withdrawing from Muong Heim and Na Khang. Even though the NVA weren't engaging the Lao military, there was plenty of truck movement along Routes 6 and 7. Apparently the Communists were busily continuing to lay in supplies for the rainy season offensive; because once the rains began, the roads would become rivers of mud unfit for truck traffic.

On April 4, the FAR and Kong Le set up a joint command at Muong Soui. The plan was to have the Neutralists defend the center of the town and the military camp, while VP's Hmong troops would defend the flanks. The FAR would be there also, in reserve of course, when and if they were needed. Upon hearing the plan, the Americans were skeptical, given the Neutralist propensity for cutting and running when the fighting got tough. Nevertheless, time was on the side of the Lao, so the U.S. military got busy scheduling hundreds of sorties for Steel Tiger and Barrel Roll.

Later, on April 21, the FAR Commander In Chief, Ouane Rathikone, complained that Thao Ma was still being stubborn. Ouane was fed up and intended to replace Thao Ma with the former RLAF commander, Brigadier General Sourith Don Sasorith, who was currently in the United States attending U.S. Army training. Some in the U.S. Embassy were concerned about the prospect of Thao Ma being replaced with a ground officer like Sourith, and wondered if being led by an Army officer would dampen the spirit of the RLAF aviators. In an attempt to shore up support for Thao Ma, it was suggested that Ambassador Sullivan intervene on the general's behalf with Souvanna.

But Sullivan knew the die was already pretty much cast against Thao Ma; he believed that Thao Ma would be pushed aside into a position that would, in effect, render him powerless. But finally, after many meetings, negotiations and compromises, Thao Ma was allowed to remain as the head of the RLAF, but the headquarters was moved to Vientiane, and the T-28s were dispersed to four different locations throughout Laos. In addition, the C-47 transports were taken out of the RLAF inventory and reassigned to the Director of Operations under the FAR general staff. This would, no doubt, allow Ouane to use the transports for his criminal enterprises, consisting of smuggling opium and gold.

During the summer of 1966, Thao Ma remained quiet for the most part, accepting his assignment; and behind the scenes, Ouane continued to develop a plan that would keep the RLAF commander out of the transport business altogether. And as the rainy season of 1966 approached, the NVA elected not to engage in any drawn out battles. With their heavy equipment and need for constant replenishment, they spent most of their time bogged down in the mud from April to October. This was also the time of year that VP would normally take the initiative to recover ground lost during the dry months. But this year, that would not happen—because VP was on his way to Hickam AFB Hospital in Hawaii for additional surgery. In May, however, VP returned to duty, ready to fight. His first order of business was to recall the 201st battalion from the field for a special meeting.

Everyone presumed that VP's recent injuries were the result of a sniper or errant rounds at Na Khang, but VP himself believed it was an officer from the 201st who had fired the shots that took him down. Later, after the battalion assembled at Long Tieng, it was discovered that the officer whom VP suspected was not among the group. It appeared that the man had resigned from the military and moved to Vientiane. In order to make sure the rest of the battalion remained loyal, VP required them all to take a sacred oath of allegiance, which they did.[58] He considered the action sufficient to close the book on the incident.

VP then arranged for the airlift of his troops to Muong Hiem, which would act as the staging base to retake Na Khang. Moung Hiem was just about the only area VP still controlled in northern Laos. Settling into his headquarters, VP wasted no time in launching his 1966 rainy season offensive. He divided his fighters into smaller units for safety, and began by probing several smaller villages and towns in the area. He was somewhat surprised that his teams met with little resistance, and wasn't sure if it was a trick on the part of the NVA. At any rate, his men continued to probe slowly and carefully. Ultimately, VP determined that the NVA had retreated to safety in North Vietnam to regroup and wait for the rains to stop.

After reoccupying the deserted villages, Vang Pao's men shifted their focus to retaking Na Khang. Intelligence disclosed that the NVA were still in Na Khang and were heavily fortified. Later, after receiving authorization, U.S. jets and RLAF T-28 fighters pounded the base for two days with iron bombs, also strafing it with cannon fire. In addition, Air America began bringing in additional Hmong fighters from Moung Hiem in H-34 helicopters. On one of the last flights on May 19, the flying was unusually tough because the mountains were draped in a heavy cloud cover. The NVA shot the chopper down, and an Air America pilot by the name of Bill Wilmont and almost a dozen Hmong guerrillas perished as the aircraft burst into flames and burned. The only survivor was the aircraft mechanic, who was thrown from the helicopter.

On May 23, Vang Pao's guerrillas reached the perimeter of Na Khang. The USAF jets and RLAF T-28s worked their guns against the NVA, and with the combined effort, Na Khang was retaken on May 25. After taking Na Khang, VP sent a guerrilla unit to Houei Thom. The team met some resistance, but the village was taken with little effort. Not taking anything for granted, and in true guerrilla fashion, VP again broke his men down into several smaller teams and continued to probe. One of the teams went towards North Vietnam and met no resistance. The other teams retook San Tiau, and continued on to Phou Pha Thi and Nong Khang. The only Communist activity detected was a caravan moving supplies. VP called in air support, and the caravan was eliminated in short order.

While activity in Laos was limited, there was plenty of activity across the border in North Vietnam. The enemy was organizing two new regiments of infantry troops, to be put use in northern Laos when the dry season came. Anticipating the fall offensive, the CIA tried to get ahead of the Communists by adding an additional case officer by the name of Frank Odom, code named "The Bag," to the region. They also created Road Watch Teams consisting of Thai mercenaries, and a new battalion of Hmong guerrillas was trained and would be airlifted to the area when needed.

Meanwhile, on June 11, eight Douglas B-26K bomber aircraft arrived at NKP, where they were assigned to the 606th Air Commando Squadron (composite), the "Lucky Tigers," in a temporary duty status as part of a project called "Big Eagle." Big Eagle would evaluate the B-26's night interdiction capability with a possible deployment of 12 additional aircraft depending on the results of the project. But one problem required attention first: the Thai Government didn't permit the U.S. to station bombers on its soil in those days. So the USAF changed the aircraft designation of the B-26 to A-26; the letter "A," of course, refers to attack aircraft.

Produced by the Douglas Aircraft Company, the B-26 first flew on July 10, 1942, and entered combat for the first time in late 1944, but didn't see much action. After World War II, the Air Force selected the B-26 as its mainstay of light bombardment squadrons, and in 1948, it was designated as the B-26B, and subsequently flew 12,000 sorties in Korea from 1950-53. It inflicted significant damage, and few were lost. But after the Korean War, most of the B-26s were either sold to foreign countries or mothballed. The B-26's next appearance was in

South Vietnam in 1953, when it flew air missions against the North Vietnamese at Dien Bien Phu. Later, the B-26 was used during Project Mill Pond in 1961, at which time the aircraft flew missions over the Plain of Jars. It also flew missions in South Vietnam in Operations "Jungle Jim" and "Farm Gate." Its in-commission rate, however, was low, and later, two incidents involving wing separation led to the aircraft being pulled from service.

In 1963, 40 B-26B aircraft were modified with new engines, wingtip gas tanks, weapons pylons, and new nose guns; the cockpits were also modernized, and the wings reinforced. The aircraft were then designated the B-26K, and eight of the upgraded aircraft were deployed to Thailand on June 11, 1966 under Project Big Eagle.

The aircraft began its evaluation period by flying interdiction missions over the Ho Chi Minh Trail in southern Laos, in the operational area referred to as Steel Tiger. Essentially, the A-26 would fly alone over the trail, looking for targets of opportunity, and when a NVA truck convoy was spotted, the "Nimrods," as the A26s were called, would attack the trucks using bombs, napalm and .50 caliber

Figure 23. B-26K (A-26) Aircraft
(Photo from the Public Domain)

machine guns. The evaluation period lasted six months, and during that period, over 1,000 sorties were flown, about 2,000 tons of bombs were dropped, and roughly 500,000 rounds of ammunition were expended. The Air Force evaluation was considered successful, and the Nimrods became a permanent part of the 606th ACS. The Nimrods were later separated from the composite squadron, and became the 609th Air Combat Squadron (ACS).

As the number of aircraft flying missions over Laos increased, the U.S. decided that some form of airborne control of these sorties was needed to provide an airborne information link and assistance in a timely manner. Both the U.S. Ambassador to Laos and the 7th Air Force were also concerned that without airborne control, aircraft flying north might not be able to communicate with the existing ground control center in Laos. Initially, the aircraft selected to temporarily bridge that communications gap was the RC-47, call sign "Dogpatch." The venerable old converted transport aircraft had been retrofitted with cameras and radio relay equipment, and was already being used to send and receive intelligence information from the road watch teams operating in eastern Laos. The only problem was, the Dogpatch crews weren't specifically trained for airborne command and control, and were unfamiliar with the terrain in Laos.

Operations using Dogpatch as airborne command and control centers began around the end of April 1966. Initially, the aircraft would take off from their home at Udorn and fly to NKP, where they would top off their fuel and pick up additional intelligence specialists. Then the aircraft would head out to fly specific orbits (or racetracks as they were called) while receiving and relaying radio traffic from the air and ground. At first, the operation was somewhat fluid, because all the aircrew personnel were on temporary duty (TDY) assignments to Thailand and weren't exactly sure what was required of them.

Prior to flight, CIA and USAF operations specialists briefed the crews, and orbits were selected more or less based upon where the fighting was taking place at that moment. Routes were selected at random to avoid a fixed or predictable pattern, to avoid antiaircraft fire and bad weather.

Soon, the airborne command and control aircraft began regular operations, and continued to operate over northeastern Laos, and on occasion over the border in North Vietnam. At first, airborne control activities and equipment were rudimentary at best. But by July, the TDY personnel were in the process of being replaced by permanent personnel, and many of the initial operational problems were being worked out. Also, by July and August, most aircraft flying north were checking in and out with Dogpatch on a regular basis. Originally, there was only one Dogpatch mission each day, out of Udorn, but after a couple of weeks there were two missions a day operating under the call signs "Cricket" and "Alley Cat." Later, in June 1967, the new EC-130 Airborne Battlefield Command and Control Centers (ABCCC) aircraft replaced the RC-47s, and the SEA fleet of ABCCC aircraft was rapidly increased to seven.

The low-flying, slow-moving aircraft were attractive targets to Communist antiaircraft gunners, as they proved on July 19 when Dogpatch 2 departed Udorn Air base enroute to Sam Neua. The USAF crew consisted of pilot Captain Robert E. Hoskinson and crewmen Galileo F. Bossio, Vincent A. Chiarello, Bernard Conklin, Robert J. Di Tommaso, James S. Hall, Herbert E. Smith, and John Mamiya. When the aircraft was approximately ten miles from Sam Neua, the crew reported that they were under attack by enemy fighters. Radio contact with the aircraft was then lost, and the details of what happened afterward remain unknown. Troops operating in the area at the time believe that Dogpatch 2 either got too close to the air defenses at Sam Neua and was shot down, or may have inadvertently strayed into North Vietnam and met its demise. No specific details were reported of the crash, but quite a few reports were received, some conflicting with others. It was later unofficially reported that as many as five crewmembers might have survived by bailing out, and were later captured and held as POWs. Many years later, in 1998, the remains of Conklin, Chiarello, Hall, Mamiya and Smith were recovered and returned to their families; but the status of the other members of the crew is still classified as MIA.

The year 1966 also brought a new specialty into the war. In April, the AIRA increased the number of FACs to four, and a FAC program was initiated. It was initially called "Butterfly" and originated in VP's MR 2. The Butterfly FACs would fly in the backseat of Air America light transport aircraft and radio instructions to ground commanders. There were initially three FACs: one USAF combat controller, a Thai controller, and a Hmong controller. The controllers used SSB radios to communicate with ground forces. The USAF controller would relay information to and from the orbiting Dogpatch airborne command center; the Thai controller would also relay the same information to Thai commandos on the ground, and of course the Hmong controller would relay all appropriate information to Vang Pao's guerrillas.

Meanwhile, the FAR General Staff presented plans for an operation named "Prasane," scheduled to commence on July 18. The objective of Prasane was to sweep the Pathet Lao from Nam Bac and the Ou River valley. The operation would use troops from the FAR, VP's Hmong SGUs, and the RLAF. The first phase of the operation would soften up the Communist troops who had recently taken three Lima Sites at Nam Thouam, Nom Lak and Pha Thong. While these sites were being softened up, the Hmong and FAR troops would attack. Phase Two of the operation would then airlift several hundred Lao soldiers into Nam Thouam and two battalions into Pha Thong. Then, in Phase Three, the troops would sweep the three sites, while the Hmong guerrillas blocked the escape routes to the east. The U.S. Embassy was supportive of the operation because it required little U.S. effort, and would hopefully result in important ground being retaken.

For the helicopter airlift effort required to support Prasane, it was hoped that the USAF at NKP could provide several CH-3 helicopters and crews to transport Lao troops, because Air America was already tied up airlifting war supplies to VP's troops in northern Laos. In addition to the helicopter assets, Thao Ma also requested two USAF observation aircraft to provide FAC and reconnaissance support. He envisioned using USAF pilots and Lao observers riding in the backseat. When first approached by Thao Ma, the U.S. balked at providing the airlift helicopters, but agreed to provide the observation aircraft. So Air America would once again have to pick up the slack, even though they were already stretched thin.

Operation Prasane began on schedule, and met with less resistance than anticipated. By July 30, all Phase One goals were completed. Phase Two then got underway, and Nam Bac was retaken on August 7. Again, little resistance was encountered, with the Pathet Lao simply melting away into the hills. But as the monsoon rains intensified almost all operations ceased, except for some patrols which encountered almost no resistance. By August 23, the rivers were out of their banks and Vientiane was knee-deep in water. Wattay Airport was unsuitable for air operations, so Air America temporarily operated out of Udorn. The situation did not improve until late September.

Meanwhile, as the war expanded, it was recognized that precise navigation was required for delivery of munitions and ordnance on targets in Laos—and it became apparent that the TACAN located on Skyline Ridge wasn't adequate to control air resources. Vang Pao recommended LS-185 (Phou Tia), with an elevation of 4,500 feet, but the site was unsafe due to hostilities in the region. LS-36 (Na Khang) was ruled out for that same reason. Ultimately, the USAF 1st MOB out of Clark Air Base was brought into the discussion, and asked to survey several sites in Laos as potential candidates to house the new TACAN facilities. Later, when the 1st MOB arrived in Laos, they surveyed potential sites at LS-50 (Phu Cum) and near Skyline Ridge, Luang Prabang and LS-85 (Phou Pha Thi). From the sites surveyed, it was determined that LS-85 would be the best location for the TACAN equipment. Ambassador Sullivan agreed, considering security at the site to be good; but he did not want Americans involved with maintaining the TACAN equipment once it was installed and operating. In addition to TACAN equipment, the ambassador recommended that a low-frequency radio beacon also be installed to provide navigational aid to aircraft with TACAN. On July 14, Admiral Sharp approved installation of the equipment at LS-85.

In the summer of 1966, a Top Secret operation known as "Heavy Green" was initiated. Few U.S. personnel in SEA even knew it was taking place; it was performed in secrecy on the summit of Phou Pha Thi, or Pha Thi, as the Hmong refer to this mountain. Pha Thi is located in northeast Laos, twenty miles west of Sam Neua and 15 miles from the border with North Vietnam. The U.S.

Figure 24. Phou Pha Thi
(Photo from the Public Domain)

wasn't the first foreign nation to use this site. As early as 1953, French commandos had used the summit as an assembly point for their Hmong guerrilla network. At 5,800 feet, Pha Thi isn't the tallest mountain in Laos, but its strategic location made it a natural choice for the covert activity presently underway.

There was a village and a dirt landing strip at the bottom of the mountain, and it was designated a Lima Site (LS-85) for resupply purposes. Most of the mountaintop was protected by a near-vertical face of limestone, making it extremely difficult, but not impossible, to scale. The top of the mountain was accessible by walking and climbing, but it took a long time and a lot of effort to make the trek up the back way. Also, partway up the mountain was a helicopter landing pad and living quarters for the Hmong guerrillas. The CIA also utilized a small command post and bunker at the landing pad as well. From that location, they would meet with the Hmong guerrillas, provide them with daily tasking, and debrief them upon their return from their intelligence missions. To facilitate the installation of the communications equipment under Heavy Green, the top of the mountain was cleared and leveled to the extent possible using Hmong villagers living near the mountain. From the mountaintop, VP was able to use his Hmong fighters to visually monitor NVA personnel coming into Laos from North Vietnam.

Meanwhile, construction activity on the Top Secret facility on the summit of Pha Thi had just begun. A small group of 1st MOB personnel had recently arrived, to begin the installation project that would allow the United States to provide the first all-weather bombing capability to aircraft participating in Rolling Thunder and Barrel Roll. After installation of the equipment at Pha Thi was completed, U.S. aircraft could be navigated to and from their targets in any weather conditions. The could also put their bombs directly on the target every time, even if they couldn't see what they were bombing—which was the case most of the time in Laos.

As 1966 ended, the 1st MOB was rapidly moving construction supplies to the site through Sam Thong, Long Tieng and Na Khang, and no one was the wiser. We'll talk about what happens at LS-85 a bit later in the story, but for now, let's look at other activities also taking place in Laos.

In mid-1966, USAF Captain Richard (Dick) Secord arrived at Udorn. Secord was a West Point graduate, and had flown over 200 air combat missions in South Vietnam in the venerable T-28, where he was assigned to a project known as "Farm Gate." Farm Gate was intended to provide a cover story for U.S. personnel flying air combat missions in Vietnam and to teach South Vietnamese pilots how to fly. But when he arrived at Udorn, Secord was detailed to the CIA, and his assignment at Udorn was to oversee Air America's airlift role in SEA. Captain Secord had barely settled in at Udorn when he was loaned to the CIA Station in Vientiane, Laos. His role there would be to oversee the Road Watch Teams along the Ho Chi Minh Trail. Once settled, Secord dived into his work with great passion. As the months passed and CIA agents departed, his role expanded. Ultimately, Secord became practically a one-man show, coordinating air activities over Laos with the 7th/13th Air Force. He was considered to be a tenacious and pugnacious individual. One thing was always apparent to those who dealt with Captain (later Major) Secord, and that was that he always kept the best interests of the troops on the ground as his first priority, and foremost in his thoughts and deeds.

Meanwhile, on September 17, 1966, Communist forces retook San Tiau (LS-1), the Hmong support base south of Ban Ban. VP counterattacked, and four days later the base was back under Hmong control.

In early September, it had been recommended by the AIRA in Vientiane that the A-26K Nimrods be used for air interdiction strikes in the Barrel Roll area; Ambassador Sullivan agreed, and the first strike was subsequently flown on October 10. It was credited with eliminating 10 North Vietnamese trucks and over 50 enemy personnel. In late September, the NVA truck traffic increased in northern Laos near Sam Neua, and the A-26s responded again, but could not locate the trucks under the dense foliage. Later, on October 15, the U.S. Embassy in Vientiane requested that eight more A-26s be added to the existing fleet in Thailand to interdict the rapidly expanding number of NVA trucks along the roads in northern Laos.

The 7th Air Force Commander, USAF General William W. Momyer, disagreed with the request and recommended disapproval, citing a need for faster-moving jet aircraft due to the increasing number of NVA artillery positions in Laos. Admiral Sharp, however, agreed with the embassy, overruling Momyer. On October 25, at a meeting held at Udorn to discuss air interdiction in northern Laos, Momyer recommended that the Bango/Whiplash alert mission be discontinued and replaced with a daily mission profile consisting of 12 A-1 Skyraiders, 18 F-104 fighters, and four A-26 Nimrods. Ambassador Sullivan concurred, and procedures were established for emergency strikes.

Even as Momyer and Sullivan made their plans, there was trouble brewing back in Laos. With Thao Ma in check, the FAR General Staff had turned their attention to Kong Le. It was no secret that Ouane and Kouprasith had always wanted control over the Neutralist forces, which presently numbered over 10,000. In early October 1966, while Souvanna Phouma was in New York speaking at the United Nations, Ouane seized the opportunity to neutralize Kong Le. Ambassador Sullivan got wind of the planned coup, but decided not to directly intervene. The State Department in Washington did, however, brief Souvanna on Ouane's plan.

The plan would reorganize the Neutralists into four mobile groups, with one group being roughly the size of a regiment. A Neutralist staff function would remain at Vang Vieng, and all Neutralist officers would be retained at their present rank until confirmed by Royal Decree. Three of the four groups would be commanded by Ouane's cohorts, Colonel Soulivanh Singhavara, Lt. Colonel Sing Chanthakouman, and Colonel Somphet Sotsavan. The fourth group's commander would be named at a later date.

With his plan in place and Souvanna still in New York, Ouane set the wheels in motion on October 16. Kong Le was confronted and told that he was to leave the country straightaway. Seeing the handwriting on the wall, he was soon on an RLAF C-47, being flown to Thailand and into exile. Just like that, the coup was over, without a drop of blood having been shed.

Looking back, Sullivan had seen this day coming for over two years. In early 1960, Kong Le's drive and ambition inspired the 2d Paratroop Battalion to victory, and his men idolized him. But more recently, the paratroop commander had lost his ambition and will to fight. In fact, Kong Le hadn't even been present at Muong Soui during the two previous Neutralist attacks on Phou Kout. He had lost the respect of his officers and men, and they turned against him in the end. Souvanna had also seen this day coming for quite some time, and therefore he made no move to avert the coup.

As soon as Kong Le left the country, other dramatic events began to unfold. In the early morning hours of October 21, Thao

Ma and Colonel Bounlet Saycocie seized Savannakhet AFB. Later, at approximately 8:00 A.M., Thao Ma's T-28 fighters were in the air over Vientiane, strafing and bombing FAR Headquarters and the barracks at Chinaimo Air Base. The attacks left approximately 80 people either dead or injured. Thao Ma called Ambassador Sullivan, asking for his assistance in persuading Generals Kouprasith, Bounpone, and Oudone to resign. The ambassador refused, referring Thao Ma to the Lao Deputy Prime Minister, Leuam Insisiengmay. After talking to Leuam, Thao Ma agreed to suspend any further attacks, and to participate in mediation talks. On the afternoon of October 21, Lao Prince Boun Oum, the British ambassador, Sullivan, and the FAR General Staff flew to Savannakhet to talk to Thao Ma.

But the talks did not go well; Thao Ma was still defiant, even though his coup never really got any support. After the meeting, the ambassadors, Boun Oum, and the General Staff returned to Vientiane, where they met with Leuam. After weighing all the options, it was decided that order would have to be restored at Savannakhet. On the following morning, Brigadier General La Pathammavong and his men walked into the air base in Savannakhet—and met no resistance. Thao Ma was no longer there, because after the meeting on October 21, he realized that he had run out of options, and none of the brass would back him up. So just prior to dusk that afternoon, Thao Ma and about a dozen of his loyal followers got into their fully loaded T-28s and flew to Udorn, where they were allowed to land, and remain in Thailand as political refugees. As expected, back in Vientiane Ouane postured and symbolically demanded Thao Ma's return; but from then on, the Chief of Staff would always need to be looking over his shoulder, wondering what his three exiled generals might be planning in Thailand. The three—Phoumi, Kong Le and Thao Ma—had once been powerful and popular leaders in the kingdom of Laos, and could be planning for a return in the future.

As chaos reigns in Vientiane, construction atop Phou Pha Thi by the 1st. MOB continued.

Meanwhile, in October, another secret program was underway in Laos: the so-called "Steve Canyon Program." It was the forerunner for a group that later became known as "The Ravens." The Ravens were a tough group of FACs who directed air strikes from small Cessna O-1 Bird Dog aircraft with no armament and no weapons, except their USAF issued side arms and the M-16 rifles they carried for personal protection. You'll read more about Steve Canyon and the Ravens in a later chapter of this book.

On November 2, 1966, Hmong Road Watch Teams contacted an A-26 Nimrod and relayed target information on five NVA trucks spotted about ten miles east of Sam Neua. The Nimrod pilot diverted to the location, and visually confirmed the presence of the trucks. He then rolled in and took out four of the trucks before proceeding on down that road in search of others. Soon, he discovered and eliminated four more trucks. The Nimrod pilot then radioed for A-1 support and they diverted to assist the Nimrod. When the smoke cleared, approximately 50 NVA trucks had been taken out, and several hundred Communist troops were dead. For the remainder of the month, however, bad weather curtailed most of the American air strikes against the NVA and Pathet Lao forces. The Communist troops took full advantage of the weather, and began

Figure 25. Cessna O-1 Bird Dog
Photo from the Public Domain

to move large quantities of war supplies into northern Laos for the anticipated dry season offensive, which was fast approaching.

On November 24, several Pathet Lao battalions attacked Tha Thom and took the town by the end of the day. The FAL responded, and after four days of heavy fighting, the town was back under government control.

As November ended and December began, things grew relatively quiet in northern Laos, as the Communists continued to resupply. VP also took advantage of the lull, using it to his advantage by attacking and taking Muong Het (LS-13) on December 18. He then dispersed his men along the Laotian border with North Vietnam. Meanwhile, the NVA continued their build-up around Na Khang and Phou Pha Thi.

Late in 1966, Pathet Lao informers reported to the CIA that three American pilots were being held at a well-known NVA site in north-central Laos. The informants were able to provide specific verifiable facts about the POWs, including their names, which were checked on the official list of missing airmen. Since combat intelligence information tends to be transitory in nature, Dick Secord, Pat Landry and Bill Lair immediately planned a raid, in coordination with CIA and US military officials. Unfortunately, after too much analysis, the raid didn't take place, and the POWs were reportedly moved.[59]

Meanwhile, in the last two weeks of December, the NVA began a large build-up of supplies and equipment in the Sam Neua area. Later, dozens of Soviet trucks were sighted in Xieng Khouang Province on Route 7, making their way to the Plain of Jars. It was apparent the Communists were planning to expand the war in 1967. The move did not escape VP's attention either, and he rapidly deployed guerrilla units to harass the enemy.

In the meantime, Colonel Heine Aderholt returned to Thailand to activate the 56th Air Commando Wing at NKP.[60] The base would soon become a place reminiscent of an air museum: the aircraft parking area was lined with old propeller-driven aircraft such as the C-123K Providers, A-1 Douglas Skyraiders, Cessna O-1 and O-2 forward air control aircraft, HH-43 Huskies, EC-47 electronic monitoring aircraft, and an occasional T-28 trainer-turned-fighter. And, of course, the A-26 Nimrods were also there. But as the days and months passed, NKP proved to the NVA and everyone else involved that they were a force to be reckoned with. People no longer referred to NKP as being the "Home of the Antique Airlines." It became a potent, in-your-face adversary that was responsible for effectively supporting the Secret War in Laos, and its presence, capability and successes did not go unnoticed by Hanoi.

As 1966 winds down, the complexion of the Secret War in Laos has begun to change. It's no longer a small insurgency where opposing factions exchange minor blows. The Communists have steadily increased their hold on northeastern Laos, and the NVA keep coming. The U.S. has continued its build-up in Thailand, and is trying a variety of methods to deal with the Communists. But it still appears that America isn't taking the war seriously enough. No large operations have taken place, and the U.S. approach appears to be piecemeal.

A new year is just around the corner, and if aggressive steps aren't taken by the United States, the Communists may become unstoppable. Keep reading to see how everything unfolds.

Chapter 7

Turning Up the Heat

As 1967 arrived, President Johnson found himself frustrated with both the overt war in Vietnam and the Secret War in Laos. Washington continued to pour money and U.S. personnel into the MACV, hoping to break the will of the Viet Cong; but in Vientiane, the situation was a bit more difficult. The CIA had tried to loosely adhere to the Geneva Accords of 1962, and they were fairly successful in that effort. But now, LBJ had directed them to turn up the heat on North Vietnam. This meant not just listening and reporting, but launching action operations. For that purpose, the CIA assigned one of its best men, Ted Shackley, to run the station in Vientiane. Many new American faces soon followed Shackley into Laos, where they would take over and manage the Secret War.

In MR 1 (northwestern Laos), two additional paramilitary case officers arrived to augment the CIA personnel in the northwest. Pat Sharone, a former U.S. Army Airborne soldier in World War II, and Chuck Campbell, a former U.S. Marine, were the two officers selected. Their job was to organize the hill tribes, collect intelligence, and occasionally launch operations against the Chinese, NVA and Pathet Lao in the Nam Bac Valley. Later, Eli Popovich—a former CIA officer in Burma and the Balkans—was selected to lead the Nam Bac CIA unit. Popovich's job was to set up Lao home guard units to collect intelligence, provide local defense, and occasionally take part in offensive operations against the Communists. Tony Poe, having worn out his welcome in MR 2, transferred to MR 1 to train local Lao defense units in the Sayaboury Province. And in addition to their other duties, the CIA unit in MR 1 became the launch point for forays into southern China to collect intelligence information and tap telephone lines.

In MR 2, General Vang Pao's responsibility was northeastern Laos, including the Plain of Jars and the areas southward to Vientiane. At this point Bill Lair was the CIA officer in charge of operations, and he needed many case officers under him to attend to a multitude of new duties. With the demands from the Agency, Lair's staff grew significantly to cover a myriad of other tasks, including recruiting and expanding the Hmong SGUs to collect intelligence information, oversee Road Watch Teams, and conduct offensive operations against the Communists.

In MR 3 (Central Laos, including the panhandle and Ho Chi Minh Trail), a seasoned CIA case officer named Walt Floyd was selected to set up and manage Road Watch Teams. He was also tasked to collect intelligence and oversee offensive operations against NVA personnel, using the Trail to move war fighting equipment and supplies to South Vietnam. Working with Floyd was another recent addition named George McGrath, a former U.S. Army Airborne officer and former Special Forces Green Beret.

Last but not least, was MR 4 (southern Laos), where Paul Barb, another seasoned case officer, was selected to lead the CIA team. In conjunction with George Doty and Duncan Jewell, Barb was tasked with setting up Road Watch Teams and interdicting war supplies flowing down the Ho Chi Minh Trail. Among other things, the interdiction effort entailed seeding the trail with antipersonnel and anti-vehicle mines. Later, Barb and his team were joined by Wayne McNulty and several other well-qualified former paramilitary officers.

With the influx of new CIA personnel, the paramilitary prospects looked promising for the Lao Government in early 1967. By this time, friendly forces had successfully captured and occupied the Nam Bac Valley in Luang Prabang Province, for the first time since the war had begun. It was now under government control. The valley was rich in rice production and fruit orchards even though, historically, it had provided a route for invasion from the North. Besides the potential for bounty, holding Nam Bac gave the impression that Communist control of the area had lessened in the high population areas.

In January, seven Lao military sectors, A-G, delineated reconnaissance and target areas in Barrel Roll, Steel Tiger and Tiger Hound. In these areas, American aircraft were authorized to conduct air strikes against moving targets of opportunity under the Rules of Engagement, as long as they were a certain distance from villages and occupied structures. These targets could be struck day or night, provided they were not within 200 yards of an improved trail or road. To carry out the strikes, the aircraft could use airborne or ground FACs, or radar-guided resources. A FAC was required, however, on close air support missions, when required by the Embassy in Vientiane.

It was also compulsory that aircraft carrying out air strikes without FAC or radar support confirm their position by radar or TACAN in advance. If any doubt existed about the target, the pilot was not authorized to use his ordnance. Given the excessive number of rules and controls, it was almost impossible to comply

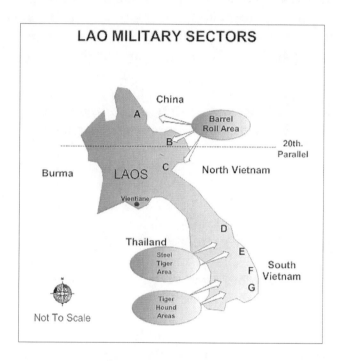

Figure 26. Lao Military Sectors
(Drawing by the author)

with all the Rules Of Engagement (ROE). There were many, and they continually changed based on the situation on the ground and the whims of the generals in charge. In order to meet the ROEs, all pilots took periodic examinations to prove they understood the rules. If a pilot failed the test, he couldn't fly until the exam was successfully completed. Ironically, it wasn't the simple villagers tending their land who benefitted from the ROEs, as was intended, but the Communist troops who knew them better than any pilot. And once again, the bad guys used the rules to stay one step ahead of the good guys.

Speaking of the bad guys: by early 1967, there were signs that the Pathet Lao was a force in decline. Many observers believed they would soon disappear altogether, were it not for the North Vietnamese stiffeners. In fact, the Pathet Lao had been reinforced with over 10,000 front-line NVA troops, bringing the total Communist troop levels in Laos to approximately 50,000. That number included the Pathet Lao, dissident Neutralists, and regular NVA troops. Added to the total was another force of roughly 20,000 advisors, engineers, transportation, and communications personnel. It should be noted that a large number of this latter group directly supported the movement of supplies and weapons transiting the Ho Chi Minh Trail into South Vietnam.

Even though the number of Communist troops appeared large, the Lao forces were improving their tactics with an eye toward making large-scale military gains. But events unfolding on the ground would soon refute that prospect.

On January 1, 1967, election results in Laos gave Souvanna Phouma's United Front roughly two-thirds of the seats in the National Assembly: 32 out of a total of 59, based on a 60% turnout of the nation's 800,000 registered voters. As usual, the Pathet Lao rejected the results, but if nothing else, the election showed that Souvanna was better off politically than before. The Rightists lost some strength, but the Neutralists picked up some seats. It was significant that the FAR supported the United Front, because they played an important role behind the scenes.

Early 1967 also saw some changes to the military hardware used in SEA. To achieve the Johnson Administration's new goals of breaking the Viet Cong and booting the NVA out of Laos, significant upgrades of the U.S. aircraft stationed in Laos were required. Washington wanted to replace the F-104, F-105 and F4-C with new F4-D aircraft, making things easier by having only one weapon system to support instead of three. Other assets would need to be rearranged and upgraded as well. For example, in January, twenty two O-1 Bird Dog FAC aircraft were assigned to NKP, Thailand; and by February, the O-1s were already being replaced with the two-engine O-2 Cessna Skymasters.

At about this same time, Lao Government, and CIA officers were busy debriefing a Pathet Lao defector in late December 1966. To show good faith, and hopefully avoid a lengthy prison stay the defector provided information regarding the location of a Pathet Lao prison camp near the town of Ban Naden, in central Laos. The defector indicated that the prison was in a cave at the base of a limestone cliff, and covered by dense vegetation. The information sounded believable, and tended to somewhat validate previously obtained regarding a prison camp in that general geographical location. Based upon this new information, a reliable team consisting of a seasoned, Lao military personnel, led by a dependable sergeant was put together to attempt a rescue. Several possible scenarios were discussed. Finally, it was decided that the team would be taken to the general area by helicopter, and dropped off. The team was then make their way to the prison using counter-surveillance techniques, free the prisoners, and lead them a safe distance away to a safe location where a pick-up by helicopters could be made.

The team later rehearsed the plan, without knowing the actual target. Later, during the first week of January, 1967 the team was flown by helicopter to a landing zone near the target area. After exiting the helicopter, the team quickly disappeared into the jungle and began their trek to the alleged prison. For the next couple of days, the team of followed their predetermined route to the general vicinity of the prison. After verifying the existence of the prison, the team rested and waited until just before daybreak of the following day. They then attacked the sleeping guards, and opened fire on the prison defenders. When the guards had been silenced, the team went to work forcing their way into the cave-like confinement facility, and freed dozens of prisoners. Some panicked and ran, but the others remained and were quietly led away form the prison towards the extraction location.

Shortly after they began their trek, the Pathet Lao regrouped, assembled a search party, and began tracking the rescue team and the freed prisoners. It didn't take long for the Pathet Lao troops to locate the fleeing prisoners, and they closed in to recapture the group, and deal with the Lao soldiers who freed them. But, fortunately for the fleeing prisoners, RLAF T-28s working in the area arrived on the scene, and shot up the Pathet Laos troops chasing the freed prisoners. And, thanks to the RLAF pilots, and sympathetic villagers, the prisoners were safely loaded onto Air America helicopters and flown to freedom. The freed prisoners were then fed, received medical treatment as required and returned to their loved ones.

After all was said and done, not much publicity was given to the successful raid. But, this rescue was significant in that few prisoner rescue attempts were successful.

Meanwhile, in northeastern Laos, Communist activity around Na Khang (LS-36) increased. LS-36 was a particularly important installation for both Lao and U.S. forces, because as we've mentioned before, its location helped the Lao control Route 6, and it also served as a launch facility for guerrilla teams and U.S. MACV SOG units operating covertly in North Vietnam.

The Communists were well aware of the importance of LS-36, and wanted to retake the installation again as soon as possible in order to cripple the American and Lao elements operating in the area. To that end, and using inclement weather for cover, the NVA began to infiltrate the site's perimeter on the night of January 5. Their plan was to avoid contact with the Lao defenders at the perimeter as they slowly moved towards their target, the installation's command post. As the attack began, the Communists troops crept into the installation from three sides, slowly crawling up to the inner perimeter in the dark of night; and there they waited for daylight to strike. As morning approached, most of the people in the camp were still asleep in their bunks; the weather was ugly, and the area was socked in by heavy clouds that would hamper air support.

. As the sun began to rise on January 6, the NVA began their attack on Na Khang, dropping mortar rounds on the base from the north. The CIA case officer at the site tried desperately to radio for air support, but it wasn't easy to reach anyone who could help. Meanwhile, Don Sjostrom, a USAID employee who worked for Pop Buell, went outside with his weapon to assist in the defense of the site. But Sjostrom was no combat soldier, and he was quickly cut down by an errant round. In the meantime, contact was made with other CIA personnel, and air support was requested—but the nearest aircraft were at least an hour away in Thailand. The first aircraft to arrive over Na Khang were four F-105 Thunderchiefs from Takhli Air Base.

At the time, LS-36 was still socked in, and the cloud level was too low to permit dropping bombs. But the flight leader was able to get below the clouds and made several noisy passes over Na Khang before having to rejoin his flight. Even though he wasn't able to drop any bombs or do any strafing with his cannons, his passes overhead definitely raised the morale of the Hmong guerrillas on the ground; those passes at 200 feet in a mountainous area were an extraordinarily brave effort. But by this time the Thunderchiefs were running low on fuel, and they had no choice but to return to Thailand. Operating further south in the panhandle area of Laos, two A-1E Skyraiders from Udorn were conducting close air support missions when they were diverted to help at Na Khang. Upon arriving a short time later, the pilots circled above LS-36, which was still socked in by low clouds.

By this time, one of the A-1s had managed to find a hole in the clouds and dropped down to take a look. Upon receiving clearance to strike at will, the pilot began making passes over the installation, strafing with his cannons and firing rockets into groups of NVA troops. After firing out his ammunition and rockets, the A-1 climbed back up above the clouds and then led his wingman down through the clouds.

The second A-1 picked up where his wingman had left off, and made numerous passes before running out of ammunition and ordnance. All the while, both Skyraiders were taking hits from automatic weapons and small arms fire, and doing their best not to slam into the surrounding mountains. Later, as the two pilots climbed above the clouds, more A-1s began to arrive over the site, ready to fight. Realizing they were outgunned, the Communists broke off the attack and retreated into the tree line near the base. NVA sniper fire continued, but the base was able to reopen the airstrip. Arriving shortly thereafter, VP took control of the ground action. While searching the bodies of the dead Communist troops, he was able to determine that the attackers were a mix of NVA and Communist Chinese soldiers. All of the dead attackers were believed to be new to the area, because each carried a detailed map in his pocket depicting infiltration and departure routes from Na Khang. If VP's hunch was right, the retreating soldiers would take the exact same route out that they had used to come in. VP quickly briefed the CIA case officers about his suspicions, and the USAF was notified to attack the retreating Communist troops. The subsequent fighting continued throughout the day. There was little activity during the night, but the USAF erred on the side of caution and scheduled a C-130 "Lamplighter" to fly overhead all night, dropping illumination flares.61 A-1 Skyraiders from NKP also loitered in the area, in case they were needed.

By about noon on the following day, most of the Communist attackers had retreated from the area—and were soon discovered wandering around lost, and spread out, in a canyon-like area. The valley floor was heavily wooded, but enemy troops could be observed moving about. Soon, a flight of Skyraiders from Udorn showed up overhead, armed to the teeth with cluster bombs, napalm, white phosphorous rockets, and 20 millimeter cannons. The A-1s then went to work on the bad guys below; and when it was all said and done, nothing on the ground was moving, and the entire area was engulfed in flames from the napalm. No American aircraft were lost on this mission, but most were hit numerous times by machine gun and small arms rounds. After the fight, the A-1s departed and flew home to safety back in Thailand.

Na Khang was spared, for now, and the NVA were repulsed. But the Communists weren't done. They soon regrouped, and during the night of January 22, they attacked the FAR/Hmong site at Nong Khang (LS-52), about ten miles north of Sam Neua. The attack began at about 3:00 A.M. with a mortar barrage, followed by an NVA assault resulting in hand-to-hand fighting which continued until dawn. The Communist troops finally broke off the attack when RLAF T-28s and American A-1s showed up and began strafing runs against the enemy. When the NVA finally retreated, more than 60 of their troops were left behind, either dead or dying.

Later, on February 2, a small Communist force of approximately 30 men conducted a sneak attack against the RLAF airfield at Luang Prabang, using rockets and automatic weapons. The well-planned attack lasted only 10 to 15 minutes, after which the Communist retreated. A subsequent inspection revealed that six T-28 aircraft and two H-34 helicopters had been destroyed, with three other T-28s and one additional H-34 damaged. Additionally, the AOC was partially destroyed. Human casualties on the Lao side totaled five soldiers killed and six wounded; no Communist casualties were observed. Although this attack might appear to be negligible in terms of losses, the attack itself was unprecedented: the Royal Capital at Luang Prabang had never been attacked before, which made the event particularly frightening and unexpected.

As the month of February 1967 worn on, the Communists continued to take advantage of the heavy cloud cover enveloping northern Laos. On the night of February 12, the NVA probed the defenses at LS-36 again, firing over 70 rounds from an 82-millimeter recoilless rifle; but the attack was repulsed by an A-26K Nimrod which strafed the enemy troops, causing them to break off the attack. The Hmong defenders did not suffer any losses in the attack, but their barracks was completely destroyed.

Later, on March 20—and continuing every rainy season thereafter in SEA—the USAF 54th Weather Reconnaissance Squadron, operating out of Udorn Air Base and using WC-130 aircraft, began conducting cloud seeding operations using silver oxide pellets. The project, called "Operation Popeye," was designed to extend the rainy season and increase its intensity. It was hoped that the increased rainfall would literally bog down the NVA in the mud, bringing traffic on the Ho Chi Minh Trail to a halt. Operation Popeye was classified at the Top Secret level, and few people in either the USAF or Washington were briefed on the program. The results of the program were reported as moderately successful, but the negative aspects of the program probably outweighed its perceived success. Some of the negative aspects will be mentioned later in the story.

In any case, the bad weather continued well into March, giving the Lao troops a chance to plan an attack against the Communists. Their target was Ban Mok Plai (LS-193), in the Nam Hieng area near Nam Bac, which they wanted to retake and use as a launch point to retake Muong Soui. The plan was to use five Hmong battalions and a 105mm artillery section; the Lao felt this was sufficient to defeat the enemy troops, estimated to be equivalent to three battalions. But the NVA made other plans, and decided to attack the Lao forces on March 10. They began by advancing on government forces north of the airstrip at Nam Bac, following up with an assault against other Lao artillery sites to the southeast.

The Communists managed to establish control of a small area near the airstrip, but the attack on the artillery site was repelled. On the following day, the Hmong mounted a counterattack, driving off all but a handful of Communist troops near the airstrip. This action was followed by American and RLAF air support; by March 12, the airstrip was reopened, operations rapidly returned to normal. and, the mission to retake LS-193 finally got underway. The Hmong and Lao government troops began their attack on the village of Ban Mok Plai on March 12, and it appeared they would take the objective with no difficulty; but the Communist troops put up a stiff resistance, and the attack stalled. On the following day, a Lao Neutralist paratroop battalion encircled the enemy and they retreated. It now appeared the village of Ban Mok Plai was in Lao control again. But the question remained as to how long they could hold the position.

The NVA subsequently began to resupply their troops in the Nam Bac area, and added two fresh infantry battalions to their ranks. By March 20, the Communist troops at Nam Bac were ready to fight, and they attacked the Lao and Hmong defenders at Ban Mok Plai. The Lao government responded by flying almost 100 sorties against the Communists, using the venerable T-28s. But the NVA increased its pressure on LS-193; and as the level of fighting increased, some Hmong defenders mistakenly assumed they were surrounded and began to retreat, as they customarily did, leaving weapons and equipment behind. But this time would be different, because the Communist troops were waiting for them . . . and they continued to wait until the Lao troops were completely ensnared. Then they systematically began to cut down the retreating troops, leaving more than 40 dead and 60 wounded. Recognizing the dire situation, the Lao government later airlifted a battalion of government troops into Ban Mok Plai, and the battle ended in a stalemate.

Also in March of 1967, USAF General Momyer paid a visit to NKP to inspect the troops and to assess the progress of the air war firsthand. While at the base, Momyer stumbled upon the fact that enlisted personnel and non-rated officers were being used as FACs to control air strikes over northern Laos. He was reportedly shocked and angered that he had not been briefed on the program, and ordered it to stop at once. Of course, his decision was made without benefit of any knowledge about the FAC program at all. Later, he cancelled the program completely; and as far as he was concerned, if FACs were needed, they would be selected from the pool of "rated" officers who had received FAC training. Just that quick, a successful program was cut short, leaving a void in FAC coverage until resources could be reassigned to satisfy the requirement.

Thirsting for more combat, the NVA initiated another attack on Nong Khang on April 3, in an attempt to retake the position. The bad weather since December 1966 had given the Communists ample time to resupply and regroup, and their confidence level was high. At first, the Hmong defenders held their ground; but as the fight intensified, the defenders became weary. They badly needed air support in order to repel the Communists, but no aircraft could respond because the area was completely socked in by dark, heavy clouds. As the day wore on the fighting continued, and by early evening the Hmong began to run out of ammunition. Without ammunition and air support, it was time to withdraw. Anticipating a retreat, the NVA left only one avenue of escape open for the defenders—and of course, as the weary Lao retreated, the Communists were waiting to finish them off. A good number of the defenders did survive the ordeal, but they were so demoralized they just simply walked away and went home.

That same month, Souvanna authorized the Neutralists to retake the Plain of Jars, inasmuch as they had controlled the Plain when the Geneva Accords had been reached back in 1962. Likewise, General Ouane wanted to occupy Muong Sai during the upcoming rainy season in order to protect Luang Prabang and Nam Bac. He also wanted enemy supply lines into Laos cut, and requested massive air power to destroy Communist armor on the Plain. Ouane believed that if the Plain was secure, the FAR could occupy the hills around the Plain and protect the residents living there. VP wasn't happy with Ouane's plan; however, because in his opinion the Hmong would do the majority of the heavy fighting, while the FAR would get all the credit. Instead, VP believed the Hmong guerrillas should concentrate on retaking lost Lima Sites and harassing the enemy.

Meanwhile, VP didn't waste any time in striking back at the Communists. On April 9, Hmong guerrillas attacked Chik Mok Lok; a 4,000-foot tall hill near Muong Penn. VP was backed up by about ten A-1 Skyraiders and about the same number of F-105 Thunderchiefs. By midday, the Hmong attackers were on the summit, after fierce hand-to-hand fighting and plenty of napalm and anti-personnel bombs—courtesy of the USAF. Having had enough, the NVA fled down the hill to safety. Later in the afternoon, the NVA retaliated by lying on a barrage of mortar fire, wounding a Hmong commander. The Communists then counterattacked and took the hill, forcing the defenders to flee in the direction of Phou Pha Thi.

Later in April, the NVA once again probed the perimeter of Na Khang. They were shocked to find that all the vegetation had been removed by the Americans, using a new defoliant called "Agent Orange." Without the cover of vegetation, the Communists were soon discovered and quickly routed by Hmong defenders. They retreated to the safety of the jungle, and waited for a better time to attack Na Khang.

In the spring of 1967, Vang Pao initiated several operations against the NVA. He also rotated the protectors at Na Khang with fresh troops and moved the other guerrillas to Phou Pha Louom, where the troops proceeded northward. These troops confronted the NVA on approximately ten occasions, and each time the Hmong held their ground. VP then used his militia forces in the vicinity of Phou Pha Thi, and they probed to the east towards Sam Neua. While this activity was taking place, VP joined forces with other guerrilla units from MR 5 to probe the mountainous region northeast of Vientiane. All the activity kept the NVA and Pathet Lao off-balance, and they were unable to mount a large offensive. Additionally, nighttime air sorties by A-26K Nimrods from NKP exacted additional losses on the Communist. By the end of April, the NVA had terminated their dry season offensive, electing to retreat to North Vietnam to resupply, refit, and prepare to fight another day.

In June, nightly air raids around Xieng Khouang and Phongsaly Provinces were flown by the Nimrods and flare ships. Using the Lao Forward Air Guides, NVA truck kills increased along Routes 6 and 68, and the total number of vehicles destroyed was estimated at about 90. Also, as mentioned earlier, the RC-47 ABCCC aircraft were replaced with the Lockheed EC-130. The EC-130 was basically a C-130 Hercules transport aircraft modified to carry a Communications module, and it flew in designated orbits, providing airborne command and control capability. Numerous tests were conducted to determine the best possible orbits, with safety and communications effectiveness being the primary factors. An ABCCC with the call sign "Hillsboro" orbited in southern Laos and controlled the air assets in Tiger Hound. "Cricket" was the daytime call sign for the ABCCC further north, and it controlled the air assets in Steel Tiger and Barrel Roll. Relieving Cricket at night was "Alley Cat." Similarly, "Moonbeam" relieved Hillsboro each day as the sun went down.

While in orbit, the ABCCCs were delegated authority to exercise command and control in areas controlled by the 7th Air Force. The primary mission of every orbit was to assure proper execution of all the assigned missions, and to control aircraft diverted to secondary targets. A typical work day for an ABCCC crew member lasted more than sixteen hours. The day usually began with a briefing for supervisors and crews, and included weather, intelligence, operations, and the sorties—or "frags," as they were called. After the briefings, the crew would obtain their personal gear and survival equipment prior to take-off, then make their way to the aircraft to get ready to fly. After takeoff, and upon reaching their orbit, the ABCCC would have many assets available to them, including FAC, illuminator, fighter, bomber, reconnaissance, and tanker aircraft. They also had a myriad of helicopters available as well. The communications module aboard the ABCCC included HF, VHF, UHF, secure voice, and secure data. They could contact all military, CIA and U.S. Embassy personnel as needed from the aircraft, eliminating delays and providing real-time instructions to the aircraft at their disposal.

Operationally, the ABCCC consistently improved its performance and more than fulfilled expectations. There were minor problems, of course, concerning personnel, maintenance and command and control; but these issues could all be worked out behind the scenes by the management types running the program. Initially, all ABCCC aircraft were assigned to Da Nang, but a case was later successfully made for moving the ABCCCs to Udorn. Back-and-forth territorial feuding soon developed, and continued until October 1968, when it was finally decided to house most of the assets at Udorn.

The rainy season of 1967 was late in coming that year, not arriving until July. The Lao and the NVA both welcomed the arrival of the rains, because by then, everyone was exhausted and just wanted to rest. But the NVA had failed to score any major victories during the dry season, and the Neutralists were still holding on at Muong Soui, if only because they were not being attacked. By 1967, generally speaking, the fighting ability of the Lao had improved, and even though corruption still ran deep in the government, the RLG had also improved. The departures of Thao Ma and Kong Le did not seem to affect the morale of the troops all that much; as a matter of fact, the Lao military appeared to be functioning rather smoothly. The other factor that weighed heavily in favor of the Lao at that particular moment was the American air power brought to bear against the Communists. Its effects were substantial. At the beginning of the year, the USAF had more than 400 aircraft in Thailand, flying missions in Laos and over North Vietnam almost every day.

Bolstered by gains made during his spring offensive, VP planned to initiate a strong rainy season offensive. As usual, he was promised additional air support from Barrel Roll assets, and was told he could also utilize the resources of the newly activated 56th Air Commando Wing at NKP. By July 23, the rainy season began in earnest. VP used his reserve guerrillas to probe Hua Moung, and then applied pressure at Samadhi and achieved victories at Sam Neua and Xieng Khouang. The Hmong were even able to stop fighting long enough to harvest rice in Moung Ngan, and seized the high ground in the region.

The CIA contingent in Vientiane was impressed with VP's gains, so they intended to increase the size of the guerrilla units and mold them into a light conventional force. The agency wanted to engage the NVA on an even larger scale and draw them into bigger battles, exposing them to even more devastating air assaults. VP also requested that the U.S. allow his Hmong pilots to fly the potent T-28s. The idea wasn't warmly received at first, but VP persisted, and eventually the U.S. relented. The first two Hmong pilot trainees were sent to the Waterpump training facility at Udorn. As predicted by VP, the program was a success, and the Hmong pilots received high marks. In fact, by 1971, over 60 Hmong pilots had graduated from Waterpump, and flew the T-28s on hundreds of sorties each. Of course, quite a few of these brave pilots perished under relentless NVA antiaircraft fire.

There was other activity occurring during the second half of 1967 that concerned the U.S. Embassy in Vientiane. Among other things, the NVA was working hard to improve Route 19 leading southwest from North Vietnam through Dien Bien Phu and into Laos—and historically, the Communists preferred to build a road first, and then use it to bring their army to the fight. It appeared that something big was in the planning process. Meanwhile, back at Nam Bac in northwestern Laos, the CIA's Eli Popovich was training Lao guerrilla units. Popovich was a seasoned paramilitary specialist with combat experience in Burma, Korea and China; he must have been pretty good at what he did, because his well-trained commandos soon conducted several successful hit-and-run attacks against NVA supply lines in the north. The Communists were not amused, however, and assembled a substantial force to retaliate.

Shortly thereafter, a North Vietnamese construction battalion began work on a road running from the border of North Vietnam directly to Popovich's headquarters in Nam Bac, and the NVA provided security for the construction team until the road was nearly finished. And sure enough, in July 1967, the NVA began their march towards Nam Bac—but rather than engaging the Lao guerrillas, the Communist troops continued on through Nam Bac to Luang Prabang. On July 16, a more destructive raid than the one executed in February was launched against the Luang Prabang airfield. A dozen sappers quietly entered the base and placed individual explosive charges on most of the T-28 aircraft located at the airfield. The intruders also rigged explosive charges near a portion of the ammunition dump.

Later, when the timed explosives detonated, three Lao soldiers were killed and eight were wounded. A portion of the ammunition dump also exploded, but fortunately the main portion of the dump failed to ignite. Nine of the eleven T-28 aircraft were completely destroyed in the attack, and once again, no Communist troops were killed or wounded.

In mid-September, Communist forces attacked the base again—and this time they overwhelmed the defenders, taking and holding the airfield. In response, the United States hastily diverted fast-moving jet fighters from the Plain of Jars to the Luang Prabang area, and the NVA was driven back northward. The RLA then decided to move a large mobile force into the Nam Bac valley to discourage any further NVA hostilities, while Ambassador Sullivan promised Souvanna that the lost T-28 aircraft would be replaced by assets from the MAP program as soon as replacements could be located. Shortly thereafter, the replacement aircraft began to arrive, a couple at a time, until all nine had been replaced, just as promised.

Meanwhile, in late July, the USAF began Operation "Knight Watch" to increase pressure on the enemy's lines of communications. Essentially, the operation consisted of utilizing Rolling Thunder jet fighters diverted from their primary missions due to weather reasons. If they couldn't hit their assigned targets in North Vietnam, they would be given new orders to divert to northern Laos, where waiting A-1s from NKP would guide them to priority targets. One such popular target was the NVA Command and Control Center complex near Sam Neua. A typical Knight Watch mission would begin with a group of fighters following the FAC to the target. After the targets were marked by the FAC, the jets would roll in and drop their bombs. This process would continue until the FAC was satisfied the maximum force had been expended, and then he would join up with other fighters waiting to drop their ordnance and guide them to other targets of opportunity. This scenario was played out over and over until all fighters dropped their bomb loads, whereupon they would scramble for home.

In the meantime, other designated A-1s loitered nearby in the event a SAR was initiated. The intent was for the A-1s to handle the rescue until it was either resolved, or they were relieved by other A-1s with fresh fuel and ordnance. During Knight Watch, however, no American aircraft were lost, so no SAR activity was ever launched for the operation. In fact, Knight Watch was quite successful, in that it was responsible for eliminating over 100 Communist antiaircraft weapons, more than 50 trucks, several storage depots, and various petrol farms, ammunition dumps, caves and buildings.

As Knight Watch continued, the RLG moved fresh troops into northern Laos to supplement the Hmong guerrillas . . . but the NVA matched them man for man, battalion for battalion. The CIA quickly recognized the problems associated with the build-up, and cautioned the Lao generals in Vientiane about any further escalation. But as usual, the Lao didn't listen. Colonel Pettigrew, the new AIRA in Vientiane, was also concerned, and blamed the Lao government's Tactical Headquarters, North—or "TAC North," as it was called. The problem was that Lao troops were only loosely controlled, considering themselves individual operating elements, each reporting directly to TAC North. This lack of unified command caused a rapid deterioration on the ground. Later, on August 31, the situation deteriorated even further when an RLAF T-28 mistakenly bombed a friendly position, causing the troops to flee in the direction of Nam Bac. Unfortunately, their hasty withdrawal left a big hole in the defenses, and the Communist troops literally walked in, paving the way for the complete capture of the valley.

By the time the Hmong guerrillas joined the fight, only one RLA battalion remained, and the defenders were completely surrounded by NVA soldiers pressing towards the Lao troops. The final assault began shortly thereafter. The RLA troops fought valiantly to the last man, and the NVA clean-up began in earnest. Fortunately, the Hmong guerrillas were eventually able to break out of the valley and escape, but by then, over 300 were dead. Nam Bac was subsequently lost to the Communists, and nothing stood between them and the Royal Capital of Luang Prabang.

In September, Souvanna appealed to the Americans for help in getting the situation under control. He wanted an immediate shipment of arms and ammunition, and he also wanted a senior American advisor assigned to Tac North. But the only available officer at that time was USAF Major Karl Leuschner, who ran the AOC at Luang Prabang. Nonetheless, he was assigned to the position—and it proved just as tough for him to get anything done as it had been for his U.S. Army counterpart previously. In order to accomplish the goals set by the Lao commanders, a large dose of air power would be required of the American and RLAF pilots, but unfortunately no effective air management system existed at that time. Instead, there were several layers of approval required to get anything done, and even then, the individual pilots were not permitted to correct discrepancies on the spot when the situation changed. Meanwhile, the NVA continued to tighten the noose, and by the end of the rainy season, everything in northwestern Laos, except the village of Nam Bac and a RLAF airstrip, was in Communist hands.

One of the biggest obstacles to having effective air power on the part of the RLAF was the fact that Thao Ma's departure had left the RLAF splintered into several groups. The fighter pilots considered themselves patriots who fought and died for their country. Then there were the transport pilots, who were more interested in making fortunes in opium smuggling than they were in defending the homeland. Below the pilots were the enlisted men, who got almost nothing and had no incentive to go the extra mile. Then there was the fourth group, the General Staff, headed up by General Sourith. This group talked a lot, but didn't follow their words up with action.

Meanwhile, in the northwest corner of Laos where Myanmar (Burma), Laos and China come together in what is commonly referred to as the "Golden Triangle," a different kind of war was about to erupt. Northwestern Laos was in Military Region I, and the Lao general in charge was Ouane Rathikone. General Ouane was a person who excelled in taking care of his own needs, desires and wants first; the Lao and the Secret War came second. Ouane's primary business was the drug trade, and opium was the jewel in the drug crown. When it came to drugs, Ouane would do whatever it took to monopolize the drug activity in the Golden Triangle. It was rumored that he often traded guns, equipment and ammunition provided by the CIA for the Secret War to the drug lords in exchange for opium and protection. There were other power brokers in the drug trade as well, but Ouane wanted it all for himself. So, in a cleverly devised scheme, he gave the appearance of providing a safe sanctuary for caravans of mules hauling over 16 tons of opium from Burma to a lumber mill he owned in northern Laos.

When the caravans arrived, they were being chased by Chinese bandits; and ultimately, all the players ended up in the lumber yard facing each other for a showdown. Ouane wasn't present; he was on a two-way radio ordering an air strike by RLAF T-28 aircraft. As the smugglers faced off against the Chinese, the T-28s strafed the lumber yard with machine gun fire, dropping their loads of cluster bombs on everyone below. The bombs did their job, wiping out just about everyone in the lumber mill yard, including the loaded mules. After it was all over, Ouane came in and took the opium for himself. This event became known in the media as the Opium War of 1967.

.According to other independent sources, the drug caravan butchered by Ouane belonged to Khun Sa, a Shan tribal warlord of Chinese descent also known as Chan Chi Foo. One recollection was that Khun Sa lost 70 mules, 37 men, and approximately 15 tons of opium in the Opium War. Another source indicated that 200 pack horses, more than 80 men, and about 10 tons of opium was lost during an assault by Kuomintang mercenaries and RLA troops loyal to Ouane Rathikone. In any case, the massacre brought the drug trade into the international spot light, and opened the door for many false reports of warlords being drug lords as well, so that everyone was tarnished by the publicity. Vang Pao was no exception; he was guilty by association.

We'll cover the drug trade in more detail in a later chapter. Meanwhile, we turn our attention back to events taking place in the Secret War. The USAF continued to plan and carry out air strikes while the RLAF floundered. On average, the Americans flew approximately 30 sorties a day against the Communists, while the RLAF, on a good day, might fly less than 20. Also during this period, construction of the Top Secret radar site at Phou Pha Thi (LS-85) was completed, and operational testing had begun. As mentioned earlier in the story, Admiral Sharp had approved the installation of the TACAN and TSQ radar equipment in early 1966, and construction began shortly thereafter. In November 1967, the installation was complete and the site was ready to go operational. The USAF personnel manning the site were all sheep-dipped and temporarily given jobs with Lockheed Corporation, the civilian contractor supporting the radar systems at the site. The nickname for the operation under direction from LS-85 was "Commando Club."

Figure 27. Radar Equipment for Phou Pha Thi (LS-85)
(Photo from the Public Domain)

The TACAN and TSQ-81 radar facilities[62] were situated on the western rim of a steep ridge above a helicopter landing zone about 300 yards away, at an elevation 200 feet below that of the facility. Near the helicopter pad, the CIA erected a command post and bunker which also served as a residence for the two CIA case officers assigned to LS-85. There were also several shacks where the local Hmong guerrillas and their families lived. From this location, the 200-man Hmong force protecting the top of the mountain gathered and received their daily briefings and assignments.

Early on, the United States developed a concept for the defense of the radar navigation facility at Pha Thi that relied on the remote location of the facility, the locals providing intelligence information in the area, and American airpower. The concept was based upon the belief that sufficient time would exist to anticipate an attack by the Communists. In other words, the brass felt that by the time the bad guys reached the summit of the mountain, the technicians running the site would already be evacuated to safety. This flawed belief also relied heavily on the local Hmong guerrilla leader and his knowledge of the terrain and people, including a network of local informants who kept their ears and eyes open to detect the enemy before they reached the mountain. The assumption was made that the commander would have sufficient time to communicate any threat to the CIA case officers on top of Pha Thi.

The plan for defense of LS-85 assumed that the Hmong would notify the Embassy when the attack was anticipated, and provide the Americans with target data. The embassy would then authorize the Hmong commander to notify the USAF team operating the radar navigation facility at the summit. The TSQ technicians would, in turn, relay the information to 7th Air Force and request air support. When air support arrived, they would deal with the advancing Communists; and as a last resort, the USAF personnel at the site would be evacuated and the equipment itself destroyed. In fact, the equipment at the facility was reportedly already rigged with explosive charges to facilitate destruction. On paper this entire scenario was a good one, but would the enemy follow the script, in the event they wanted to eliminate the TACAN/Radar site?

As soon as the North Vietnamese became aware of the radar site at Pha Thi, they realized the significance of the effect it could have on their efforts to expand the war in Laos and South Vietnam. After all, the radar site was only seventeen miles from their border. Not wasting any time, NVA engineers immediately began work on a road running from Sam Neua to Phou Pha Thi. As construction progressed, reconnaissance photos depicted the progress clearly—but the road's progress didn't alarm many of the American leaders, because it was assumed the airmen manning the site could be evacuated and the radar destroyed should an attack take place. Ambassador Sullivan believed it also, although he didn't feel comfortable with a radar navigation facility being located on the summit of Pha Thi.

By October 1967, the rains had ended in Laos and the roads were dry, in spite of efforts by Operation Popeye to extend the rainy season. The rainy season had in fact been light, allowing the NVA to hold most of their strong positions. Taking advantage of the dry conditions, the Communists immediately began an ambitious program of road repair throughout northeastern Laos. Hmong Road Watch Teams observed the activity, and reported increasing amounts of heavy equipment working on Routes 6, 7 and 19. The roads leading to Nam Bac and Pha Thi were also being rapidly repaired. But there had been little progress on the ground by Lao government forces during the rainy season, except for some success on the part of Vang Pao's Hmong guerrillas. Meanwhile, the situation in Nam Bac continued to deteriorate, and dissension within the ranks of the Lao military continued. Also, at the rapid rate that the roads were being repaired, the NVA would be ready to begin resupplying their troops in the field by November.

In order to deal with the expanding Communist threat, a meeting was called at Udorn between Ambassador Sullivan, Generals Westmoreland and Momyer, and representatives of the State Department. During the meeting, a three-phase attack plan was agreed upon to interdict supplies and NVA troops flowing into South Vietnam. The first phase was a concentrated bombing of stockpiled Communist supplies in the mountain passes where North Vietnam enters Laos. Phase Two would entail interdicting supplies flowing down the Ho Chi Minh Trail, while Phase Three would focus on bombing stockpiled supplies where the Trail left Laos and entered South Vietnam. This plan did not suggest that interdiction efforts weren't previously underway; rather, its intent was to concentrate more strikes on the Communists in order to stem the flow of supplies to the NVA troops in the south.

In an effort to clarify U.S. policy as related to Laos, the American Embassy in Vientiane developed a position paper intended to provide broad guidance to the various U.S. agencies involved, but did not specify approaches to policy. The paper, entitled "U.S. Policy with Respect to North Laos," was then placed in the coordination cycle; but by the time it was actually published, it was nothing more than a watered-down philosophical document offering little substance. After the document was published, it was largely ignored by the CIA, which always pursued its own objectives in any case. Their focus was the Secret War, managed by a handful of case officers, contractors and VP's guerrillas. Meanwhile, the military attachés at the embassy were busy trying to support the Lao military without stepping on the toes of the CIA or the State Department. It was a delicate balancing act, but somehow it always seemed to work.

These U.S. military officers also walked a fine line between the military brass in Saigon, Udorn, Honolulu, and the Philippines, in that the attachés had to find some way to keep all the brass happy. Somewhere in this dysfunctional bureaucracy were hard-working officers and enlisted men trying desperately to combat the expanding

Communist presence in northern Laos—but they were hard to find. There were some bright spots in this chaotic environment, however. The USAF was averaging approximately 30 sorties a day in northern Laos, and impressive results were tallied during the dry season of 1967. Almost 200 NVA trucks were attacked, and many of those were crippled or eliminated. During the first two weeks of November, for example, almost 30 targets were eliminated, including supply depots, ammunition dumps and fuel storage areas. Also, in one air attack on NVA soldiers, over 300 were killed. In the latter part of November, air attacks eliminated more than 40 buildings and resulted in almost 20 large secondary explosions. The raids continued into December, with major raids against truck parks and Communist military complexes.

Meanwhile, the situation at Nam Bac became critical. The Lao defenders were taking no action to thwart the Communist build-up; instead they just hunkered down in place. Meanwhile, the NVA quietly continued to build up their forces around the valley, and simply waited until they were ready to attack.

In late November, the Communists beefed up their forces in Laos with several more NVA battalions, and began clearing operations in the vicinity of Routes 6, 68 and 611. All three of these roads were vital to North Vietnam, because they fed traffic from the DRV into Laos through the Plain of Jars. First the Communists attacked Ban Nhot Phat (LS-179). Next, they moved on to Phou Pha Louom (LS-220) and then Phou Den Din, which was only 12 kilometers from Pha Thi. Sporadic fighting continued into December 1968. Meanwhile, the radar/TACAN site at Phou Pha Thi was completely operational, directing air strikes on a daily basis. Simultaneously, construction of the Communist road towards LS-85 continued unabated.

In December 1967, a CIA representative briefed CINCPACAF of upcoming Communist objectives in Laos. According to the official, the NVA would continue to provide stiffeners to the Pathet Lao, and would send as much help as the Pathet Lao needed on short notice. Of course, the enemy depended almost completely on dry roads, so any large offensive operation would have to take place during the dry season (October thru June). The CIA representative also indicated the NVA would continue to clear out all of Vang Pao's guerrillas in most of northern Laos, and try to keep the Hmong general tied up in the areas around Vientiane to reduce the likelihood of reinforcements being sent to the north.

On December 28, an F-4D Phantom from Ubon was flying a night mission in Laos under FAC control and making a run over the enemy using rockets, when it was hit by heavy machine gun fire from the ground and burst into flames. The crew of two safely ejected, with one airman landing on the ground and another landing in a tree when his parachute caught the upper branches. Both crewmen activated their survival radios and reported their positions. A SAR was subsequently initiated and rescue aircraft scrambled to reach the scene, and an airborne flare ship, Lamplighter 1, was sent to offer illumination support. Upon arrival over the crash scene, an assisting A-1 Skyraider began to take ground fire. Not long after that, it began to get dark, and it couldn't be determined how many troops the NVA had in the area. For those reasons, the SAR was suspended until daybreak on December 29.

The rescue force returned the following morning, and the pilot was picked up safely. A USAF Para rescue specialist was then put on the ground near the crewmember hanging in the tree. The rescue specialist was able to cut the injured crewmember out of his parachute, and he was hoisted safely onto the hovering SAR helicopter along with the rescue specialist. All aircraft and crews then safely returned to their bases, and both of the downed airmen were safe, thanks to the heroic efforts of the SAR team.

Meanwhile, at Nam Bac, the situation had become grave. The Lao troops outnumbered the enemy three to one, but additional NVA troops kept arriving to bolster the Communist ranks. They also controlled the roads leading into the Nam Bac valley, so supplies to the Lao troops had to be air-dropped by Air America and the RLAF. Harassment attacks by VP's guerrillas at Muong Sing, Nam Tha, Muong Sai helped, because they caused the NVA to keep their heads down. VP also moved almost 300 troops close to Muong Ngoi to support the other Lao troops, but he held short, waiting for assurance that the Lao forces were ready to assist in any attack.

But help from the RLG troops would probably not be forthcoming, because the Lao commander—Colonel Savatphayphane Bounchanh, a protégé of General Ouane—had not even developed a plan of attack. And the assistant AIRA couldn't plan any air support, because Bounchanh hadn't given him any requirements. It didn't really matter in any case, because in late December, the Lao had decided to abandon Nam Bac; instead of defending the valley, they planned a breakout. Essentially, their plan was to airlift large numbers of Lao troops out of the Nam Bac valley and have the remainder fight their way out, eliminating as many Communists as possible in the process.

Later, during the last days of 1967, President Johnson once again ordered a Christmas pause in the bombing of North Vietnam, in hopes that Hanoi would agree to peace talks in the coming year. As we have pointed out previously, the NVA had no intention of seriously talking peace, but were thrilled about the bombing pause because, it would give them plenty of time to complete the installation of hundreds of new Surface to Air Missile (SAM) sites in North Vietnam. Many American fighter aircraft and crews would soon be lost due to the existence of these new SAM sites.

In the meantime, the NVA got wind of the Lao plan to break out of Nam Bac, and rushed approximately 5,000 fresh troops to engage the remaining Lao. In late December, the Lao evacuation operation got underway as planned, with a large number of Lao troops being airlifted out of Nam Bac to Muong Ngoi, where they joined up with Vang Pao's troops. When this happened, the remaining troops at Nam Bac suddenly lost the will to fight, refusing to engage the Communist troops in a breakout. Instead, they retreated further into the valley, and began to disband and look for possible avenues of escape.

But as more NVA troops continued to arrive, the noose around the necks of the remaining Lao troops began to tighten. Soon the Communist troops began their advance, systematically eliminating all resistance. By January 14, 1968, the entire valley was in Communist hands, and the only thing left to do was to call in the fast-moving American fighters to destroy the supplies and equipment left behind by the retreating Lao troops.

The American Embassy in Vientiane was stunned. They couldn't believe what had happened. In fact, Ambassador Sullivan stated that it was the largest military disaster in the history of Laos—and the loss of over one million dollars worth of MAP equipment and supplies didn't bolster his spirits either. Then, about two days after Nam Bac fell, Colonel Bounchanh and two of his officers were found walking out of the valley on foot. The trio were picked up by helicopter and returned to a safe location. After the fiasco, many demanded action against Bounchanh; but inasmuch as he was an associate of General Ouane, no action was taken, and his military career did not suffer.

Chapter 8

The Ravens

While the fighting continues to escalate in northern Laos, we should pause for a moment to discuss two subjects that greatly influenced the Secret War: the Forward Air Controller (FAC) group that called itself "the Ravens," and the drug trade. In this chapter we'll address the significant role played by the Ravens during the latter half of the Secret War; in Chapter 9, we'll take a look at the ways that the inescapable drug trade impacted the war and everyday life in Laos.

The Ravens[63] were officially formed in approximately 1966, and started showing up in Laos in 1967. By then, the U.S. Embassy in Vientiane had begun to realize that with the increased bombing in the kingdom, permanent FAC support was needed to maximize bombing accuracy and to minimize damage to civilians—and that as the war expanded, a continuing supply line for replacement FACs would be required. Furthermore, as Vang Pao expanded his forces, he would also require more air support.

Prior to 1967, the United States had tried to handle the FAC requirements by using enlisted USAF combat controllers, non-rated officers, and AOC personnel riding in Air America STOL aircraft. The airmen would sit in the back seat and, using air-to-ground radios and intelligence data, direct American strike aircraft flying interdiction missions. This method of forward air control worked in the beginning, when the war was small and the NVA were conducting operations on a smaller scale; but with the increasing numbers of NVA troops in Laos, it soon became much less effective. In addition to FAC support requirements, the U.S. military needed their own FAC aircraft; and last but certainly not least, early in 1967, General Momyer had ordered an end to the use of enlisted and non-rated officer personnel as FACs (see Chapter 7). Unfortunately, there was a problem with expanding military FAC support in Laos, because the Geneva Accords prohibited the presence of U.S. troops in country. But not to worry, since the U.S. had already violated the Accords (as the NVA had done from the very beginning) by introducing sheep-dipped U.S. military personnel to handle some specialized tasks. Since the horse was already out of the barn, the decision-makers reasoned, why not just continue on down that path?

Given the need for dedicated FACs in Laos, and also to provide *some* appearance of adhering to the Geneva Accords, the USAF created the Steve Canyon Program. As you may or may not recall (depending upon your age), *Steve Canyon* was a comic strip that ran from 1947 to 1988. The lead character, Steve, was a handsome young man with a clean-cut, square-jawed appearance. He usually wore flight coveralls and slept in his office, he had a soft spot for attractive women—and he was always looking for adventure. It was a perfect cover story for the Ravens, given the similarities.

At this point in time, USAF military FACs were already operating in South Vietnam, using Cessna L-19 observation aircraft. (The military version of the L-19 was called the "O-1 Bird Dog"). It was a modified Cessna Model 305A: a single-engine, lightweight, strut-braced, high-wing monoplane with tail-wheel landing gear. It also had only two seats in tandem, with angled side windows to

Figure 28. Comic Strip Depictions of Steve Canyon
(From the Public Domain)

improve ground observation. Other differences included a redesigned rear fuselage, allowing a view directly to the rear; transparent panels in the wings' center sections, allowing the pilot look directly overhead; and several minor modifications to fulfill military requirements. The O-1 cruised at 178 miles per hour, its range was 530 miles, and it flew at roughly 20,000 feet. During the Vietnam War, the USAF lost more than 170 Bird Dogs in combat, and in 1974, the USAF replaced them with the two-engine Cessna O-2 Skymaster. The Ravens also used a slightly more powerful Cessna, called the U-17.

Early on, in order to get volunteers for FAC duty in Laos, personnel already performing as FACs in South Vietnam were told, in very general terms, about the new program. They weren't told much—just enough to pique their interest and provide fuel to generate discussion. Frankly, they *couldn't* be told very much about the program, because it directly violated the Geneva Accords. But the small amount of information given to the FACs in South Vietnam was enough to entice the most adventuresome pilots. Most of them were tired of flying around South Vietnam anyway, and needed fresh stimulation.

So it didn't take long for the FACs to ask for more information about Steve Canyon. Those expressing genuine interest would be given a cursory briefing, still without much detail; it provided just enough well-placed information to leave them wanting more. The pilots were also told that when, and if, they volunteered for the program, they would be given only one chance to back out. Usually they didn't. Those who persisted were given another cursory briefing and told they were to continue their duties in South Vietnam, pending contact at a later time. Their names were then forwarded to the program managers. Those selected for duty in the program subsequently disappeared from the rolls in their units of assignment, and later mysteriously reappeared in northern Laos.

As it turned out, there weren't enough volunteers coming from South Vietnam to fill all the Raven FAC slots in Laos; so back in the United States, aviators who were finishing up initial pilot training also began to hear about the Steve Canyon Program. Soon volunteers began coming forward. But the path from the U.S. to Laos took bit longer to negotiate than the one from South Vietnam. After acceptance to the program, the new pilots went to the Special Air

Warfare Center (SAWC) at Hurlburt Field #9 in Fort Walton Beach, Florida for training in the O-1 Bird Dog. After qualifying in the O-1, the pilots were sent to southern Florida for water survival training. Next, they were shuffled to Fairchild AFB in Washington for survival training. From there they traveled to the Pacific Jungle Survival School (Snake School) at Clark Air Base in the Philippines to learn how to evade, escape, and survive in a hostile jungle environment. After all these obstacles had been successfully negotiated, the selectees were flown to Thailand with instructions to report to Detachment 1, 56th Special Operations Wing, Nakhon Phanom, Thailand. Detachment 1 wasn't actually located at NKP, but at Udorn Air Base. Upon arrival at Udorn, the pilots were required to turn in all identification and all their military uniforms and gear. Each pilot's personal effects were then stored away in wooden lockers.

A day or so later, bright and early in the morning, the pilots—now sporting casual civilian attire—boarded an Air America aircraft for a short flight to Vientiane. Upon arrival in Laos, they received yet another briefing at the U.S. Embassy, where they learned exactly what their job would entail: flying the O-1 Bird Dog over some of the most inhospitable territory in the world, while performing FAC duties.[64] They were also given new documents identifying them as forest rangers who worked for USAID in Vientiane. With all that completed, they were officially sheep-dipped. That same night, other sheep-dipped U.S. military personnel in Vientiane would take the newcomers out for dinner and drinks on the town. Early the next morning, the pilots would climb into another Air America aircraft for a short flight to one of the five RLG military regions (MRs).

Once they reached their destinations, they reported to the AOC commander, who brought them up to speed on conditions in the area. Then, for the next six or more months, the pilots performed Raven duties in the hostile Laotian skies. Usually, Military Regions 1, 3, 4, and 5 were assigned one Raven each, though depending on the level of fighting, more than one could be assigned. But at Long Tieng—or Secret War Central, as it was also known—it wasn't uncommon to find anywhere from 6-12 Ravens assigned to support Vang Pao. After all, this was the hub of all action in Laos. Realistically, it didn't matter where in Laos a Raven was assigned, because they could be just about anywhere in Laos in less than an hour by air. In other words, on any given day, if something was going on in a particular region, any number of Ravens could be sent there to help carry out the mission. These brave airmen soon became a close-knit group, working together for the common good.

The center of activity in each region was the AOC; everything started and ended there. On most mornings, the AOC commander held an informal meeting with the resident Raven(s), the Intelligence officer, and all other personnel involved in the daily prosecution of the Secret War. Targets, NVA activity and all known threats were discussed. Upon adjournment, they would all leave and go immediately to work. For the Raven FAC, that meant getting in his Bird Dog and climbing into the sky for a long day of excitement—and terror.

Essentially, what a FAC did was to fly over areas of known or suspected Communist activity, looking for a number of things: troop movement, equipment movement, enemy storage facilities, or anything else that needed to be eliminated. When he spotted something important, the information was radioed to the AOC. The information was evaluated, and higher headquarters was notified when an air strike was required. If fighters were summoned, the FAC would loiter near the target and wait for the fighter aircraft to arrive overhead. Once the fighters were on station, the Raven would describe the target and its exact location. The fighter aircraft then lined up for their bomb runs.

When everyone was ready, the Raven would swoop down towards the target and fire wing-mounted smoke rockets to mark the target, then climb to a safe altitude overhead and call in the fighter aircraft. One by one, the fighters would dive in and make their bomb runs while the Raven watched from above. As the bombing progressed, the Raven would call in corrections to the fighter pilots, if necessary, and the bombing and strafing would continue until all ordnance had been expended.

Then the fighters would scramble for home, because by then, they would be running low on fuel. The Raven would return to the target area and make repeated passes to complete a Bomb Damage Assessment (BDA). After completing the BDA, he would radio the information to the AOC, which would, in turn, notify all the appropriate agencies.

If a Raven's work day sounds like a long one, that's because that's exactly the way it was. He started his day at just about daylight by going over weather reports and intelligence summaries. Then he had the informal meetings with the AOC staff. Next, he went out and checked his aircraft from nose to tail. He also performed minor repairs if needed, because for the most part, onsite mechanics were not available. Next, he made sure the bird was fueled and armed with smoke rockets. Later, as the sun came up and the thick clouds parted, the Raven took to the air with a USAF-issued .38 caliber, five-shot Smith & Wesson revolver strapped on his hip for protection. After that he would fly to his designated area, direct air strikes all day, and then land for the final time just as the sun disappeared over the horizon.

In MR 2, planning the war was accomplished informally at VP's residence every evening. The key players were usually there: the CIA, the senior Raven, Hmong officers, Air America personnel, the AOC commander, and occasionally Pop Buell. When a new Raven arrived at Long Tieng, the senior Raven would bring him along for introductions to all the key players. A meal would be served at a long table, low to the floor in the main hall. There would be baskets of sticky rice, vegetables, and spices placed at intervals along the table. If it was available, there would also be plates of meat.

VP would sit in the center of the table with his advisors beside him. The other attendees would then spread out around the table, and the meal would be consumed. After the meal, everyone would move to VP's operations room, where he would brief the group. He would go over the events of the day, including what had gone wrong, what had gone right, and other important information. Plans for the next day would follow, with VP pointing out the scope of operation and the logistics required. He would let the key players know what was expected of them, and answer any questions before concluding the meeting.

After dinner, the new Raven would be taken to the Air America bar at Long Tieng for introductions and a drink, and then over to the CIA bar for more introductions and drinks. In order to enter the latter bar, you had to pass by a large cage containing two black Himalayan mountain bears named Floyd and Mama Bear. Over the years, it seemed that Floyd had developed a taste for beer. He would drink as much as he was given, so during any given evening, many cans of beer would be opened and placed on a shelf near the cage. Floyd would pick up the cans, one by one, and drink them down. After

Floyd had consumed large quantities of beer, he would spend much of the following day nursing a hangover in a cave behind the cage.

Meanwhile, inside the CIA bar, the new Raven would meet many unusual and quirky individuals who worked for the CIA, the Department of State, USAID and Air America. The conversations were usually lively with tales of heroism, misfortune and conquest. There might also be a game of pool in progress, and of course the endless card games that took place nightly. After a whirlwind tour of Long Tieng, the newcomer would be taken back to the Raven's bungalow to ponder events of the day and prepare for the following day.

In addition to flying Forward Air Controller duties, the Ravens also participated in search and rescues, and provided support to Air America. If needed (or if desired), they could go fly the T-28 Trojan, and drop bombs and shoot real bullets at the Communists.

To say that the Ravens were among the most hard-working and dedicated professionals you could meet would be an understatement. By the end of the Secret War, many downed pilots and thousands of troops on the ground owed their lives to the Ravens.

A little earlier, we mentioned that most volunteers for duty with the Ravens had certain traits that were advantageous for FAC duty. For example, a Raven needed to be able to take care of himself. This wasn't a job for whiners or the faint of heart. Most of the pilots who volunteered were adventurous and individualistic, with a hint of disregard for the spit-and-polish image of most military personnel. They didn't wear uniforms, their hair wasn't always neatly trimmed, and their moustaches extended past the corners of their mouths. It also wasn't wise to walk around exchanging salutes either, what with the occasional snipers lurking in the hills overlooking Long Tieng. Needless to say, the Ravens' typical persona didn't sit well with the military brass at Udorn, and certainly not with the generals in Saigon and Hawaii. But the ambassador himself was pleased with the Ravens, and didn't want them to be other than the way they were. And remember: roughly half of the Ravens assigned to Laos came home in aluminum caskets—and some were never found after being shot out of the sky.

In the latter half of 1969, the USAF brass began to take an interest in the Secret War. They all wanted to see this mysterious place called Long Tieng, and naturally they wanted one of the much-prized pictures showing them standing next to Vang Pao. Not only that, they wanted very much to take more control of their pilots operating out of Long Tieng. But the generals weren't the only ones who wanted to see the place that had become famous as Secret War Central: Congressmen, Senators, and other do-gooders also came to visit.

As the story goes, one nosey general from Udorn arrived at Long Tieng without even telling anyone he was coming. Suffice it to say, when the general showed up unannounced, he was, for the most part, ignored. But he didn't stand back and remain silent, because after all he was a general, and should have some influence over the pilots who served at Long Tieng in the famed Ravens unit. So the general went around asking a lot of questions—to the point that he irritated some of the CIA personnel. In fact, they reportedly wound up throwing the general's aide out of the Agency's bar, and onto the top of a cage holding the two wild bears.

Not being one to take this sort of treatment lying down, the general returned to his office at Udorn and made it known to everyone who would listen that he objected to the obnoxious behavior of the Ravens, whom he considered to be "uncivilized, and no better than common bandits." It didn't take long for this information to get back to the Ravens at Long Tieng, and so they reportedly sent the general a holiday greeting card, containing a thank you note and a photograph of several of the Ravens dressed up like Mexican bandits.

To outsiders, it may have appeared that the Ravens were a gang of undisciplined, crude misfits who spent most of their time drinking and behaving in an obnoxious manner—but that simply wasn't the case. They were all true patriots, who defended freedom and gave their all for America. It cannot be denied, however, that the war did harden them psychologically; if it hadn't, their survival rate might have been even lower than it was. Half of the Ravens were killed while assigned to Laos, and they all witnessed death and destruction every single day—so it was no wonder their behavior was viewed by some as being somewhat odd.

In addition to the brave USAF pilots who flew and fought against Communism in Laos, there was at least one U.S. Army Raven. His name was Joseph K. Bush, and he was from Temple, Texas. Bush was officially assigned to JUSMAGTHAI as an advisor in northern Laos, but he also flew the O-1 Bird Dog as a Raven. His duties were essentially the same as the other Ravens at Long Tieng: he flew in support of VP and the Hmong guerrillas. But Captain Bush's life was unfortunately cut short on February 10, 1969 at Muong Soui. Early that morning, NVA soldiers attacked the compound where Bush worked with grenades, automatic weapons and satchel charges. The site was only lightly defended, and Captain Bush fought valiantly to save the others in the compound, sacrificing his own life while doing so. For his gallantry, he was posthumously awarded the Silver Star.

Another example of good lives being cut short involved Captain Richard Elzinga, a brand new volunteer who had arrived in Laos on or about March 24, 1970, and First Lieutenant Hank Allen, whose tour as a Raven was nearly finished by then. Hank had flown roughly 400 air combat missions, and was eager to return to his fiancée, marriage and the good old US of A.

Earlier in 1970, Long Tieng had been attacked. It was no longer a safe place to park airplanes overnight, so the Ravens had been bunking down in Vientiane. They would leave Wattay Airport when the sun came up, fly to Long Tieng, plan their missions, fly all day, and return to Vientiane as the sun went down. On the morning of March 26, Hank Allen and Dick Elzinga departed Wattay early. Elzinga was in the front seat of the plane, Allen in back, headed for Long Tieng on what was supposed to be Elzinga's check ride. As they took off, they radioed the tower that they were in the air. It was the last time anyone ever heard from the two Ravens. When they didn't show up at Long Tieng later that morning, the other Ravens became concerned, but they were already busy flying sorties in support of VP. At the end of the day, however, they started flying the route Allen would have taken from Vientiane, diligently searching for some clue as to what happened to the two aviators. But no trace whatsoever could be found of them or the plane.

They continued searching for days, without success, and Allen and Elzinga were subsequently listed as MIA. Days turned into weeks, weeks into month, and months into years. A few years later, on March 10, 1973, a Pathet Lao soldier was captured—and while he was being searched, three traveler's checks in Elzinga's name were found in the prisoner's pockets, along with currency from three countries. The prisoner was subsequent interrogated, but he did not reveal any information that could be used to determine either Captain Elzinga's fate, or Lieutenant Allen's.

Death was the Raven's constant companion—and despite the fact that half of them eventually succumbed, most Ravens wouldn't hesitate to fly into its teeth in order to get the job done. Death was the Raven's constant companion—and despite the fact that half of them eventually succumbed, most Ravens wouldn't hesitate to fly into its teeth in order to get the job done. A typical example involved USAF Captain Michael E. Cavanaugh, who participated in the evacuation of Muong Soui in June 1969. Cavanaugh and his Hmong backseater (observer) were directing air strikes near Ban Ban. As the day slowly wound down, it was time to head for Long Tieng and call it a day. While enroute to the Alternate, Captain Cavanaugh realized that he needed fuel. He notified Vientiane of his situation and was told that the nearest fuel was stored in a bunker near the end of the runway at Muong Soui. He was also told that the NVA were all over the site and it wasn't safe to land. Nonetheless, Cavanaugh turned his aircraft in the direction of Muong Soui, headed for the airstrip and the much-needed fuel. An A-1 Skyraider was also in the area, and he also proceeded to Moung Soui, where he hosed down the Communists at the airstrip with cannon fire. Cavanaugh landed his O-1 and taxied to the far end of the runway. He jumped out of the O-1 and ran for the bunker. He quickly found a 55 gallon drum of fuel and began rolling it towards the O-1. His backseater grabbed a hand pump and prepared to pump the fuel. By this time, the NVA began firing in the direction of the bunker where the O-1 was parked. Cavanaugh was had a difficult unscrewing the cap on the drum so he grabbed his .38 caliber revolver and began pounding on the screw cap. Finally, the cap began to turn, and he removed it. He and his backseater then took turns with pumping fuel into the O-1. Meanwhile, incoming automatic weapons fire continued. After filling of the wing tanks, Cavanaugh fired up the engine. By this time it was dark, and his aircraft lights and instruments did not work. Fortunately, another A-1 dropped napalm at the other end of the runway, and Cavanaugh turned his O-1 in the direction of the flames. He jammed the throttle forward, and released his brakes. Having no instrument lights, he did not know what his speed was, so when the engine sounded right, Captain Cavanaugh pulled back on the stick, and the little aircraft began to climb. Once airborne, he then headed for Luang Prabang, and landed safely a little while later. For Mike, It was just another day at the office.

In the final analysis, the Ravens were outstanding aviators, and their bravery and sacrifice were unmatched. Everyone who took the opportunity to watch the Ravens work would vouch for that. Those Ravens fortunate enough to return from the war have gone on with their lives. Some went on to achieve their original goals of accomplishment in the Air Force; others were unable to achieve the level of success they desired, many because they felt they just didn't fit the traditional career officer mold. And then there are those like Fred Platt, who sustained debilitating wounds during the war and lives in excruciating pain every day of his life.

During the Vietnam War, more than 130 pilots participated in the Steve Canyon Program. More than 170 USAF O-1 Bird Dogs were lost, with three of those being shot down by NVA SAMs. But thousands of FAC missions were successfully flown by the Ravens.

After the Secret War ended, the surviving Ravens agreed to meet once each year, to reminisce about their experiences during the war and to salute those who hadn't been able to make it home. To this day they're still getting together, and they're involved in many worthwhile charities and public services. They gave their all for freedom, in support of our great nation, and they keep giving. That's what sets them apart from others, and makes them true heroes.[65]

Chapter 9

The Drug Trade

At this juncture, we also need to address the drug trade in Laos, inasmuch as it was intertwined with the Secret War—so much so that at times, it was hard to separate one from the other. The drug trade took place throughout the country, and helped to fuel the widespread corruption that permeated the Laotian government. But we should be clear as to what we're talking about when we use the term "drug trade." We're not referring to the production or sale of drugs such as marijuana, Thai Sticks, or hashish. While these drugs were all very popular with American military personnel and Western visitors, they were hardly the big ticket item in Laos. What we're talking about here is opium.

By the time Laos became embroiled in the Secret War, opium had been legally grown, harvested and sold in the little kingdom for centuries. The drug itself is a resinous narcotic formed from the latex released by lacerating (scoring) the seed pods of opium from the species *Papaver Somniferum*. It contains up to 16% morphine, an opiate alkaloid. Cultivation of opium for food, anesthesia, and ritual use dates back to the Stone Age, and ancient empires used opium as a potent form of pain relief. Morphine, a derivative of Opium, is still used extensively throughout the world today by surgeons and hospital staff as an anesthesia and painkiller.

By the early 1500s, however, opium was consumed in China for recreational purposes, and by the eighteenth century, it became even more popular after users began to mix it with tobacco for smoking. At about this same time, addiction also began to surface as a serious problem, and so the Chinese

Figure 29. Opium Poppy Field and Harvesting
(Photo from the Public Domain)

government banned the use of opium for recreational purposes in 1729. That's not to say that the use of opium stopped, because it didn't; it was still used extensively, albeit illegally. Its use as a recreational drug in other countries, however, remained rare into the late nineteenth century.

Prior to World War II, all countries in Southeast Asia had government-controlled opium monopolies, similar to our tobacco monopolies today; but it was illegal to smuggle opium and to trade it without a license. Following China's lead, Thailand had banned its use in 1811. Meanwhile, the British East India Company initiated large-scale production of opium in India, and was looking for new export markets in Southeast Asia. In 1852, King Mongkut (Rama IV) of Siam (Thailand) gave in to pressure from Britain and established a royal opium franchise, run by wealthy Chinese traders. Opium, lottery, gambling, and alcohol permits soon began to spread, and by the end of the 1800s, taxes on these monopolies provided nearly fifty percent of the Siamese government's revenues.

Lack of access to the Chinese opium trade led the British to attack China in July 1842, and a month later China was defeated. A treaty was subsequently signed, and China paid Britain $21,000,000 in reparations, ceded the island of Hong Kong to Queen Victoria, and opened five ports to the British. Friction persisted between the two countries, however, and Britain attacked again in 1856. By 1860, China was defeated a second time.

International regulation of opium did not begin until about 1870, leading to the formation of the International Opium Commission in 1909.[66] The global production of opium peaked in approximately

1906, when over 40,000 tons were harvested. Most of the opium produced was consumed in China, leaving only about 2,000 tons available to the rest of the world for recreational and medical use. Since that time, production has steadily decreased.

Even after China banned the recreational use of opium, it continued to be used legally in the form of patent medicines. The Mao Zedong government is credited with eradicating both consumption and production of opium in China in the 1950s, during the Cultural Revolution. Addicts were forced into treatment and the dealers were executed, forcing opium production to move south into the region known as the Golden Triangle, where Myanmar, Laos, and China meet.

During the French occupation of Indochina, from approximately the mid-1800s until 1954, the French government firmly controlled the opium market, encouraging its cultivation, sale, and usage. The French military became the purchasers, or middlemen, buying directly from the farmers. They would then take the opium to Saigon, and sell it to organized Vietnamese syndicates that controlled the opium smoking dens. The French even encouraged the proliferation of opium dens. As the primary, and just about only, cash crop in Laos, opium represented the only real avenue for the French to make any money there. A portion of the profits from their sale of opium went into their operating budget, and the monies were also used to finance their military operations against the Vietminh.

Make no mistake about it: there was big money to be made in the opium business, especially in the Golden Triangle region. After the French departed Laos, the Corsicans, Vietnamese, Chinese, and some Lao businessmen moved in and took over the purchase and resale of opium produced in the mountains, to a large extent by the Hmong. One such businessman was General Ouane Rathikone. As the demand for opium increased rapidly, even as the supply decreased, the opium poppy became a valuable cash crop to the hill tribes in Southeast Asia. It soon replaced other traditional crops, because the average farmer could earn more than five times his normal income by cultivating opium.

The leading producer of illegal opium in the world is currently Afghanistan, followed by Pakistan and the Golden Triangle region. In addition, India and Turkey still legally produce opium for export to licensed pharmaceutical companies around the world.

In the introduction to this book, it was explained that Laos lacked expansive areas of land suitable for agriculture on a large scale; as a matter of fact, only about five percent of the land was arable. Also, the country was poor in natural resources; in other words, there were no large deposits of gold, silver, and other minerals available for exploitation. By default, opium became, essentially, the only cash crop. Otherwise, the Hmong were, for the most part, subsistence farmers. They tended small plots of land where they planted vegetables, rice, and opium. The rice and vegetables were consumed by the farmer and his family, the opium by others. The drug was not widely used in Laos as a recreational drug, but it was occasionally used for medicinal purposes, and as a pain reliever for old people suffering from disease.

The opium was harvested by the farmer, taken to the local village, and sold to a middleman for roughly the equivalent of $50 (U.S.) per kilogram.[67] After the middlemen purchased the opium from individual villagers, they would combine the small lots into kilogram-size "sticky bricks." Later, at a particular time each year, the opium buyers would travel to Laos and purchase the sticky bricks from the local dealers. As mentioned previously, roads in Laos were few and unimproved, so most buyers would fly into the towns with an airstrip. They would then set up shop, and the dealers from around the area would bring their opium in for resale. A good example of this type of transaction involved the town of Phong Saly in northern Laos, which had a large market and its own airfield. This led to it becoming a center of the Laotian opium trade.

After buying all the available opium in Laos, the buyers would get back in their airplanes and fly the opium to Saigon, where it would be sold again to large-scale buyers with access to laboratories in Vietnam and Europe. Meanwhile, the farmers who had grown and harvested the opium would take the money they earned and buy salt, spices and staple food stuffs they couldn't otherwise grow. They might also buy cloth for making clothing, or a couple of piglets or chickens. Any leftover money they used to purchase silver and silver jewelry, which they could convert into cash later if the need arose. The Hmong considered the accumulation of silver jewelry to be a sign of affluence.

In order to put this into context, let's examine the income potential of the average Hmong farmer. As a rule of thumb, a farmer could harvest up to three kilos of opium per year on an acre of land. The three kilos would yield the farmer roughly $150 for the year's work. If he cultivated more than one acre, his annual income would, of course, be higher; some put more effort into the enterprise, and thus made more money. To show the bigger picture, let's look at the income potential for a corrupt RLA general like Ouane Rathikone. By virtue of his military rank and family status, he had money and followers to do the work for him. Ouane then became a buyer who paid the farmers $50 a kilogram for the opium. Next, he turned the small lots into sticky bricks. Then, with the RLAF C-47 transports at his disposal, he loaded up the sticky bricks and hauled them directly to Saigon, cutting out the middleman. There he sold the opium to the large buyers for $300 per kilogram. He didn't have to pay for fuel or the aircraft rental, because that was already paid for, unknowingly, by the United States. All he had to do was to slip the pilot and copilot a few hundred dollars to keep their loyalty.

In an earlier chapter, we mentioned the Opium War of 1967. In that incident, Ouane's soldiers and the RLAF pilots flying T-28 fighters intercepted Khun Sa's caravan after it crossed the Mekong River into Laos and arrived at the lumber mill. Approximately twelve tons of opium disappeared that day—probably showing up in Saigon on one of Ouane's RLAF aircraft, where it was sold. Using simple math, the bounty would have yielded roughly $2,880,000 in U.S. dollars.

The purpose of this exercise is to give you some idea of the earnings potential from the sale of opium, and why corruption and violence was so tempting within the Lao military and governmental structure. We don't mean to imply that the United States condoned or approved Ouane's activities, because that was *not* the case. It never was, despite the claims of some observers and authors. The U.S. military attachés did everything in their power to discourage opium smuggling by Ouane and the RLAF, and when possible, they did their best to preclude U.S.-provided assets from being used in the opium trade. But it wasn't considered our place to interfere with the simple Hmong farmer who was cultivating and selling opium. His activity was legal in Laos, and that's how he fed, clothed, and sheltered his family.

Some Westerners who traveled to Laos and studied the opium trade during the Secret War have attempted to portray Vang Pao as a drug lord. They've also claimed that the Secret War in Laos was all about opium. But that's simply not the case, and the evidence doesn't support that notion. There have been accusations that VP used two C-47 aircraft donated by the CIA to haul opium to the marketplace, but this appears to be more conjecture than actual fact. It's also rumored that VP stored opium in the basement of his residence at Long Tieng; but again, even if he did, it was legal to grow, cultivate, and sell opium in Laos. So if VP used the C-47 aircraft to transport the drugs to Long Tieng for storage and sale, it would have been perfectly legal and acceptable at that time. As for the opium stored in VP's basement, if that were true, it could have been considered insurance of a sort, in the event the U.S. bailed out and left VP and his troops to fend for themselves. In that case, VP could sell the opium to defray the costs of keeping his troops paid and armed.

It was rumored, also, that Air America was involved in opium smuggling during the Secret War. Certainly, there were journalists and correspondents who referenced Air America when talking about the opium trade—but none were able to provide specific evidence of a link. In fact, many Air America pilots and crewmembers have vehemently denied any such link. But most would likely agree that, on any given day, they could have *unknowingly* transported opium. After all, the personal items carried by their passengers were not inspected, because there was no reason to inspect them. A cardboard box was just a box, after all, and a valise was just a piece of luggage. The pilots had many more immediate concerns when flying their aircraft; their safety, and the safety of their passengers, was paramount in their minds. There were also the ever-present Pathet Lao and NVA troops shooting at the Air America aircraft, not to mention the unpredictable weather and all the mountains sticking up into the sky. Also, the primary job of Air America pilots was to fly men and equipment around the country at the direction of either the CIA or USAID. Their days were long and busy, and usually there weren't enough aircraft and crews to handle the large number of missions ordered—much less to search luggage for contraband.

Another example of assumed participation in the opium trade by the United States involved the USAF. A former Assistant AIRA assigned in northern Laos recalled that in early 1969, upon arrival in Laos, he was required to fly airstrikes against caravans transporting unknown cargo (opium) from Burma into Laos. He and other USAF pilots flew strikes against the caravan using T-28 fighters to satisfy RLA generals. Apparently, the generals needed to keep the other warlords in check to assure their cooperation, so they picked the USAF to deliver the message.

In 1971, Alfred W. McCoy, an investigative journalist, visited Laos for a brief period while conducting research for a book he was writing, *The Politics of Heroin in Southeast Asia.* For this research, he picked the Long Pot district in northeastern Laos, which contained approximately a dozen villages. The district's high altitude made it the perfect climate for growing the opium poppies. While conducting his research, McCoy reportedly interviewed officials in the villages, and villagers themselves, through an interpreter. It was also reported that he talked to Pop Buell and Don Schanche, who was in Laos writing a book about Pop. In fact, Pop reportedly invited McCoy to accompany him in an Air America aircraft to visit Sam Thong. McCoy took that ride, and did visit LS-20. It appears that McCoy spent about one month total in Laos, usually in the company of an Australian by the name of John Everingham. At the conclusion of that visit, McCoy reportedly was convinced that the CIA and Air America were involved in the opium trade, along with the Hmong and VP.

During his research at Long Pot, Mr. McCoy reportedly learned that the average household produced about 15 kilos of opium each year, and was told that VP received the opium and transported it on Air America aircraft. The transactions were supposedly handled by Hmong officers, so that the Air America crews knew nothing of the cargo riding in their aircraft. After the opium was purchased, it was supposedly flown to Long Tieng, where VP reportedly took possession of the cargo. These transactions reportedly continued from approximately 1965 to 1972, at which time the NVA occupied Long Pot and ended the activity.

Mr. McCoy published his book in 1972, and he has also written and published additional information on this subject. It should be pointed out, however, that McCoy's claims were later called into question based upon the limited amount of time he spent in Laos. Additionally, all interviews of local citizens were through an interpreter, without benefit of additional corroboration. The reported yield of 15 kilograms per household for the Long Pot area is also questionable, in that the average farmer would need to tend approximately five acres of land annually for such a yield. That is unlikely based upon the scarcity of arable land in Laos.

On July 30, 1973, *Time Magazine* published an article entitled "Victory over Opium." The purpose of the article was to highlight the arrest of Lo Hsing-han, a Burmese citizen believed to be one of the largest heroin tycoons in the world. Lo, who had privately funded Burmese General Ne Win's battle against the Communists for many years, became a casualty of the Drug Wars in SEA. With threats from the United States of withholding aid unless he neutralized Lo, Ne Win quietly asked Lo to get out of the opium trade. Lo refused to shed his opium interests, so Burmese forces drove him out of the country and into Thailand, where Thai special narcotics officers were waiting. Lo was subsequently tried, convicted, and held in a Thai prison until 1980, then released back to Burma. He subsequently reinvented himself by becoming a successful business tycoon, and apparently stayed on the correct side of Burmese authorities thereafter.

With Turkey's decreased production of heroin after 1970, pressure on the Golden Triangle region of Laos and Burma was brought to bear, and the production of opium increased dramatically. And, as history reflected when Lo was arrested in 1973, there were plenty of smaller drug lords waiting to move up in the ranks.

In 1991, Alfred W. McCoy published a second book, entitled *The Politics of Heroin: CIA Complicity in the Global Drug Trade.* The book cover indicated that it was a revised and expanded edition of his first book, mentioned above; the publication outlines twenty years of research, leading to the publication of the second book.

But over the years, Mr. McCoy's assertions have been refuted repeatedly by a number Americans who were actually on the ground in Southeast Asia during the Secret War in Laos. Listed below are individuals who have disagreed with McCoy:

Christopher Robbins, author of *Air America* and *The Ravens*, has stated, "It just isn't so."

Peter Kann, publisher of the *Wall Street Journal* (and formerly its reporter in Indochina from 1967 to 1975) and **Phillip Jennings**, an Air America pilot in Laos during the Secret War, both flatly challenge Mr. McCoy's assertions of Air America's involvement in any opium smuggling.

William E. Colby, former Chief of CIA Operations in SEA during the Secret War, has stated, in part, "The Royal Lao Army never really entered the conflict directly, remaining in the Mekong Valley where some of their generals—not Vang Pao or his officers, and certainly not the CIA or Air America—profited from the opium trade rather than joining the battle." Mr. Colby was, of course, referring to Ouane Rathikone and his cronies as the generals who profited from opium.

B. Hugh Tovar, former Chief of Station in Vientiane (1970-1973), has stated, in part, "Briefly, the U.S. mission in Vientiane under Ambassador G. McMurtrie Godley did everything humanly possible to put the kibosh on narcotics traffic. The CIA station as part of that mission was fully committed and involved in the effort under Godley's direction. Sustained hell-raising with top officials of the Royal Lao Government led to passage of a law proscribing all forms of narcotics traffic. Pressures were applied down-echelon to see that the law was enforced. Air America and other contractors were fully integrated in the process, and inspections of all aircraft were conducted rigorously and consistently. There were no exceptions, and this included Lao officials (generals) active in military operations".

James Quigley, former Air America and Air Asia Employee, has stated, regarding both books written by Mr. McCoy, "The allegations cited in these books that Air America knowingly engaged in drug trafficking are false."[68]

Ever since the Vietnam War and the Secret War in Laos ended, the U.S. Department of State has continued to work with the Lao Democratic Republic (LDR) to reduce and eliminate opium production in Laos. As an incentive, farmers are compensated for growing alternative crops. Laos has also enacted laws making opium production illegal. These efforts are paying off. In 1989, Laos produced 230 metric tons of opium. By 1993, that number had dropped to 180 metric tons. In 1996, the production total was 20 metric tons, and in 2007 it had dropped to 9.2 metric tons. That reduction in availability has resulted in a price per kilogram estimated to be $974 in the year 2007.

The bottom line, as it applies to the opium trade in Laos, is that the United States disapproved of the criminal enterprise, and did its best to discourage the production and sale of opium. But it *was* legal in the Kingdom of Laos to cultivate, sell and transport the drug. And anytime there are vast sums of money to be made from any enterprise, there are people who will take advantage of the opportunity. Whatever happened, and to what extent, is for the most part immaterial. The United States was in Laos to halt the spread of Communism, and the CIA and the U.S. military worked very hard in that regard.

In any case, thanks to the continuing efforts of the United States, opium is no longer the cash crop of choice in Laos.

Chapter 10

Turning Point

In Chapters 8 and 9, we left the Secret War briefly to discuss the Ravens and to talk about the drug trade, and how both tied into events taking place on the ground in Laos. Now it's time to get back to northeastern Laos, where the fighting has become intense.

The Nam Bac debacle had resulted in a complete erosion of FAR competence and ability. The beating they took wiped out at least a third of the Groupe Mobile forces, and years of confidence building by the Americans was suddenly gone. The Lao government troops simply lost the will to fight. Instead, they congregated near large towns where they felt more secure, refusing to go out and engage the Communists in the field. The CIA's guerrilla war was also impacted, because many of their assets had been tied up defending Nam Bac. Even the Road Watch program along Route 19 was suspended. But the war raged on, and the U.S. advisors and embassy personnel began to immediately rebuild the FAR.

The loss of Nam Bac also diverted RLG resources intended for use in the remote northern areas near the Chinese border. This created a vacuum that the Chinese rushed to fill, by beefing up their resources on the previously-mentioned road building project from Meng La, China to Pak Beng, Laos and the Mekong River. The project was called The Chinese Road, and nobody knew quite what to make of it. It had begun in approximately 1962, ostensibly as an economic aid gesture from China to Laos, but many suspected China of having other plans for the road after its completion. Most believed it would become a corridor for resupply for the Pathet Lao. Souvanna had previously authorized construction of the road, even though he, too, believed the Chinese had a hidden agenda. Heretofore, construction had proceeded slowly, due to hostilities in the area and poor workmanship on the part of the Chinese—not to mention the fact that RLAF and U.S. aircraft periodically bombed the road to further harass the builders.

But that was about to change, because China had begun to install antiaircraft guns along the path of the road to discourage the bombings. In so doing, the Chinese essentially took control of northwestern Laos—and were prepared to do whatever it took to maintain that control. Anticipating this move, the U.S. quickly designated the area as off-limits to over-fligh, and bombing. The only exception made was for periodic flights by CIA U-2 reconnaissance aircraft. Even with the restrictions in place, an American aircraft would occasionally stray off course, and the navigational errors usually resulted in the aircraft being downed by Chinese antiaircraft fire.

With the FAR in disarray, Ambassador Sullivan depended more and more upon Vang Pao and his guerrillas for support. Sullivan also depended on the USAF. Since his arrival in Laos, he had lobbied for control of all U.S. air support assets, but had been thwarted at every turn. Among other things, the USAF leadership was leaning more toward the use of jet fighters than propeller-driven aircraft. Sullivan preferred prop aircraft due to the thick jungles, limited visibility, and the unusual terrain of Laos. Furthermore, prop aircraft could loiter over the target for long periods of time, and did not need refueling as often as jets.

As related to operational control, there were four areas of responsibility in SEA. First, there was Rolling Thunder, consisting of bombing missions over North Vietnam. Then there were South Vietnam and southern Laos, where air interdiction was required. Finally, there were Barrel Roll and the other missions in northeastern Laos. In an attempt to clear up any doubts as to priorities and control, in 1966 President Johnson decreed that the JCS and NSA would control Rolling Thunder operations. MACV (Westmoreland) would be responsible for South Vietnam and southern Laos; and last but not least, Ambassador Sullivan would call the shots in Laos, to include approving the Rules of Engagement. The USAF's 7th Air Force was responsible for supporting all these areas, with first priority going to Westmoreland, then Rolling Thunder, and finally Barrel Roll.

In reality, Sullivan was responsible for all operations in Laos, but lacked the resources (i.e., aircraft) necessary to prosecute the war. The 7th Air Force possessed the resources, but lacked the operational responsibility. Both the AIRA in Vientiane and the 7th/13th Air Force in Udorn were caught in the middle, but neither was responsible for air resources. This arrangement was imminently unworkable, but heretofore nobody had been able to come up with a better plan. The USAF wanted to provide the air support, but objected to being left out of the planning process. The CIA, veiled in its shroud of secrecy, declined to allow the USAF access to its plans, implying that the Air Force should just send their aircraft to wherever they were told to send them, do what they were told to do, and not question anything. In other words, the CIA did not consider the USAF to have a "need to know." Not surprisingly, the Air Force objected, and this slipshod method of control continued.

In late 1967, the debate over jets versus props began to come to a head. A recent USAF study had indicated that prop aircraft were better suited for operations in Laos, and enjoyed a better kill ratio than the jets. Sullivan pressed this issue with USAF General Glen Martin, Deputy Chief of Staff of Plans and Operations, during a meeting in November. Martin made no commitments, but relayed the message to USAF Chief of Staff McConnell upon his (Martin's) return to Washington. General Momyer seized this opportunity to commission another props-versus-jets study, and of course the results leaned substantially toward jets this time, except in some interdiction situations in which the A-1 would be the better performer.

At this point, it is important to mention a little known aspect of the Secret War. In fact, scarce mention is made of this military unit which contributed so much to the efforts of interdicting the movement of NVA troops and materials down the Ho Chi Minh Trail, and into South Vietnam. What we are talking about is the U.S. Navy's Observation Squadron Sixty-Seven (VO-67), affectionately known as the "Ghost Squadron"

It was indeed a strange sight on November 15, 1967 when three U.S. Navy OP-2E, "Neptune" aircraft touched down on the runway at NKP, Thailand. The event left many U.S. Air Force personnel scratching their heads, and wondering if the Navy was going to be hunting for enemy submarines in the Mekong River. The three aircraft were the first group of twelve aircraft that would soon be flying dangerous missions over the Ho Chi Minh Trail. The OP-2Es were actually modified P-2 Neptune submarine hunters that had been reconfigured to implant acoustic sensors in the dense jungle treetops along The Trail.

The P-2 aircraft was designed and manufactured by the Lockheed Aircraft Company, and first flew in 1945. It was designed to fly at an altitude of approximately 20,000 feet, and cruise at approximately 174 miles per hour. It carried a crew of approximately nine personnel, and flew extensively until it was retired in approximately 1984. The modifications to the P-2, in order for it to be designated at the OP-2E was accomplished initially by Martin Aircraft Company, and many additional modifications were accomplished by the U.S. Navy. Upgrades included improved electronics, self-sealing fuel tanks, armor plating, under-wing mini-guns, chaff dispensers, LORAN, and internal mounts for M-60 machine guns. Their bomb bays were also modified to carry the acoustic sensors for implanting along The Trail.

When all 12 aircraft were in place at NKP, the squadron required just over 300 personnel to maintain, and fly the OP-2E. Of those 300 men, more than 200 were enlisted rated aircrew members. The OP-2E was intended to be an interim measure until fast-moving jet aircraft could be modified to implant acoustic sensor as a part of the Muscle Shoals and Igloo White programs. The VO-67 began flying immediately upon arrival at NKP and flew missions on an almost daily basis until they were relieved of duty on July 1, 1968. And, during their period of service in Southeast Asia, three of the aircraft, and 20 personnel were lost in combat. Little official documentation was originated regarding the Ghost Squadron because their activity was classified at the Top Secret level, and upon deactivation, members of the unit were told that they could never discuss what they did in support of the War in Vietnam, and the Secret War in Laos. One thing is known, however, and that is VO-67 was instrumental in the battle at Khe Sanh, South Vietnam in January, 1968. Leading up to, and during that battle, the VO-67 implanted acoustic sensors all around the perimeter of the base allowing the United States to detect, monitor, and destroy the Communist as they attempted to wipe out the American military troops at Khe Sanh.

OP-2E Neptune
Photo from the Public Domain

Meanwhile, things continued to heat up in northern Laos. Another event took place in the south at Muong Phalane (LS-61) near Savannakhet, in an area that heretofore had been quiet in comparison to northern Laos. When it happened, the event didn't attract a lot of attention, but it certainly should have made the U.S. embassy in Vientiane aware that Phou Pha Thi might be destined to fall soon. Previously, there had always been an American presence in Savannakhet, including the AIRA, USAID, Air America, and the CIA. USAID also stored and distributed relief supplies from Savannakhet, and Air America operated a radio station there. In addition, the Air Attaché provided advice to the RLAF at Savannakhet, and the CIA ran Road Watch Teams out of the area.

Prior to December 1967, there was an unwritten agreement that if the FAR troops limited their forays in the area of the Ho Chi Minh Trail, then the Communists would leave Savannakhet and Muong Phalane alone. But on December 25, that all changed. The U.S. leadership ordered the USAF 1st MOB to install a TACAN site at the airstrip adjacent to Muong Phalane. The navigation site was scheduled to be a part of a new highly classified DoD countermeasures program called "Muscle Shoals," using electronic sensors along the Ho Chi Minh Trail. We'll discuss Muscle Shoals a little later in the story, but for now we need to fully explain the event we're leading up to.

Due primarily to an excellent network of spies and informants, North Vietnam suspected that the TACAN site at Moung Phalane was connected to a new American sensor program, and decided to teach the United States and the Lao government a lesson. So in the early morning hours on Christmas Day, an NVA infantry battalion and a company of DAC Cong commandos (sappers) swept over the TACAN site, firing automatic weapons and rockets. They first took out the TACAN unit and then turned their attention to the small wooden building where two USAF technicians from Detachment 1, 1043rd Radar Evaluation Squadron out of Udorn slept. The two technicians were reportedly surprised and killed. The NVA then reportedly moved to the nearby town of Muong Phalane, where they attacked and damaged the Air America radio station and burned the USAID warehouse to the ground. During the attack, one Philippine national and three Thai citizens were reportedly killed. Initial reports from the area differed regarding how the technicians actually died; however, it was clear that fast retaliatory action was required.

The attack took everyone by complete surprise, but the U.S. acted quickly, dispatching a search party to the area. The group was led by the local CIA case officer, and they were flown into the town on an Air America H-34 helicopter. Upon reaching the site, the helicopter began to take ground fire, and the case officer knew that he didn't have much time to investigate. Once he was on the ground, he ran to the TACAN unit and determined that it was heavily damaged. He then ran into the building where the technicians had lived, and then returned to the waiting helicopter in less than a minute. He got back into the aircraft, which continued to take small arms fire, and the chopper struggled into the air. A minute or two later, small arms fire again riddled the helicopter, ultimately causing it to crash-land some distance away from the town. Fortunately, none of the personnel on the helicopter were severely injured, and they were subsequently rescued by another Air America aircraft in the area.

After the attack at Muong Phalane, there was disagreement as to the events that took place on December 25, 1967. One report indicated the attack actually took place on Christmas Eve. Other reports as to the fate of the USAF technicians, and other persons killed or captured during the attack, also differed. But, one thing is certain, however: the two USAF technicians were never seen or heard from again.

Subsequent to the attack, and out of an abundance of caution, a new TACAN station was installed across the river from Savannakhet near the small town of Mukdahan, Thailand, where it would temporarily be safe from the Pathet Lao and NVA. As history would later show, the U.S. should have removed the USAF technicians from Phou Pha Thi out of the same abundance of caution. As a matter of fact, the technicians at Muong Phalane were from the same unit as the technicians at LS-85, and were, in fact, their coworkers.[69]

Meanwhile, in Washington, the debate over props versus jets dragged on into early 1968, with Ambassador Sullivan pushing for operational control of the 56th Air Commando Wing at NKP. He wanted the 56th to be dedicated to the operations in northeastern Laos. The USAF disagreed completely with Sullivan, and, of course, the ambassador did *not* get dedicated use of the wing at NKP. Finally, in March 1968, the JCS put the issue to rest (at least temporarily) by putting Momyer in charge of all fixed-wing air assets in Southeast Asia.

Meanwhile, a feud developed between General Momyer and Colonel Heinie Aderholt, the commander at NKP. There were many differences between the two officers, and the prop-versus-jet debate caused an even deeper rift between them, with Colonel Aderholt being a strong advocate for the A-26. In fact, Aderholt received several written reprimands from Momyer during the 1966-67 timeframe, and was banned from important staff meetings by Momyer himself.

While the situation in northern Laos continued to deteriorate, not too far away, at Phou Pha Thi (LS-85), a new situation was developing. Pha Thi was almost 6,000 feet in elevation, and there were sheer cliffs on three sides protecting the summit. On the fourth side, there was a footpath up the mountain, but it was very steep and heavily wooded. If the terrain did not deter the curious from trying to climb the mountain, it was believed, the many poisonous creatures along the way would.

Not to be deterred, however, the USAF had begun construction of an all-weather USAF radar navigation facility on the southwestern facing ridge of the summit in mid-1966, and completed the project in November 1967. Even though the USAF officially classified the project as Top Secret, the construction activity in the area did not go unnoticed. One clue indicating that something was going on was the increased amount of air traffic transiting the site. Large helicopters came and went almost daily, hauling personnel and supplies. Also, on a fairly regular basis, even larger helicopters could be plainly seen in the sky, carrying large pieces of sling-loaded equipment to the top of the mountain. Word rapidly reached North Vietnam and Sam Neua of the increased activity on the mountain. The NVA and Pathet Lao also had paid informants in the Pha Thi area who reported regularly on the construction of the facility as it progressed. As a matter of fact, the Hmong guerrilla commander at LS-85 was suspected of being a Pathet Lao collaborator.

In response to the USAF activity at Phou Pha Thi, the Communists began construction of an all-weather road towards Phou Pha Thi from Sam Neua. The progress of the road continued daily, even though the U.S. regularly bombed it. As soon as the bombs stopped falling, the engineers were right back on the road, repairing the damage and pressing forward. It didn't take long for everyone to realize that it would only be a matter of time before the road reached the mountain—and that an NVA attack would come along with it.

But back at LS-85, construction continued. Ambassador Sullivan did not object to the installation of the TACAN and radar equipment, because there were already several other units installed in northern Laos. Furthermore, the TACAN device was passive, in that it did not require full-time attendants to run it. The radar equipment, on the other hand, *did* require full-time operators; and since Lao personnel were not trained to use and maintain the equipment, it would have to be attended by Americans. Souvanna Phouma approved of the installation, but went on the record stating that he would disavow any knowledge of the activity at Phou Pha Thi if it was compromised. The USAF also knew the risks of having the site at LS-85, but considered the potential benefits to outweigh the danger. In other words, the personnel were expendable. The CIA also recognized the danger, but believed that in the event of an attack, the equipment could be destroyed and the American personnel evacuated before the NVA reached the top of the mountain.

In any case, approximately 1,000 Hmong guerrillas were stationed at the base of the mountain to deter any ground attack. An additional 200 Hmong guerrillas and a handful of Thai commandos were also assigned as a defensive unit at the helipad area near the top of the mountain, some 300 meters from the summit and to the southeast. From the helicopter landing pad area, two CIA case officers ran a Road Watch and intelligence collection program from a fortified bunker, using Hmong guerrillas. They had radio and other communications gear to support the USAF technicians on the summit of Pha Thi if required.

Soon, intelligence information was received indicating the Communists might attack Pha Thi at any time, using ground troops and possibly Soviet AN-2 Colt aircraft. In December 1967, the NVA began clearing operations in the areas around Phou Pha Thi. Meanwhile, construction of the road from Sam Neua to Phou Pha Thi by the NVA continued, inching closer each day.

On January 1, 1968, Hanoi announced that it had agreed to peace talks with the United States in Paris, contingent upon the cessation of all bombing over North Vietnam. In the spirit of cooperation, President Johnson quickly extended the bombing pause that had been mandated just prior to Christmas. Fast forward a few days later on January 7, 1968, when two MiG-21s jumped two A-1 Skyraiders participating in a SAR in the Sam Neua area. The A-1s reacted quickly and took evasive action as one Skyraider was fired upon but not hit. After several more unsuccessful attempts by the MiGs to engage the Skyraiders, the Soviet aircraft retreated to North Vietnam. Three days later, on January 10, a five-man Communist patrol was discovered only about a mile from Phou Pha Thi. They were fired upon, and retreated northward. Later still, on January 12, the CIA transferred Jerry Daniels from Na Khang (LS-36) to Phou Pha Thi.

On that same day, two vintage 1947 Soviet-built AN-2 biplanes appeared in the sky over northern Laos, flying in the direction of LS-85. At first, no one bothered to look up into the sky because everyone assumed that the two aircraft belonged to Air America, and that they were approaching on a regularly scheduled supply run.

Figure 30. Soviet AN-2 Colt
(Photo from the Public Domain)

As the Soviet aircraft neared the site, they made radio contact with a Dac Cong sapper team hidden at the base of the mountain. The team then used their radio to visually guide the aircraft to drop mortars on the mountain. As the Colts passed over Phou Pha Thi, the antique craft sprayed the summit with fire from crudely mounted mortar and rocket tubes. The Hmong guerrillas detailed by VP to protect the site then began firing at the Colts; so did Jerry Daniels.

While the attack was taking place, an Air America UH-1 helicopter was sitting on the CIA helicopter landing pad, unloading ammunition. The crew quickly took off to get into the air and away from the biplanes. Once airborne, a UH-1 crewmember grabbed an AK-47 assault rifle and began firing on the same biplane that Daniels was firing at. That Colt was subsequently hit and exploded as it crashed nearby. Meanwhile, the second biplane continued to fire on the mountain, and the Air America crewman began firing at it. Amazingly, the small arms rifle rounds tore into the canvas skin of the old biplane, causing it to crash into a ridgeline a short distance away. The biplane did not explode like the first one did, but its wings were ripped off.[70] Hmong defenders then stopped firing and ran to the crash site. They found the pilot and one crew member still alive, and a third crew member dead. They summarily executed the pilot and copilot on the spot, and the bodies of all three crewmen were subsequently taken to Long Tieng and placed on public display for all to see. After baking in the sun for the next three days, the bodies of the dead North Vietnamese fliers were taken to the North Vietnamese embassy in Vientiane, where they were unceremoniously turned over to the staff.

After the attack, the radar site itself was relatively unscathed, but several Hmong guerrillas and villagers were wounded, and two Hmong defenders and two villagers were killed in the airstrike. A subsequent inspection of the radar/TACAN site at the top of the mountain confirmed that little damage had been done; it was believed that one reason for this might have been the excellent use of camouflage netting around the equipment.

The assault by the AN-2 biplanes was the first NVA air strike over Laos during the Secret War. Suddenly, everyone back at the embassy in Vientiane realized the vulnerability of the radar site at Phou Pha Thi. After the incident, the USAF stationed a Combat Controller at the site to coordinate air strikes against NVA troops operating near the base of the mountain.

After the NVA aerial attack at Pha Thi on January 12, several fresh battalions of NVA and Pathet Lao soldiers departed Sam Neua and marched in the direction of Phou Pha Thi. They soon defeated the Lao troops at Phou Den Din, and began shelling in the vicinity of LS-85. The USAF retaliated by flying more than 100 sorties in the area during January 1968. The strikes did not, however, deter the Communists, who continued their slow advance. Also after the January 12 attack, the Hmong defenders moved two captured NVA antiaircraft guns to the site, and established a twelve-kilometer defensive perimeter around Phou Pha Thi. A 105mm howitzer was relocated to the CIA helicopter pad at the site for defensive purposes, and the Hmong stepped up their patrols around the area.

Later, on approximately January 15, the NVA struck again at Muong Son, capturing the runway and the Lao government resupply base. Meanwhile, other Communist troops pushed northward to within approximately 12 kilometers of Phou Pha Thi. On January 19, intelligence sources reported that five battalions of NVA and Pathet Lao troops were advancing on LS-85. The size of the forces confirmed beliefs the radar navigation site was a high-priority target, and that the Communists would attempt to eliminate it at all costs. VP took the news seriously, dispatching two of his top commanders and 300 additional Hmong personnel to defend the site. Later, on February 18, Hmong defenders patrolling the area at the bottom of the mountain ambushed and killed NVA artillery troops near the site. A subsequent search of the dead troops' belongings disclosed documents and detailed sketches outlining an attack on Phou Pha Thi. Not only that, but one of the dead troops was a Major in the NVA, indicating that LS-85 was an important target indeed.[71]

In late January, the CIA case officers at LS-85 had conducted their own inspection of the USAF radar navigation site on the summit of the mountain, and found the northwestern approach to the summit via the footpath lacking in security safeguards. They were surprised by the deficiencies, and immediately set about installing concertina wire and claymore mines in the area between the summit and the northwestern approach.[72] They also set up a Hmong security outpost between the radar navigation facility and the northwestern perimeter of the summit. Meanwhile, the NVA and Pathet Lao battalions crept closer.

On January 31, 1968, the Communists launched the Tet Offensive in South Vietnam, and most of the available American airpower was diverted to support the American and South Vietnamese fighting there. The 7th Air Force did not forget about the threat at LS-85, however. Even though their air support resources were stretched thin, it did not mean that air strikes were withheld from northern Laos; indeed, the USAF offered assistance on any priority Laotian targets. The embassy in Vientiane then submitted a list of desirable targets in the vicinity of LS-85, but added that none needed to be struck at that moment. Nonetheless, when aircraft were available, strikes were flown in the Barrel Roll area, including targets within 25 miles of LS-85. As a matter of fact, over 150 strikes were flown in Laos in January 1968.

After reviewing all the information about the vulnerability of LS-85 to enemy attack, the CIA office in Vientiane decided the site should be abandoned and the equipment destroyed in place. The areas around the site, including the approach via the footpath, were also mined. All the equipment and facilities at Phou Pha Thi were reportedly rigged with explosives and thermite charges, assuring that when and if the site was overrun, the NVA would not be able to salvage anything of intelligence value. Vientiane then transmitted their plan to Washington, and it was immediately overruled. They were told to stay put and await further instructions. Meanwhile, the NVA and Pathet Lao slowly advanced.[73] The CIA ordered still more guerrilla units to the site, and by that time the mountain was braced for whatever was to come its way. To slow the NVA advance, artillery rounds were fired in the direction of the enemy at a range of about 20 miles.

But NVA and Pathet Lao troops continued to advance, and began to pour into the areas around Phou Pha Thi, prompting U.S. intelligence sources to predict that LS-85 would probably fall to the Communists by mid-March. The U.S. embassy in Vientiane hurriedly put together a plan for the inevitable evacuation of LS-85. The plan called for five helicopters to evacuate the 15-20 USAF technicians atop Phou Pha Thi after the radar navigation equipment had been destroyed by the airmen. Next, the helicopters would evacuate the two CIA case officers and the USAF Combat Controller at the helicopter pad down the slope from the radar navigation facility, and other selected defenders would also be evacuated at that time. The

Hmong defenders would then melt into the countryside and make their way back to friendly locations for regrouping. Finally, the USAF would strafe and bomb the entire summit of Phou Pha Thi to destroy all the equipment and structures.

The plan looked good on paper and sounded feasible, so it won out over having no plan at all.

On March 1, an NVA Dac Cong sapper team consisting of Lt. Truong Muc and approximately 32 other Communist soldiers departed Moung Cau and moved for two days and four nights to its assembly point near LS-85. The team consisted of Lt. Muc, two second lieutenants, 15 non-commissioned officers, and 15 soldiers. The team's ethnic make-up was six Hmong, six Thai, three Nung, three Tay and 15 Vietnamese. They were equipped with three B-40 rockets, AK-47 assault rifles, satchel charges and hand grenades. Their mission was to take the summit of Phou Pha Thi, eliminate the technicians, and render the radar navigation facility inoperable. The team carried their own rations, and received instructions not to interact or have contact with any of the local population along the way to Phou Pha Thi. This was a wise edict, because it was common knowledge that VP used many sources in the villages around LS-85, and would learn of the mission rather quickly if the NVA had contact with the locals.

On March 7, the sapper team split into two assault elements and advanced to the base of the mountain. There they rested and waited for the sun to go down. Later that night, the team moved in closer, where they encountered two horses grazing. At about that same time, several flashlights were observed, and the team retreated to a safe distance and waited. After lying low until about 2:30 A.M., the sappers then silently moved past a Hmong outpost and into an old growth forest. At approximately 10:00 A.M. on March 8, they encountered a mine field, where they stopped. There the team mostly rested for the remainder of the day, though Muc sent a small group of sappers to reconnoiter the area ahead and confirm the safety of the route and the direction of attack.

On March 9, U.S. Intelligence officials in Vientiane dispatched a cable to Washington, reporting their suspicions that the NVA was methodically preparing for an attack at Phou Pha Thi. They also suggested that the Communists were probing the site. The NVA was believed to have as many as seven battalions in the area that could be brought to bear. The cable concluded that the enemy was in position to launch his attack, once sufficient ammunition was available; a mortar barrage, followed up by a ground assault and possible air assault, could take place at any time. In the cable, embassy officials gave the impression that the Hmong defending the mountain could hold their ground, even if the radar and other electronic devices were neutralized by the NVA.

Also on March 9, the CIA advisor at LS-85 briefed the USAF technicians at the radar navigation facility that an attack could likely come at any minute. The evacuation plan was again reviewed, and it was agreed that if the attack came, the technicians would destroy the equipment and proceed down the footpath approximately a quarter of a mile to the CIA helicopter pad for evacuation. If they could not proceed down the path, the technicians were to remain at the radar navigation facility and evade until they could be picked up by rescue helicopters. It was noted that near the facility, there were cargo nets stretched out over the cliff and dangling down to a ledge of sorts. It was recommended to the technicians they should not consider this ledge below the summit as a safe place to hide and await evacuation.

At that point in time, Phou Pha Thi was completely surrounded, even though the USAF had flown over 300 sorties against the enemy advancing on the mountain. Meanwhile, Jerry Daniels left LS-85 and returned to Na Khang, and the USAF brought in additional USAF technicians to man the radar site on a round-the-clock basis. On March 10, at approximately 6:00 P.M., the USAF technicians held a meeting inside the radar navigation facility to go over the evacuation plan once more. At about that same time, a well-placed or extremely lucky NVA artillery round took out the 105mm howitzer protecting the mountain. At the summit, another round damaged the USAF technicians' living quarters, and their bunker took a direct hit. A dozen or so technicians working at the site then grabbed their personal weapons and ran for cover in the trenches at the site. Prior to doing so, they managed to notify 7th/13th Air Force personnel at Udorn via radio that they were taking incoming fire, and that they were abandoning the radio. The CIA's portable radio at their command post next to the helicopter pad did remain on, however, and the technicians could maintain contact with the command post with their own portables.

By this time, the Hmong defenders further down the mountain were also under attack and were defending the trails. Then, as suddenly as the fight started, at approximately 6:45 P.M. it stopped. After a while, the USAF technicians returned to their trailers at the radar navigation facility and resumed work. Several of those who were not on duty took their weapons and climbed down the cargo nets from the top of the mountain's sheer face to a small cave-like depression on the abovementioned ledge to spend the night, even though they had been explicitly cautioned against doing so by the CIA.

The Hmong troops waiting at the base of the mountain for the next assault had no idea sappers were already scaling the face of the mountain to attack the radar navigation site from above, even as a USAF C-130 Lamplighter arrived in the area and began dropping illumination flares in the vicinity.[74] The sapper team reached the mountain's summit at approximately 8:30 P.M. They crept past a Hmong guard post and entered a mature forest, where they rested and waited. At 9:05 P.M., the USAF command center at Udorn was notified that Ambassador Sullivan in Vientiane was considering ordering an evacuation of LS-85. At 9:21 P.M., intermittent NVA artillery shelling began again, but the technicians continued to direct air strikes from the radar navigation site atop Phou Pha Thi. At 9:50 P.M., the command center at Udorn notified Vientiane that LS-85 should only be evacuated as a last resort, and that the 7th/13th Air Force Commander should be notified prior to any evacuation. That decision sealed the fate of the USAF technicians working at the facility.

At about 1:00 A.M. on March 11, the NVA sapper team left the wooded area and approached to a distance of about 300 feet northeast of the radar navigation facility. Then they moved into position midway between the facility and the CIA command post/helicopter pad, and began their attack. At about 2:00 or 3:00 A.M., the Hmong defenders below began to hear small arms fire coming from the top of the mountain. At about that same time, the telephone lines from the bottom of the mountain to the top were severed.

A second group of sappers then slowly and quietly climbed the North Slope in the direction of the Thai outpost, in order to cut off any advance. Another element of the team moved southward towards the helicopter pad to cut-off any Hmong/American advance from that direction. Then, Lt. Muc and his element moved into the radar navigation site, where the American technicians lived and worked. Muc's group fired a rocket into the main power generator station, setting it on fire and knocking out the power to the site. Grenades were lobbed into the trailers where the crew lived, but bounced off the camouflage netting and back in the direction of Muc's team, wounding one commando slightly.

After that, more rockets were fired into the radar navigation site trailers, and Muc's team also opened fire with their AK-47s. The Americans, taken completely by surprise, ran outside into the open and scattered. A few of them stood and fought, even though their training for such an eventuality had been minimal at best.[75] The resisting Americans, outnumbered, were quickly killed where they stood. The sapper team blocking support from the helicopter pad then moved forward, taking heavy mortar fire. During the fight, several Hmong defenders were killed in the vicinity of the helicopter pad, and the sapper team then rejoined Muc and the others in the main radar navigation site area.

The sappers soon discovered the cargo nets hanging down to the outcropping, and began firing their weapons onto the ledge where some of the technicians had taken refuge. The Americans below returned fire, and it was believed that several NVA troops were hit. The sapper team then moved out of the line of fire and lobbed a dozen or more grenades down onto the ledge, whereupon it was believed that several of the Americans were killed. By this point, the embassy in Vientiane had been notified of the grim situation, and had immediately dispatched Air America helicopters to rescue the Americans.

At first light, the incoming artillery fire began to diminish. The U.S. rescue helicopters began to arrive in the area, and waited to come in to initiate rescue actions. They could not approach, however, because they were taking AK-47 fire from the radar navigation site. Meanwhile, one of the CIA advisors and the Hmong guerrillas from the CIA command post area cautiously approached the radar navigation facility using the footpath, and saw smoke rising from the modular trailers housing the radar navigation equipment. The CIA advisor did not see any Americans along the path, but did encounter several NVA troops, at which time fire was exchanged.

Realizing they were outgunned, the Hmong guerrillas and the CIA advisor retreated back down the path to the command post area. Convinced the radar navigation site was in enemy hands, the CIA advisor called in air strikes on the sappers to silence their guns. Finally the firing diminished, the sappers withdrew, and the helicopters approached to attempt rescue of the USAF technicians at the site. At first it was reported that 19 Americans were missing, but the number was later changed to 16. Of those, only five were extracted; one was hit by small arms fire and died during the flight to Na Khang (LS-36) and Udorn. The remaining 11 Americans were presumed dead. It was soon discovered that the explosive charges that had been set to destroy the radar equipment had not exploded, and thus had not destroyed the equipment. It was later determined that the fuses had never been rigged to set off the charges.

After the five technicians were rescued, helicopters continued to come and go, evacuating the two CIA advisors, the USAF Combat Controller, and a few Thai and Hmong defenders; the helicopters also removed the dead. The area was still hot, and the rescuers were taking small arms fire all during the rescue phase. Later, when the rescue and recovery effort on top of Phou Pha Thi was completed, the Hmong guerrillas at the base of the mountain melted away into the hills to relocation points at other Lima sites.

Meanwhile, the NVA and Pathet Lao forces systematically took control of Phou Pha Thi and most of the other Lima sites in northern Laos. The fate of some of the missing Americans at the site would not be known for many years, because the site was firmly in the hands of the NVA. For the next few days after the attack, the USAF sent all the jet fighters that it could muster to relentlessly bomb and strafe the site in order to destroy the equipment left behind. Much later, during May-June 1968, yet another TACAN unit, to replace the one destroyed at Phou Pha Thi, was installed in a remote area north of Na Khang.

It will probably never be known exactly what happened at Phou Pha Thi on March 11, 1968; but in the end, approximately 11 Americans lost their lives, after being assured they would be evacuated before trouble came. It was the largest single loss of U.S. troops in a single incident during the entire Secret War in Laos. Was it worth it? Or course not; it never is. But, the bigger question was, what benefit did we get from the radar site while it was in operation? The answer is "not much," because the final numbers showed that while in operation, only 27% of the air strikes in North Vietnam and

Barrel Roll were directed from LS-85. Many believe the fall of Phou Pha Thi was the pivotal event that signaled the beginning of the end for the United States in SEA.

Many years later, in October 1994, The United States Joint Task Force, Full Accounting (JTF-FA)[76] office in Honolulu, Hawaii interviewed Lt. Colonel (retired) Truong Muc. The former NVA lieutenant did not recall many specific details of the 1968 attack, but his responses to the interviewers' questions essentially corroborated the information outlined above and later published in the North Vietnamese book mentioned earlier, *Military Region 2: Several Battles During the War of Liberation 1945-1975, Vol. III*, published in 1996. During the interview, Muc denied taking any prisoners. He advised that his team did attempt to bury the dead Americans at the site by placing their bodies in depressions in the ground and covering them with dirt, rocks and sandbags from the bunkers. Muc also denied taking any equipment, documents or personal effects from the site. The only exception, according to Muc, was that his team took a map from the wall in one of the trailers at the site. He related that the bombing by the Americans after the NVA seizure of the site pretty much destroyed everything of any intelligence value.

Of course, after Muc's interview by JTF-FA in 1994, the so-called experts dissected the testimony and drew vastly different conclusions from his comments. But the truth is, these "experts" were not at Phou Pha Thi—and Muc was. In the final analysis, the truth may well reside somewhere between what Muc said and what the experts believe.

While the information regarding what happened at Phou Pha Thi in March 1968 is still hard to accept for those of us who were involved in the Secret War in Laos, we should take pride in several things. First, VP was doing everything he could to protect Phou Pha Thi. He positioned many of his troops on and around the mountain. He also used informants in all the villages around the area. He established listening posts, and every troop he could muster was looking and listening for information about NVA and Pathet Lao movements. The NVA knew this, which is why so few people knew the real plan. Secondly, the NVA sapper team was extremely careful: they carried all their rations, weapons, ammunition, and equipment with them. They were specifically instructed not to have contact with any local personnel along the way, and it appears that they obeyed orders.

This was not a sophisticated operation, which made it very difficult to detect. The NVA team scaled the face of the mountain using their bare hands and pieces of rope. They carried only light weapons, grenades, and satchel charges. They didn't have air support or two-way radios. There was only one radio, held by a back-up troop on the ground where reassembly would take place after the operation. After the attack, Muc and his men walked out carrying their wounded with them.

Bill Lair, Pat Landry and Dick Secord of the CIA at Udorn did everything they could behind the scenes to support the defenders at Phou Pha Thi. In his book *Honored and Betrayed*, retired USAF Major General Secord wrote about the strategy of the U.S. Embassy in Vientiane. Essentially, the plan boiled down to requesting air strikes from the 7th Air Force in the event an attack appeared imminent on Phou Pha Thi. But as General Secord points out, waiting until an attack was imminent would have been too late. He also points out that when an attack *was* imminent, and even before that, each time he requested air support from 7th Air Force for Phou Pha Thi his requests were denied, due to higher priority targets.

While Lt. Muc claimed that he and his men did not take any equipment from the site, and that in fact they tried to bury some of the dead who were killed in the attack, we do know that equipment from the radar navigation site was taken by someone. Information in the public domain indicates that as Muc and his men were finishing up their initial attack on the site, other Communist troops began arriving on top of the mountain to assist the sappers. In fact, photographs of recovered equipment and NVA troops going through the facility after the attack are available for viewing on the Internet.

Additional information is also available in the public domain from a former USAF Para Rescue Specialist (PJ) who was actually in one of the rescue helicopters sent to Phou Ph Thi to rescue the technicians. The airman related that upon approaching LS-85 on the west side of the cliffs, at around 9:00 A.M. on March 11, he observed the radar navigation site complex off to his left. He could see people crouched down and moving through the buildings, and assumed they were enemy troops, but they did not appear threatening. Then, turning his attention to the north, the PJ saw what appeared to be a dead enemy soldier slumped over, almost in a sitting position. The former PJ also recalled looking down along the cliff onto a flat ledge with large boulders, where he saw several bodies. He recalled that some dead Americans were grouped together near the boulders. Some of the bodies appeared to be Asian, clad in dark clothing. Minutes later, while he was on the ground, the PJ was able to locate one wounded USAF technician, who was hoisted up a cable, along with the rescuer, to safety.[77]

After Phou Pha Thi fell, the usual finger-pointing took place. In a letter to Ambassador Sullivan on March 14, General Momyer asked for a postmortem analysis. He wanted to know how such a small team could take such a well-defended installation. He implied the American embassy in Vientiane had relied on faulty intelligence information, and had not effectively planned or targeted the enemy.[78] Sullivan replied that the Communists outnumbered the defenders; he also defended the embassy assessments. In fact Sullivan was correct, because we now know that several NVA/Pathet Lao battalions participated in the assault on Phou Pha Thi. While it's true that only 20 NVA Dac Cong soldiers scaled the face of the mountain initially, there were hundreds more proceeding up the footpath. And, of course, there were also several NVA battalions shelling the mountain and performing clearing operations in the villages and outposts around the base of the mountain.

What Sullivan didn't say, however, was why the embassy didn't do more to manage the threat. Ultimately, the ambassador pointed fingers also, this time at the Hmong and the USAF for not providing better support. But the 7th Air Force countered that they had hit every target identified to them, flying over 1,000 sorties in defense of the radar navigation facility. Later, when the survivors themselves began to complain, the USAF conducted its own investigation and conveniently concluded that there was no negligence on the part of the Air Force or the embassy.

Back in Vientiane, the mood began to change; the Lao General Staff realized that the war was becoming serious business. They also came to the realization that they had better work more closely together to keep their country from becoming another domino in the Communist domination of Asia. The general staff soon reported directly to Souvanna Phouma, even though Ouane was still the Commander in Chief—a title without any authority. And even though improvements were beginning to take place, the ways of corruption still ran deep.

An illustrative example of that corruption occurred on March 21, 1968, when an RLAF C-47 sat on the ramp at Savannakhet while its cargo bay was filled with opium and gold destined for Saigon, South Vietnam. The cover story put forth by the RLAF base commander was that the aircraft was flying a routine mission from Savannakhet to Vientiane. The assistant American AIRA, however, became suspicious, and notified U.S. authorities in Vientiane and Saigon; and sure enough, when the aircraft took off, it proceeded directly to South Vietnam. On board were the RLAF base commanders from Savannakhet and Vientiane, and upon arrival in Saigon, the aircraft, its cargo and the crew were seized. The aircraft and crew were later released, but the gold and opium were not returned. The base commanders were subsequently reduced in grade, but kept their commands. The pilot was also mildly sanctioned, but was flying again shortly after the incident.

Meanwhile, back in Laos, while still basking in the glow of their victory at Phou Pha Thi, the NVA decided to bring in nine fresh battalions to Sam Neua and take as much territory as possible before the rainy season started. The Communists also developed a new strategy of attacking the Hmong villagers in their communities and destroying their crops, homes, and will to fight. As a part of their offensive, the NVA also initiated a drive against Na Khang, where the last remaining TACAN system in northern Laos was located.

As the situation in Laos deteriorated, the Americans began peace negotiations with North Vietnam in Paris, where Averell Harriman was selected to speak for the U.S. Later, on March 30, President Johnson appeared on national television, announcing an end to the bombing north of the 20th parallel, which included not just two-thirds of North Vietnam but also northern Laos—an ambiguous reference that had the Americans in Vientiane especially concerned. Johnson also announced during his speech that he would not run for reelection as President of the United States. Apparently, he had had enough.

For several days after the speech, the Americans in Vientiane used the chain of command to challenge the bombing halt in northern Laos. After much persistence, the Pentagon finally relented and authorized strikes by U.S. fighter jets, but they would not authorize strikes over northern Laos using the B-52 bombers.

On April 10, VP initiated his dry season offensive by retaking Moung Son. Meanwhile, the Communist troops encircled Na Khang using four battalions; by the end of April, the NVA had completely surrounded LS-36, and were poised to strike. An added bonus for the Communists was that the weather cooperated: the skies were filled with dark clouds, preventing retaliatory air strikes by the U.S.

On April 19, the 7th Air Force initiated a new interdiction program to slow the flow of war supplies flowing down the Ho Chi Minh Trail. It was called "Operation Turnpike." Using fast-moving fighter jets and B-52 bombers, the U.S. conducted round-the-clock bombing of all known storage areas and way stations along the Trail. The operation continued through October 1968, and would lead to another program, similar in nature, called "Commando Hunt."

Meanwhile, back at Long Tieng, VP was in a precarious position in which he faced a minor political crisis. His senior officers were troubled about both the recent loss of Pha Thi to the Communists and the current problem at Na Khang. In addition, Hmong communities were being attacked, their homes and crops burned. Some recommended moving the Hmong women and children to safety at Sayaboury. It was the only area of northern Laos that was on the west side of the Mekong River, and was considered safe because the river was a natural barrier that would protect the Hmong from the Communists. VP did not offer an immediate opinion one way or the other, because he was just too tired and overwhelmed to make any decision without first getting approval from Vientiane. He asked for time to consult with the Americans and his Lao counterparts from the other regions, prior to making any decisions about quitting the war.

Further south, the NVA launched a series of small actions, overrunning outposts at Tha Thom and Moung Ngan. During the fight, VP was able to use his newly graduated Hmong pilots, who were flying the converted T-28 trainers, to provide air support. While flying in support of VP at Tha Thom, one of the new pilots, Vang Tua, and two Thai wingmen lined up for a bombing run and flew into a thick layer of clouds—whereupon they all perished when the T-28s crashed into a concealed ridgeline. Their remains were recovered approximately two months later.

Up north at Sam Neua, the NVA marched south down Route 6 towards Na Khang. In April, the Communists were pounded with air strikes. At the time air support was plentiful, because the fighters that would have been used over North Vietnam were idle and eager to support the U.S. effort in Laos. Finally, in May, the NVA gave up the offensive and retreated north.

The rainy season was now approaching, and everyone was ready for the annual ritual in which the NVA would retreat to North Vietnam to regroup and refit. The Hmong also needed the time to rest and regroup, so they could fight another day. However, this year would be different. While the NVA did move north in the face of the increased bombardment in April and May, they did *not* withdraw back to their home country; and worse, they called for even more reinforcements. Soon, fresh new Communist troops began flowing into Sam Neua to reinforce the NVA troops already in place.

After the Communist victory at Phou Pha Thi, Hanoi decided to break new ground. The NVA wanted to turn up the heat in Vang Pao's MR 2 region. They intended to use the summer months to strengthen their position in the region, and use it to their advantage to influence the peace talks taking place in Paris. By June, with the monsoon rains falling, the NVA had increased its troop strength in northern Laos to over 13,000, an increase of over 3,000 troops. In order to provide supplies to these troops, the construction crews of North Vietnam began improving the small roads and trails over which the supplies would flow into Laos from North Vietnam. In an attempt to thwart this build-up by the NVA, VP went on a recruiting campaign of his own, training and equipping two new battalions of Hmong guerrillas.

The NVA began their assault during the early morning hours of May 5, by simultaneously attacking Hmong positions at guerrilla outposts a few miles to the east of Na Khang. After only ten minutes of fighting, the guerrillas withdrew; the embassy in Vientiane reported to Washington that three Lao soldiers were wounded, and one 81mm mortar launcher was lost. The embassy also advised that at approximately 0430 hours that same morning, an NVA unit attacked Lao armed forces about 30 kilometers northwest of Na Khang, near Moung Hiem. Both positions were apparently lost to the Communists, and Lao forces retreated southward. On May 6, the CIA station in Vientiane advised Washington that large numbers of enemy troops had moved into the area east/northeast of Xieng Khouang Province. The USAF responded with 35 sorties, directed by

Raven FACs. According to the CIA, General Vang Pao climbed into the backseat of one of the Raven O-1s and personally provided targeting information to the FACs. The next day, the NVA advance began to stall, with more USAF air strikes taking place. For the next week, the Ravens flew over the battlefield in their slow-moving O-1 Bird Dogs, directing air strikes against the NVA. Slowly and methodically, the jet fighters, A-1 Skyraiders and Hmong-piloted T-28 aircraft pounded the Communists.

Between May 5 and May 13, over 275 sorties were flown, almost wiping out the NVA attackers. Finally, after suffering heavy casualties, the NVA began retreating on May 10. The Hmong guerrillas pursued them and struck before they could regroup, pushing the enemy back about five miles. Ambassador Sullivan then requested strikes by the USAF B-52 bombers to cripple the NVA once and for all, but the White House disapproved, stating that it might jeopardize the peace talks in Paris.

Meanwhile, the NVA brought in four additional battalions of fresh troops to mount a new offensive planned for May 20. The CIA quickly compiled a list of 24 priority targets and about 50 secondary targets, then requested more than 50 air strikes each day to discourage the Communists. Just as expected, the NVA attacked on May 20, and for several days thereafter continued the assault. But on May 27, after making little headway, they called off the offensive. VP's guerrillas then slowly moved out to retake lost territory, but were just too exhausted to continue. The most they could do was harass the enemy.

While all this was taking place, and with more USAF air support available due to the bombing halt over part of North Vietnam, the U.S. turned its attention to serious interdiction efforts along the Ho Chi Minh Trail. Operation Turnpike was already underway, having begun in April. Using tactical fighters and B-52 bombers, the USAF waged constant warfare against the known truck parts and storage areas along the Trail. Also, by June, the USAF was busy testing a new gunship over the skies of Laos: a converted AC-130 transport called "Spectre," which was designed to complement and eventually replace the AC-47 Spooky. A prototype had already flown over 50 sorties, and had taken enemy fire on almost every mission. The only problem was that the NVA had increased the number of anti-aircraft artillery guns by 400%—and the size and range of the big guns was increasing, too. Spectre crews were forced to adjust their tactics to negate the enemy defensive measures.

By late June, the rainy season was in full force, and VP was ready to launch his rainy season offensive. His first goal was to locate a new site for an American air radar navigation site in the Sam Neua Province; his second was to devise a plan to retake Phou Pha Thi. In order to accomplish the second goal, he needed a place from which to launch his attack. He decided that Moung Son would be a good place, but the area had been lost to the NVA in April. Ambassador Sullivan didn't see the need for a rainy season offensive at all—and he no longer considered Phou Pha Thi a viable strategic objective. Nonetheless, VP was determined to undertake a campaign to restore his reputation. After the defeat at Pha Thi and the beating the Hmong had taken in other parts of northern Laos, it was imperative that VP redeem himself in the eyes of his people.

Sullivan remained adamant, and threatened to withhold helicopters required to airlift the Hmong guerrillas into action. VP persisted, and even threatened to have his troops walk to the battle if necessary. Sullivan blinked first, eventually approving VP's request for helicopter support. On June 27, over 700 Hmong guerrillas were airlifted to Houei Tong Ko (LS-184), about 30 miles southwest of Phou Pha Thi and 10 miles southwest of Moung Son. At the same time, he positioned additional Hmong forces south and east of Moung Son

The immediate goal was to take the airfield at Muong Son, and then stage troops at that location for the assault on Phou Pha Thi. By controlling the airfield, VP figured he would be able to have supplies, equipment, and additional troops brought in as necessary. By July 9, his troops had taken Moung Son, even though the weather conditions were horrible and the resistance substantial. Fortunately, the Hmong guerrillas were able to obtain USAF air support this time; in fact, VP received as much support as he needed, from a USAF primed and ready to fly and fight. Another bonus for VP was that the USAF had already installed a new TACAN unit north of Na Khang, and it had already come in handy during the unusually ugly weather that had plagued the Hmong guerrillas.

Now, with Moung Son under his control, VP turned his attention to Phou Pha Thi. The USAF flew almost 300 air strikes in July 1968, and in August, they flew an additional 800 sorties in support of Barrel Roll operations, with almost half supporting VP's initiatives. By then, the NVA was frustrated and tired of the fight. After being pounded by the monsoon rains and the other American strike aircraft, they had had enough. They fell back to regroup and rest—and brought their artillery to bear on Muong Son. The resulting barrage was so intense that it made resupply to Vang Pao's troops impossible; wounded troops couldn't even be picked up and taken to medical facilities for treatment. VP's troops were now cut off from outside help.

After the loss of Nam Bac, Phou Pha Thi, and most of the other Lima Sites in northeastern Laos, Phong Saly and Sam Neua quickly became centers of power for the enemy. As mentioned earlier, when Nam Bac fell, the FAR became an ineffective and demoralized entity. They had little to offer as a fighting force, and the Hmong were only able to launch small conventional operations. And, as the NVA speeded up construction of all-weather roads for year-round use, the Secret War became a desperate struggle for survival for the Lao.

Even as the FAR and FAL tried to find their directions, the United States had reached a decision in South Vietnam. As a result of the Tet Offensive, Washington decided to gradually pull out, leaving the South Vietnamese to fight the Communists alone. The bombing over North Vietnam would remain suspended. Meanwhile, the USAF continued to redirect its resources to interdicting the flow of supplies down the Ho Chi Minh Trail and into South Vietnam. This left northern Laos in a precarious position, requiring more study. It was also the time of year for many U.S military personnel in Laos to rotate back to the United States. That would soon bring new faces into Vientiane, and relationships would have to be reestablished all over again.

In June 1968, USAF Colonel Robert Tyrell returned to Laos for a second tour as the Air Attaché. What he found upon his arrival was a disorganized, ineffective, and corrupt RLAF. His immediate tasks would be to rebuild the RLAF, and eliminate the use of its C-47 aircraft for transporting opium and gold. On July 17, in a meeting between high-ranking Lao military officers and the American personnel at the embassy in Vientiane, Ambassador Sullivan told them that he was shocked at the extent of corruption among the senior officers. Sullivan also told them they needed to prove to all Lao citizens that the government was good; if they didn't do that, he noted, the Communists would win the war for sure. Some of the generals complained about the sacrifices they had already made, but the ambassador countered by pointing out that the lower-ranking soldiers were the ones making all the sacrifices, not the generals. To reinforce his position, the ambassador told them that the King and Souvanna Phouma agreed with him. To further emphasize the importance of stepping up to the plate, Sullivan told the generals that until he saw real progress, no new U.S. aircraft would be delivered to the RLAF.

A week later, Colonel Tyrell unveiled his new plan, which required all USAF advisors to be realigned as necessary at all the RLAF bases. Additionally, all transport missions utilizing the RLAF C-47s would be scheduled out of a centralized Combined Operations Center (COC). The five existing AOCs would be expanded, and mobile aircraft maintenance training teams would provide upgrade training. When Tyrell's plan was forwarded up the chain of command, the USAF quickly approved it. The plan provided for a USAF AOC commander, a medic, a radio operator, aircraft maintenance chief, an intelligence officer, and a Raven FAC at each AOC.

The additional American troops would be provided under a program called "Palace Dog," which was under the Waterpump program at Udorn. The staffing process consisted of having the SAWC at Eglin AFB locate, recruit and train the active duty personnel for Palace Dog. Then the specialists would be sent to Udorn, where they would be sheep-dipped, given orientation training, and assigned to the AOCs in Laos. These AOCs were located at Vientiane (Lima-08), Savannakhet (Lima-39), Long Tieng (Lima-20A), Luang Prabang (Lima-54), and Pakse (Lima-11). Additionally, the specialists (except for the intelligence officer) would be assigned to Laos on 179-day temporary duty assignments; the intelligence officer would be assigned to Laos for one year. The chain of command for this revised organization structure was arranged so the specialists would report to the commander of the AOC, who reported to Colonel Tyrell; and, of course, Tyrell reported directly to the Ambassador. The AOC concept had been adopted after the Geneva Accords in 1962, but Palace Dog made it a more formal program, and expanded the staffing.

To further enhance coordination between the RLAF and ground forces, a Joint Operations Centers (JOC) was also established in each Military Region. The JOC would be the place where Lao military and U.S. embassy personnel would meet and discuss current and upcoming operations. The leaders would then return to their respective offices and disseminate the information to their subordinates. The intention was to have the information from the JOC passed to the AOCs, and then passed down to the crews supporting the ground troops.

One additional layer of control was adopted: the Combined Operations Center (COC) in Vientiane. The COC concept had existed for quite a while, but lacked decent communications and staff and, most of all, good direction. To correct this deficiency, Colonel Tyrell recruited an airlift expert using the SAWC. The result was the assignment of USAF Lieutenant Colonel Howard K. Hartley to Vientiane. The FAR welcomed this addition, but the RLAF field commanders were only mildly receptive to the new officer. It appeared that with the addition of Colonel Hartley, control of the RLAF C-47 transports would finally result in the aircraft actually being used as intended, and not as air taxis for transporting contraband.

The new COC was soon established, but got off to a slow start; in time, however, it began to function effectively, and as expected, dramatically reduced smuggling. Of course, it was always possible for the RLAF to ignore the required scheduling protocol and simply direct a crew to fly an unspecified load to a certain destination. But for the most part, smuggling was limited to the degree that other essential combat operations were not impacted. But for all that it improved; the COC did have its limitations. It could not change attitudes, personalities, or predispositions; and any RLAF regional commander could ignore the edict coming from the COC and wage war his way. But there were successful joint operations between the regions, so some progress was made.

As the RLAF infrastructure improved, the U.S. AIRA proposed that a C-47 mobile training team be established to enhance the RLAF transport capability. Ambassador Sullivan agreed, and subsequently asked JUSMAGTHAI to request approval from the Thai government allowing the mobile training team to operate out of Udorn. The Thai government approved the request, but opted to locate the team at Phitsanulok, in northwest Thailand, instead of at Udorn. JUSMAGTHAI then forwarded the request to CINCPAC. The package was approved on February 19, 1969, after the location was changed back to Udorn, and soon members of the team began arriving at Udorn, where they operated out of the Waterpump facilities. Training commenced on March 8, with the first class consisting of 18 RLAF students.

As expected, the training program was later expanded to address assault operations, aerial resupply, psychological operations, and AC-47 gunship familiarization.

In addition to Tyrell's reorganization efforts, there were other operational changes to the way the air war was waged in the second half of 1968. Earlier, on July 6, General Brown, the new 7th Air Force Commander, had sent a memo to Ambassador Sullivan proposing changes to the Rules Of Engagement (ROE) for the region. Sullivan responded that he saw no need to change the ROE, but that he would be willing to discuss the matter. Sullivan suggested that he and Brown also discuss upcoming operations requiring air support in northern Laos. Brown was no more interested in northern Laos than his predecessor, General Momyer, had been, but he agreed to the meeting out of political correctness. It was later held at Udorn Air Base on September 9.

Representing the embassy were Ambassadors Sullivan (Laos) and Unger (Thailand), Colonel Tyrell, Colonel Sonnenberg (Tyrell's assistant), the CIA station Chief in Laos, and two of his regional paramilitary advisors. On the U.S. military side were Brown, Brigadier General George Keegan, Brigadier General Bob Holbury, Major General Louis Seith, Brigadier General John Baer, and finally Major General Chesley Peterson. The USAF took the floor first, and for the remainder of the morning and into the afternoon they discussed interdiction in southern Laos, along with a new operation called Commando Hunt. At about mid-afternoon, the floor was finally yielded to Sullivan, who reminded the group that he also spoke for Souvanna Phouma, who had been unable to attend the meeting. The ambassador made it clear to the military brass that any expanded air operations in southern Laos would only be approved if greater air support for operations in northern Laos was also forthcoming. The ambassador went on to say that Souvanna would only defend the increased USAF activity in southern Laos if it was conducted in accordance with the ROE. Brown assured Sullivan that 7th Air Force would support the fighting in northern Laos, but insisted that General Seith (Deputy Commander, 7th/13th Air Force) become the focal point for all such activity. Sullivan agreed without reservation, much to the surprise of some of those in attendance.

Not surprising, however, was the fact that Brown and Sullivan both walked away from the meeting thinking they were winners.

Brown later wrote that the ambassador agreed to give the USAF a say in planning future operations, along with stronger command and control. Meanwhile, Sullivan reported that Brown consented to allowing him (the ambassador) to execute operations requiring USAF support, and to relax command and control. But for all that the meeting on September 9 didn't accomplish, in the end it did clear the air and gave visibility to existing issues that had been left unresolved for years. The meeting did not define the roles of either the Air Attaché in Vientiane or the 7th/13th Air Force, but in the final analysis, it was still beneficial.

Shortly after the meeting, a 7th/13th Air Force photo interpretation shop was established at Udorn, allowing General Seith and Colonel Tyrell to immediately evaluate current photo intelligence data. This capability also allowed for the creation of an updated target list that could be quickly dispatched to FACs in a particular area for further evaluation. High value targets could then be flagged and struck in a timely manner. In addition to striking high value targets sooner than later, lower priority targets were evaluated, distributed to the field, and struck as alternate targets when priority targets were not reachable.

But, there was one disadvantage to targeting in this manner. While a target could be prioritized, there was no means to determine what targets complemented or applied to an ongoing ground operation. So while a target could be successfully eliminated, was it of value to a particular ground commander? In other words, the air arm was still not talking to the ground pounders. And, of course, the CIA did their targeting without consulting the USAF at all. To resolve this issue, the targeting group at Udorn expanded their scope to include the Barrel Roll area of northern Laos. All the military and embassy personnel could then meet twice monthly to discuss operations and coordinate activities. This approach was adopted, and ultimately led to a better collective understanding by the entire group, and actually improved overall operations.

Meanwhile, a noteworthy event took place in Southeast Asia: Bill Lair announced that he wanted a transfer back to the United States. It was no secret that Lair disapproved of the way the Secret War was currently being managed by Vientiane. He thought the level of fighting and broad use of air strikes was unnecessary, and also believed there were too many Americans involved in directing the war. In other words, the war was too large. Lair feared that the Hmong would ultimately be the losers, and he didn't appreciate the brave little mountain fighters being used as cannon fodder to satisfy the embassy's hierarchy. In short order, Lair's transfer back to the U.S. was approved, and shortly thereafter, he left SEA. Pat Landry, Lair's former assistant, took his job.[79]

At about that same time, the second RLAF C-47 transport mobile training team had arrived in Laos. Fortunately, six students from the first class decided to stick around and assist in training the second class; and so the training continued into the succeeding years, with one team training the other, similar to the way Waterpump worked. The training began to improve C-47 operations, but poor maintenance and logistics were still hampering effective management of the RLAF air transport capability. Periodic and phased maintenance were the areas of primary concern. When maintenance was done, its thoroughness was in doubt, and in some cases it was being signed off as accomplished without being done at all. To combat the problem, the U.S. Embassy in Vientiane took firm control of the process. The maintenance facility at Savannakhet was moved to Vientiane, and most of the aircraft maintenance was contracted out to a company headquartered in Bangkok. The RLAF mechanics were still allowed to take care of some tasks, such as changing the tires and minor repairs, but for the most part they were out of the heavy maintenance business.

The RLAF were also poor managers of the logistics pipeline. When a replacement part was needed, the item might, or might not be in stock; for other items, the shelves were overflowing. And then there was the problem of nice-to-have personal items that were ordered and pilfered by the employees running the system. This problem was fixed by turning the logistics management process over to USAID and strictly controlling access to storage areas.

Back on the battlefield, the NVA were attacking aggressively, and the reason for the stepped-up action was directly attributable to the Tet Offensive. Hanoi could not allow the war supplies flowing down the Ho Chi Minh Trail to be delayed by U.S. interdiction actions. To that end, they directed their forces to keep the RLG tied down around Saravane, Savannakhet and Attopeu. But as the rains pounded the area, the NVA became disgruntled and lost their motivation. Their combat activity at that time consisted primarily of conducting small raids and sniping.

Looking for revenge, the Hmong SGU in Savannakhet was selected to retake Moung Phalane. On August 6, the guerrillas boarded helicopters and were flown to Phou Sang He, a mountain some distance northeast of Moung Phalane. The troops slowly worked their way along the ridgeline, finally arriving at Moung Phalane, where they met little resistance in retaking the site. Later, while conducting mop up operations in the area, Lao troops discovered a large cache of enemy weapons and tools. Air America helicopters were then called in to confiscate the war supplies and take them to Savannakhet. During this process, a CIA case officer named Wayne McNulty was killed by enemy gunfire while riding in one of the helicopters. It was believed that McNulty was the first CIA officer to be killed by enemy fire in Laos.

As September approached, the fighting in Laos was completely deadlocked, with neither side having an advantage. VP's troops were in bad shape, many were ill, and they were still pinned down at Moung Son. Meanwhile, the dry season was fast approaching, and fresh NVA troops began to pour into the Sam Neua area. Some estimates placed the number of NVA at more than 15 battalions, including three battalions positioned near Phou Pha Thi.

It was then that VP decided it was time for a direct attack against LS-85. Ambassador Sullivan still wasn't optimistic that the attack would be successful, and frankly just couldn't understand VP's obsession with retaking the mountain. With the Hmong guerrillas pinned down at Muong Son, Sullivan traveled to Udorn to talk to the USAF brass about air support. At first, the Air Force wasn't optimistic about being able to provide air support in the quantities needed by VP and the ambassador; but, after some discussion, they agreed to the plan. The brass also wanted to hit the NVA hard at the Sam Neua military staging area. By doing the latter, the generals believed they could disrupt the NVA plans to the extent that the Communists would not be able to mount their annual dry season offensive.

In September 1968, an exhausted Vang Pao was invited to visit the United States. He accepted, and Jerry Daniels, the CIA advisor at Long Tieng, accompanied him, along with one of VP's wives. As a goodwill gesture, VP carried with him a handcrafted Hmong musket as a gift to outgoing President Lyndon B. Johnson. While in the US, VP got the chance to see his old friend Bill Lair. He also visited the John Deere Tractor Company, CIA headquarters, and the White House, not to mention Disneyland and the colonial town of Williamsburg, Virginia. In addition, he visited Colonel Aderholt, who was stationed at Eglin Air Force Base in Florida. On his visit to the White House, VP didn't get the opportunity to meet President Johnson, but he did meet with members of Johnson's staff. Later, President Johnson sent him a thank-you note for the Hmong musket.

D.C. was a half a world away from the Secret War in Laos, which continued unabated despite VP's absence. The North Vietnamese kept moving war supplies and Communist troops down the Ho Chi Minh Trail to South Vietnam, and the brave airmen of the USAF continued to seek out and interdict that movement. One such airman was Captain Michael J. (Bat) Masterson, assigned to the 602nd Special Operations Squadron at NKP. Captain Masterson flew the A-1 Douglas Skyraider on interdiction missions in northern Laos. On October 13, 1968 he took to the skies over NKP in the late afternoon, bound for yet another mission along the famous Route 7, near the border between North Vietnam and Laos. It was approximately 6:00 P.M. when Captain Masterson started his take-off roll. The A-1 moved slowly at first, as the wings were loaded down with bombs and rockets; the aircraft also carried a full fuel load, and the internal weapons bays were full of ammunition. Slowly the Skyraider picked up speed, and finally took to the air as the aircraft crossed the perimeter fence of the airfield. Masterson and his wingman, USAF Major Pete Brown, slowly climbed to altitude, crossed the Mekong River, and entered the unfriendly skies of Laos.

The two aircraft continued to wing their way towards their destination, flying into and out of the cloud-filled skies. As they neared the target area, the clouds got thicker and visibility more limited, but they continued on. When they were about 15 minutes from Route 7, Captain Masterson called Brown on his radio and reported that he had lost his artificial horizon. Soon he called Brown again, reporting that he was experiencing vertigo, and would have to abort the mission.[80] Major Brown instructed Captain Masterson to call him again when he was out of the clouds, and headed back in the direction of NKP.

A few seconds later, Masterson called again and reported that he was "losing it and was getting out." Brown then began to make a 180 degree turn to make sure he was clear of Masterson's aircraft in the event he ejected. But as Brown was making the turn, he observed an orange fireball on the ground. Subsequent attempts to contact Captain Masterson were unsuccessful, and Major Brown remained in the area until relieved by a USAF C-130 Blind Bat flare ship that had heard the radio transmissions and headed to the location. Using a night-vision device called a Star Light scope, the crew could see the wreckage on the ground, but there was no sight of Captain Masterson, and there were no signals coming from his emergency rescue beacon. It appeared to the Blind Bat crew that Masterson's aircraft had impacted the ground at a high rate of speed and exploded. As it did so, it had buried itself in the jungle, and wreckage could be seen for a good distance from the point of impact.

During the hours after the crash, no emergency beeper signal could be detected, and no parachute canopy was observed. Major Brown and the Blind Bat aircraft stayed in the area until they began to run low on fuel, and then departed for their respective bases. At first light on the following morning, a formal SAR mission was initiated by four A-1 Skyraiders and an Air America UH-1 Huey helicopter. Upon arrival over the crash site, visibility was good, and the helicopter was able to get within a distance of about thirty feet above the crash site. The crew observed smoldering wreckage, wings, and a crater, with the fuselage appearing to be buried. They saw no evidence of Captain Masterson, his parachute, or ejection seat. Other aircraft were also orbiting the area around the crash site, and reported that no parachute or ejection seat could be located. And still, no emergency signal had been received, and no emergency voice transmission from Masterson was ever received.

A team on the ground also tried to reach the crash site, but hostile fire in the area precluded a personal examination of the crashed aircraft. The search was then suspended, and Captain Bat Masterson was officially listed as Missing in Action. A few days later, a team was able to reach the site, but could find no trace of Masterson or his ejection seat. No other information was received concerning Captain Masterson, and when the POWs were released from North Vietnam in 1973, Bat Masterson was not among them.

Many years later, on August 9, 1993, a U.S.-led Joint Task Force (JTF) team visited the crash site and conducted a thorough search of the area. They were able to verify that an A-1 Skyraider had crashed there, but they could not find any trace of Captain Masterson. In 1999, it was discovered that a Defense Intelligence Agency memorandum dated January 14, 1972 listed Masterson's status as POW, but it was later determined that a mistake had been made and Captain Masterson was still MIA. Still later, in the late summer of 2005, the Joint POW/MIA Accounting Command (JPAC) in Honolulu initiated another search for Captain Masterson's remains. Using maps pinpointing the exact location of the crash some 37 years earlier, a team set out to get to the bottom of the mystery.

The team located the site and cleared away all the dense vegetation. They located the remnants of a crater, and small pieces of aircraft wreckage strewn about the area. The JPAC specialists were able to determine that the remnants were from an A-1 Skyraider. They also found several U.S. coins minted prior to 1968. As they dug, they found live ammunition for the A-1 cannon, and ammunition for a .38 caliber handgun, much like the one Masterson would have carried. They also found a military identification tag with Captain Masterson's identifying information stenciled on it. In addition, they recovered very small bone fragments, which were burned to the point that positive identification was unlikely. As the search continued, they found a metal flight boot insert, of the same size that Captain Masterson would have worn, and a parachute still packed and unused—as well as metal zippers consistent in appearance with those from USAF flight suits of the 1960s. From all the evidence found, it was fairly obvious that Captain Masterson had perished in the crash.

Unfortunately, as with many other brave pilots who disappeared while on missions over northern Laos, it will probably never be known for sure exactly what happened to Bat Masterson.

Meanwhile, in Paris, Hanoi continued its talks with Washington. But back in Laos, the NVA were gearing up for their dry season offensive. Moung Son was back in Communist hands, Vang Pao's troops were pushed south to Houei Hinsa, and two NVA battalions were conducting operations near Na Khang.

As the war in Laos continued to show increased Communist involvement, Washington became concerned, and asked the Department of Defense for an analysis of the situation on October 17. The JCS was selected to provide the assessment. They later submitted a report indicating that the NVA possessed the capability to overrun Laos at any time, but had not for political reasons; and that as long as Hanoi adhered to that policy, the U.S. needed to provide only limited air support to the Lao government. But if North Vietnam escalated their offensive operations, it would show a lack of good faith in the Paris peace talks. If that should occur, the JCS pointed out, the U.S. would need to step up its own air campaign to discourage the Communists.

The JCS also reported that should North Vietnam attempt to overrun Laos, U.S. combat troops might be required in Laos to deter a large-scale offensive. The Joint Chiefs also reminded the White House that the cost would be enormous, not to mention the possibility of drawing China into the conflict. In short, the JCS recommended that the U.S. continue the piecemeal approach heretofore followed, hoping that Hanoi would see the light and give up the fight. But as we now know—and should have known then—Ho Chi Minh and General Giap would not be deterred. They were in it to win, regardless of how long it took or how many lives were lost in the process. Either the leaders in Washington had not studied what the Vietminh had done to the French at Dien Bien Phu, or they were simply oblivious to what was going on in Vietnam and Laos.

This became blatantly obvious on October 31, when President Johnson addressed the United States in a televised speech. He began by announcing that there were important developments in the search for peace in Vietnam, and indicated that North Vietnam had begun to talk after his bombing halt on March 31. The President also claimed, "We could not stop the bombing, so long as by doing so we would endanger the lives and safety of our troops." But that's exactly what did happen. Every time he paused the bombing, the NVA seized the opportunity to become stronger and deliver even more lethal blows to U.S., Lao, and South Vietnamese troops. President Johnson went on to say that he had spoken with all the diplomats and military leaders, and they had agreed on his course of action, believing that peace would be the fruit of their endeavors. Again, we now know that would not be the case; Hanoi only had one objective, and that was to win. Johnson then decreed in his speech that all air, naval, and artillery bombardment of North Vietnam would cease at 8:00 A.M. on November 1, 1968. The President went on to state that South Vietnam had grown stronger through the leadership of the United States. It appeared clear that Johnson was convinced that the way he ran the war in Vietnam had yielded positive results, and that peace was near—but nothing could have been farther from the truth.

One thing was clear, however: Johnson was washing his hands of the war and walking away, leaving a mess for the next President to cleanup. It was time for him to return to Texas, and hopefully do a better job of running his ranch than he had done of running the country. A few days later, on November 5, 1968, Richard M. Nixon was elected the 37th President of the United States.

Meanwhile, on October 20, 1968, VP returned to Long Tieng, having completed his month-long vacation in the United States. He was refreshed and ready to return to the fight. His troops, however, had not gotten a vacation while VP was away, because they were busy fighting the NVA. They were all exhausted, and just about half of the guerrilla army no longer even existed. Most had been killed fighting the Communists, and others had just walked away. A recent recruiting program had yielded some replacements, but for the most part they were too young and had no fighting experience. Some were as young as 13 years old.

After his return from the U.S., VP organized an offensive he called "Operation Pig Fat." He anticipated that the operation would last about a week, beginning in November. One of his objectives was to retake Phou Pha Thi and recover the bodies of the dead USAF technicians for return to their families. A second objective was for Lao government troops to relieve pressure on Na Khang and Houei Hinsa, where NVA and Pathet Lao troops were massing. VP knew that with the bombing cessation over North Vietnam, more jet fighters would be available to help in the Barrel Roll area; and he could always count on air assets from NKP's 56th Air Commando Wing, now renamed the 56th Special Operations Wing, in Thailand. Their slow moving A-1 Skyraiders invariably came to his aid, bringing heavy loads of ordnance.

But VP would not be starting Operation Pig Fat under optimum conditions. The dry season was approaching, and the NVA were gearing up for heavy combat. VP's troops had already been decimated, and the replacement guerrillas were all green and very young. One additional issue to contend with was the fact that while peace talks continued in Paris, the Communists might attempt to grab up as much territory as possible for use in the future as bargaining chips. And it as the fighting in South Vietnam decreased, more NVA troops would become available to help the Pathet Lao in northern Laos. In fact, by then the Communists had already seized Moung Son, and had pushed the Hmong as far south as Houei Hinsa. Phou Pha Thi was still held by the NVA, Communist battalions were settling in near Na Khang, and Moung Oum was under Communist attack. And last, but certainly not least, 16 fresh NVA battalions were staged in the Sam Neua area, with plenty of big guns and equipment.

Operation Pig Fat was scheduled to begin on November 1, with Lao government forces relieving pressure on Na Khang and Houei Hinsa and then sweeping east across Route 6. But during the Secret War, things did not always go as planned. Even though the dry season was in full swing, it began to rain something fierce in November 1968. In the face of both inclement weather and continuing logistical problems, VP was nonetheless able to begin his attack to retake LS-85 on November 28. He planned a four-prong assault, and his troops fanned out in the direction of the Lima sites around LS-85. As fate would have it, the NVA wasn't expecting such a move, and VP caught them completely off guard. The Lima Sites around Phou Pha Thi began to fall, one after the other.

As the operation gained momentum, VP decided to put more resources into the fight, and also to make it his dry season offensive. The new plan called for three battalions to attack Phou Pha Thi, supported by a substantial number of USAF air strikes. The three battalions were to divide up into four groups and advance on the mountain, and this they did. Over the next several days, the groups made good progress, but the availability of air power was reduced significantly due to increased emphasis on interdiction missions along the Ho Chi Minh Trail in southern Laos. Eventually, VP and his men found themselves at Houei Ma (LS-107), near Phou Pha Thi—in fact, they were within artillery range. The Hmong general then brought up a 105mm artillery piece so he could lob shells onto the mountaintop. VP's troops were able to retake Houei Ma, but heavy NVA mortar fire soon began to fall on their position.

Shortly thereafter, another group of Hmong guerrillas were directed to climb the footpath to the southeastern slope of Phou Pha Thi, and work their way up to the summit. The guerrillas followed their orders, and were able to make it quite a ways up the footpath and establish a position—but the NVA soon discovered the climbers and began to spray the area with machine gun fire, driving the guerrillas back down the path to the valley floor. The NVA gun was subsequently silenced by artillery fire from Houei Ma, but the climbers were unable to reestablish a foothold.

By November 30, the NVA had regained their composure and gone on the offensive. The NVA 148th Regiment sent three battalions to join the fight near LS-85, and the rest of the NVA troops at Sam Neua went on alert, though for the most part they had already dispersed. At about that same time, the USAF began to drop bombs on the NVA staging areas at Sam Neua, but fortunately for the Communists they didn't sustain much damage. Meanwhile, the air strikes on LS-85 were taking a toll, but the Communists held on to the last man. On December 8, the USAF lost two A-1 Skyraiders and two helicopters in the fight for the mountain. The NVA then began to find their range, and on December 21 the Communists managed to retake Houei Ma, destroying VP's artillery piece and the ammunition that was stored nearby, killing a Hmong commander in the process.

Meanwhile, the Hmong guerrillas finally reached the summit of LS-85, but didn't find much to mop up once they got there, because the Communists had already moved on. With that, the Hmong offensive rapidly began to wither, so the NVA went on the offensive once again. Pressure from the NVA continued to increase, and soon VP left the fight, returning to Long Tieng to celebrate his birthday and to plan a new offensive. By early January 1969, the weather and additional reinforcements of NVA troops caused Operation Pig Fat to stall and slowly fall apart.

As the NVA began their mop up at the Lima sites around LS-85, VP's troops retreated to Na Khang (LS-36) and waited for the expected attack—which did not come. Instead, the NVA surprised everyone by striking in southern Laos at the town of Tatteng, near the Bolovens Plateau. When the attack started, the Lao defenders retreated to a small fort on the edge of the town to await their fate. When the news reached Vientiane, USAF fighters were summoned and they harassed the enemy at Tatteng all night long. Over the next week, the Communists attacked the fort repeatedly, trying to cut a path through the minefield around the compound and the barbed wire protecting it.

Meanwhile RLAF and USAF fighters and gunships pounded the NVA around the clock. The fort held, but the village around it was practically blown to pieces by all the exploding ordnance. Nonetheless, the fighting continued through the month of January and into February 1969. The NVA troops then slowed their attack, resorting to occasional mortar fire and probes. Later, on February 2, the Communists went back to all-out assaults, but still the fort held, thanks to continued air strikes. As February wore on, the USAF supplied generous quantities of airdropped antipersonnel mines and rolls of barbed wire that essentially deployed while falling to earth. Fortunately for the defenders, the mines and the wire seemed to do the trick, and the NVA attacks slowed again.

Finally, on March 9, 1969, the attack was broken and the NVA retreated. When all was said and done, the defenders literally walked out of the fort without incident, and the NVA troops who were left standing simply walked away from the fight, dragging their wounded with them. Left behind were hundreds of dead Communist soldiers, rotting in the sun.

Meanwhile, the new covert 7th Air Force and U.S. Navy aerial interdiction program known as "Commando Hunt" had begun in November 1968. The new program targeted the entire Ho Chi Minh Trail, from its origin in North Vietnam to its terminus in South Vietnam. The program would use the lessons learned from Operation Turnpike and the latest technology, including Igloo White, Operation Popeye, the MSQ-77 Combat Sky spot laser guided bombing system, MACV-SOG, and the new AC-130 Spectre gunships.

Commando Hunt had actually been conceived back in 1966, after Secretary of Defense Robert McNamara became disenchanted with bombing efforts over North Vietnam, and their failure to stem the flow of war supplies on the Ho Chi Minh Trail. Even at that time, McNamara had reportedly considered an electronic barrier to infiltration from the Demilitarized Zone (DMZ) to southern Laos. The electronic barrier would consist of acoustic and seismic sensors that would pinpoint enemy locations and movement. A scientific group was later established to develop the electronic technology. It was first called "Practice Nine," then "Illinois City," "Dye Marker," "Muscle Shoals," and finally "Igloo White."

Igloo White consisted of three integral components. First, battery-powered sensors, implanted by either aircraft or MACV-SOG troops, would monitor movement and then report this activity electronically to an ABCCC flying above. The airborne control center would then relay the data to the Infiltration Surveillance Center (ISC) at NKP, where giant mainframe computers would analyze the data. Next, the computers would transmit target coordinates back to the ABCCC which would, in turn, direct air strikes on the targets. The anti-infiltration effort would also be supported by the MSQ-77 Combat Sky Spot ground-based radar bombing system, which would direct air strikes in any weather, even complete darkness.

The initial test of the new Igloo White sensors had previously taken place in November 1967, in support of U.S. Marines at Khe Sanh Combat Base in South Vietnam, near the DMZ. After implanting over 300 sensors around the perimeter of the base, monitoring personnel were able to locate and target the attacking NVA troops. With that information, U.S. aircraft were able to come in and successfully bomb the enemy troops, breaking their will and sparing the U.S. troops at Khe Sanh.

When Commando Hunt was employed along the Ho Chi Minh Trail, it was never assumed that the operation would completely stop the flow of NVA troops and supplies into South Vietnam. The goal was simply to limit the flow to the extent possible. The initial thrust of Commando Hunt 1 envisioned two objectives: first, to substantially reduce the flow of troops and supplies, increasing the amount of time required for those resources to reach the battlefield; and second, to destroy as many NVA trucks and supply caches as possible during transit. The undertaking would be a monumental one, because the Trail was controlled by the North Vietnamese 259th Logistics Group. The 259th was composed of tens of thousands of NVA troops dedicated to protecting the Trail, along with thousands of civilian engineers who directed the Trail's maintenance. That was coupled with 40,000-50,000 civilian laborers employed to maintain the motorability of the Trail utilizing at least 20 bulldozers, 11 road graders, three rock crushers, and two steam rollers.

By the end of Commando Hunt 1 in April 1969, the USAF estimated that over 7,000 NVA trucks had been destroyed, and over 20,000 enemy personnel had been killed by air strikes. On the U.S. side, over 50 aircraft had been lost. Nonetheless, the flow of traffic on the Trail continued unabated. And to make matters worse, the NVA had installed hundreds of larger antiaircraft guns along the route, and some of those used radar-guided technology.

Meanwhile, on December 24, 1968, an F-105 Thunderchief, call sign "Panda 01," was shot down and crashed in Laos near the town of Ban Phaphilang. The pilot was USAF Major Chuck Brownlee, who successfully ejected. Unfortunately, however, his parachute drifted into an area known to be occupied by Communist troops. Brownlee's wingman made radio contact with the downed pilot, who reported that he was injured. Two HH-3 Jolly Green Giants on airborne alert quickly proceeded to the crash site, and could see Major Brownlee's parachute in the trees. They made numerous attempts to contact the pilot, but received no response. By that time, darkness was closing in. The Jolly Greens did not have nighttime rescue capability, so they departed and returned to their assigned base at NKP.

At first light on December 25, an all-volunteer crew departed NKP in an HH-3 Jolly Green Giant helicopter, with A-1 Skyraider escort and a second HH-3.[81] The pilot of the primary rescue or "Low" HH-3 was Major Reinhart, the copilot was Captain Gibson, and the flight engineer was Sergeant Gallagher. The Para Rescue man was Airman First Class Charles D. King. When they arrived over the crash site, the A-1s trolled the area for enemy fire, but the waiting Communists were not taking the bait. Having not taken any fire, the lead A-1 directed the Low HH-3 to go in and attempt a rescue. The Jolly Green then navigated directly over the parachute of Major Brownlee, and Sergeant Gallagher could see Brownlee in the harness. Brownlee was not moving, and his feet were only about twelve inches off the ground. Airman King then volunteered to go down and rescue Brownlee, so he was lowered by cable with a jungle penetrator.

No sooner than King's feet had touched the ground than the Communist troops opened fire on him, Brownlee, and the HH-3. Somehow, King managed to get Brownlee onto the penetrator, but in the process, King was hit by enemy fire. He called Major Reinhart on the radio and related that he was hit, and recommended that Reinhart immediately ascend and depart the area. Sudden ascents were not standard operating procedure, due to the potential danger to the rescue troop and to the person being rescued; but in this case, the chopper was taking automatic weapons fire and could have gone down at any moment. So Reinhart quickly ascended straight up, and in the process the penetrator cable caught on a tree and snapped. The helicopter continued to ascend, but King and Brownlee fell to the jungle floor. King got on the radio again and told Reinhart to leave the area immediately due to the heavy enemy fire. Reinhart then moved the control stick forward and applied power, taking himself, the helicopter, and the rest of the crew away from the intense small arms fire.

The enemy then swarmed over King and Brownlee, but Reinhart's men could not fire on the enemy troops for fear of hitting the two Americans. For the next two days, additional rescue efforts at the crash site continued, but King and Brownlee could not be located. Years later, it became known that Airman King had initially survived the attack and was taken prisoner. Many years after that, his Geneva Convention identification card was located in a war museum in Hanoi. No information was ever received on Brownlee, but the rescue crew believed that he had died while hanging in tree, still attached to his parachute harness. Other reports indicated that King died of his wounds while trying to rescue Brownlee. But we'll never know for sure what actually happened to King and Brownlee. And, as previously mentioned, it was not uncommon for the NVA to unceremoniously bury Americans who died during capture or during captivity.

As 1968 drew to a close, the situation in northern Laos appeared grim for the Americans and the Lao alike. The NVA had positioned many thousands of troops in the region, and they weren't going to leave. Vang Pao was running out of options and troops. Meanwhile, the U.S. government was slowly backing away from the war, and the United States was about to inaugurate a new President. Meanwhile, Averell Harriman was in Paris trying to get Hanoi to negotiate an end to the war in SEA. Sadly, it did not appear that Communism could be stopped in the tiny kingdom of Laos; but it was clear that a lot of fighting and dying would continue to take place before things eventuality played out.

The 1968 gains made by the Communists put new strains on the RLG. There were fears of rebellious conduct on the part of the Lao soldiers in Vientiane and Luang Prabang, but for the most part, that did not happen. And, at about this same time, reorganization at the upper levels of the Lao military command began to take place, resulting in some of the older generals being transferred to prestigious positions in Vientiane. This was viewed as a positive development, because it cleared the way for the younger officers to have more authority, as well as a voice in the planning and execution of the war.

Let's hope that 1969 brings better news for those fighting to keep Communism out of Laos.

Chapter 11

Erosion of Confidence

In early January 1969, Pop Buell returned from home leave in the United States and made the rounds, checking on the refugees in the Lao villages before reporting his findings to USAID. While doing so, Pop discovered that about one-third of the areas previously controlled by the Hmong had been lost. Over 50% of the schools he had started earlier were gone, and most of the fighting men had been killed. To Pop's way of thinking, there were just no available options to the Hmong; in other words, no more mountains to flee to, and no place to hide.

Pop's assessment was correct. The NVA had begun to take the fight to the Hmong. With the cessation of bombing over North Vietnam by President Johnson, the NVA were free to bring larger antiaircraft weapons into Laos. The big guns were then positioned along the Ho Chi Minh Trail in southern Laos, and at key locations in northeastern Laos.

Also in early January 1969, Vang Pao issued orders to form a defensive perimeter encompassing Houei Tong Ko, Moung Hiem and Na Khang. In order to get the civilians out of the line of fire, the USAF 20th Special Operations Squadron (SOS), the "Pony Express" from Udorn, flew hundreds of missions in their CH-3E helicopters, moving civilians out of harm's way so Pop Buell could take care of them at Sam Thong. At the same time, VP was busy rotating troops in the field, providing them with a break in the action and allowing some to return to Long Tieng for rest and relaxation.

Meanwhile, the NVA developed a new plan of action. They kicked off their dry season offensive by probing Phou Fa, Phou Vieng, Sam Thong and Phu Cum. They covered their advance with 37mm, 57mm, 12.7mm and 23mm antiaircraft weapons. This made the area too hot for the slower propeller-driven U.S. strike aircraft, so fast-moving F-4 Phantom jets were called in to provide close air support.

The Communists also sent troops into Phong Saly in the north, and to the southern edge of Xieng Khouang Province. But the NVA's main focus was Moung Soui. The base had been a thorn in the side of the Communists ever since Kong Le had occupied the site a few years earlier, after being driven out of Khang Khay (Khang Khai). Muong Soui had also become an operating location for the RLAF T-28 aircraft, and they had been harassed by the NVA for months. It was a different ballgame now, however. Kong Le had long since given up and fled to Thailand, where he was living in exile. On two occasions in the past years, NVA sappers had unsuccessfully tried to take Muong Soui. And, more recently, huge stockpiles of bombs and ordnance had been staged at Muong Soui for anticipated RLAF raids around the Plain of Jars. To make matters worse, the USAF also stationed about ten USAF technicians at the site to assist the RLAF. With the build-up and the presence of American troops, it was time for the NVA to take the site once and for all.

On January 17, a Pony Express CH-3 helicopter flew USAF Communications technicians to a remote area just north of Na Khang to work on the TACAN system, which had been installed after Phou Pha Thi fell. Periodic maintenance of the TACAN unit was required, and had been performed from time to time; but previously, smaller UH-1 helicopters had been used to transport the USAF technicians to and from the site. On this day, however, the smaller helicopters weren't available, so the decision was made to use the CH-3. As the helicopter hovered in preparation for landing on the small mountain helipad, it took small arms fire. When the landing gear came in contact with the ground, the helicopter rolled over the edge of the pad and down the side of a hill, coming to rest in a ravine below. Three USAF personnel were thrown from the aircraft, but the five crew members and one technician were still on the helicopter, and were killed as it exploded on impact.

Also in January, a detachment of several EC-47 airborne radio direction-finding aircraft was assigned to NKP. The "Electric Gooneys," as they were called, could monitor NVA ground radio transmissions, identify their exact locations, and provide that information to the ABCCC for targeting. The ABCCC would then scramble USAF jet fighters to bomb the NVA by homing in on the location of the outgoing radio transmissions. The USAF personnel flying on the EC-47s would listen to NVA conversations and glean valuable intelligence information regarding their operations plans. These aircraft were manned by airmen assigned to the USAF Security Service who were fluent in

Vietnamese, French, and other languages commonly used in that area of the world.

On February 10, just after midnight, the NVA initiated their attack on Muong Soui. Approximately 30 NVA Dac Cong commandos crept into the village near the base and attacked the perimeter of Muong Soui with rockets and grenades. Next, they penetrated the perimeter fence and began moving through the compound, lobbing grenades and raking the area with AK-47 assault rifles. Going from tent to tent and shack to shack, the Communists inflicted heavy damage to the site. When it was over, eleven Lao troops and one American were dead. Twenty others were wounded, and the surviving Lao troops fled, disappearing into the jungle. Shortly after the NVA attack began, a USAF flare ship showed up overhead with fighters following close behind. Sporadic fighting continued during the night, but by the next morning, Muong Soui was back in government hands. During the attack, two helicopters had been able to land and successfully extract eight USAF technicians.

The Communist offensive at Muong Soui was a major concern to embassy officials in Vientiane, because the U.S. plan was to slowly de-escalate the level of warfare in Laos. The last thing they wanted was an escalation. But in northern Laos, the fighting was beginning to intensify, because the NVA were not marching to Washington's drumbeat. Disturbed by events in Laos, the White House then sent William Bundy, the Assistant Secretary of State, to see the folks at the Russian embassy in DC. Bundy was asked to deliver a message to the Soviets indicating that the incoming Nixon Administration might not approve of the measures being taken by the NVA in Laos. It was hoped that this move would persuade the Soviets to apply pressure on the NVA to stop fighting and seek peace, but the Soviets failed to take the bait—and they responded by showing Bundy the door.

Meanwhile, back in Laos, VP's resources were rapidly diminishing. He had no choice but to reallocate his troops to protect the Hmong heartland southwest of the Plain, because he knew that a concentrated push by the Communists could not be contained. On a more positive note, Na Khang was temporarily back in Lao hands, and VP hoped that the site could weather one more attack, as it had for the past two years.

Meanwhile, on February 12, Souvanna Phouma admitted to the media for the first time that the U.S. was dropping bombs on the Ho

Chi Minh Trail and in northern Laos. He told the reporters that Laos had no option but to seek the help of the Americans, because North Vietnam had violated the conditions of the Geneva Accords. He also offered to stop the bombing if North Vietnam removed their troops. The Pathet Lao's response to Souvanna's statement was to promptly demand the cessation of all bombing, without addressing the issue of NVA troop withdrawal.

Later, on February 28, the 174th Regiment of the NVA moved against Na Khang. This time, however, they did not use the obvious entry route through the trees as they had in the past; instead, they decided to gain entry by crawling through a new stand of elephant grass along the perimeter of the base. Not expecting an attack from the tall grass, the Lao defenders were intently watching the tree line for the approaching Communists. By the time they realized what was taking place, it was too late. After penetrating the perimeter, the NVA set up a machine gun on the runway and began chewing up the buildings and shacks in the compound. Many defenders began to fall. Meanwhile, the USAF sent two flights of F-4 Phantoms, and later two F-105 Thunderchief flights, with strikes directed by a FAC. As night fell, the A-26 Nimrods from NKP and the new AC-130 Spectre gunship from Ubon also showed up to assist the defenders at Na Khang. But there wasn't a lot of progress made, because the NVA were all over the site, making it hard to distinguish them from the Hmong.

Meanwhile, the 20th SOS Pony Express also arrived with their CH-3E helicopters to evacuate the civilians. Fighting continued through the night and into the following morning, when USAF fighter craft returned, along with A-1 Skyraiders. One of the Skyraiders was shot down, but the other took out two NVA machine guns. The fighting continued, with many Hmong defenders being killed—but few Communist soldiers appeared to be losing their lives. Later, during the night of March1, an errant incoming mortar round landed directly on the Hmong command post, killing all the officers. When the word got around the compound that the officers had been killed, the Hmong guerrillas stopped fighting, and quietly slipped out of the compound and through enemy lines towards Long Tieng. When the sun came up on March 2, the USAF fighters returned to help the defenders, but soon discovered that all the surviving Hmong soldiers were gone, with only the dead left behind. With no other alternative, the fighters destroyed what they could of the site and its contents to deprive the NVA of equipment and supplies. Na Khang was in Communist hands.

With the fall of LS-36, nothing stood in the way of the NVA all the way from the Plain of Jars to Long Tieng; and except for Bouam Long (LS-32), Phu Cum (LS-50) and Phou Vieng (LS-6), there wasn't anything to block the Communists from walking into Muong Soui. Out of the four battalions defending Na Khang before the recent battle, only about a hundred Lao troops were able to escape and survive. All the others were dead. As history would later show, VP and his troops would never hold Na Khang again.

After LS-36 fell, the USAF sent in wave after wave of fighter aircraft to level the site. Meanwhile, the NVA moved over 30,000 troops into eastern Laos along the Ho Chi Minh Trail. NVA troops also poured onto the Plain of Jars, the area around Bouan Long, and as far south as the hills around Long Tieng and Sam Thong. Meanwhile the talks in Paris continued, and in America the protests against the war in Vietnam and Laos grew louder.

Back in February, Colonel Tyrell had submitted a formal request for additional T-28 aircraft. At the time, the American embassy in Vientiane was pleased with the RLAF, so they supported the request. The JCS in Washington, however, did not agree and disapproved the request, citing a worldwide shortage of T-28 Trojans. But embassy personnel would not take no for an answer, and escalated the issue to the Secretary of State. The request subsequently stalled, and for the time being, there would be no additional T-28 aircraft forthcoming.

Also in February 1969, the AIRA requested that AC-47 gunships be assigned to Laos to help fight the Communists. As an interim measure, he recommended converting existing RLAF C-47 transports using existing machine guns and other equipment. As usual, correspondence continued to flow back and forth for several months; and in the interim, the 7th Air Force agreed to make four USAF AC-47 gunships available for use in Laos.

Later, on approximately March 13, 1969, the four AC-47 "Spooky" gunships arrived in northern Laos, and were put to work that same evening. Apparently, an area near Muong Ngai (LS-01) was under heavy attack and needed help fast. Spooky 01 quickly took to the air, and showed up at about the same time as the exact location of the bad guys was confirmed. The gunship then went to work, spraying the enemy with cannon fire, and stayed over the target until it was completely out of ammunition. Then Spooky headed home. When the sun came up the next morning, the devastation of the gunship attack was apparent, and the good guys were convinced that Spooky would be their weapon of choice in future defenses.

After that incident, the Spookies continued to impress the Americans and the Lao troops, and during the period from March through October 1969, the AC-47s flew hundreds of missions in northern Laos in defense of more than 300 Lao government positions. None of the positions were lost. One specific example was apparent at Bouam Long (LS-32), an isolated Hmong outpost in northern Laos. At that location, on March 20, 1969, Spooky beat off two heavy NVA attacks, killing close to 200 NVA and Pathet Lao soldiers.

To help shore up Lao defenses, four additional AC-47s, their crews, and support personnel were subsequently assigned to Udorn Air Base. Colonel William H. Ginn, Jr, the Deputy Commander for Operations at Udorn, then flew to Long Tieng to visit with VP, to explain how the Spookies could be utilized. The meeting was productive, and Colonel Ginn left believing that he had been able to boost VP's morale, and that the Hmong's combat effectiveness would be improved with the use of the Spooky gunships. The gunships would be controlled by 7th Air Force Headquarters in Saigon, South Vietnam. The "Blue Chip" Command Center would direct the AC-47s over Laos through "Alleycat," the nighttime orbiting airborne battlefield command and control center. One AC-47 would be airborne nightly, backed up by another Spooky on the ground.

As morale plummeted among the Hmong government troops in early 1969, many began to desert. Many others simply retired, having served their time in VP's army. New recruits were still hard to come by, and thousands were needed right away to fill the ranks of the approximately 20,000 killed in action; but even with significant recruitment efforts, only a few hundred troops were found to replace those already gone. Even worse, about one-third of the new recruits were younger than fourteen years old.

The loss of Na Khang and Phou Pha Thi didn't help the situation. Many began to question VP's leadership abilities, VP among them. After all, 1969 had started miserably. Phou Pha Thi, Muong Soui and Na Khang had been taken by the Communists, and VP felt that he had lost face again. He was humiliated, and depression set in. Even his CIA advisors became concerned. The general wandered around Long Tieng aimlessly; it was said that he did not bathe often, and wore the same clothes day after day.

Meanwhile, the NVA doubled their troop strength in Laos to approximately 100,000. The Communists then pushed their way into the foothills of the Plain of Jars, where they could reach Long Tieng with their large artillery pieces. They intended to establish a position that would allow them to stay in the country through the annual monsoon season, breaking the tradition of turf-swapping with the changing seasons.

Pop Buell heard about VP's depression so he traveled from Sam Thong to Long Tieng to hopefully boost the General's spirits. What he found when he got there was pretty much what he had expected: VP was in a sullen mood, and hadn't shaved, bathed, or changed his clothes recently. For the most part, VP was sitting by himself, as he did from time to time, stewing in his own juices and hoping for a vision. Pop tried to talk to VP, but it didn't do a lot of good. So he stayed with VP for quite awhile, and began recounting all the good things that VP had accomplished.

At about that same time, a Raven FAC operating over the Plain of Jars discovered large caches of explosives and ammunition being stockpiled by the NVA for future operations. While flying overhead, the Raven had observed the explosives in newly-dug trenches, before they could be concealed. He then called the orbiting airborne control center, requesting an air strike. The request was approved immediately, and soon U.S. fighters rolled in and found their targets. The Raven watched from high above as the bombs struck the trenches—and then the sky lit up and the hills shook as the explosives and ammunition began to cook off. The munitions continued to explode throughout the night and into the next day. When it was finally over, it appeared that the NVA would be deprived of essential munitions for their planned 1969 attacks.

Hearing the news, Vang Pao's mood quickly changed. All of a sudden, he was his cheerful self, chatting away and rattling off instructions. Long Tieng was back in business. All of a sudden, the house where VP and Pop Buell sat began to come to life. There was activity in the kitchen, and people began to appear in the room. Soon, there was food on the table and people to eat the meal. Pop then smiled to himself, confident that his visit might have had something to do with VP's quick recovery.

After losing Na Khang, VP's fallback position was Bouam Long (LS-32), but it was presently under siege by the 148th Regiment of the NVA. LS-32 was the northern most Lao position, and sat deep in enemy territory, its bowl-like rim at the 5,000 foot elevation. From this fortification, the Hmong defenders could monitor NVA truck traffic transiting Laos from North Vietnam via Routes 6 and 7. Also, inasmuch as it was the northernmost Lao fortification and near North Vietnam, it was used for other covert United States operations as well.

After the fall of Na Khang, the 7/13th Air Force in Saigon held an air support conference. All the important officers from the U.S. military services in Vietnam and Laos were there, and the objective of the conference was to make sure that air support was being used where it was needed most. Of course, Vietnam was the priority, but there was plenty of support to go around. After the normal pleasantries, the meeting got underway, and progressed with each entity expressing their needs and wants as related to air support. The air sorties were then assigned as requested, and after everybody received the air support they requested, there was still an enormous amount left over.

Finally, the general in charge of the meeting turned to the U.S. officer from Laos and asked him what he needed. The officer said that he would gladly take all the leftover air support. He got what he asked for—and then some. Suddenly, the pace of the war effort increased in Laos. More FACS arrived to become new Ravens—and VP didn't know it yet, but more help was on the way.

Meanwhile, the RLAF generals appealed to the U.S. Embassy for American troops, but with the United States beginning to draw down its forces in Vietnam, there was no possible way to get a commitment for U.S. troops in Laos. Having no other choice, the generals appealed for help from VP and his Hmong guerrillas. To sweeten the deal, they agreed to give VP an additional eight T-28 aircraft. The deal was quickly approved, and VP soon controlled his own small air force. He stationed the aircraft at Long Tieng.

By March 1969, the USAF had begun to use more jet aircraft to perform forward air controller duties, because the propeller-driven O-1 and O-2 aircraft weren't fast enough to avoid the big antiaircraft guns recently relocated by the NVA to northern and southern Laos. Typically, unarmed RF-4 and armed F-4 Phantoms would arrive at the same time over the target area. The unarmed Phantoms would conduct photo and visual reconnaissance runs prior to the armed Phantoms making their bomb runs. The armed Phantoms would then drop their ordnance, and the RF-4s would make another pass, conducting post strike photo reconnaissance. Later, after returning to base, the USAF technicians on the ground would process the film and forward the photographs to the intelligence staff for analysis.

To compliment the FAC, a new navigation system called LORAN was employed. It consisted of a computer on the Phantom and two radio transmitters at fixed locations on the ground. The onboard computer would measure the time difference between signals received from the two transmitters to establish a reference point (the target). With this information, the pilot of the strike aircraft was then able to drop the bombs on target, pretty much regardless of weather conditions. Still another effort to improve air operations, adopted in January 1969, was something called airborne radio direction finding.

Using the EC-47 surveillance aircraft, airborne radio operators with foreign language training would monitor radio transmissions from NVA ground stations. The intercepted radio transmission could then be used to plot a fixed position. The fixed point on the ground could then be relayed to strike aircraft in the area. Once armed with the location, the pilot could then find and eliminate the target, using bombs or onboard machine guns. The radio intercepts also provided valuable intelligence information on Communist strength, logistic structure, and hostile intentions.

With all the advances in capability provided by electronics, the Plain of Jars became of vital importance from a strategic standpoint. The Plain was fairly level and covered approximately 500 square miles. This land was different from most of Laos, which was mountainous and rugged, with small valleys scattered throughout. For many years before the war began, the climate on the Plain had supported large plantations and offered good grazing for livestock. It was also a historic place; scattered over the plain were large stone containers that resembled jars, hence the name. The stone jars, which were almost as tall as the average man, had always been there, as far back as the people could remember;

Figure 31. Urns on the Plain of Jars
(Photo from the Public Domain)

but the history and purpose of the jars was unknown. The popular belief was that the jars had been used as burial urns for a long-dead civilization.

Several airfields were also located on the Plain, and important roads crossed it—including Route 7, which connected the Vietnamese border to Route 13. The Plain also connected the royal capital of Luang Prabang with the business capital of Vientiane. Meanwhile, north of the Plain, the NVA 148 Regiment continued their attack on Bouam Long. VP wanted to draw the NVA away from Bouam Long, so he launched an attack against another Communist-held position at Phou Koum. His diversion appeared to work, because the NVA broke off the attack at Bouam Long and rushed to Phou Koum to assist their forces there. Vang Pao knew the diversion wouldn't last long, but it would

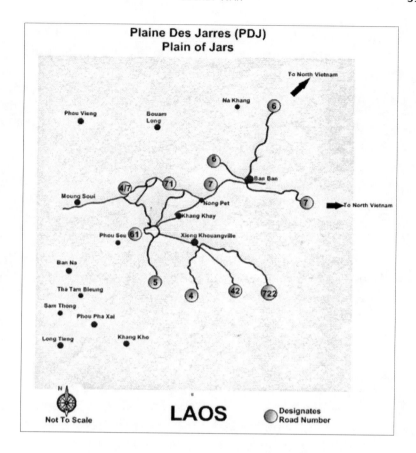

Figure 32. Plaine Des Jarres (Plain of Jars)
Drawing prepared by the author

hopefully at least buy him a little time until he could figure out more options. He then developed a bold plan to retake the Plain of Jars. He briefed Tom Clines, the resident CIA advisor at Long Tieng, but Clines did not like the plan. VP persisted, and traveled to Vientiane to brief the plan to the CIA Station Chief at the embassy. The station chief also didn't like the plan, so he declined to elevate it to the Ambassador. By this time, Ambassador Sullivan had left the country, and the new ambassador, G. McMurtrie Godley, had not yet arrived; but others in the embassy were not impressed with VP's plan, either. Historically, the embassy had avoided large operations on the Plain, preferring smaller strikes against isolated targets. Not only that, but the Plain was now heavily fortified with NVA and Pathet Lao troops, who would try to hold the Plain at any cost.

As discussed earlier in the book, the Secret War was run primarily by the Ambassador in Vientiane, who retained complete authority and control of the conduct of the war. In an attempt to bypass the embassy, VP went to see the Prime Minister, Souvanna Phouma, who reviewed the plan but rendered no opinion. Not content to be ignored, VP then went to see the King (Savang Vatthana). The King listened to VP's plan and indicated that it sounded reasonable to him, but neither approved nor disapproved it.

While VP continued to beat the drum about his plan to retake the Plain, President Richard M. Nixon had settled into the White House and had his own ideas about the war in Laos. He wanted the Lao generals to take the fight to the Communists, and he wanted the United States to back the Lao generals up with air support. When VP learned this information, he was convinced that his plan fit right into the framework Nixon proposed.

The U.S. Embassy in Vientiane then suggested a more modest plan, one which would last for approximately three days. The plan would target Communist transshipment points, base camps, and storage areas on the Plain of Jars, areas which had traditionally been off limits as delineated by the ROE. The objective of the embassy's plan was to make the NVA think that VP had launched a large counteroffensive on the Plain. This would, hopefully, cause the Communists to forget about Bouam Long, and focus their efforts on holding the Plain of Jars. If they bought the ruse, they would most likely return to defend their sanctuaries, giving the troops at Bouam Long a breather and time to regroup.

Hmong, CIA and 7th/13th AF personnel subsequently collaborated on the plan, which was called "Rain Dance," and more than 300 air strikes were scheduled. The purpose of Operation Rain Dance was to initiate an attack against the NVA on the Plain of Jars, using U.S. and RLAF air support. This preemptive strike was intended to surprise the Communists. Later, after the first strikes, VP's plan was to continue the offensive in the air, and then add ground forces to keep the NVA off-balance so he could retake lost territory.

On March 17, 1969, Operation Rain Dance got underway. All the towns occupied by the Communists were hit: VP himself attacked Khang Khay, Phong Savan and Xieng Khouangville. In the weeks that followed, over 500 sorties were flown. Vang Pao also took this opportunity to retake Xieng Khouangville near the Plain, because the earlier air strikes had pretty much reduced the town to a pile of rubble. Most of the buildings were completely gone, except for an occasional standing wall, and huge bomb craters pocked the streets. A later assessment indicated that over 1,500 structures had been destroyed by the bombings. Naturally, the locals had fled when the bombing started and were living in the woods and caves nearby. But a few NVA soldiers still remained in the area, and began firing on VP and his men as they entered the town. Jet fighters were called in again, and soon the NVA guns were silenced. After wiping out the last resistance, an investigation of the area yielded tons of supplies, ammunition and equipment left behind by the NVA as they retreated.

VP confiscated the usable equipment for later use, but rigged everything else with explosive charges and destroyed it. Later, a large NVA medical facility was discovered in a cave near the town. The entire facility was underground, and came complete with stores of medical supplies, X-ray machines and a surgical facility. This facility was also destroyed after salvageable items were taken. Meanwhile, the NVA regrouped, as they always did, and counterattacked. VP and his men then pulled out of Xieng Khouangville and melted into the hills.

During the next few weeks, VP's troops took the town of Kong Dane on Route 4, giving him control over all road traffic. He also took Phu Khe, with the USAF flying hundreds of sorties, resulting in the destruction of numerous enemy bunkers, trenches and supply depots. The next successful target was Phu Nok Kok, a mountaintop overlooking Ban Ban and Route 6. VP also positioned troops to interdict all enemy convoys attempting to resupply the Communist troops on the Plain of Jars. The NVA then tried to retake Phu Nok Kok, but once again US air power was called in and they retreated. For additional insurance, AC-47 Spookies were also called in to discourage the enemy from returning.

By the time Operation Rain Dance ended, it had exceeded everyone's expectations. Not only had it pushed the Communists back and recovered some of their territory, but by April 7 the air strikes had caused almost 500 secondary explosions and over 200 secondary fires, having destroyed more than 500 buildings outright.

Even the EC-47s produced very good intelligence information during this period. For example, on April 15, radio operators located a major NVA communications complex on the Plain of Jars. About two dozen American fighter jets were called in, and they completely destroyed the complex. A few days later, an underground fuel depot was also located; again, USAF fighters were dispatched. One of the responding F-105s was able to put a Bullpup missile squarely into the mouth of the cave where the fuel depot was housed, causing a tremendous secondary explosion. Explosions continued in the cave complex for more than twelve hours.

Given all the recent successes by Vang Pao and American aircraft, the embassy and the USAF brass became concerned, because the NVA had not mounted any significant counterstrikes. They wondered if the heavy use of U.S. airpower in recent weeks had given the Lao troops a false sense of safety. And, with all the successes, some American generals believed that the Lao may have become too dependent on U.S. air support. It was hard to know exactly what was going on with the NVA at that point, because good intelligence information had not been forthcoming. But the embassy didn't have to wait very long, because the NVA soon began to strike back, systematically retaking ground lost during Rain Dance. By the end of May, they had recaptured all their lost territory; but at least Muong Soui had been spared a little while longer, and the NVA were deprived of valuable war supplies.

In May, the U.S. Army Attaché at the embassy in Vientiane convinced the Deputy Chief of Mission that the US Army OV-1 Mohawk (call sign "Spud") could provide additional intelligence collection capability in Laos. The aircraft currently operated in South Vietnam and southern Laos, but with the increased use of Igloo White sensors in southern Laos, some of the Mohawks had become available for use up north. With its side-looking airborne radar and infrared sensors, the OV-1 could not only provide accurate information to the radar officer in the right seat, but that information could also be recorded for later analysis by intelligence officers. After reviewing its options, the embassy immediately requested that OV-1s be stationed at Udorn for use on a regular basis in northern Laos. The Army Attaché was thrilled, and arranged for the transfer of two OV-1s to Udorn.

Soon, OV-1s were operating over northern Laos, but the information they collected seldom reached the USAF in time for them to use it effectively. That was due, in large part, to the inter-service rivalry between the USAF and the Army. More specifically, the information would be collected and analyzed by U.S. Army Intelligence personnel, but not disseminated outside Army channels, so it seldom reached the USAF planners. In other words, the United States had valuable intelligence information sitting on the shelf instead of being distributed to the field where everyone would have benefitted.[82] Meanwhile, on May 22, 1969, "Operation Stranglehold" commenced. Stranglehold was conceived as a short-term operation designed to choke off

Figure 33. U.S. Army OV-1 Mohawk
(Photo from the Public Domain)

Communist resupply routes feeding supplies to the Plain of Jars. The plan was to focus on interdiction of Routes 6 and 7, and included approximately 100 air strikes each day. For maximum effect, the strikes were timed to take place in mid-afternoon, when the most NVA troops and equipment would be moving about. At the same time the air strikes were taking place, Hmong guerrilla units at other important road junctions would also be attacking the NVA. While it was realized that these small attacks would not stop the Communists, it was hoped that they would slow the NVA down.

The operation commenced shortly thereafter; but as usual, the Communists were undeterred by the strikes delivered during Operation Stranglehold. On the positive side, however, more than

300 Communist structures were destroyed, and approximately 250 secondary explosions and fires were observed. So while Stranglehold didn't stop the Communists, it did slow them down a bit.

By early June 1969, the annual rains had returned to Laos—but the Lao and NVA troops continued to fight each other for territory, and no significant gains on either side were recorded. The NVA was able to resupply its troops without USAF interference, because the bad weather kept the U.S. jet fighters on the ground. By June 18, the NVA had positioned three battalions on the perimeter of Muong Soui; this time, they brought tanks, the iron monsters that the Hmong feared more than anything else. Later, on June 24, the NVA launched their primary attack on Muong Soui, supported by their iron beasts.

Fortunately for the Hmong, at that moment there was a break in the clouds, allowing the Americans to bring in air support in the form of jet fighters, A-1 Skyraiders, RLAF and Hmong T-28s. The good guys were able to destroy several of the tanks and temporarily hold the NVA at bay. At this juncture, the Neutralists defending Muong Soui could read the handwriting on the wall, and began to desert in large numbers. Meanwhile, the fight dragged on into the night, whereupon Spooky showed up and put on quite a show, breaking up a combined attack by the NVA and Pathet Lao. But as morning came, the weather deteriorated once again, precluding any additional US air support.

By June 26, most of the Neutralists had deserted, leaving only a few hundred troops to defend the site. When the information reached the embassy in Vientiane, the ambassador decided to end the fight and evacuate the remaining personnel. A fleet of about 20 American helicopters was assembled, including helicopters from the 20th and 21st SOS, the 40th Air Rescue and Recovery Squadron (ARRS), Udorn, and more than 10 Air America H-34s.

Sure enough, at daybreak on June 27, the NVA renewed their attack, using the remaining tanks to lead the charge. The weather had improved somewhat by this time, and USAF jet fighters once again swept in to bomb the Communists. They did a good job, but the fate of the site was already determined at that point. Realizing the end was approaching, the U.S. launched the waiting helicopters, and the evacuation of Muong Soui commenced. By nightfall, all the Lao troops and civilian personnel had been evacuated, and the NVA was already celebrating their victory. With Muong Soui firmly in their hands, the NVA reached the conclusion that they could hold all of the Sam Neua Province and still have enough power to penetrate deep into Xieng Khouang Province.

The embassy in Vientiane considered the Communist assault on Muong Soui to be a major escalation of the war, and demanded an instant response. Later, on July 1, Vang Pao led a force of approximately 1,500 Lao government troops, made up of Hmong, Neutralists and RLA personnel, in an effort to rout the NVA from Muong Soui. The United States helped by providing ample air support: approximately 50 sorties were flown, and over 30 structures were destroyed. But the weather soon deteriorated once again, precluding additional air strikes; and with the monsoon season in full swing, the Lao troops were reluctant to renew the attack. By July 5, however, the skies had cleared enough to allow the RLAF, Hmong and USAF fighters to conduct additional air strikes at Muong Soui.

Fighter aircraft subsequently pounded the NVA, allowing VP's Hmong guerrillas to advance within a mile or so of Muong Soui. Then the clouds returned, halting the air strikes. VP then radioed Long Tieng and ordered his own T-28s into the air. His best two pilots, Ly Lue and Vang Sue, quickly scrambled two fully loaded T-28s, lifted off, and were soon over Moung Soui, awaiting instructions. VP personally got on the radio and began to direct the two aircraft on their bomb runs. After his first pass, Ly Lue was directed to go around again and hit the command bunker on the ground. The pilot explained to VP that he didn't have the ordnance he needed to take out the bunker, and that he should go back to Long Tieng, and rearm with bigger bombs.

Vang Pao disagreed, and insisted that Ly Lue go again, this time even lower, and take out the bunker. Ly Lue dutifully complied, and VP directed him as he flew lower and lower towards the bunker, finally dropping his remaining bombs. They were right on target: the bunker was hit—but at a cost. While shouting praise to Ly Lue, Vang Pao noticed that Ly Lue's aircraft was hit and flying out of control. He shouted into the radio microphone for Ly Lue to head southward, but at first there was no response from the pilot. Finally, the aircraft did slowly turn towards the south, and flew directly towards Vang Pao's position, crashing a few hundred feet away. VP and his men scrambled to the downed aircraft, only to discover that Ly Lue was dead and trapped in the wreckage of his T-28. His body was later

BILLY G. WEBB

removed from the aircraft and flown to Long Tieng for burial. VP was devastated; some believed that he never really got over the loss of Ly Lue. For the next three days the Hmong burial ritual was observed, and finally Ly Lue was buried at Long Tieng, in a beautifully carved mahogany casket. Meanwhile, the attempt to retake Muong Soui had failed.

After VP's failure to retake Muong Soui, the NVA began to rapidly build up their forces in the area. Intelligence indicated that the NVA had massed more than 7,000 combat troops and several thousand support personnel around the site. They also beefed up their forces at Xieng Khouangville, reportedly planning to resupply their troops directly from North Vietnam, using Route 7 instead of Route 6. In addition, they were rapidly constructing Route 72, which would also be used to transport war supplies, from Nong Pet to Xieng Khouangville,

On July 16, the Lao cabinet met with Souvanna Phouma. They insisted that Laos sever relations with North Vietnam, and arrest all Pathet Lao officials in Vientiane. They also insisted that Souvanna order a general mobilization order and request more U.S. air strikes, to include the big B-52 bombers. Souvanna himself considered the NVA attack on Muong Soui a major violation of the Geneva Accords, and wanted to deliver a clear message to the Communists. He also wanted an air strike on the Chinese mission at Khang Khay; heretofore, the area had been off-limits as a target.[83] The embassy forwarded the request to the 7th Air Force, who then forwarded it on to the State Department in Washington.

The request finally reached Washington on Saturday morning, and was received by a deputy assistant, who advised Vientiane to hold off on conducting the strike until the request could be reviewed by higher-ups on the following Monday. Officials from Department of State, the Department of Defense and the CIA subsequently met on Monday and disapproved the request, arguing that the NVA would retaliate in force, possibly escalating the conflict yet again. Upon hearing the news in Vientiane, the embassy notified the 7th Air Force—which did not plan to strike the Chinese mission anyway, regardless of whether or not it had been approved by Washington.

Meanwhile, U.S. government officials mulled over the situation in northern Laos. The JCS provided their standard rhetoric that an all-out Communist offensive in Laos could not be stopped, and that ultimately it was up to the Lao to defend their own country. So the Joint Chiefs recommended that air strikes continue, but that no B-52s should be provided. They also recommended continuing diplomatic, political and economic efforts to contain the conflict. Back in Laos, Ambassador Godley more or less agreed with Washington. He believed that the Communists had no plans for an all-out assault; he also believed that the NVA would isolate Luang Prabang and then wipe out the Neutralists at Vang Vieng, effectively controlling most all of northern Laos.

As it turned out, it didn't make much difference one way or the other, because the request to bomb the Chinese mission was overcome by other events. In early August, U.S. intelligence began intercepting Pathet Lao radio transmissions that reportedly originated from a building fairly close to the Chinese mission at Khang Khay, prompting a planned retaliatory air strike from the USAF. The planners also went to great lengths to make sure that only the radio station from which the transmission emanated would be taken out, and not the building where the Chinese mission resided.

To carry out the attack, they used a Raven FAC to mark the target. Then a USAF fighter marked the target with a laser, providing a direct path for a laser-guided missile. At first, everything appeared to be going just as planned—until the release of the missile. As the missile took flight, clouds suddenly appeared over the target, reportedly obscuring the laser beam. The missile, which was already in flight, then became confused and went directly for the Chinese mission. The projectile struck the building solidly, resulting in massive secondary explosions that leveled every structure in the vicinity, including the radio transmitting station.

After the dust settled, information coming out of Khang Khay mentioned nothing at all about a missile strike on the Chinese mission. In fact, the Chinese never made a complaint to anyone, or even acknowledged that the building had been eliminated. It was as if the building had never even existed. But in a strange sort of way, justice had been served, and the Lao were very pleased. As it turned out, this wasn't the first time that the Chinese mission in Khang Khay had been hit by an air strike. In fact, it had been bombed years earlier, after the town became a Pathet Lao stronghold—when Kong Le and the Neutralists hastily departed for Muong Soui, allowing the Communists to literally walk in and take over the town. Later, the

RLAF bombed the town, again destroying the Chinese mission and the Pathet Lao headquarters, reportedly killing one Chinese national and injuring six.

But getting back to 1969: that summer, intelligence information came to light indicating that the Communists planned several moves to secure northern Laos. Their first objective was reportedly to move west and cut the road between Vientiane and Luang Prabang, isolating the Royal capital. Then they would move on Vang Vieng and Muong Kassy. Later, another force would move down Route 4, completely encircling the Hmong settlements.[84] By taking these actions and stringing out their troops, however, the NVA would leave themselves vulnerable to attack in their rear areas, which were only lightly defended.

As the month of August began, Vang Pao was busy making plans to retake the Plain of Jars and drive the NVA back across the border, because he believed the enemy was overextended. Later, as the rains came, VP cut the enemy's rear supply lines. At this stage of the war, many thought that defeat would soon come for VP and the Hmong; but VP believed that by pushing the Communists out of Laos, Ly Lue's death would be avenged. But to accomplish the task, VP needed the help of the USAF.

He named his operation "About Face," and his plan was to initiate the attack on August 15. The plan would call for interdicting Route 7 between Ban Ban and Nong Pet using a generous amount of U.S. air strikes, followed by armed reconnaissance along roads entering Laos from North Vietnam, and destruction of enemy supply bases. Many believed the rains would not let up, and that it would be impossible for the U.S. to bomb what could not be seen beneath the thick clouds.

Nonetheless, VP was adamant about that start date of the attack—and sure enough, on August 15, the clouds parted and it was bright and clear. To some, it seemed almost as though VP possessed some magical power to control the weather. Operation About Face then literally started with a bang as VP's troops from Bouam Long moved south and harassed the enemy from behind their own lines. Meanwhile, American air support arrived and fighter jets began making pass after pass. Some said that it was the heaviest bombing ever seen in northern Laos.[85]

Meanwhile, the bombing continued unabated, taking out NVA troops, weapons and equipment, and, in one case igniting a Communist ammunition storage area that continued to cook off for more than 24 hours without stopping. By this time the NVA troops had not received any supplies for three months due to the monsoons. Some Communist troops were out of ammunition; many were without food and near starvation. In short, they were only interested in retreating, not fighting, so that's exactly what they did. But as they retreated, the relentless Hmong guerrillas followed, cutting them down from behind.

With all the fighting, the Plain of Jars had become a wasteland. The dead and dying were everywhere. Not only were Communist soldiers killed, but so were Lao villagers on the Plain. Some said it resembled an open mass grave. After the bombing, U.S. aircraft flew over the Plain spraying Agent Orange, which would keep the NVA from being able to occupy the Plain anytime in the near future; and for the most part, it was not fully occupied again after Operation About Face.

By September 9, Hmong guerrillas had also captured Phong Savan and Khang Khay, meeting only light resistance. They continued on and proceeded to reoccupy Xieng Khoungville and Muong Soui, meeting no resistance at all. By the end of September, the Plain of Jars and surrounding towns were in the hands of VP's forces once again. One U.S. Embassy official was quoted as saying that it was the first major victory in the history of the Royal Government. General Vang Pao had finally become the big man he had always wanted to be.[86]

Meanwhile, on September 2, 1969, while Operation About Face was in progress, the infamous Ho Chi Minh quietly died from heart failure. News of his death, however, was withheld from the public for two days, because North Vietnam was celebrating the anniversary of the founding of the so-called Democratic Republic of Vietnam, and did not want that celebration to be interrupted. After news of Ho's death was released, no replacement was named to fill the office of president. Leadership of the country was shared thereafter by several North Vietnamese cabinet ministers.

While the RLG basked in the warmth of their recent successes in northeastern Laos, significant Lao successes had also taken place in southern Laos along the Ho Chi Minh Trail. But once again, the bigger question was, what were the long term benefits to the Lao? The NVA had plenty of troops, and a steady flow of supplies from China and Russia, staged for use in Laos. In fact, North Vietnam possessed a seemingly endless supply of fresh troops and weapons. But in Laos, most of the local able-bodied men had already been killed, captured or maimed by war. Even VP's troops were depleted and weary.

Meanwhile, the embassy staff in Vientiane put their heads together and developed a plan for better utilization of RLA troops to augment the Hmong forces. They also wanted more aircraft, pilots and technology, and recommended eliminating the use of Thai pilots. Their plan was sent to Washington, where the usual players did the usual review and essentially reiterated their standard philosophy. After reviewing the plan, President Nixon disapproved the use of B-52 aircraft in northern Laos, but did agree to give the Lao additional T-28s.

Back in Hanoi, losing the Plain of Jars was viewed as a setback. With the drawdown of American troops in South Vietnam, General Vuo Nguyen Giap, Commanding General of the North Vietnamese Army, began to take a personal interest in the Secret War in Laos, particularly the war being fought in Military Region 2—Vang Pao's backyard. Giap wanted to inflict the same kind of damage on VP and his troops that they had inflicted upon the NVA. For the assignment, Giap selected General Vu Lap. Vu Lap was an educated man who distinguished himself in combat and had subsequently come up through the ranks.

Giap gave Vu Lap two divisions, an armored regiment, and four battalions of North Vietnamese Special Forces (Dac Cong) troops. The operation was named "Campaign 139." In preparation for beginning the offensive, the NVA units positioned themselves near the Vietnam/ Laos border in October 1969. Occasionally, one of their units would cross the border to probe the Lao defenses; this increased activity soon got the attention of VP and the CIA. The probes were also noticed by the JCS in Washington. Towards the middle of October, the Joint Chiefs announced that the buffer zone, previously ten miles wide, would be pushed back five miles.

VP then quickly briefed the Ravens and told them that everything outside the new five mile band could be attacked. Of course, the U.S. hoped that preemptive strikes would destroy the war supplies of the NVA and discourage the Communists from mounting a large offensive. Then, for three straight days, the USAF provided an extra 80 sorties a day—and the enemy was caught off guard. What had been a sanctuary before was now fair game, and the bombs fell like rain from the fast-moving fighters, resulting in many secondary explosions.[87]

On October 27, USAF Captain James W. Herrick, Jr. of the 602nd Special Operations Squadron departed NKP in his A-1H Skyraider on a routine air interdiction mission, using call sign "Firefly 33." His wingman was First Lieutenant James G. George. Their mission was to locate and interdict enemy activity along Route 7 in northern Laos (Barrel Roll), in the Ban Ban Valley of Xiangkhouang Province. The weather conditions that day were overcast, with clouds at the 7,000 foot level. Upon arrival in the target area, both aircraft spiraled down through the clouds to approximately 2,000 feet, where they were able to break out and begin searching the valley below for potential targets.

They worked the valley eastward towards the Lao/Vietnam border in tight canyons with towering, jagged limestone peaks. As the two Skyraiders worked the valley, weather conditions deteriorated even further. While scouring the valley, Lt. George radioed Captain Herrick, advising him to break off the search and follow him up and out of the valley. George then proceeded through the clouds to clear air above the clouds but did not see Herrick behind him; so he called Herrick again, who radioed back with his position.

George quickly switched channels to check in with the airborne command center, and then switched back to the operating frequency and called Herrick again. This time there was no answer, and George contacted the airborne command center requesting a SAR. A subsequent search of the area, however, failed to disclose the location of Captain Herrick, and the SAR was discontinued. About five days later, in the same general area where Herrick had been operating on October 27, aircraft wreckage and a scorched area were observed from the air, but the type of downed aircraft could not be determined. Unfortunately, subsequent efforts to visually search the crash site were not feasible due to heavy enemy activity on the ground. Captain Herrick was later classified as MIA, and to this date his remains have not been recovered.

At about this same time, the availability of American air support in northern Laos began to decrease, because support for the U.S.

withdrawal from South Vietnam took priority in the allocation of sorties. The embassy in Vientiane complained, but was overruled. Notwithstanding, the USAF still promised sufficient air support to VP and his guerrillas. Later, on November 6, VP called his field commanders together for a strategy meeting. He also used the meeting as a forum to press the CIA for more weapons and artillery. At this point in time, it was common knowledge the U.S. had begun using the newer M-16 rifle and 155mm howitzers. VP also wanted these new weapons for his Hmong guerrillas in battles yet to come.

Also in early November, the NVA kicked off their dry season offensive for 1969 by boldly crossing the border into Laos. One division traveled down Route 7; the other division used Route 72. Both were headed in the same direction: towards the Plain of Jars. Within a week, the NVA's 316 Division reached the village of Nong Pet, which provided direct access to the Plain. The Communists took Nong Pet easily, but Hmong reinforcements soon struck back and retook the village, taking heavy casualties in the process. Further south, the NVA's 312 attacked Xieng Khouangville. There, the Hmong defenders were greatly outnumbered, but they held on for eight days. Later, they retreated and melted away into the jungle until they received reinforcements, whereupon they counterattacked, again taking heavy casualties.

Meanwhile, the NVA continued their advance towards the Plain. To stall the advance, the USAF bombed the eastern Plain with everything they had. The bombings soon moved north all the way to the Vietnam border. Some of the bombing restrictions were again lifted by the embassy in Vientiane, and sanctuaries which had been previously off limits were now approved for bombing. The result was unbelievable: the USAF hit many ammunition and fuel depots in the bombing, and secondary explosions went on for hours and hours. But the NVA advanced nonetheless, prompting Ambassador Godley to contact Washington and request B-52 strikes. VP did not believe the request would be approved, so he pushed to get the old airfield on the Plain at Lima Lima (also called Lima 22) repaired for use by his T-28s.

Lima 22 was an old French airfield that had not been used for years, but the location was ideal and would benefit the Hmong. The existing runway had been constructed using Pierced Steel Planking (PSP), large steel planks with holes in them. PSP had been used extensively in the past, and provided an almost instant runway. Numerous usable structures also still existed at Lima 22. Meanwhile, the request for the big bombers stalled again in Washington, but VP's progress had not, and the airstrip was now ready for use. After the airfield was repaired, Air America fixed-wing aircraft and helicopters began shuttling in people and equipment to maintain and protect Lima 22. The NVA were also aware that Lima 22 was reactivated, and every night they shelled the airstrip. For safety, therefore, all aircraft were flown out at the end of every day so they would not be easy targets on the ground at night. Indeed, this was pretty much standard procedure throughout Laos every night for just about every airfield, as we have mentioned previously. At night, the Lao aircraft would usually go to Vientiane, while the USAF aircraft returned to Thailand. The Hmong T-28s would remain overnight (RON) at Long Tieng.

After Lima 22 was activated, older cargo planes like the C-47 and C-123 brought in heavy weapons and ammunition. And, with the daily supply flights, the T-28s could fly many more missions every day, because they could easily refuel and rearm at Lima 22.

Later, in early December, Dac Cong commandos struck at Phou Nok Kok. At dawn, the NVA commandos were poised to take the city when a CIA advisor in the area by the name of Will Greene decided to take action. He radioed for air support, and then personally directed air strikes by the USAF from his position on the ground. The bombing continued all morning, and finally the Dac Cong advance was stopped. Subsequent contact with the Dac Cong continued sporadically until later in December, when the Communists attacked Lima 22 again. But VP's troops were braced for the attack.

Meanwhile, Spooky 1, an AC-47 gunship, lifted off the runway at Vientiane, and winged its way northward. The gunship was later on station near Lima 22 before midnight, and went to work with its machine guns. About three hours later, Spooky 1 left Lima 22 because he was low on fuel, and Spooky 2 was on the way to replace him. With Spooky support temporarily unavailable, the NVA began an all out assault on Lima 22. The Communists advanced with tanks firing at point blank range; NVA commandos and infantrymen followed the tanks. The outer perimeter fell quickly. Then one tank crawled over a land mine that exploded, taking out the tank. A second tank stalled but kept firing. Now the NVA commandos exposed themselves in the open, and machine guns from inside Lima 22 started firing. Many Communists were cut down, but the advance continued.

Soon, the sound of an old propeller-driven aircraft could be heard in the distance, and shortly thereafter, Spooky 2 arrived on station. He immediately called for Spooky 3 and 4 to get airborne and join him at Lima 22. Spooky 2 then began dropping flares to illuminate the enemy, and the gunship's machine guns opened up on the NVA below. Meanwhile, the fighting on the ground continued until the first light of day appeared over the horizon.

The NVA knew that when daylight came, the T-28s would return to bomb them—so they broke off the fighting and retreated, dragging their casualties with them. Meanwhile, just after dawn White Star personnel (U.S. Army Green Berets) came to the site by chopper to assist the Hmong. Rescue choppers also came in to begin the evacuation of the wounded. At about that same time, a C-47 transport from Vientiane, piloted by an American advisor by the name of Bill Keeler, arrived to also assist in the evacuation of the wounded.

Meanwhile, near the junction of Routes 7 and 71, NVA troops of 316 Division moved against Lao forces, where recent intelligence indicated that NVA truck traffic was transiting Route 6. As the Communists turned up the heat, Vang Pao became frustrated, and declined to go along with plans for a phased withdrawal from Lima 22. He did agree, however, to remove some troops from the Sam Neua area. To complete the withdrawal, Air America and the 21st SOS (Knives), combined their talents on January 4, 1970 and successfully evacuated thousands of civilians, guerrilla troops, livestock and personal items from the Sam Neua area to safety further south.

As the civilians and guerrilla troops were being relocated, the NVA conducted harassment raids in the Sam Neua and Xieng Khouang Provinces. Caught in the crossfire, VP brought in additional Lao forces from other areas, but this only made the NVA more determined to increase the intensity of their attacks. By this time, the Communists had begun to use their long range artillery pieces to pound the Lao forces at Phou Nam Phong. After nine days of intense bombardment, the Lao guerrillas began to melt away into the jungle and head towards Nam Xan. As VP's troops moved out of the area, the NVA engineers set about repairing and improving Route 72 in the direction of Xieng Khouangville.

Meanwhile, in the northeast, a company of Dac Cong commandos initiated another attack on Phou Nok Kok. The Lao were able to contain the sappers, but on January 10 a second group of Dac Cong commandos scaled the northern face. After reaching the highest point of the mountain, the sappers set up mortars they had brought up the mountain with them. The commandos then began to shell the Lao elements further down the mountain. It didn't take long for the already exhausted Lao to get their fill of the fight, and they gathered their equipment and abandoned the position.

Even though VP's defenses were thin, he wanted to make one more stand before the NVA began their heavy offensive. Meanwhile, pleas for help from other areas of Laos did not meet with much success. The Pakse region did send one battalion of Lao guerrillas, but it wasn't really enough to make a difference. Realizing he was in a precarious situation, VP finally accepted the inevitable in early February 1970, and ordered the evacuation of more 10,000 civilians from the southern Plain, using Air America and Continental Air Services aircraft.

At this point, the NVA had demonstrated that they were prepared to match or better any offensive moves by Vang Pao and the Americans. With their continual infusion of troops and heavy weapons, the NVA had positioned themselves for the eventual capture and control of all of northern Laos—and the Lao finally realized that it was only a matter of time until Laos would be under the complete control of North Vietnam.

Chapter 12

The War Grinds On

By the end of November 1969, Operation About Face was winding down. The operation hadn't been planned to last as long as it did, but its success was far greater than expected. Even so, the Hmong guerrillas were exhausted and spent—conversely, the NVA had been gearing up for a new dry season offensive. But the reason for what appeared to be success for Vang Pao in Operation About Face was because the NVA had intentionally avoided significant contact with his troops during the operation. Instead, they focused on other blocking initiatives outside of the Plain.

In other words, the Hmong were duped.

Toward the end of 1969, Souvanna had tried to persuade Prince Souphanouvong—the figurehead for the Pathet Lao—to agree to an end in the fighting on the Plain of Jars. Souvanna even offered to halt all U.S. bombing if the NVA withdrew to North Vietnam. But the Pathet Lao refused, demanding a complete cessation of all bombing prior to any negotiations.

The embassy in Vientiane realized that VP's 5,000 battered troops would be no match for the tens of thousands of NVA and Pathet Lao troops that were expected to sweep over the Plain in the coming months. As an alternative, U.S. leaders decided on a phased withdrawal, leaving only four strong points of defense scattered across the Plain. Again, the lessons of history were ignored: apparently, the American planners had forgotten what had happened to the French when they experimented with strong points as a strategy back in the 1950s. During that war, the Vietminh simply passed up the strong points, cutting the French off from resupply. Then the Communists returned at their convenience, and wiped out the defenders at the French strong points.

The key to holding any strong point depended upon VP's ability to retain control of Phou Nok Kok, which overlooked Route 7. The NVA apparently realized this also, and attacked the Hmong troops holding that position on December 2, 1969. For four days the battle raged, and U.S. fighter aircraft and gunships helped to break the attack. Two weeks later, the NVA struck again; but this time they created a diversion by first striking Xieng Khouangville and Lima 22. Once again, however, the NVA attack stalled, so they withdrew.

On January 2, 1970, Dac Cong commandos initiated another attack on Phou Nok Kok. They began by pounding the mountain with artillery fire, breaking the Hmong's will. This was followed up with a more conventional attack. By mid-January, the mountain was in Communist hands. After Phou Nok Kok was lost and the Hmong lost the will to fight, the other three strong points were simply abandoned. The Hmong then retreated to the western rim of the Plain, much to the Americans' chagrin. In fairness to the Lao, however, the loss of Phou Nok Kok wasn't their fault. The weather had precluded about 60% of the planned protective air strikes, and the NVA capitalized on that fact. Furthermore, most of the defenders had only recently relocated from Pakse, in the south, to Phou Nok Kok, and were unfamiliar with the terrain.

On January 21, the USAF came up with an alternate bombing plan, using LORAN (reference points). The LORAN method was later employed, but the results could not be validated visually due to the continuing poor weather. Efforts to verify strike results on the ground also failed, because the troops could not get to the target area on foot. Also, in late January, Ambassador Godley renewed his request for B-52 bombers to fly strikes in support of ground forces in Laos. Based upon recent developments in Laos, the JCS changed their previous stance, supporting the ambassador in his request. Final approval would have to come from the President, so the JCS deferred, pending that approval. Anticipating the President Nixon's approval, the Strategic Air Command (SAC) was directed to conduct photo reconnaissance and initiate the planning process for the strikes.

Assuming that he could not retake Phou Nok Kok, VP used as many reinforcements as he could find and established a chokepoint near Nong Pet at the junction of Routes 7 and 71. He was also provided with a second SGU battalion from Pakse; he dispatched them immediately to Xieng Khouangville, to reinforce Neutralist troops already in position. As January gave way to February, the Communist noose continued to slowly tighten around the necks of the Lao. On February 11, Dac Cong commandos crept into the Route 7-Route 71 road junctions and overpowered the Hmong troops using tear gas. The overwhelmed Hmong troops fled in the direction of Lima 22.

The following morning, under a thick blanket of fog, two NVA regiments arrived at the junction; at about this same time, the MR 2 Hmong position at Lima 22 was attacked by Dac Cong commandos. Fortunately, the defenders were able to hold off the Communists—for the time being, anyway. Meanwhile, the NVA quietly gained complete control of the 7-71 junction, and on February 17, NVA tanks moved on Lima 22. Fortunately, the CIA had already seeded the area with anti-tank mines, and all the Communist tanks were disabled.

Meanwhile, on February 14, MACV commander General Creighton W. Abrams, Jr., had dispatched a SAC "Arc Light" planning team[88] to Udorn to evaluate Ambassador Godley's proposed B-52 target list. The team subsequently reviewed the list, but didn't consider any of the targets worthy of B-52 strikes due to their low material value. Nonetheless, MACV decided to authorize one strike on the Plain of Jars. The target would be the most lucrative one on the proposed list, and the strike was designed for shock value. It was anticipated that approximately 35 of the giant bombers would be used in the strike.

The strike was executed on February 17, using B-52s staged at Utapao, Thailand, just outside of Bangkok. It produced spectacular secondary explosions, but not many bodies could be found on the following day by a ground team in the area. Despite the low body count, MACV authorized almost a dozen more B-52 strikes between February and May. The strikes were later suspended due to the increased U.S. and South Vietnamese activity in Cambodia.

After the B-52s bombings, information regarding the strikes was leaked to the press, and in less than two days, articles began to appear in newspapers in the United States, Thailand and other nations. Suddenly, Laos was big news, and the little kingdom was invaded with even more war correspondents hungry for a scoop. They soon began to forage for information outside of Vientiane, and apparently three correspondents somehow wound up on the base at Long Tieng, taking pictures and talking to anyone they could find who spoke English or French. Of course, it didn't take long for the CIA to realize that the reporters were on base. They were quickly rounded up, their film and notes were confiscated, and they were unceremoniously returned to Vientiane. Shortly thereafter, President Nixon publicly admitted that the U.S. was assisting the Lao military.

All the publicity was also noticed by the U.S. Congress, of course. Many lawmakers already had their suspicions about Laos, and some had even been briefed on the U.S. involvement there. Suddenly, Laos became a must-visit for many Congressmen. To appease the lawmakers, a "special" tour was hastily arranged. As the Congressmen and Senators arrived in Laos, they were taken on a sightseeing excursion of Vientiane and Luang Prabang, and some were even given courtesy rides in Air America aircraft for an aerial overview of Laos. Then they would be flown to Sam Thong, where Pop Buell would meet them. He would brief the lawmakers on the refugee program and take them on a tour of the hospital, schools and storage warehouses. After the tour and briefings, the guests would be herded back onto waiting aircraft for their return trip to Vientiane, and then home to the United States. Of course, Long Tieng was not included on the tour, for obvious reasons, and it was hoped that none of the lawmakers would notice.

It was fortunate that they did not, because on February 17, a squad of Dac Cong commandos was able to penetrate Long Tieng. When the attack was over, three NVA commandos were dead, and one O-1 Bird Dog and two T-28 aircraft were damaged. But the damage wasn't the issue; the problem was that Long Tieng had been penetrated. The psychological impact could be devastating.

Also on February 17, the AC-119K "Stinger" gunship completed its first mission over the skies of Laos at Lima Site 22. The Stingers were developed as a follow-on weapon system to the AC-130 Spectre, designed to support Troops in Contact (TIC) and to supplement the Spectres in attacking targets along the Ho Chi Minh Trail. The basic airframe used for the Stingers was the old C-119 "Flying Boxcar." The Stingers were fitted with two Wright R-3350-85 "Duplex Cyclone" radial engines, each capable of providing 3,500 hp. Each aircraft also carried four GAU-2A/A mini-guns and two M61 20mm cannons. In addition, the Stingers had improved Electronic Counter Measures (ECM), Forward Looking Infrared (FLIR), AN/APQ-133 side-looking beacon tracking radar, and AN/APQ-136 search radar, as well as night observation capability and flare launcher tubes. The gunships carried a crew of six, operated at approximately 23,000 feet, had a range of 1,600 miles, and flew at 130 knots.

As February 1970 dragged on, the NVA continued their assault on the Plain of Jars. In response, the USAF, 7th Air Force increased the number of air attacks on the Communists, averaging more than 100 strikes per day. But many of the strikes were ineffective because of the clouds, and haze from agricultural clearing fires hampered accuracy. In many cases, the fighter jets had to divert to secondary targets of lesser value.

Figure 34. AC-119K Stinger Gunship
(Photo from the Public Domain)

On February 20, the NVA moved against Lima 22 once more. Even though several previous attempts had been thwarted, the Communists were determined this time, and more calculating as well. The attack began with the NVA using their 122mm rockets to soften up the base. They followed the rocket attack with a ground assault that night. At first the NVA were discouraged by intense small arms fire from the Neutralists. Somewhat surprised, they fell back to regroup. Several hours later, they came at the northern position again, this time using several tanks.

As the tanks reached the perimeter wire, the Neutralists did not hesitate to react—they all broke and ran to the south, straight through the rest of the defenders. As the Neutralists troops passed the other guerrillas, they also bolted, running after the fleeing troops ahead of them. It didn't take long before the position was almost deserted. Shortly thereafter, air strikes had to be called in to destroy all the equipment, ammunition and explosives left behind to deprive the NVA of its use against the Lao. Meanwhile, VP deployed hundreds of Hmong guerrillas on the hilltops between the Plain and Long Tieng. He took this action because he knew that the next move by the Communists would be to head south towards the secret war headquarters at LS-20A.

With the fall of Lima 22, the Communist offensive had crested. The NVA and the Pathet Lao had captured the Xieng Khouang airfield, and then continued west and took Muong Soui. By February 24, the Communists had again occupied the Plain of Jars, with Hmong defenders holding onto a defensive perimeter southwest of the Plain.

Later, on March 12—as Vang Pao was trying to hold the NVA at the Plain—Communist troops from the 148 Regiment managed to maneuver around the defenders and move south into Tha Tham Bleung, a long valley north of Long Tieng. As VP's guerrilla fighters retreated southward, they established strong points along the ridgelines between the Plain and Long Tieng. The USAF also provided additional air strikes, but it was doubtful that the weather would cooperate. An additional AC-119K Stringer was also dispatched to Udorn, and all-night gunship support of VP's troops was promised by the Americans.

Meanwhile, the NVA continued their move southward, aided by bad weather that inhibited U.S. airstrikes. By approximately March 15, the Communists had occupied the Tham Bleung valley. But rather than striking Long Tieng, the NVA went after Sam Thong (LS-20) on March 17. As mentioned previously, LS-20 was a USAID facility that included a hospital, schools, an airfield, and warehouses where refugee supplies were stored. Inasmuch as Sam Thong was not considered a likely target for the NVA, it was only lightly defended by a small group of Hmong guerrillas. As Dac Cong commandos and NVA regulars arrived at the perimeter of Sam Thong, a general alarm was sounded, and the civilians were all airlifted to safety. The Hmong guerrilla contingent then managed to stall the Communists for one day, before quickly departing to safety at Long Tieng.

By early morning on March 18, 1970, the airstrip at Sam Thong was under attack, and the remaining Lao civilians fled into the hills. The NVA then began their destruction in earnest by blowing up and torching first the hospital, then the school and warehouses. When they finished sweeping over the site, at least half the structures were destroyed. Artillery pieces had been available at Long Tieng, but of course there wasn't anyone at Sam Thong trained in directing artillery or air strikes—so the T-28s at Long Tieng were not effective either. Wisely, however, the staff and others at Sam Thong had fled into the jungle, and slowly made their way to safety. Having accomplished their task, the 148 Regiment retreated to safety back into the valley at Tha Tham Bleung.

By March 20, the Communists were within a mile of Long Tieng, and their artillery was positioned to shell the base. Meanwhile, Thailand had offered several hundred troops to assist in the defense of Long Tieng. VP also had more than 1,000 troops already in place to defend LS-20A, but the NVA had brought more than 3,000 troops to the fight about to take place. On March 22, the rains began, temporarily delaying ground action. As March 23 dawned, the overcast skies cleared; and for several days, the USAF pummeled the Communists. Meanwhile, VP received additional replacement troops, putting him on an equal footing with the NVA.

On March 24, the USAF provided substantial air resources to VP, allowing him to retake several positions around Long Tieng; and Sam Thong was retaken as well. Later, as March 1970 ended, the first NVA troops arrived at Skyline Ridge above LS-20A, but the thick haze and smoke of the burning season precluded further air attacks on the enemy.

With the Communist troops on Skyline Ridge, the local villagers panicked. Air America C-123 cargo aircraft began arriving shortly thereafter to evacuate the civilians and the families of the Hmong fighters. The villagers slowly made their way to the airstrip, loaded down with their personal belongings. After landing, the C-123s would taxi to the end of the airstrip, turn around, and, with engines running, the cargo ramp would be lowered. The villagers would quickly make their way onto the aircraft, the ramp would close, and away the aircraft would go. Minutes later, another aircraft would land, and the procedure would be repeated.

Meanwhile, the NVA began to probe the location by firing 122mm rockets into Long Tieng. A 20-man NVA sapper unit also made it onto the runway, but was driven away before they could do any damage. Meanwhile, rockets continued to pound the base for several days.

While the rockets rained down on Long Tieng, the USAF wasn't able to provide air support to Vang Pao, because visibility was almost zero due to the smoke created by clearing fires. This was, after all, the burning season, and there were fires for miles. The burning season was an annual occurrence, just before the rains began. After the small trees, brush and grass were burned off, the rains and the ash helped to stimulate the soil to start growing grass, or whatever else had been planted.

Just when it seemed that nothing could be done to deter the Communists, a breeze began to blow, the clouds lifted, and the smoke and haze disappeared almost instantly. Now the air support could be called in. Two Ravens, Brian Wages and "Weird" Harold Mesaris, took to the sky in their O-1 Bird Dogs to direct the air strikes. The T-28s were also called from Vientiane and soon arrived overhead. The fast moving jet fighters and A-1 Skyraiders from Thailand also came—and the bombing commenced.

As fate would have it, the NVA were caught completely off guard and in the open. Hundreds of sorties were subsequently flown, pounding the NVA troops, and the Communists began to pull back. By this time, the Ravens who had left Long Tieng the day before had also returned, and were in the air directing air strikes. For additional insurance, several hundred more Thai military personnel were brought in to assist the depleted Hmong forces. This engagement represented the first time that Thai regulars (ground troops) had been used in the Secret War. Thai mercenaries, of course, had been used for years, and would continue to be used throughout the war; but this was the first introduction of Thai Army troops. With the decreasing supply of Hmong warriors, the Thai regulars would be used extensively for the duration of the war.

Meanwhile, VP called in an air strike on Sam Thong on March 29 to rout the NVA there—but this time it would be more than a rout. As a lone C-130 cargo aircraft winged its way towards Sam Thong, it carried a single item: a giant steel drum packed with highly explosive chemicals. This new weapon was called a BLU-82 Daisy Cutter[89], and it had not previously been used in Laos. Later, as the aircraft descended towards Sam Thong, the rear ramp of the cargo aircraft was lowered. Then, at the appointed time, the aircraft began to climb—and the giant drum, strapped to a pallet, was pushed out of the back of the aircraft. A parachute then deployed, and the big bomb floated earthward. When it was about three feet above the ground, the bomb detonated.

The effect was similar to a miniature nuclear explosion. The blast leveled everything within a radius of several hundred yards, including hills, trees, and whatever else was in its path. Every living creature within that radius was vaporized instantly. Later, when the smoke cleared, Sam Thong was very quiet . . . or rather, what *had been* Sam Thong was very quiet. All that was left was huge circle of scorched earth.

The fight for LS-20A and Sam Thong was temporarily over, and the NVA didn't bother to launch a counteroffensive. They had been unsuccessful in taking Long Tieng, despite an 11-day assault using mortars, artillery and 122mm rockets. The rainy season would arrive within a month, and any subsequent operations would have to be small in scale, with obtainable objectives. The main force of the NVA soon withdrew to North Vietnam to rest and refit, as was the annual custom in this see-saw conflict. When the rains came, the NVA had just two objectives: to maintain a presence on

Figure 35. BLU-82 Bomb
(Photo from the Public Domain)

the Plain of Jars and at Tha Tham Bleung, and to take Bouam Long, (LS-32).

Throughout the war, Bouam Long had the singular distinction of never having been taken by the Communists. Other sites, like Na Khang, were taken annually in the whipsaw of warfare, and the control of most of the other Lima sites had changed hands regularly over the years—but not Bouam Long. The NVA had been trying to take LS-32 for years, but the geography of the area precluded the site's capture. Bouam Long was on a plateau atop a rugged mountain rising above dozens of smaller mountains, and it was nestled within sheer cliffs, hidden grottos, and razor sharp limestone ridges.

In order to get to the site, the NVA would have to negotiate the near mountains and then advance up a steep rise to the plateau. The main village was located in a bowl-like setting with sheer limestone peaks around it. It was also heavily protected by razor wire and mine fields. LS-32 was used primarily as a radio intercept facility to monitor radio communications by the Communists in North Vietnam and northeastern Laos, and it was also a jumping-off point for MACV-SOG forays into North Vietnam.

On February 23, the NVA initiated contact at Bouam Long. The initial attack was surprisingly effective, with the Communists making their way up the plateau to the razor wire. The defenders subsequently contacted the embassy in Vientiane, and a defoliation mission was authorized to eliminate heavy vegetation, denying the NVA the cover of the overgrowth. The NVA then dropped back and waited. On April 10, the Communists attacked at Phou Then, a mountain seven kilometers south of Bouam Long, and drove the Hmong fighters from its summit. The NVA then began shelling the village in the bowl of Bouam Long. Dac Cong commandos also tunneled inside the perimeter and into the very trenches the Hmong defenders used to move around the site. The fighting continued unabated into May 1970.

Meanwhile, on April 10, a C-130 assigned to the 21st Tactical Airlift Squadron crashed into Phou Bia while on approach to Long Tieng, in the course of flying a routine supply run out of Takhli Air Base. The aircraft was hauling fuel and ammunition to the troops when it crashed, and the six-person Air America crew aboard perished. Phou Bia is the tallest mountain in Laos, and most of the time visiting aircrews managed to skirt it successful. But on this day, that just wasn't the case.

Meanwhile, in southern Laos, the ground situation remained somewhat static. The NVA continued to transport war supplies down the Ho Chi Minh trail uninterrupted; there was no serious attempt to interdict the traffic on the trail, except for minor pinpricks by the Lao and U.S. In Cambodia, Prince Norodom Sihanouk had been removed from power in a coup, and replaced with General Lon Nol. Upon taking office, Nol immediately cancelled the NVA's permission to transit Cambodia, causing even more activity along the Trail.

The only obstacle to expanding the NVA activity in southern Laos was the Lao government outpost at Attopeu, a garrison of several hundred Lao troops. The NVA attacked Attopeu on April 28—and the so-called defenders literally laid down their weapons and retreated. When the word of the Attopeu attack got out, other Lao troops also quickly vacated other garrisons in southern Laos, including Saravane.

Meanwhile, in northern Laos, the fighting continued at Bouam Long, and VP had additional fighters brought in by helicopters. One of the groups brought in was a new team of Hmong commandos, who were about to be tested by the persistent NVA. Later, enemy troops stormed the slopes at Bouam Long after successfully going through the mine fields and razor wire. Some NVA troops even made it into the village in the bowl, but they took many casualties.[90] The fighting was fierce, and the Hmong were rapidly running out of supplies. Desperate calls for air support and supplies didn't help, because the mountains and valleys were socked in with fog and clouds, precluding resupply from the air.

Finally, on May 16, the skies over LS-32 cleared, and supplies were dropped to the Hmong defenders. T-28s and AC-130s also pounded the NVA troops from the air. Slowly, the air support began to make a difference, and the NVA fell back. In the aftermath, there were dead and dying Communist troops lying everywhere, and the air was permeated with the stink of gunpowder, rotting flesh and cordite. At that juncture, the NVA, having finally had enough, broke off the attack and retreated south to their headquarters on the Plain of Jars.

By mid-May, the Communists were as far west as they had ever been at that time of year—and some American officials believed the NVA would press on to take Phu Cum and Bouam Long. Having already taken Houie Sang and Phou Sam Soun, they could then secure the north rim of the Plain of Jars. And, by holding the territory they already controlled on the southern part of the Plain, the NVA would be in an excellent position for the next dry season offensive.

VP's wet season offensive plan was viewed with pessimism by U.S. officials, given the beating that the Hmong guerrillas had sustained during the early months of 1970. Later, as the rainy season approached, Lao and U.S. air strikes helped VP's troops stop the enemy's attack and force his withdrawal to the mountains along the south and west rim of the Plain of Jars. Also, with Sam Thong liberated (at least temporarily) and Long Tieng once again secure, the residents of the valley began to return. In short order, life in MR 2 returned to a somewhat normal level.

Leading up to the dry season of 1969/1970, the Lao guerrillas had enjoyed more than 100 air support sorties a day, which resulted in tons of enemy equipment and supplies being eliminated, and several thousand Communist soldiers being killed. But like everything else in this war, air support was also changing. The 22nd SOS (Zorros) from NKP, flying the A-1 Skyraider on close air support missions, was disbanded on July 18, 1970, their aircraft and equipment transferred to other squadrons. Other units in Thailand would soon follow the 22nd into oblivion.

Meanwhile, VP had finally received an increase in the number of USAF sorties allocated to Barrel Roll, and the command and control approval process at Udorn was reportedly simplified. The rainy season was also beginning, so VP went about his annual routine of striking the Communists hard. He also took several new Thai mercenary battalions and put them in defensive positions along Skyline Ridge above Long Tieng, and also placed Thai soldiers on Zebra Ridge, Phu Long Mat and Ban Na.

For offensive operations, Vang Pao relied on his depleted Hmong defenders. With the Hmong he began to probe enemy positions and also established blocking forces. The Hmong later probed Moung Soui, Ban Na and Nong Pet, but the probes were met with stiff resistance and the NVA defenders held. When they initiated probes on the Plain, the Hmong guerrillas were repelled immediately by the heavily fortified NVA troops. The Hmong guerrillas then attacked the NVA troops left behind in the Tha Tham Bleung Valley, but again the NVA held.

Prior to 1970, the heavy fighting against the Communists in Laos had been undertaken by the Hmong guerrillas. But their numbers had dwindled to near-extinction, and their role as guerrilla fighters had slowly transitioned to conventional warfare, a type of fighting for which they were not well-suited. It was clear that the FAR would have to step in and shoulder most of the load in the future.

Thanks to Colonel Tyrell, the RLAF at least had improved dramatically, and was flying thousands of sorties every month. But, that still wasn't enough, so the role of the USAF in Laos would need to expand also. At the same time, however, budgets in Washington were decreasing, the American people did not support the war, and Congressional opposition had increased. The summer of 1970 would also signal the beginning of the end, with reductions in USAF assets. Units at Udorn also began to draw down, the AC-119K Stingers were transferred to NKP, and staffing at 7th/13th Air Force was cut in half.

The Secret War in Laos continued unabated. As the rainy season advanced, the Hmong and CIA advisors at Bouam Long dug deeper trenches and installed another layer of sandbags around the gun positions; they also seeded more mines in the fields, and added more razor wire on the slopes. The summer days were hot and humid, and the rain was unrelenting. Body bags containing the remains of Hmong warriors continued to arrive at Long Tieng for identification and burial—but recruit numbers continued to drop, because there weren't any resources to draw from.

Also during the rainy season, the U.S. air sorties allocated to northern Laos (Barrel Roll) were reduced from more than 100 a day to slightly over 30. This reduction was made to free up assets to support interdiction along the Ho Chi Minh Trail in southern Laos, which was the priority at the time. In addition, historical data indicate that weather conditions also hampered U.S. air strikes during most of that rainy season.

As the monsoon rains increased during June and July, reports from the field revealed that fighting had dwindled to the point that only occasional skirmishes were taking place. Also, during the month of June, the RLAF flew only 35 air strikes, and were forced to stand down due to weather more than 60% of the time. Likewise, the Ravens only flew about 50 sorties a week. But, later, in July, the weather improved somewhat, allowing the Ravens to at least fly half-day schedules. In one particular week, the T-28s flew 58 sorties, and the USAF flew 245 air strikes in the area.

With activity limited in the air, the Ravens found themselves acting as fire adjusters for VP's artillery. And, as the Lao commanders became more familiar with what effective artillery could contribute, they were suddenly sold on the use of the big guns. In the first week of August, the Ravens directed over 200 rounds from one 105mm gun, and over 400 rounds from another. VP was so impressed with the effectiveness of the guns that by the end of the wet season, he was regularly including artillery support in his operational orders for the first time.

In August, VP launched an offensive called "Operation Leap Frog," using Air America and USAF helicopters. The Hmong guerrillas subsequently initiated their attack on Ban Na, and the weather was terrible, with constant rain, heavy cloud cover, and fog hampering the Hmong efforts. Even though the NVA were small in number during the rainy season, they were able to hold Ban Na, so VP retreated. Next, the Hmong guerrillas attacked Moung Soui, where they were able to establish temporary control of the airfield. And once again, still few in number, the NVA held and retook the airfield. Once again, VP's troops retreated.

During Leap Frog, VP was supported by Chuck Engle and Craig Duehring from the Ravens. On one of their sorties, Engle's O-1 Bird Dog was hit with AK-47 fire, and he was shot through the lower leg. He and Duehring left the fight and headed for Long Tieng. Even though he was losing a lot of blood, Engle was able to land the aircraft before passing out, and he was flown to the USAF hospital in Udorn, where they patched him up. Later, after he had sufficiently healed he returned to Long Tieng, and to the fight.

In retrospect, Operation Leap Frog proved less than successful, for a number of reasons. For one thing, the weather failed to cooperate, and there were a number of reverses in the ground fighting. During one such fight, a series of NVA mortar rounds and ground attacks by NVA sappers on a Lao artillery position near Phou Long Mat resulted in the loss of 33 Lao irregulars, the commander, and an air guide. There were also more than 50 irregulars wounded. After losing the artillery position, the Hmong guerrillas tried to retake it and lost another 20 or so troops with the wounded numbering about 35. Meanwhile, the RLAF was trying to help, but in one week they were only able to fly fewer than 100 sorties. The USAF contributed only another 30 or so during that same week.

After failing to achieve his objectives at Ban NA, Vang Pao initiated another offensive called "Counterpunch, Part II." Later, on August 31, a guerrilla patrol advanced to the eastern edge of the Moung Soui airfield and encountered little Communist resistance. After a brief engagement, the guerrillas were reinforced with several hundred fresh troops. They also received additional reinforcements by troops moving south from Phou Fa. Although Moung Soui was not heavily defended by the NVA, they were able to drive the guerrillas back to Xieng Dat. Later, after a month of intense fighting, the guerrillas finally took Moung Soui.

In September 1970, Combat Skyspot was reintroduced in northeastern Laos. But the problem with Skyspot and LORAN D was the inaccurate maps of northern Laos; in order to make pinpoint bombing successful, reliable maps were required. To that end, in the summer of 1970 RF-4 reconnaissance aircraft began photo-mapping northern Laos. Each time a photo was taken, the exact LORAN coordinates were captured by the onboard computers. Later, after photo mapping the entire area of northern Laos, the information was consolidated, an accurate grid overlay map was completed, and it was all uploaded into the U.S. aircraft computers. When tests were done to determine the accuracy of the maps, they proved reliable 98% of the time.

Meanwhile, on October 13, USAF Major Joseph L. Chestnut, a Raven operating out of MR 1 in northwestern Laos, was flying a RLAF T-28 when his aircraft mysteriously disappeared. One report indicated that Chestnut was on an orientation flight, and smoke was observed coming from his wing. The report also indicated the T-28 was observed flying over the top of a large hill and crashing on the other side. A subsequent ground search located the aircraft, but Major Chestnut was not found and no distress signal had been received. Another eyewitness reported that Chestnut's aircraft was hit by ground fire prior to crashing, and that a ground search could not be immediately initiated because there was not enough daylight left. But later searches spanning several days after the crash failed to disclose what happened to Major Chestnut, and he was classified as MIA. Many years later, however, his remains were recovered, and were returned to his family on July 25, 1995.

By October 23, 1970, Ban Na had been retaken by the guerrillas, along with the western rim of the Plain of Jars. In the process, large quantities of rice, ammunition and personal equipment was found and confiscated by the guerrillas. They were also able to capture recoilless rifles, small arms, and mortars. Furthermore, as the dry season approached, some NVA troops abandoned their positions—simply walking away, leaving materiel and supplies behind.

Meanwhile, the flow of NVA trucks onto the Plain was increasing daily, and there were signs of a Communist build-up in the central and eastern areas of the Plain. In spite of that fact, VP was able to push the NVA back approximately 30 miles during the rainy season. Nonetheless, the Communists were still in an excellent position to begin their dry season offensive. One good reason for the effective positioning of war supplies on the part of the NVA were the two new roads that had been recently constructed. These were Routes 72 and 73, both of which bypassed the road junction of Route 7 between Ban Ban and the Plain of Jars. During each of the two previous years, the U.S. had been able to interdict the NVA trucks at the road junction, so the NVA simply built new roads skirting the junction, allowing direct access from North Vietnam to Laos. For additional insurance, the NVA brought in more large antiaircraft guns to protect their trucks on the new roads.

As the rainy season drew to a close, it was obvious there was little reason for optimism on the part of the Lao troops. The guerrilla forces had been beaten up badly, and were tired and worn from the constant fighting. Also, they had achieved very little success, relatively speaking. Conversely, the NVA was still present in Laos in large numbers, and those numbers continued to increase. Furthermore, the United States was scaling back its day-to-day air support. With the Communists beginning their dry season offensive, the campaign could well prove to be the guerrillas' last. If the irregulars were to fail, it could result in Laos being partitioned into Communist and non-Communist areas, much as North and South Korea had been. That result would end all hopes of Laos acting a buffer to Communism, and the threat to Thailand would be significantly increased.

In October, the NVA began to pull back from their forward positions in northern Laos. They formed a new defensive line along Route 4, cutting just about across the middle of the Plain of Jars. This action allowed Vang Pao to get some traction on the Plain, allowing him to retake Muong Soui on October 11 and LS-15 (Phong Saly) a week or so later. He was also able to retake Phou Seu by the end of October. The NVA's pullback was odd, and the reasons for it remain uncertain, but it could have taken place for two reasons. One, their supply lines had been severely interdicted in previous months, leaving them short on supplies. By pulling back, they could shorten those supply lines. The second reason may have been to avoid another one of VP's dry season offensives, something like Operation About Face during the previous year.

A little later, on November 21, 1970, the legendary Green Beret Colonel Arthur D. (Bull) Simons led a team of 56 Army and USAF Special Operations troops on a raid of the Son Tay prison camp in North Vietnam. The raid was called "Operation Ivory Coast." Although the raid was a tactical success, not a single prisoner was rescued, because just days before the raid, extremely heavy rains and the possibility of flooding had prompted the NVA to move the prisoners to another prison camp on higher ground. Sadly, the information never got to the raiding team, even though one intelligence estimate the day before the raid had indicated the prisoners were probably no longer at Son Tay. The raid did, however, get North Vietnam's attention, and they subsequently moved most prisoners to larger, more centralized facilities, and most were treated better than they had been previously.

Ironically, the heavy rains necessitating the prisoners' removal from Son Tay might have been at least partially due to Operation Popeye. Popeye was a weather modification program that was launched on March 20, 1967 by the United States Air Force, and lasted until July 5, 1972. The project was assigned to the 54th Weather Reconnaissance Squadron at Udorn Royal Thai Air Force Base. Using WC-130 aircraft, the mission was to seed the clouds using a 40mm aluminum cartridge and a candle assembly. After the cartridge was dropped, a firing mechanism would ignite the candle and mix with chemicals to produce silver iodide or lead iodide.

The iodides would permeate the clouds, and ideally heavy rains would be produced. The objective was to limit the ability of the NVA to move people and equipment over the roads, minimizing their ability to fight. This may have also resulted in the Son Tay prisoners being moved to higher ground. But the problem with Operation Popeye was that Colonel Simons and his men would probably not have known of its existence, because it was Top Secret and compartmentalized—which meant that even Simons' weather officer may not have been privy to the information. In fact, the program was so sensitive that it took many years for Congress to get access to the information so that hearings could be held. To make a long story short, the United States had Colonel Simons and his men trying to rescue prisoners of war at the same time that we had WC-130 aircraft flying overhead, seeding the clouds.[91]

Meanwhile, back in northern Laos, as the NVA pulled back in October, Vang Pao saw an opportunity to go after the Communists and gain additional ground. He was backed by the King of Laos and Souvanna Phouma, but the embassy in Vientiane wasn't so sure it was good idea. The number of USAF air sorties was still dwindling, and the NVA retained a very large presence in northern Laos. But, ultimately, Ambassador Godley did consent to a raid on Ban Ban, to interdict the NVA supply line along Route 7.

VP's operation, named "Counterpunch III", began on November 26, and it appeared to be doomed from the start. Low clouds and haze limited U.S. air support, and the hearts of the Hmong just weren't in it. The operation quickly fizzled, although it technically continued into January 1971. The attempt to draw large numbers of NVA into the fight didn't work, and Route 7 was only closed for a few days during the operation. Another possible explanation for the lack of success of Counterpunch III could have been the ongoing problem of the CIA planning its operations without fully briefing the U.S. military, and not asking for or accepting their input in most cases.

To add other grim information to all the other bad news of 1970, the United States had begun its withdrawal of troops from South Vietnam and, at the end of the year, only 280,000 troops remained. Also, on November 16, the last RF-101 Voodoo left Southeast Asia. The Voodoo had been among the first U.S. tactical jet aircraft involved in the Southeast Asia conflict, and it flew with distinction for more than eight years under combat conditions. During that period, approximately 35 Voodoos were lost.[92] It was described as "a pilot's airplane."

On December 20, 1970, the 602nd SOS (Firefly), flying the A-1 Skyraiders out of NKP, was disbanded; and the last class of Thai "B Team" pilots had graduated from Waterpump at Udorn back on April 17. As these resources disappeared, the void was filled by the 23rd Tactical Air Support Squadron (TASS) from NKP, flying the new twin engine OV-10 "Bronco." The Bronco was a very fast aircraft, and it also had extended range. In addition, the 1st SOS (Hobos) out of NKP was still supporting the Secret War with their A-1 Skyraiders.

As the year began to wind down, the future of the Secret War appeared to be grim. America wasn't behind the war, and many in Congress didn't support it either. The Hmong guerrillas were depleted, their numbers nearing extinction. Conversely, the NVA troop strength was growing, and they were remaining in Laos even during the rainy season. Meanwhile, the USAF presence was decreasing, and U.S. government agencies continued to compartmentalize information without sharing it. They also didn't talk to each other effectively. As a matter of fact, the USAF Chief of Staff, General John D. Ryan, met with the other Joint Chiefs on December 17 to discuss that very subject. He wanted to make sure that sufficient dialogue and planning took place prior to future operations.

The Joint Chiefs agreed with General Ryan, and asked Secretary of Defense Melvin Laird to restate the military's position to the Secretary of State in Washington. Meanwhile, VP prepared for the dry season offensive ahead. To contain the NVA would require more than 2,000 air strikes, but the U.S. was only prepared to authorize less than a thousand. Other special missions such as rescue, escort, and flare drops would be flown by the USAF and would continue on an as-needed basis—so the bulk of the air interdiction sorties would fall to the RLAF. It was obvious, however, that they were not up to the task. Out of fewer than 50 aircraft total, several had been recently lost, and many others were not current on maintenance and refurbishment.

As the year 1970 ended, the future didn't appear to be bright for Laos—and only time would reveal the end result. But in the meantime, the Hmong, and Vang Pao, had to continue to fight and bleed.

Chapter 13

Aerial Reconnaissance

While events on the ground continue to deteriorate, let's turn our attention to the skies above Laos and North Vietnam. Up to this point in the story, we've occasionally mentioned aerial or airborne reconnaissance; so this may be a good time to pause and address the subject, in order to adequately relate its value to the overall war effort.

Aerial reconnaissance wasn't new to either the Vietnam War or the Secret War in Laos; in fact, its use goes all the way back to 1794, when the French first used balloons to observe an enemy's maneuvers. Similarly, the U.S. military utilized balloons for aerial reconnaissance during the Civil War, and the use of balloons for aerial reconnaissance continued into the 1950s. One of the more famous "balloon" programs was called Project Mogul, which utilized high altitude balloons for a variety of classified military purposes. Mogul was reportedly exposed by an event in Roswell, New Mexico in 1947, when a downed Project Mogul balloon was mistaken for an alien flying saucer. High altitude reconnaissance balloons were also used by the U.S. Government as late as 1952, in two other programs, Project Moby Dick and Project Genetrix.

The first known use of airplanes for aerial reconnaissance was in 1911, when an Italian pilot flew over Turkish lines in Libya to gather military intelligence using cameras from the air. Other nations soon followed suit, using both airborne cameras and human observers in a variety of aircraft to gather intelligence information. Recognizing its potential value, the United States began to get more serious about aerial reconnaissance after World War II, and it was used extensively during the Cold War.

As the Cold War heated up, the United States needed to know what the Russians were doing in regards to their airpower and intentions. Human spies were used extensively for gathering intelligence information, but their usefulness was limited, and a better method of verifying intelligence information was required.

In order to covertly monitor Soviet activities, the United States also developed the U-2 "Dragon Lady" reconnaissance aircraft in the early 1950s. The aircraft was designed and built by the Lockheed Aircraft Corporation and first flew in 1955 at Groom Lake, Nevada. The CIA oversaw the development of the U-2, but during its operational life the CIA and the USAF shared ownership of the aircraft. The U-2 was very successful at obtaining imagery intelligence (IMINT) of Soviet intentions, but the aircraft was susceptible to long range Surface to Air Missiles (SAMs). The whole world became aware of the existence of the U-2 when USAF pilot Francis Gary Powers was shot down over Soviet territory on May 1, 1960. The Russians paraded the captured pilot in front of news cameras from around the world, and even tried Powers in a Soviet court of law. Fortunately, he was later released and returned to the United States. Two additional U-2 aircraft were also lost while flying high altitude reconnaissance combat missions: one was shot down over Cuba during the Cuban Missile Crisis in 1962, and the other was lost over North Vietnam in October 1966 due to mechanical problems. Later versions of the U-2s

Figure 36. U-2 Dragon Lady
(Photo from the Public Domain)

are still operational today, and are still used to gather imagery intelligence data over low-threat hostile countries.

Recognizing the vulnerability of the U-2, The CIA began development of the high-flying SR-71 Blackbird in the early 1960s. Lockheed was awarded that contract as well, and the aircraft first flew on April 2, 1965 at Groom Lake (also known as Area 51). During its lifespan from 1964 to 1998, 32 Blackbirds were produced and flew extensively over hostile territory—and not a single aircraft was lost due to hostile fire. Twelve of the Blackbirds were lost, however, due to mechanical problems.

Approximately ten years prior to the development of the U-2, the U.S. military had begun to embrace another form of aerial reconnaissance, with the advent of something called Unmanned Aerial Vehicles (UAVs). Several

Figure 37. SR-71 Blackbird
(Photo from the Public Domain)

aerospace companies were later contracted to produce UAVs, or drones, as they were also called. At first, the vehicles were produced for use as surface-to-air and air-to-air targets. Essentially, the targets contained an engine, fuel, and a guidance system, and the drone was shaped more or less to look like a missile. The drone would be fueled, programmed with flight data, and then launched from under the wing of an aircraft or fired from an apparatus on the ground. The objective was for either aircrews or gun crews on the ground to recognize, engage, and shoot down the drone.

From the numerous participating contractors, one aerospace company stood out from the rest in successfully developing drones which, time and time again, fulfilled government requirements perfectly. That company was Ryan Aeronautical of San Diego, CA. In

1948, Ryan also developed a jet-powered target drone for the USAF. After initial development, Ryan made improvements, and the first successful flight of the "Fire Bee" took place in 1951. The Fire Bee was just over 17 feet long, powered by a Continental J69 jet engine, and its swept wings spanned about 11 feet. It had a top speed of just under Mach 1, and was capable of operating remotely at 50,000 feet, with a range of 400 miles.

Over the years, improvements and innovations were designed into subsequent unmanned vehicles produced by Ryan, and the Fire Bees continued to fly and meet all operational requirements. At about this same time, the USAF also recognized the importance of aerial reconnaissance, and was also utilizing numerous existing piloted airframes for aerial reconnaissance. In the 1960s, the USAF began to take steps to use the Fire Bees as more than just target drones.

Meanwhile, in Southeast Asia, some of the venerable C-47 cargo aircraft were fitted with cameras, utilized for aerial reconnaissance, and renamed the VC-47 and the SC-47. T-33 jet powered trainers were also fitted with cameras and renamed the RT-33. As mentioned elsewhere in this book, manned reconnaissance aircraft were also used extensively, and at least one SC-47 was lost over the Plain of Jars on March 23, 1961. Also in 1961, the USAF contracted with Ryan to produce the first reconnaissance version of the UAV. The project was codenamed Fire Fly, and the vehicle first flew in the summer of 1962.

The "Lightning Bugs," as these Ryan UAVs were called, were subsequently deployed to SEA and utilized by the CIA and the USAF. The UAV were used on high-altitude reconnaissance missions between August 1964 and December 1965. During these missions, it was determined the Ryan Fire Bee could operate very effectively on low altitude missions. In fact, it was less apt to be detected and shot down on low-level missions, because it flew below the radar. By the time the enemy gunners saw the Lighting Bugs, they were gone.

Recognizing the potential value of the UAV, the USAF initiated reconnaissance activities under very tight security in a program named "Buffalo Hunter." As Buffalo Hunter emerged, the environment in North Vietnam and northern Laos was changing. The NVA gunners had become very effective in shooting down reconnaissance aircraft like the RF-101 and RF-4C, using the latest in Soviet and Chinese technology. Notwithstanding, photo reconnaissance mission using aircraft continued over northern Laos under a USAF program called

"Yankee Team." At about this same time, a CIA reconnaissance program called "Oxcart" was undertaken over North Vietnam using the SR-71.

Buffalo Hunter was under the cognizance of the USAF Strategic Air Command, and the operational drones were assigned to the 350th Strategic Reconnaissance Squadron (SRS) out of Davis-Monthan AFB, Arizona. The 350th SRS was responsible for launch, control and recovery of the drones, and they operated from Bien Hoa Air Base, South Vietnam. The actual recovery of the drones after flight was handled out of Da Nang Air Base in South Vietnam. In 1970, the drones were relocated to U-Tapao Air Base, Thailand with recovery of the drones being handled out of NKP. And although the SEA-based SRS squadron handled the actual launch, control and recovery of the drones, the mission planning and control of the program was handled by the Strategic Reconnaissance Center (SRC) at Offutt AFB, Nebraska.

Although SAC controlled mission planning and scheduling, the drones were considered to be national assets assigned to the JCS in Washington, D.C. The JCS controlled these assets in support of the overall national reconnaissance requirements levied on them by the U.S. Intelligence Board, but the operational control was delegated to the SRC. The process used to actually initiate a Buffalo Hunter mission began with a request submitted to the 7th Air Force, Deputy Chief of Staff. The requests would then be forwarded to MACV for consolidation with other requirements, and then transmitted to the CINCPAC. CINCPAC would then forward the mission request to the SRC. The SRC would combine the military request with requests from other agencies. Later, all the requests would be prioritized and mission planning conducted in a manner to get the most value out of each mission, while satisfying as many customers as possible. The approved requests would then be sent to the 350th SRS for mission planning and execution.

Upon receipt of an approved mission request, the 350th would plot the mission course using current topographical maps and charts. The data itself was then programmed into the drone's computer, including altitude settings for the specific path to be taken by the drone. Allowances were made for weather, terrain, elevation and enemy air defenses. When mission planning was complete, the drone would be fueled and attached to a pylon under the wing of a DC-130 mother ship. The mother ship would be manned by a standard crew consisting of pilot, co-pilot, flight engineer and navigator. Additional crew members on the drone launches included two launch control officers (LCO), an Airborne Recovery Control Officer (ARCO), and a radar technician to monitor the Microwave Command Guidance System (MCGS). In addition to monitoring the drone's flight, the radar technician could and would make mid-course corrections as necessary while the drone was in flight.

The DC-130 would then take off and proceed to the launch point, at which time the drone would be powered up and released. Upon releasing the drone, the mother ship would travel to a safe distance, where the aircraft would loiter, observe and make mid-course corrections as necessary while monitoring the drone's flight and the data transmitted back to the DC-130. On a typical mission, the drone would proceed along a twisting imaginary track at varying altitudes and headings in order to cover all the targets, consisting of from five to fifteen. Upon completion of the mission run, the drone would climb rapidly to about 45,000 feet, then slowly climb an additional 12,000 feet and prepare for recovery. At this point, the ARCO would pass control of the MCGS to a ground station in the recovery area to the Drone Recovery Officer (DRO). The DRO would then send a command to the drone to shut down its engine. At that point, a parachute would deploy from the drone to slow its decent.

Upon descending to approximately 15,000 feet, a second chute would deploy, separated by a 200 foot cable. When the drone had descended to approximately 10,000 feet, a CH-3 helicopter would snag the drone's recovery line and retract the cable, capturing the drone. With the drone safely snagged,

Figure 38. Ryan Firebee (Lightning Bug)
(Photo from the Public Domain)

the CH-3 would proceed to the recovery location and gently lower the drone to the ground. The waiting ground crew would then load the drone onto the appropriate conveyance and return it to base, where the film would be removed and processed for intelligence evaluation. Upon removal of the film, it was packaged for transport aboard a T-39 "Scatback" courier aircraft for processing at Tan Son Nhut Air Base, South Vietnam.[93] There the film was developed and forwarded to the appropriate customer(s) for evaluation.

As can be imaged, the drones were susceptible to artillery and small arms fire, as well as MiG aircraft and SAMs. Operational experience, however, had taught the route planners that a low, fast mission profile dramatically increased the drone's survivability against enemy forces. And inasmuch as the drones flew low and fast, any retaliation would have to be accomplished within 10 seconds of seeing the drone, because it would be gone from view rather quickly. Overall, the drones fared well in the hostile environment of North Vietnam and northern Laos. Of the almost 300 drones launched in 1970, only nine were confirmed lost due to enemy action. An additional five were also lost during 1970 to unknown causes, which may have included enemy action. In 1971, 286 drones were launched, with six being lost to enemy action and eight to unknown reasons. Later, in 1972, almost 500 were launched, with 52 being lost for a variety of reasons.

To look at the drone's success rate in a different context, during 1970-1972 almost 13,000 targets were attempted, resulting in success gained in over 5,000 of those attempts. In other words, the drones were about 40% successful. The really good news, however, was that during that period, no pilots were lost on the reconnaissance missions, because the drones were unmanned. Had it not been for the drone capability, manned aircraft would have had to make most of those same flights, and hundreds of additional pilots could have been lost over North Vietnam and northern Laos.[94]

Not all the drones were recovered as planned, however; and occasionally, mechanical failure or other electronic glitches caused drones to stray off course and fall to Earth in undesired locations. One such drone landed on its own after a mission over northern Laos in 1971. Shortly after it landed, an HH-53C (Jolly Green), believed to be aircraft number 68-8285 from the 40th Air Rescue and Recovery Squadron at Udorn Air Base, was dispatched to recover the drone. The crew consisted of the pilot, co-pilot, flight engineer and two Para-rescue specialists (PJs). The crew was reportedly told the recovery would be a "piece of cake" and there were no hostile troops in the area.

The aircrew launched on July 21, and soon arrived over the general area of the downed drone in northern Laos. They were assisted in pinpointing the location of the drone by a Raven FAC. But by then the weather had deteriorated, and there were many very tall trees surrounding the area where the drone had landed. The Jolly Green pilot was concerned about having enough fuel for the return trip, and called an airborne tanker for more gas. The helicopter linked up the tanker a safe distance away, took on more fuel, and then returned to the area of the downed drone. By this time the weather had deteriorated even further, and visibility was very low. The Raven was contacted on the radio, and returned to assist in pinpointing the location once again.

After the drone had been located, the two PJs were then lowered to the ground by the flight engineer, using the onboard hoist and cable system. The PJs went to work hooking up the sling, and it was soon discovered the straps holding the sling were not long enough to reach the cable. The flight engineer asked the pilot to lower the helicopter, and finally the straps were able to reach the cable. Unfortunately, the belly of the helicopter was now literally in the canopy of the trees. At any rate, the straps were finally attached and the sling was ready to be raised. The flight engineer had also just lowered another cable to bring up the first PJ—when all of a sudden, the flight engineer heard a loud explosion, and the helicopter began to fall into the trees below.

The flight engineer released his gunner's belt and dove for the hatch to release the sling holding the drone as the rotor blades beat and chopped at the trees on the way down. Upon impact with the ground, the helicopter then began to roll down a hill, tearing off parts of the aircraft. When the helicopter finally came to rest on the ground, the engineer was able to crawl out of the aircraft and get a safe distance away, even though he was in great pain from his injuries. An Air America UH-1 (Huey) soon showed up, and the flight engineer and an injured PJ were placed on the helicopter for airlift to a hospital in Vientiane. The engineer had suffered a broken back and other injuries, and the PJ had been hit in the face by one of the rotor blades. His entire lower jaw was nearly cut-off, and he was bleeding badly.

The rest of the crew was banged up and bruised, but otherwise ambulatory. They were later picked up by an Air America H-34 helicopter and taken to safety. The crew was later flown to Udorn, where the badly injured PJ and engineer were hospitalized for treatment. The next day, another helicopter from the 21st Special Operations Squadron at NKP was sent to inspect the downed chopper. Upon arrival over the site, they took tremendous ground fire and had to withdraw. It was then apparent that the downed helicopter could not be recovered, so USAF strike aircraft were called in to destroy both the aircraft and the people on the ground shooting at the helicopters.[95]

After the Paris peace talks ended in 1973, the drones continued to operate, and some were even equipped with real-time television imaging. During the period of 1973-1975, over 180 low-level missions were flown using the Lightning Bugs, and an additional 200 missions using a later-model Ryan drone. The overall success of these missions was estimated at approximately 97 percent. But the missions later ended in 1975, when Vietnam and Laos fell to the Communists.

It should also be mentioned that early in 1971, under the "Have Lemon" project, some Ryan Fire Bee drones were experimentally armed with air-to-ground missiles and the drones were reportedly 100% successful in tests at Edwards AFB, California. That technology, although available during the Vietnam War, was not employed. After the war, the remaining serviceable drones were used for other operations; during the opening days of Gulf War II in March 2003, for example, some of the Vietnam-era Ryan drones were used to lay chaff corridors through Iraqi airspace to shield American cruise missiles and manned strike aircraft on missions to Baghdad and elsewhere. Through the years, Ryan Aeronautical remained one of the premier UAV producers in the world, with current successes under the Global Hawk and Fire Scout programs.

As mentioned earlier, in addition to the drones and the high flying reconnaissance aircraft, manned aircraft were still needed to conduct aerial reconnaissance on a daily basis, in order to satisfy the intelligence needs of military commanders on the ground. One tactical jet aircraft to see action in SEA was the RF-101 Voodoo, manufactured by the McDonnell Aircraft Corporation. It was officially billed as a day reconnaissance jet, but also functioned well in all-weather conditions, and could also be used at night under certain circumstances. During its operational life, it extracted much of the photographic intelligence information for the bombing of North Vietnam and the planning of military operations in Laos and Cambodia.

The Voodoo was designed in 1946, and two prototypes were developed in 1948. Not surprisingly, however, funding snags and politics precluded production until the first aircraft finally rolled off the assembly line in May 1955. Purchase Orders then began to flow, and a total of 203 aircraft were built. The Voodoo was the first supersonic aircraft produced in the United States, and it had a top speed of 875 knots. The pilots said that it handled well and was very responsive; but the aircraft was completely unarmed, with cameras taking up all the space in the fuselage, precluding the installation of defensive weapons.

Actually, the Voodoo couldn't have come along at a better time. The Communists were bent on taking control of SEA, and their aggressive posture had the United States on edge. As mentioned earlier, by the early 1960s aerial reconnaissance was conducted covertly, using a variety of existing airframes such as the Douglas DC-3 transport. The aircraft were also flown by the U.S. State Department on routine transport runs between Saigon and Vientiane to haul embassy personnel and supplies. While flying the skies of Laos, reconnaissance would be accomplished using hidden cameras to photograph military objectives.

Due to the limited number of SC-47 or VC-47 aircraft available, an RT-33 from Thailand was loaned to the RLG in Laos and flown by a Thai volunteer. The aircraft flew a total of six successful reconnaissance missions. As luck would have it, at about the same time the RT-33 was being used in the skies over Laos to collect photo intelligence information, several RF-101s were already in nearby Thailand participating in joint military exercises. Several other RF-101s were also on temporary duty in Saigon. Given the urgent need for photo reconnaissance support and the recent arrival of Voodoo aircraft in SEA, a decision was made to utilize the RF-101s to support existing aerial reconnaissance requirements. The project was called "Pipe Stem."

The first Pipe Stem aerial reconnaissance mission was flown on October 21, 1961, and two days later the RF-101s flew four sorties over Tchepone, Laos. From those sorties, photographic intelligence clearly depicted Soviet IL-14 aircraft dropping war supplies to NVA and Pathet Lao troops. Two days later, another RF-101 sortie was flown, and again clearly showed the IL-14s dropping supplies to Communist troops. The photos were flown to Washington, D.C. and shown to President Kennedy, who ordered the recon flights to continue.

After Kennedy's order. two sorties were flown each day over northern Laos, with the aircraft taking ground fire on every mission. The missions continued until November 21, 1961, at which time the ICC complained and the missions were halted. As of that date, over 60 successful missions had been flown. Meanwhile, the United States relocated four RF-101s to Don Muang, Thailand for use in Task Force "Able Mable."

When Able Mable was conceived, there were two bases in SEA that had operational RF-101 aircraft and the infrastructure to support them. The first was the 15th Tactical Reconnaissance Squadron at Kadena Air Base, Okinawa. The other unit was the 45th Tactical Reconnaissance Squadron at Misawa Air Base, Japan. These two bases would provide the majority of RF-101 aircraft utilized at Tan Son Nhut Air Base, Saigon, Don Muang Air Base, and Udorn Air Base on a rotational basis.

On all reconnaissance missions, weather was usually a factor, and antiaircraft fire to 5,000 feet could be anticipated—not to mention small arms fire from semi-automatic weapons. At that time, navigational aids were rudimentary at best, and electronic navigation aids were not yet in existence. In most cases, the pilot had to use visual landmarks and maps. unfortunately (or perhaps fortunately, depending on one's perspective), the only available maps of Laos were those previously compiled by the French Motor Club. Also, the pilots were forbidden to enter the airspace of Burma, China, North Vietnam or Cambodia on their reconnaissance missions. Combine all those factors with the fact that there were no formal SAR procedures or capability in place, and that's essentially the dangerous environment in which the Voodoo aircraft had to operate.

Notwithstanding, by the end of 1961, over 100 Able Mable missions had been flown in Laos and South Vietnam using the RF-101. To ease the maintenance load and get more pilots exposed to the missions, crews and aircraft were rotated every six weeks. The Able Mable missions continued into 1962, and on August 14th an RF-101 over Route 7 in northern Laos took a direct hit from antiaircraft fire at an altitude of approximately 10,000 feet. The blast blew off a camera bay door and severed hydraulic and electrical lines in the fuselage of the aircraft. The pilot was uninjured in the attack, and was able to nurse the aircraft back to Don Muang. Upon landing the nose gear collapsed, but the aircraft stopped safely. Out of an abundance of caution, however, all Able Mable flights were temporarily halted pending further inquiry.

The flights resumed again on September 1, 1962 over Vietnam, though flights over Laos were still suspended. All RF-101 flights were again halted on September 14, because the U.S. government was concerned about North Vietnamese radar capability and wanted to conduct a study before continuing the reconnaissance flights. The RF-101 crews weren't concerned much about the enemy's radar, and were confident that it was not a show—stopper. They believed in their aircraft and their flying skills, and considered themselves capable of dealing with the issue. By late December 1962, reconnaissance flights over Laos remained suspended, but the RF-101 resumed flights out of Tan Son Nhut on a daily basis in order to provide photographic intelligence of the build-up of Communist troops and supplies in areas bordering the Demilitarized Zone separating North and South Vietnam.

The reconnaissance flights over Laos remained suspended throughout 1963 and into early 1964. On January 22, 1964, the JCS urged the Department of Defense to insist upon resumption of the Able Mable flights over northern Laos. Ambassador Unger agreed, and supported resumption on the recon missions. But the U.S. Department of State was adamant that no flights would be conducted unless the Lao government approved. A few months later, on May 17, Pathet Lao forces suddenly attacked Lao Neutralists troops on the Plain of Jars and sent them fleeing southward. By nightfall, the Plain was completely occupied by Communist troops.

Laos was suddenly thrown into crisis mode, and something had to be done. Seizing upon the opportunity, the United States leadership recommended resumption of the aerial reconnaissance missions over northern Laos; and the Prime Minister, Souvanna Phouma, finally consented. With any luck, Able Mable would soon be back in business. Not wasting any time, the JCS directed the USAF and the Navy to get ready to fly. The airmen and sailors quickly complied, and two days later, the USAF was directed to conducted aerial reconnaissance of the Communist infiltration routes from North Vietnam through Laos and into South Vietnam via the Ho Chi Minh Trail. They were also told to place special emphasis on the Ban Thay military installation east of Muong Phine, and the contiguous roads and trails. No limitations as to the number of sorties to be conducted were mentioned, but the aircrews were reminded not to fly into North Vietnam's airspace.

A short time later, in the early morning hours of May 19, four RF-101 Voodoo aircraft took to the sky, and shortly thereafter were flying fast and low over the Plain of Jars and other parts of northern Laos. Their cameras rolled, and it didn't take long to cover the entire area. Having performed their mission, the aircraft headed back to Ton San Nhut so the film could be developed and processed for evaluation. Two days later, on May 21, a U.S. Navy RF-8 aircraft joined the RF-101s on photo reconnaissance missions over northern Laos and the roads connecting it with North Vietnam. The photographs were handed over to the RLG so they could provide them to the ICC to demonstrate that the Pathet Lao were violating the terms of the Geneva Convention.

Seizing upon this opportunity of mutual cooperation, MACV proposed a continuing program of two daylight and one night reconnaissance flights using the RF-101 and Navy RF-8 aircraft. The USAF agreed, but cautioned that two additional RF-101s would be needed to handle the workload. With the military in agreement, the plan was submitted to Souvanna Phouma and Ambassador Unger. They both approved, and a program called "Yankee Team" was initiated on May 22, 1964.[96]

On the following day, the program was briefed to the JCS. They approved the program and outlined four objectives:

1) Acquire timely tactical intelligence for the RLG.
2) Substantiate scope and extent of Communist infiltration of war materials and troops through Laos to South Vietnam.
3) Provide psychological boosts to friendly forces.
4) Convince North Vietnam the U.S. was in for the long haul, as long as North Vietnam was a threat to peace.

Additionally, the JCS was to be kept posted on all missions in advance, and specific authorization was required for more than nine sorties in any given 24-hour period. Finally, with everyone's approval in hand, the USAF and USN began the Yankee Team/Blue Tree missions. The Yankee Team missions began right after the JCS approval had been received and continued through the month of May, with the Navy providing RF-8 aircraft to supplement the RF-101s.

While conducting the reconnaissance missions, the Navy suggested the use of air refueling to expedite the recon aircraft's return to Tan Son Nhut. (This was a very good idea, because the Yankee Team aircraft usually had to divert to Da Nang Air Base in Vietnam for refueling prior to returning to Tan Son Nhut). The Navy offered to test the process by providing air tankers to refuel the Yankee Team aircraft. It was later tried and found to be not only feasible but practical, and soon the process was standard procedure.

On June 6, 1964, a Navy RF-8E was downed by enemy fire while on a Yankee Team mission over the Plain of Jars. The JCS took swift action by directing fighter jets to escort unarmed reconnaissance aircraft during their missions, and to protect them from ground fire or any other airborne threats. But, unfortunately, another Navy F-8 escort aircraft was shot down on the following day. In retaliation, the JCS directed an air strike on all antiaircraft batteries around the Plain of Jars, using USAF F-100 Super Sabers as a warning to the NVA and Pathet Lao.

The strike was carried out successfully, and the RF-101s filmed the results, which were forwarded to Washington. Meanwhile, the Yankee Team missions were temporarily suspended, but resumed shortly thereafter. On one such mission, USAF Captain Burton Walz flew his RF-101 over Ban Phan Nap, photographing antiaircraft positions that had brought down an F-100 three days earlier. During one of his runs over the target, Walz was hit by ground fire, which caused the aircraft to burst into flames and spiral out of control. Walz was somehow able to eject, and wind drift took him into a large tree, where his parachute canopy became entangled.

Other than being entangled in the tree, Walz was okay, so he began to try and secure himself to the tree and hope for rescue. But the story doesn't end there. While securing the parachute canopy, it began to rip, and Walz tumbled to the ground—at which time he sustained a broken arm and leg. An Air America helicopter working in the area went to help, and was able to safely rescue Captain Walz and fly him to the USAF hospital at Korat Air Base in Thailand. In other words, it was just another routine day at work for Captain Walz.

Yankee Team/Blue Tree reconnaissance flights continued throughout the dry season of 1964-65. This was the busiest time of year for the NVA, and so they were moving as many troops and as much equipment as they could into northern Laos and South Vietnam. Not only that, but they were repairing bridges, rebuilding roads, building new roads, and installing more antiaircraft positions all over northern Laos and along the Ho Chi Minh Trail in southern Laos. In early 1965, the JCS decided to move one group of RF-101s to Udorn, keeping the remainder of the Voodoo aircraft at Ton San Nhut. The aircraft remaining in South Vietnam would keep the call sign Able Mable, and the RF-101s transferring to Udorn would take the name "Green Python." It was also decided that Green Python aircraft would conduct air reconnaissance over northern Laos and North Vietnam, and Able Mable Voodoos would conduct reconnaissance missions over South Vietnam. Thereafter, the RF-101s continued their missions, and the number of Green Python aircraft was increased to 12.

Then, abruptly, on May 12, 1965, President Lyndon Johnson halted the bombing over North Vietnam, hoping the NVA would opt for peace and agree to talks. Of course that didn't happen, but the Communists used the lull in the bombing to fortify their existing positions and begin the installation of SAM sites in concentric rings around the city of Hanoi. The Green Python RF-101s were directed to increase their aerial reconnaissance over Hanoi, and in three days they had flown close to 200 missions, providing photographs of the missile installations and additional antiaircraft positions.

Six days later, on May 18, the bombing of North Vietnam was resumed, and the recon flights over the north resumed as well. But on July 24, the inevitable happened: a fast moving F-4 Phantom fighter jet was shot down by a SAM a few miles west of Hanoi. A new question then arose. Based on this new threat, should the United States also be concerned about the Soviet MiG aircraft at Phuc Yen Airfield, outside Hanoi? The short answer was *maybe*. Up to that moment, the Voodoo pilots hadn't been particularly concerned, because they were confident they could out maneuver or outrun the Soviet fighters. Past photo reconnaissance had shown a few MiGs sitting on the ground, but none had actually taken off from Phuc Yen for engagement.

Nonetheless, a recon mission was ordered to see what the Communists had been up to, if anything. As it turned out, the thinkers back in Washington had been right for once. The recon photos clearly depicted 24 newly arrived crates, believed to contain MiG aircraft. Regardless, antiaircraft fire was still considered to be the largest threat to Green Python aircraft, and the number of Communist antiaircraft gun emplacements were increasing at an alarming rate.

The NVA had placed the weapons around all their major facilities, and also along known air corridors used by the United States while flying over North Vietnam. Their plan was to wait for an American aircraft and then, when it entered the target area, all the guns would open up on the aircraft, filling the sky with projectiles in the hope that one would hit the aircraft. It was certainly a bold plan, and an expensive one at that. But to survive, the American pilots simply had to stay out of range and remain very alert.

While all this activity was taking place in 1965, the RF-101 Yankee Team/Blue Tree flights continued over North Vietnam and northern Laos, and the requirement for fighter escort remained in place. It wasn't working, however, because the U.S. was using the new F-105 Thunderchief and it just didn't have enough fuel to loiter over the target while the Green Pythons did their job. In fact, the F-105s would routinely have to depart for fuel, and by the time they returned, the RF-101s had completed their sorties and were headed for home.

The Voodoo pilots then came up with an alternative to fighter escort, recommending the RF-101s fly in pairs; that way, one could watch out for the other and vice versa. If something bad happened to one aircraft, the other could remain to control the SAR effort. After much discussion, the plan was approved, and the Yankee Team sorties continued.

In October, a new aircraft arrived at Tan Son Nhut Air Base in Saigon: the brand new McDonnell-Douglas RF-4C Phantom II. The aircraft had been developed three years earlier as a supplement to, and eventual replacement for, the RF-101. The Phantoms then began working with the Voodoo aircraft, and this allowed the USAF to redistribute some of the older RF-101s to units in Japan and Okinawa. With the new Phantoms settling in, 1965 began to wind down—and President Johnson called for another halt to the bombing.

His advisors objected, as did the Pentagon, but Johnson was adamant, so the bombing halted. The North Vietnamese and Pathet

Lao were delighted. It was the dry season again: roads could be repaired, bridges could be built, and the Communists troops in the field could receive ammunition and supplies without having to worry about bombs falling on them. Of course, the continuing Voodoo reconnaissance photos clearly showed the build-up and activity. And, at the same time, more SAM sites were under construction in North Vietnam.

As 1966 arrived, the RF-101s had to deal with very bad weather during their recon missions. They did well, though, and returned excellent photographs depicting Communist activities. Of course, as the threat grew larger, it began to take its toll on the RF-101s. By the end of the year, more Voodoos had been lost to ground fire. But the reliable RF-101 continued its service right up until November 1, 1970, when all Voodoo missions ceased. The aircraft and all remaining assets were then transferred to the Air National Guard in Meridian, Mississippi. An era had ended, but reconnaissance continued using the Phantom II. After all was said and done, the United States had lost more than 30 RF-101 Voodoo aircraft in SEA.

After replacing the Voodoos, the RF-4C saw extensive service with the USAF for the duration of conflict in SEA. Seven RF-4C aircraft were lost to

Figure 39. F-101 Voodoo
(Photo from the Public Domain)

SAMs, 65 were lost to antiaircraft fire, four were destroyed on the ground, and seven were lost in accidents. More than 500 RF-4C aircraft were built, most for the USAF. The United States continued to use the RF-4C until September 1995. But the United States military was not the only customer for the famed Phantoms: they were also sold to several other nations under the Foreign Military Assistance (FMA) agreements, and some are still in use today.

Initial missions by the RF-4C, however, revealed several problems and deficiencies. The side-looking radar had major problems and was initially very unreliable in combat, and it took several years to fix this issue. There was also a problem with the infrared sensor that had to be fixed, and airframe vibrations would often result in distorted images taken by the cameras. But, for approximately eight years, the RF-4C served in SEA, with numerous USAF reconnaissance units stationed at Udorn and Tan Son Nhut. The aircraft usually

Figure 40. RF-4C Phantom
(Photo from the Public Domain)

flew alone, and most missions were carried out during the day over northern Laos and North Vietnam. None of the Phantoms were lost to Soviet MiG fighters.

A unique feature in reconnaissance operations was unveiled on April 2, 1969, when a specially equipped RF-4C lined up for a photo run over the Mu Gia Pass on the border between Laos and North Vietnam. This would mark the first time that a laser camera was used in aerial surveillance. The laser camera came to SEA along with five specially configured Phantoms, under a program called "Compass

Count." The camera had not been previously tested under combat conditions, but it was hoped the laser would provide sufficient illumination for night reconnaissance. Heretofore, the conventional method of using photo cartridges that required visible flashes of light for illumination had been used. But these flashes of light could easily disclose the location of the aircraft, potentially allowing antiaircraft gunners more time to shoot it down. If the laser worked, it would significantly reduce the threat to the pilot.

The laser camera was tested at several different locations in Laos, Cambodia, and Vietnam over the next several months. The camera itself performed with a high degree of reliability on all occasions. The laser, however, was another issue. During testing, it was discovered that moisture and haze impaired the laser's effectiveness; the result under those conditions was poor quality photographs. Having an abundance of both haze and moisture in Southeast Asia resulted in certain death for the laser camera, and its use was subsequently discontinued.

Chapter 14

The Son Tay Raid

In Chapter 13, we discussed aerial reconnaissance and the extent to which it was used in the Secret War. In this chapter, you'll be able to see how some of the technology was used.

As 1970 approached, several dynamics had come into play that would shape future events in Laos, Vietnam, and Cambodia. First of all, the people—both the indigenous peoples and the American public—were tired of war, death and destruction. As of December 1969, 47,768 Americans had died in Vietnam. Hundreds were missing, and 451 were known to be POWs. Of course, none had officially died or become missing in Laos, because the United States denied having a military presence in Laos . . . but we know the truth. In reality, hundreds had died and hundreds were missing.

Of the 451 servicemen held prisoner in Vietnam, approximately half had been in captivity for more than 2,000 days. Of the hundreds of MIAs, it was believed that perhaps half that number were prisoners. We also know that the conditions under which the prisoners were held were intolerable. The prisoners were routinely tortured, starved, denied adequate medical and dental care, and they had little, if any, contact with the outside world. America just wanted the war to end and for the POWs to come home—and, these issues had not gone unnoticed by the White House, Congress, or the Department of Defense. Everyone wanted the prisoners to come home.

But the United States had not been idly sitting on its hands regarding the POW/MIA issue. The military had been actively looking for the prisoners, as had the U.S. intelligence agencies. From a military perspective, the Pacific Command established the Joint Personnel Recovery Center (JPRC) in September 1966. For operational purposes, and secrecy, JPRC was placed under the Studies and Observations Group (SOG), MACV in Saigon. As we now know, SOG was a highly classified, multi-service Special Forces unit which conducted unconventional warfare.

This group conducted strategic reconnaissance missions, rescued downed airmen, captured NVA combatants, supervised and carried out interdiction activities on the Ho Chi Minh Trail, and conducted psychological operations. In other words, they had broad authority, autonomy, and almost unlimited resources. They could literally go anywhere, do anything they were told to do, and actually get the job done without a lot of red tape. The SOG had been actively looking for POW camps in North Vietnam for some time, and had collected good intelligence on many of the known camps. One of those camps was in North Vietnam, near the town of Son Tay. It was a small town about 30 miles from Hanoi, located very near the banks of the Song Con River.

Of all the known POW prisons, Son Tay was considered the best candidate for a POW rescue. It was not in a heavily populated area; it was a small facility, capable of housing approximately 75-100 prisoners; and it was an area that could be secured in short order. On the negative side, it was just minutes away from a military installation housing in excess of 10,000 NVA soldiers, not to mention an NVA artillery school and air defense installation. In fact, the school actively had trained Pathet Lao troops for many years.

When the weather was favorable, high-flying USAF reconnaissance aircraft photographed Son Tay on a regular basis, looking for clues as to whether or not Americans were actually being held at the site. The National Security Agency (NSA) also kept the prison under surveillance, using unmanned reconnaissance drones operating under the Buffalo Hunter program. Data from the surveillance flights indicated that Americans were being held at Son Tay, but the actual number of prisoners could not be determined. As mentioned earlier, good reconnaissance could only take place in good weather—and the year 1970 had thus far proved to have very bad weather indeed. It rained constantly, and the skies were overcast most of the time. The Song Con River near the prison compound was at flood stage levels early in the rainy season, and if the water level continued to rise, the prisoners at Son Tay would have to be relocated to another facility.

To add one more variable, the SOG may have had no idea that Operation Popeye was taking place. Earlier, in the book, we mentioned Operation Popeye briefly, but this may be the appropriate time to provide more information about this Top Secret project. Operation Popeye began on March 20, 1967 and continued every rainy season in SEA until 1972. Three WC-130 aircraft and two F4-C Phantoms, all assigned to the 54th Weather Reconnaissance Squadron at Udorn, flew two sorties each almost every day, seeding the clouds with silver iodide crystals. The crystals would make it rain harder and longer, putting more water on the ground and achieving the effect desired by the U.S. Government.

Also as mentioned previously, this highly classified operation was not talked about by people briefed to the project. In fact, they couldn't talk, because they had signed nondisclosure agreements threatening them with long terms in prison if violated. It was what the government referred to as "compartmented" information. In other words, if you weren't briefed on the project, you would have no knowledge that it existed. But this was not unusual, because during the Vietnam War, it seemed that almost everything was compartmented. In order to get access to compartmented information, two requirements had to be met. First, you had to have the appropriate security clearance, and secondly, you had to have a "need to know." If both requirements were met, then you would be accessed to the information.

In the case of Operation Popeye, SOG personnel did have Top Secret clearances, but they probably would not have been considered to have a need to know, so they were not briefed on the program. Likewise, most people in the Pentagon and Congress were not considered to have the need to know, so very few people in Washington were briefed or knowledgeable of the operation.

SOG knew about Son Tay, and they had collected hard intelligence on the prison after it was confirmed that Americans were being held there. But SOG had not heretofore acted, out of fear that a rescue operation could be compromised based upon the fact that too many people knew about the information. And inasmuch as there were known intelligence leaks in MACV, a rescue was not, heretofore, attempted at Son Tay. But by 1970, it was a different ballgame.

Many of the MACV personnel previously knowledgeable of Son Tay had rotated back to the United States, or had been reassigned to other parts of the world—and SOG would not operate alone this time around. In May 1970, updated photo reconnaissance intelligence information confirmed that Americans were still at Son Tay. Photographs of the prison disclosed that the prisoners had formed a large letter "K" in the dirt, a code symbol for "come and get us." It was also determined the prison was being enlarged to hold additional prisoners. American intelligence officials believed that speedy action had to be undertaken to rescue the prisoners. Brigadier General Donald D. Blackburn, the former SOG Chief at MACV, now stationed at the Pentagon, suggested that a small group of Special Forces volunteers could rescue the prisoners at Son Tay.

After his stint with MACV, Blackburn took the assignment as Special Assistant for Counterinsurgency and Special Activities (SACSA) in Washington, D.C. In that capacity he reported directly to the JCS, and therefore was the final authority for SOG missions. For the Son Tay mission, he recommended Colonel Bull Simons to lead the team into Son Tay. Simons was an old U.S. Army Special Forces hand, and had extensive experience in Southeast Asia. If anybody could get the job done, it was Bull Simons. Blackburn even went so far as to talk to Simons, and he agreed to take the assignment.

Blackburn also briefed the JCS, and the concept was favorably considered. The plan was then taken to Secretary of Defense Melvin Laird, National Security Advisor Henry Kissinger, and finally to President Nixon. The President liked the idea, and authorized the planning to continue. Simons then traveled to the U.S. Army's Green Beret headquarters at Fort Bragg, North Carolina, where he handpicked about 100 volunteers for an undisclosed classified operation. No other information was provided to the volunteers at the time, except that the eventual number of raiders might be less than 100.

Of course, the USAF would also be needed to fly the mission, so Brigadier General Leroy J. Manor, USAF Special Operations Commander at Eglin Air Force Base in Florida, was selected to command the operation. Included in the 100 volunteers were two Army officers whom Simons had worked with before and trusted completely. They were Captain Dick Meadows, who would lead the ground assault team, and Lieutenant Colonel Bud Sydnor, who would be the ground component commander.

The second phase of the operation, named "Ivory Coast," began in August 1970 at Eglin. Using photographic intelligence information, a full-scale mock-up of the POW camp at Son Tay was constructed at Eglin. The volunteers, still not knowing the target, erected the mock village every night and began to practice their tactics. They disassembled the village when they were done for the night. This continued through September 1970, and finally the team was ready.[97]

As the assault team of Green Berets continued to practice their tactics at the mock village, the USAF support element practiced night air refueling, night flight formations, and illumination flare-dropping. All toll, they logged over 1,000 flying hours and conducted over 200 sorties without an accident. They were also ready to go. Simultaneously, the assault team, led by Captain Meadows, conducted live fire drills throughout August and September of 1970 during daylight hours, and at night as well. It was predicted that the level of expertise gained during that period had prepared the assault team for anything the Communists could throw at them during the actual raid.

General Manor subsequently reported to Laird that the team was ready to execute the mission. Later, on October 6, 1970, the raiding team conducted a full dress rehearsal using the mock village. The rehearsal was a success, and the timed practice raid lasted approximately 25 minutes.

On October 8, General Manor, General Blackburn, and Colonel Simons traveled to the White House, where they briefed President Nixon, Henry Kissinger, and Kissinger's executive officer, Brigadier General Alexander Haig, on the plan.[98] The briefing reportedly went well, and a date for the rescue of the hostages was set for November 22, 1970. Meanwhile, Operation Popeye continued unabated over Son Tay, the rains continued to fall, and the river adjacent to the Son Tay prison was almost out of its banks.

After Simons and Manor returned from Washington, weapons, ammunition, grenades, claymore mines and other explosives-related materials were issued to the assault team. They were also issued many different types of tools and equipment items, including bolt cutters, pry bars, chainsaws, machetes, axes, acetylene torches, two-way radios, ropes, chains, night scopes and just about anything else that would aid them in freeing the prisoners. In addition, they were issued comfort items to assist the prisoners, such as shower shoes, pajamas, first aid kits, inflatable splints, cans of water and emergency rations.

On October 3, aerial reconnaissance photos had again been taken of the prison camp at Son Tay, and it appeared there was no activity there. A few days later, however, new photographs showed increased activity of some sort, but no prisoners were sighted in the compound. As the days passed, it was finally time to move the operation closer to Vietnam; and on November 12, the first contingent of raiders left Eglin Air Force Base destined for Takhli Air Base, Thailand. By November 17, the entire team was in place at Takhli. Still, none of the raiders had any idea where they were really going. They could guess, but no one knew for sure except Simons, Blackburn and Manor.

After the raiders arrived at Takhli, their compound—an old CIA facility—became a busy place. Weapons and radio checks were conducted repeatedly, and all weapons and equipment were made ready for the raid. Still, the final team had not been selected. Finally, on November 18, the entire group was assembled in the base theatre for a briefing by Colonel Simons. During the briefing, he went over the schedule for the next three days, and the final 56 Green Berets were picked for the assault team. Those not selected were understandably disappointed, but they understood the procedures, and would remain in the rear at Takhli in case they were needed. Meanwhile, General Manor also selected the 92 airmen who would participate in the airborne portion of the raid, and they were briefed as well. Still, they were not briefed on the actual target name or location.

Meanwhile, the USAF weather officer studied all the meteorological charts and forecasts. November 22 did not look good for a launch. The remnants of a typhoon were passing over Southeast Asia, and North Vietnam would be socked in on the planned date of the raid. General Manor was subsequently briefed on the weather forecasts and made the decision to move the launch date up to November 20. This decision was relayed up the chain of command, and was ultimately briefed to Kissinger and Nixon, who both concurred.

Meanwhile, back at Takhli, Simons' troops nervously awaited go time for the raid. Finally, on the day of November 20, the team was allowed to rest and get ready for the launch that evening. Prior to resting, however, the team was assembled and given their final briefing. Only then did they learn the actual target. They were quiet when first told, but within minutes they were all applauding and cheering.

The plan would be executed as follows:

Five USAF HH-53 Super Jolly Green helicopters and one HH-3 Jolly Green helicopter would fly from Udorn, over Laos, and to Son Tay, following a HC-130 tanker and navigation aircraft. They would refuel when needed from the HC-130. Upon reaching North Vietnam, various diversions would be in progress. The lone HH-3 carrying Captain Meadows and a team of 14 would be crash-landed in the prison compound, which was about the size of a volleyball court and surrounded by large trees. Meanwhile, the two HH-53 helicopters would land outside the prison, carrying the majority of the assault team. The first team, led by Simons, would breach the wall using satchel charges, assist Meadows and his team in clearing the cell block, and then make sure the prisoners made it through the hole in the wall and onto two other waiting HH-53s. The team outside the compound, led by Sydnor, would act as perimeter security and eliminate any interference from the NVA troops residing near the prison at the secondary school and at other locations around the prison compound.

While the assault team cleared the compound and rescued the prisoners, five USAF F-105 Wild Weasel aircraft would patrol the area in the event any SAM sites needed to be neutralized. Ten F-4 Phantoms would patrol higher in the sky and take out any Russian MiGs that might appear. And, last but certainly not least, five A-1E Skyraiders from NKP would patrol the Son Tay area and provide close air support as needed by Sydnor.

Additionally, just prior to the team's arrival over Son Tay, the U.S. Navy would also be used to create a diversion near Hanoi at Haiphong Harbor. Essentially, fighter jets would launch from the U.S.S. *Oriskany* nearby in what would appear to be an air raid, but the aircraft would drop only flares, not bombs. It was hoped that this diversion in the harbor would completely distract the NVA from what was taking place at Son Tay, giving the raiders enough time to rescue the prisoners. But even though the Navy fighters would only drop flares, they could use their air-to-ground missiles for self defense if necessary.

The plan was relatively simple, and that's the way it needed to be. That was the way Bull Simons worked. Meanwhile, back at Takhli, the assault team members boarded a C-130 for a short flight to Udorn, where their helicopters waited. At 11:18 P.M., the assault team boarded the helicopters and the operation commenced. Later, as the helicopters were making their way to the target, Meadows and his raiders were already aboard the HH-3.

After three hours of flying time, the assault force neared the compound; and so far, they had not been detected. As the HH-3 carrying Meadows and his team neared the compound, the pilot initiated his controlled crash-landing. The only problem was that the trees were much larger than anticipated, and the pilot almost lost control of the helicopter as the rotor blades began to chew up the trees on descent. At any rate, the chopper finally fell and then bounced off the ground, ejecting the door gunner, who only suffered a sprained ankle. The team then quickly left the aircraft. By this time NVA guards had heard the racket and were in the yard with their weapons ready. The assault force quickly eliminated all the guards (about 12) in the compound. Meadows and his men then quickly opened every cell in the compound . . . and found no evidence of any prisoners.

Meanwhile, as Meadows and his team were searching the prison compound, the HH-53 with Simons and his men aboard had reportedly gotten slightly off course, and had ended up landing at the secondary school instead of the prison compound. As the team jumped out of the chopper, the NVA and Chinese soldiers in the building began running out and grabbing their weapons. Simons then realized that he was at the wrong location, but a firefight was already breaking out, so he turned his attention to the task at hand. In short order, about 200 NVA, Chinese, and numerous other unidentified personnel were lying on the ground, either dead or dying.

By this time, the pilot of Simon's aircraft had taken off and was loitering nearby for safety. After the shooting stopped, Simons called the pilot to come and get him and the team; they quickly got aboard the aircraft and relocated to an area near the prison wall. By this time, Meadows and his team had neutralized the guards in the compound, breached the wall, and were now outside, boarding one of the other HH-53 helicopters. At that moment, everyone realized that there were no prisoners at the facility, and so there was nothing else to do but depart as quickly as possible. Meanwhile, the HH-3 in the prison yard had been rigged with explosives, and the guard shacks around the prison had been blown to bits by machine gun fire. At about that same time, the HH-3 exploded, and the raiders departed the compound in the direction of Laos. After it was all over, the total time on the ground had been less than 30 minutes.

While Simons, Meadows, and their troops were taking care of business at the prison and the secondary school, Sydnor's team had sealed the perimeter of the area, and in the process eliminated several squads of NVA soldiers heading towards the prison yard when all the fireworks started. Apparently, NVA soldiers from the air defense base nearby had also heard the noise and were headed to join the fight when Sydnor's team blew up the bridge over the Song Con River, effectively taking the Communists out of the fight. With their mission completed, Sydnor's team boarded their chopper and joined up with the rest of the assault team leaving the area.

After all was said and done, not a single American was lost or wounded—except for the gentleman with the sprained ankle. One F-105 aircraft participating in the raid had been downed by a SAM, but the crew was quickly rescued by one of the HH-53s leaving the compound. Another F-105 had also been hit, but the pilot was able to nurse his aircraft back to Thailand, where he landed safely. Meanwhile, on the way back to Thailand, all the raiders were deeply disappointed at not being able to rescue any prisoners; but on the positive side, no U.S. troops had been lost during the raid, and the NVA had taken significant losses.

Upon their return to Udorn, Simons briefed Manor and the other Air Force brass at 7th/13th Air Force. Then Manor and Simons boarded a special mission aircraft for the trip to Washington to brief Blackburn, Kissinger and Nixon. Of course, the President was already aware of the results of the raid, but wanted to talk to Simons and Manor prior to the White House talking to the press. In less than 24 hours later, Manor and Simons had arrived in Washington and briefed Blackburn. The trio then went to the White House to brief the President.

After the briefing, the President congratulated Simons and Manor on a job well done. He also applauded their tactical success, and was relieved that no team members had been lost. But he was not surprised that the prisoners had been moved away from Son Tay, because the Government had already received intelligence information confirming that fact.

After the raid, Hanoi was angry and upset that the Son Tay raiders had come so close to rescuing the POWs; they were also distressed that the choppers had arrived over Son Tay undetected. In the aftermath, Hanoi took quick action to vacate many smaller prisons around the outskirts of Hanoi and moved all prisoners to facilities in the city, such as the infamous Hanoi Hilton. Also, knowing the press would be demanding answers, Hanoi began to treat the prisoners with more respect, and more humanely.

Of course, all of this takes us back to one haunting question: why were the prisoners moved in the first place? Well, if you recall, Operation Popeye had continued unabated throughout the rainy season, which may have had something to do with the Song Con River nearly overflowing its banks . . . and as it turned out, that fact was reported as the primary reason for vacating the prison at Son Tay. Another source also suggested the potable water well had dried up at the prison, which may have also been a factor in the prisoners being moved. And, finally, don't forget about the intelligence leaks at MACV headquarters.[99]

In December 1970, American intelligence officials reported that Hanoi had taken a "War Is Hell" approach to the raid. The North Vietnamese were reportedly beside themselves that the raid had been so easily executed without detection, and they were taking steps to beef up their internal defenses. It was also estimated that North Vietnam had increased the number of outposts and sentinels, and had improved their training methods.

Months after the raid, two obvious questions came up. The first question was, why didn't we destroy the Son Tay prison camp so it would never be used again? The answer to that question is simple: a bombing halt had been called over North Vietnam in 1968, and the U.S. was motivated to end the war by means of the Paris Peace Talks. The second question that surfaced was, was the prison camp at Son Tay ever used again? Some sources indicate that it was not; other sources indicated that it was used again as a prison to hold Americans in 1975. Meanwhile, back in Laos, the Communists had stepped up their attacks, and NVA troops continued to pour into Laos in the last quarter of 1970.

The raid on Son Tay left as many questions unanswered as it answered. Did Washington already know that the prisoners had been moved from Son Tay? Available information certainly suggests that this may have been the case. Also, was the prison compound the real target, or was it the secondary school where Bull Simons landed? After all, the school's existence was known. It was a fully functional training facility where the Pathet Lao and personnel of various nationalities received training. There were also Russians and Chinese nationals there, and logically, other foreign nationals from Communist countries such as Cuba. Cuba did staff the Pathet Lao medical facilities in Laos with doctors, so therefore some could have been at the training facility adjacent to the prison compound. If the training facility was the actual target, what better cover than an attack on an empty prison compound, to take out the Communists utilizing the training facility? Simons and company did an outstanding job of eliminating those personnel: all toll, about 200 people were killed there.

Another issue is the thorough training for the raid, and the repeated drills to make sure it was done right. In other words, how could Simon's helicopter land at the training facility hundreds of yards away? Was it *really* pilot error, or careful planning with a plausible excuse?

We'll never know for sure, because dead men tell no tales. Bull Simons is long since dead, and most of the crew at the White House is gone. And even if those people were still alive and knew something, they most likely wouldn't be able to divulge it, because of the tenuous contemporary relationship between the U.S, China, and Vietnam, not to mention Russia. And in any case, if the secondary school *had* been the primary target, the information would most likely never be divulged simply because it would probably remain classified.

In any case, it is literally, and figuratively, water over the bridge. We will never know for sure, and perhaps that's the way it should be.

Chapter 15

The End is Near

As the year 1970 wound down, the NVA had not, for the most part, retreated to North Vietnam as they usually did to rest, refit, and rearm: a considerable number of troops stayed put in the mountainous area between the Plain of Jars and Skyline Ridge. As 1971 arrived, the logical next step for the Communists was to move on Vang Pao's stronghold at Long Tieng, in hopes of defeating the Lao resistance once and for all. But the Communist dry season offensive was unlikely to have much substance, because their supply depots on the Plain had been pretty much depleted.

In January 1971, Vang Pao fell into another one of his depressed moods. As we have already mentioned, he was known for his mood swings, and he recognized that. When he would get depressed, those around him would let him stew for a while, and then they would confront him to talk the issue through. VP would then be good as new, ready to reinitiate the attack against the Communists. But this time it was different, because he was convinced that he could not win the war. A short time later, after his mood improved, VP called most of the tribal elders together and told them they were losing the war; the NVA were massing in preparation for their dry season offensive. VP also advised the elders that Long Tieng would probably fall soon, suggesting that they consider relocating to a safer place further south.

But the U.S. Embassy and the Lao government had no intention of vacating Long Tieng, so the decision was made to stay put at LS-20A. Since the Hmong defenders were becoming fewer in number, the U.S. negotiated with Thailand for additional mercenaries and regular Thai soldiers to fill the void. After all, these troops were all well-trained and very loyal, just as the Hmong were. To sweeten the deal, the United States agreed to pick up all the expenses of the soldiers, and to pay their wages while serving in Laos. The deal was soon approved and, not long after, several Thai battalions were in place.[100]

VP immediately placed the Thai troops in defensive positions in the valleys and villages around Long Tieng, and northward toward the Plain of Jars for static defense. Meanwhile, further north, on the edge of the Plain at Muong Soui, only one lackluster Neutralist battalion remained to fight the Communists. Since VP was certain that another attack would soon come, he arranged for Air America to move his wives and all the civilians out of Long Tieng to safety.

Just as anticipated, General Vu Lap began his dry season campaign on February 2 by attacking Muong Soui. NVA tanks and artillery pounded the weak Neutralist battalion mercilessly; and sure enough, by sunrise of the following day, the Neutralists had abandoned all their gear and were on the run, headed south. With Muong Soui under their control, the NVA then moved south against Ban Na and Tha Tham Bleung. The Communists began their attacks by pouring in a constant barrage of artillery fire; simultaneously, they attacked Thai and Hmong positions at Phou Long Mat and Zebra Ridge, north of Long Tieng. With fewer troops and more areas now under attack, VP's forces were spread very thin. And the troops protecting Long Tieng were few in number, and woefully inadequate to accomplish the task. With no place else to run, VP requested more air support from the Americans—but unfortunately all the U.S. assets had been diverted to participate in something called "Operation Lam Son 719."[101]

Also in early February, the NVA struck RLG positions north of Luang Prabang, the royal capital. Heretofore, the town had been, for the most part, spared by the Communists, apparently because of respect for the royal family on the part of the Pathet Lao; but now that the war was in full stride and North Vietnam was in the driver's seat, there were no safe areas. A call went out for RLG reinforcements, and soon, Air America airplanes began to land at the Luang Prabang airfield. Before long, two Lao battalions were in place.

At about the same time that Lam Son 719 was underway in southern Laos, the weather in northern Laos turned strangely ugly. This was a very bad omen, because without favorable weather, the USAF and RLAF would probably be unable to provide the air support necessary to stop any enemy attack. Taking advantage of the poor visibility created by the foul weather, the NVA quickly moved against Tha Tham Bleung valley on February 7. Also, while VP's troops were completely occupied by the attacking Communists, a company of Dac

Cong commandos slipped unnoticed through the lines and headed south, straight for Skyline Ridge. By February 13, the Dac Cong had reached the ridge, and from there they directed fire from a recoilless rifle onto LS-20A. With the remaining residents at Long Tieng ducking for cover, some of the commandos proceeded down the ridge, where they set up mortar tubes. From their position in the valley, they went to work lobbing rounds onto the main part of the base. To add insult to injury, the NVA began firing 122mm and 140mm artillery rounds over Skyline Ridge and into the valley of Long Tieng.

By the time the sun came up on February 14, Hmong and Thai troops at Long Tieng were reeling from the constant NVA artillery attacks. VP had not yet arrived from his overnight stay at Udorn, and the troops were awaiting further orders. Feeling compelled to do something, a CIA advisor took action and called for air strikes, but most of the U.S. air assets were still tied up supporting Lam Son 719. One USAF F-4 phantom was available, however, and diverted to Skyline Ridge to silence the NVA artillery. But upon rolling in on the target, the F-4 became disoriented in the fog and haze, and delivered his ordnance right on top of the defenders and workers at Long Tieng. A storage warehouse, an ammo dump, a radio transmitter, and quite a few structures in the CIA compound sustained considerable damage from the cluster bombs. The casualty count totaled more than 20 dead and over 100 wounded. On a positive note, a team of Dac Cong commandos had also been killed by the cluster bombs.[102]

Fortunately, by then Vang Pao and CIA advisor Jerry Daniels had arrived at LS-20A. RLAF T-28 aircraft had also arrived overhead, and tried to help by pounding the NVA attackers; but they would not budge. The shelling from the NVA 130 millimeter artillery also continued, and so did the Communist ground probes.

After the initial shelling stopped, VP toured the base to survey the damage. Not only did he see the devastation from the cluster bombs, but he also found additional damage from small arms fire and B40 rockets. There was also damage to his residence and to most of the other structures at LS-20A. Meanwhile, two additional Thai battalions were quickly airlifted to Long Tieng for support to the outnumbered Hmong defenders. With these reinforcements in place, VP was then able to send more troops north, all the way to the Plain of Jars. He also reinforced the troops at Phu Long Mat; those forces were then able to push the NVA troops off Phu Pha Sai with the help of air support.

Also in February 1971, the big B-52 bombers returned to the skies over northern Laos, and flew more than 100 sorties against NVA supply bases on the Plain. Many of the strikes achieved excellent results, setting off numerous secondary explosions. The strikes limited the resupply efforts of the NVA somewhat, but the Communists had secondary routes of resupply and were in fairly good shape by the end of the dry season. By the end of February, the NVA's 866th Group assumed an active combat role in northern Laos. Heretofore they had acted only as a support element, providing advice and support to the Pathet Lao; but their role rapidly changed to also provide combat support.

Meanwhile, as the NVA continued their attacks between the Plain and Long Tieng in March, the 21st SOS "Knives" from NKP were called upon to shuttle Hmong and Thai troops into Sam Thong to engage the NVA. But, unfortunately, upon landing, the first of three CH-53 helicopters hit the runway hard and lost its tail. It then spun out of control across the airfield before coming to a stop and catching fire in a ditch. Sadly, the pilot and copilot were killed, along with six Lao soldiers. But two USAF flight engineers/gunners were able to survive the crash.[103]

At any rate, the airlift continued and was completed soon thereafter, and the Hmong and Thai troops moved out in the direction of Nam Ngum. By March 19, two additional battalions of Hmong and Thai troops had been successfully inserted at Phou Tham Seh, a ridge located several kilometers north of Long Tieng. The two battalions subsequently joined up with other guerrillas, but met heavy NVA resistance and eventually retreated to Zebra Ridge. Soon, other guerrilla groups consisting of Thai Regulars, Thai Volunteers, and Hmong fighters were sent to several strategic locations north of Long Tieng to engage the NVA, but deteriorating weather and a lack of air support precluded any sizeable victories against the Communists. In fact, their primary concern was one of survival until they could be relieved.

Meanwhile, NVA's 165 Regiment and 316 Division had joined the fight, and the noose slowly tightened around the necks of the guerrillas. And, once again, most of the American air support had been reallocated to striking other targets over North Vietnam, because the bombing halt had been temporarily lifted. As the month of March wound down and April began, the NVA effectively controlled the territory between the Plain of Jars and Skyline Ridge. The fighting continued until the latter part of June, when the NVA broke off the attack and slowly made their way back to North Vietnam to rest and refit.

Meanwhile in Washington, the U.S. Congress House Appropriations Committee, Foreign Operations Subcommittee, distributed the following information relative to the continuing struggle in Laos:

> *The Pathet Lao Insurgency against the government of Prime Minister Souvanna Phouma continues to be supported from North Vietnam and China. The position of that insurgency has further decreased relative to the conflict involving outside forces. The 30,000 largely ineffective Pathet Lao forces in North Laos are at present equaled by the North Vietnamese force of about 30,000 regulars.*

> *The territorial position now is close to the alignment in previous years at this time. However, a serious threat to Long Tieng has developed earlier this dry season and the enemy force is larger. The North Vietnamese may wish to overrun Long Tieng in hopes of dispersing General Vang Pao's Hmong, the most effective indigenous force in Laos. North Vietnamese/Pathet Lao troops are also closer to the Royal Capital of Luang Prabang, a political target. At present the city is effectively a hostage.*

It was also reported that members of the Senate Foreign Relations Committee had taken the position that Thai troops, which had been acknowledged by the Administration to be fighting in Laos, were in violation of the Fulbright Amendment to the 1971 Defense Authorization and Procurement bills. That legislation prohibited American financing of third country forces in Cambodia and Laos, and was designed to prevent further escalation of the U.S. role in the Indochinese War.

At this juncture, it's worth stopping for a moment to take a high-level look at the situation. Some progress had been made by the Lao in southern Laos, but Lam Son 719 had been a complete disaster. Up north, VP was only in control of Long Tieng and Bouam Long. The NVA were in control of most other areas, and were steadily bringing in more fresh troops. In Paris, the peace talks continued, and it was hopeful that a ceasefire accord could be soon reached. Meanwhile, Henry Kissinger was having secret meetings with China and North Vietnam, trying to negotiate his own backdoor deal to end the conflict. He had excluded South Vietnam and Laos from any input into the negotiations. In Washington, Congress had inserted itself into the process by demanding more say as to what took place in Laos—and the White House wanted it all to end.

While the generals and diplomats argued policy, plans and expectations, Vang Pao ran out of patience waiting for the Americans to come up with solutions. He had no other choice; he had to fight. Souvanna Phouma and the King expected VP to make a stand, regardless of the outcome. It was common knowledge that the U.S. had decided to extricate itself from the conflict, and was already decreasing its support. So VP began his dry season offensive on April 15, and by April 18, Skyline Ridge was cleared. Also on April 18, VP had a battalion of guerrillas airlifted to Pha Phai. Once in place, the guerrillas moved on foot to interdict Route 4 between Xieng Khouangville and the Plain of Jars. Later, on April 23, Vang Pao's troops attacked Phou Phaxai, but were driven back.

The NVA counterattacked, and again drove the Hmong forces off Phou Long Mat. On April 27, VP's troops retook Phou Long Mat. Also during April, field reports indicated that the NVA had suffered considerable losses without actually improving their position; but with the rains coming, the Communists began pulling back. As usual, Vu Lap left several regiments in place to hold the Plain of Jars and to make another attempt to take Bouam Long. The 174 Regiment then initiated their attack at LS-32 on May 20, as the rain began to fall.

Still, a bigger question remained: what action should the U.S. and Lao governments take during the upcoming wet season? Washington's plan was still to disengage and slowly withdraw, because they did not want to support any large battles in Laos. They recognized that Long Tieng had to be held, but outside of that they had no other plans. Likewise, the Seventh Air Force planned to reduce the number of sorties in Barrel Roll to about 30 a day. For its part, the USAF agreed to temporarily provide more than 50 daily air support sorties. They also offered to provide 40 F-4 Phantoms and four A-1s to support the

Raven FACs protecting Troops in Contact (TIC). Two more Phantoms were provided for use against NVA artillery, and another four were provided to act as a quick response force. At night, the AC-119k Stinger gunships from NKP would patrol MR-2 in direct support of VP; and when available, an AC-130 Spectre gunship could be diverted from southern Laos, if conditions permitted.

VP's plan for the monsoon offensive was to sweep across the Plain and destroy the NVA supply depots, as he had done in 1969. He also wanted to retake strong points in the hills around the Plain. At $7^{th}/13^{th}$ Air Force, the generals were not optimistic about VP's plan. They preferred to use the USAF to bomb the NVA supply depots, and for VP to establish strong points around the Plain. They also wanted VP to launch hit-and-run attacks against the NVA. In fact, the USAF had already compiled a target list, and obtained confirmation through intelligence sources. Meanwhile, the embassy in Vientiane had already approved VP's plan and notified 7th Air Force that VP would be on his own in his forays on the Plain of Jars, and that no additional air support would be requested.

There were also other indicators of bad things to come. VP knew that U.S. troop levels in South Vietnam had been reduced by 50%, to about 250,000; and he knew that the number of air support sorties allocated to Barrel Roll was similarly reduced by about 50%. Then there were the ongoing meetings between the U.S. and China, which VP and the Hmong elders considered a betrayal. But, what was the best course of action for the Hmong? No one was sure at that point, but *something* had to be done. Later, the clan elders came to VP and requested that all civilians be moved to Sayaboury. As usual, VP did not make any commitment to the elders, because he knew that Souvanna Phouma would not approve the proposal.

And, as the situation in Laos continued to deteriorate, the secret meetings continued between Henry Kissinger and the North Vietnamese officials over possible provisions for the release of American POWs held in North Vietnam.

Late in the month of April 1971, some gains were made by VP and his troops. Two of his battalions marched north from Phou Long Mat and wrested control of a high point from the NVA, and Hmong and Thai troops also reoccupied Pha Phai after stiff NVA resistance. And, by the latter part of May, VP's troops had also regained control of Zebra Ridge. At about the same time, the NVA began to disengage and head north in advance of the rainy season. As usual, they left a substantial force to launch harassment raids, and to contain any Hmong/Thai initiatives.

Meanwhile, it appeared that the Communists had planned to attack up north at Bouam Long, just as they had the year before; and while most of the NVA troops continued to depart for North Vietnam, a good portion of the 316 Division marched north from the Plain of Jars, in the direction of LS-32. From a weather standpoint, they could not have picked a better time. The rains were already starting, and the Hmong base at Bouam Long was socked in. The sky was filled with long, hanging clouds that even enveloped the tops of the trees and the hilltops. The Communists were sure that U.S. air support would not be able to thwart their attack. Not wasting any time, they sent over 2,000 seasoned troops against the defenders at Bouam Long, outnumbering the Hmong by at least two to one. In the cold, wet terrain, the going was tough, but the Communists slowly fought their way up the slopes, confident that air support would not come.

As the NVA inched closer to the site, the Hmong site commander radioed for immediate air support. Shortly thereafter, a lone USAF aircraft flew over the site and dropped a new electronic device, a mobile beacon called "Pave Mace." Pave Mace was the code name for a tracking system that utilized a ground beacon in conjunction with the Black Crow sensor mounted in the console of an orbiting USAF gunship. When the ground sensor was activated, a coded pulse from the airborne gunship would intercept the signal. It let the console operator know the type of target, its range, bearing, and other information. The information received from the ground beacon also allowed the gunship to identify and attack enemy targets in any weather conditions without the need for constant voice contact between the ground and the airborne gunship—and the gunship crew did not need a visual fix on the ground target(s).The beacon was specifically designed to be used in all weather conditions, and without any other means of communication between the aircraft and the men on the ground.

The NVA continued to advance, unaware of the Pave Mace beacon, which was emitting a signal to approaching gunships. At first light on the following day, the NVA was close enough to make their final assault. As the attack began, the Hmong site commander called for the AC-130 Spectres. The aircraft approached, following the beacon signal and voice instructions from a FAC on the ground. Even though the Spectres couldn't see the enemy, they were guided to the exact spot where the cannons needed to direct their fire upon the NVA.

By this time, the fighting was intense, with the Communists hitting the Hmong with mortars, artillery rounds, rockets, and even commandos, but ultimately, the gunships began to take their toll, and the Communists broke off the attack and retreated. Once again, Bouam Long avoided capture; the site was safe again, if only temporarily. The NVA were exhausted and had lost the will to fight, so they pulled back. But as they departed in the last days of May, the NVA left two Pathet Lao battalions behind to keep the defenders from leaving the site. This tactic would hopefully assure that the Hmong would be unable to interdict the NVA supply lines. On a more distressing note, at the end of May 1971 only two areas in northern Laos were still controlled by VP: Long Tieng and Bouam Long.[104]

Shortly after the latest attack on Bouam Long, Long Tieng received several more battalions of Thai Army troops. These guys were tough, and would complement the Hmong defenders and other Thai regulars already in Laos. With these reinforcements, VP's men were ready to move out and reengage the Communists. In June, VP began the wet season offensive, using helicopters to leapfrog his troops across the Plain of Jars in small teams. Upon insertion, they fanned out and took the fight to the enemy. At first, resistance was light, and the Hmong were optimistic that they may be able to rapidly retake lost territory. As they advanced, the Hmong troops captured and destroyed Communist supplies and equipment. Fortunately, by this time, the rains had begun in earnest, and the NVA was dispersed all over the Plain and pinned down.

VP's offensive had apparently caught the NVA by surprise, because they assumed he was still tied down fighting the 174 Regiment. Meanwhile, still thirsty for action, VP moved against the Communists on the Plain on June 3 using a three-pronged attack. The first group moved south from Bouam Long, while a second headed straight for the center of the Plain, and a third group moved in from the southwest. The CIA quickly requested more air support from the USAF, but the generals protested, stating that their orders were to reduce air support and wind down operations. Holding firm, the USAF would only commit to about 30 sorties a day. Meanwhile, VP continued to move on the Plain, and the NVA quickly retreated to its strong points along Routes 4 and 7. On July 1, VP resumed his advance. A task force of Hmong defenders moved out from Phou Teung and crossed Route 4; at about that same time, three battalions from another task force were airlifted into the vicinity of Xieng Khouang airfield.

On July 7, another three guerrilla battalions were airlifted from Phou Seu to Phou Keng, and after a week of intense fighting, they were at the base of the mountain. Vang Pao's troops had gotten within striking distance of the NVA storage depots, so the Communists had returned two regiments to the Plain. Meanwhile, VP brought up two 105mm and four 155mm artillery pieces for additional firepower, in the event USAF A-1 Skyraiders were unavailable.

The NVA also brought up their PT-76 Russian tanks, knowing the iron beasts frightened the Hmong. The Hmong defenders were quickly driven back across Route 4. For the next several days, other Hmong defenders were likewise engaged, and the battle was a back-and-forth propositions with first the NVA getting the upper hand, and then the Hmong. Hmong troops also crossed the Nam Ngum River and uncovered NVA caches of rice, which they liberated, and then moved on to Phou San, where VP finally established a foothold on July 29. By the end of July, VP's initiative began to stall, and he found himself in a tenuous position, with troops dispersed over at least half of the Plain. By the end of August, his troops were stalled in the middle of the Plain. It was clear that the NVA was determined to hold the area; and it also showed that the Communists could reinforce their troops at will, even at the height of the rainy season.

The Hmong were now in a very vulnerable position, so they dug in and hoped that air support would come sooner rather than later. The CIA then asked the USAF to provide the additional air support. The Air Force finally relented, agreeing to provide four additional sorties a day. The battle raged on through August 1971, with control of the Plain still shifting back and forth between the Hmong and the NVA.

In southern Laos, things were heating up as well. With activity on the Ho Chi Minh Trail picking up, the USAF was obligated to provide more than 200 sorties a day to support the RLG and the CIA. Meanwhile, the RLG and the CIA had planned a large offensive to retake the Bolovens Plateau. The undertaking was called "Operation Sayasila," a Lao term for the Eastern Bolovens. The first phase of the operation was to strike at Saravane on July 29, using a guerrilla force from central Laos. The second phase was to use two additional guerrilla groups from the local area to attack the Communists at Pak Song and Lao Ngum, ideally causing the NVA to essentially lose control of the war in southern Laos. At first, it appeared that the RLG was making some headway, but the effort soon began to stall. Essentially, the Communists withdrew from the populated areas, allowing the Lao troops to literally walk into deserted towns. Then the NVA would regroup in force and retake the initiative by initiating counterattacks. The fight continued for most of August; and by the end of that month, the RLG forces were isolated, confused, and had lost the will to fight.

Meanwhile, the U.S. JCS issued a directive requiring Washington's approval for any major military operations planned in Laos. All plans had to be submitted 10 days in advance of the operation(s). The directive was billed as a vehicle to get the CIA to be more forthcoming in sharing their plans with the USAF, but in reality, it was designed to further curtail U.S. activity in Laos. Notwithstanding, the directive did get the CIA to become more inclusive when making their plans.

On August 12, the Communists initiated a counterattack at Xieng Khouangville; and, by August 16, the Hmong had been driven back to Phou Teung. The NVA also recaptured Phou San.

Throughout the summer of 1971, arguments had continued over how many sorties would be allotted to northern Laos. The embassy had certain expectations, as did the CIA, and the USAF was somewhat caught in the middle while trying to do the right thing. Washington was still holding firm on its commitment to slowly withdraw from SEA. On September 13, the AIRA in Vientiane tried once again to get more sorties, but to no avail. As September wound down, the Hmong guerrillas hung on to their tenuous position on the Plain of Jars, with little activity to report. There was some NVA activity during the month, and the Hmong were forced off some strong points, but the Communists didn't even bother to reoccupy those positions.

On the Plain, hostilities continued, and VP needed help fast. Pat Landry, the CIA man at Udorn, successfully cajoled, badgered and threatened the USAF in order to get B-52 strikes authorized over the

Plain. Soon, the large aircraft crossed the Plain of Jars, dropping iron bombs on everything. Thousands of Communist troops were killed, and the few existing structures that still stood were flattened. Once again the Plain had been devastated; but still, the NVA held their positions. Meanwhile, the Hmong were weary, tired, and desperate for rest, so VP decided to begin wrapping up his rainy season offensive.

But he didn't want to just retreat, leaving his rear flank unprotected. What he planned to do was to use his artillery to trap and kill any NVA in pursuit of his retreating soldiers. VP subsequently positioned artillery pieces so that their fire would cross each other's, so that no matter what direction the NVA took, they would be trapped. When the trap was set, VP's men waited for the signal to begin their slow retreat, acting as bait to lure the NVA into the trap.

Meanwhile, in October 1971 or thereabouts, NVA General Vu Lap was replaced by General Le Trong Tan. Tan was one of the brighter NVA officers, and he was reportedly a very good tactician. He had always been at the forefront of the fighting, from Dien Bien Phu to Da Nang and on to northern Laos, and was well-respected by all North Vietnamese military and government officials. Tan was convinced the best way to capture Long Tieng was by using the powerful 130mm artillery guns. His plan was to use fresh NVA regiments and drive the Hmong from the Plain and in the direction of Long Tieng, using the large artillery pieces. As the Hmong retreated, he would follow; and when he was within range of the LS-20A, he would use the big guns to destroy Long Tieng and the Hmong, once and for all.

Coincidentally, in early November 1971, the US received corroborating intelligence information indicating that the NVA was planning a huge dry season offensive, using more than a dozen long-range 130mm artillery pieces that were already on the way to Laos. Hmong Road Watch Teams also reported large numbers of NVA troops on the roads marching into Laos. Shortly thereafter, the NVA began conducting harassment raids, and NVA intelligence-gathering patrols were discovered further south in the Long Tieng area. Meanwhile, little was being done to shore up the Hmong defenses. And on top of all this, the Hmong had lost their motivation, because the holidays were approaching and they were still in the field without their families.

As mid-December 1971 rolled around, the base at Long Tieng, and the village around it, was already celebrating the holidays. In fact, many Hmong officers had traveled to LS-20A to join in the celebration. They just left the troops to fend for themselves, which did not sit well with the guerrillas. On December 17, Generals Tan, and Vu Lap launched their dry season offensive. Tan and his men rapidly deployed around the Plain, led by Russian tanks and Chinese armored personnel carriers. As the NVA approached VP's outer security perimeter, the dispirited Hmong troops simply dropped their weapons and walked away, either in the direction of their homes or towards Long Tieng.

Also on December 17, it was reported that all hell had broken loose in northern Laos. An NVA artillery round had apparently landed on an ammunition storage bunker at Phou Theung, and the subsequent explosion could be seen for miles. The Thai defenders were able to hold off the NVA until the afternoon, and then they had to vacate the position after several of their leaders were killed. Later, Finger Ridge fell.

VP's plan had anticipated a large NVA offensive, and as mentioned earlier, it called for an *orderly* withdrawal by the Hmong in the direction of Long Tieng. His plan also intended to have the Hmong slowly retreat through the valley towards LS-20A, believing that the NVA would follow. As the plan unfolded, VP wanted his Thai manned firebases to open up on the NVA with artillery, killing them in the crossfire. But for some strange reason, it appeared that the Hmong troops had not been briefed on the plan, because when they retreated, they literally ran helter-skelter in all directions, exposing the Thai firebases to the NVA. When VP found out what happened, he was furious, and reprimanded the Hmong for not following the plan. He then sent two of the fleeing battalions of the guerrillas back onto the Plain to try again to lure the NVA into the trap—but most of the Hmong panicked again when the Russian tanks came in their direction.

As the NVA marched southward, the Thai gunners fired their 105mm howitzers as directed, but the NVA troops did not slow down. They continued to advance, taking the casualties in stride, but not stopping. In their advance, they swarmed over the Thai firebases. One by one, the bases fell, and fighting was so intense that resupply from the air was impossible. B-52 bombers flew night missions against the NVA, and U.S. fighter bombers also flew missions over the Plain, as did VP's T-28 aircraft. But General Tan had anticipated the aerial bombing, and had secreted anti-aircraft weapons across the entire Plain of Jars. He quickly put them to use, shooting down one of the F-4 Phantoms and two Lao T-28s. Russian MiG aircraft also appeared over the Plain and shot down five more Phantoms.

At first light on December 18, VP took a helicopter and headed north towards the fighting. The area was socked in with fog and clouds, eliminating visibility, but he could hear the sounds of battle below him. He then got on the loudspeaker and shouted to the Hmong troops to hold their positions and fight—but they did not listen. And, with the Hmong fighters on the run, there was nothing to stop the NVA advance. One by one, the Thai firebases continued to fall. A few days later, on, or around December 22th, an F-4 Phantom supporting a Thai position on the Plain was shot down by a MiG-21. Two other F-4s showed up and joined in, and chased the MiG as it fled. But while preoccupied with the chase, both Phantoms reportedly ran out of fuel, and the crews had to eject. Sadly, only two of the four airmen were rescued.[105]

After the Thai firebases were overrun and in NVA hands, Tan's troops continued their march south. Large caves were already being prepared to house the large 130mm NVA guns that Tan planned to hide, and later use to take Long Tieng. At about that same time, air reconnaissance photos showed large Russian trucks moving south with their cargoes covered . . . but everyone knew what was below the tarps: the big guns that could reach Long Tieng. Meanwhile, using the Russian tanks and the 130mm guns to good advantage, the NVA continued to move south, taking everything in their path. Along the way, several abandoned U.S. 105mm and 155mm guns were captured by the NVA, and the Thai firebases protecting Long Tieng also began to fall, with many Thai fighters taken prisoner.

To provide cover for their offensive, the NVA began sending MiGs into northern Laos to harass the slower, propeller-driven U.S. aircraft loaded down with bombs. Upon hearing that MiGs were spotted in the area, the slower aircraft would turn south and fly to safety. The F-4 Phantoms would jettison their bombs and get ready to engage when they were alerted to MiGs in the area. In the beginning, the North Vietnamese had the edge in these air-to-air engagements because heretofore, the USAF had focused on bombing, and had not maintained their proficiency in dogfighting. But as time passed, the USAF, with some practice and retraining, began to improve their dogfighting capabilities.

Meanwhile, General Tan continued his advance southward as NVA troops moved through Ban Ban and Nong Pet. It was still raining, and visibility was very limited. Two NVA regiments and one battalion of Dac Cong commandos, supported by an Armor Battalion, moved out first. When the Hmong saw the Russian tanks coming, many dropped their weapons and melted away into the forest. With the core of VP's defensive positions rapidly collapsing, the NVA began probing the remaining Thai and Hmong firebases around the Plain. Moung Soui hadn't been hit yet, but the defenders there abandoned their artillery pieces anyway and headed south. The NVA's 316 Division, 335 Individual Regiment, and Regiment 174 joined up and headed to Phou Keng. But an AC-130 Spectre later showed up at dark and was able to keep the NVA contained throughout the night.

Later in December, the NVA encircled Phou Keng and soon took control. The Thai and Hmong defenders were authorized to withdraw, but the intensity of the fighting was too great to attempt a breakout during daylight hours. Later that night, the remaining defenders were able to slowly withdraw in small numbers; but many of the withdrawing troops were either killed outright or captured. And after three days of heavy fighting, the Communists had retaken the Plain of Jars.

As the Plain was falling, three more fresh battalions of Thai fighters were airlifted to Long Tieng. With the Plain under NVA control again, the Thai and Hmong defenders who were left also began moving south towards Long Tieng, with the NVA following close behind. Air America helped as much as they could by flying along the path of the retreating Hmong and Thai troops, picking up their dead and wounded, as well as those who were too tired to walk. The majority of these survivors were shell-shocked, and many were suffering from various types of wounds and exposure.

On December 24, an NVA sapper team managed to get past the Skyline defenders once again, and onto the runway at Long Tieng. They destroyed two O-1 Bird Dogs and fired rockets into several of the buildings. The CIA Station Chief and Ambassador Godley were concerned, so the ambassador sought out Pat Landry at Udorn and began looking for Vang Pao. He wasn't at Long Tieng or Vientiane, so it took a while to find him. Finally, they located him in a small village. As usual Vang Pao was in one of his mood, and was sick with a cold to boot. But Godley and Landry talked to VP for awhile, his mood soon changed, and as usual he agreed to renew the fight.

Meanwhile, help was finally beginning to arrive—not that it would do much good. Two fresh regiments of RLG troops arrived in Long Tieng, and immediately deployed around the base. Morale began to improve as the troops dug in. But the determined NVA troops continued to advance. The troop strength of the advancing Communists at that time was estimated to be almost 20,000, while the Hmong and Thai defenders numbered approximately 10,000. Later, on December 31, 130mm rounds began to fall on Long Tieng. There was heavy bombardment throughout the night, and the sound of the falling rounds was deafening. As each round exploded, the shockwaves shook the buildings and huts in the valley.

Meanwhile, the NVA were busy building a new road (Route 54) from the Plain of Jars toward Sam Thong.

During the first week of January 1972, more than twenty battalions of NVA troops—led by General Tan—marched through Tha Tham Bleung Valley towards Skyline Ridge. Soon, the Communist troops were climbing the ridges around Skyline. The defenders, made up of Hmong, Thai and Lao fighters, were dug in and fought back. After three days of heavy fighting, the NVA fell back. In the meantime, however, they had retaken Sam Thong, and also controlled the road between Sam Thong and Long Tieng. At about the same time, the big 130mm NVA guns resumed their shelling of Long Tieng, quickly demoralizing the Hmong.

As the shelling from the 130mm guns continued, two Dac Cong sapper teams returned to the airfield at LS-20A, blew up the ammunition dump, and fired rockets into the CIA compound. The civilians at Long Tieng had long since fled, and the town was eerily quiet and dark. But if Long Tieng was going to survive, the big guns had to be silenced. Hmong pilots continued to fly in their T-28 Trojans, trying to locate the hiding places of the big guns. But the pieces were being fired from their maximum distance of almost 20 miles, and were constantly being moved. VP's pilots did get lucky, however, and were able to find two gun emplacements. The Hmong pilots were then able to mark their location with flares so the American fighters could take them out.

Meanwhile, on January 9, Dac Cong commandos again managed to get onto the airfield at Long Tieng and began firing rockets into the CIA quarters, VP's residence, and the radio station. Two additional O-1 FAC aircraft were also damaged. By mid-January, the NVA had stepped up their attack even more. VP was exhausted again, and had come down with pneumonia on January 4. The CIA advisors had him airlifted to the U. S. Air Force hospital at Udorn to receive medical treatment and to recuperate. About a week later, VP returned to Long Tieng well-rested, healthy, and ready to fight; but his return failed to reassure the media. They were already posting articles predicting the fall of Long Tieng and quoting military assessments of the situation.

Meanwhile, in Paris, the North Vietnamese had hardened their position by demanding an unconditional troop withdrawal and cessation of all bombing over North Vietnam. Back on the ground in Laos, the CIA arranged for additional Thai reinforcements, and several more battalions of Lao RLG units were brought to Long Tieng from southern Laos. Prime Minister Souvanna Phouma must have believed that Long Tieng was about to fall, because he ordered VP and the troops to pull back to Vientiane and defend the city—but VP resisted. He did, however, travel to Vientiane to assure Souvanna that he would be able to hold Long Tieng. He also told Souvanna that he would quit the fight if he had to pull back to Vientiane. Finally, Souvanna relented and allowed VP to stay at Long Tieng. Some of the CIA advisors also wanted to vacate Long Tieng, but others, like Jerry Daniels, did not agree. Ultimately, they had a meeting and agreed to stay and support VP in his fight for freedom. Air America, on the other hand, was not quite so agreeable. They were very reluctant to fly into Long Tieng, because the airfield had been chewed up by the shelling, the wreckage of destroyed aircraft still littered the aircraft parking ramp, and most of the buildings were either damaged or destroyed.

In the middle of January, the NVA made another advance to the ridges of Skyline. There they paused. At first, VP could not figure out why the NVA had halted, but then he realized that they were waiting on reinforcements before making their final push. He then dispatched reconnaissance teams, and they returned with information that confirmed VP's belief. One team also discovered a regiment of fresh NVA regulars marching towards the ridge. It appeared that the

Communist troops were unaware they had been spotted, because they continued to march in a tight formation.

Armed with the information, Vang Pao aimed his 105mm howitzers in the direction of the advancing regiment and almost completely wiped them out. Later, flying high overhead, waves of B-52 bombers dropped bombs on the advancing and dug-in NVA troops. During the bombing, the NVA retreated from the ridges and hurried into the forest. After the big bombers did their damage, U.S. fighters from Thailand arrived and continued to hunt out and bomb the NVA. Meanwhile, VP repositioned his howitzers and continued firing on the retreating NVA. After all was said and done, several thousand dead NVA soldiers were counted in the forest near the ridges.

On January 19, 1972, the U.S. Embassy in Vientiane finally decided to tell the media what was actually taking place in northern Laos. They wanted the journalists to see close up that Skyline was under siege by North Vietnamese troops, not the Pathet Lao. United Press International (UPI), Associated Press (AP), the *New York Times*, three major television networks, and several foreign journalists were invited to tour Long Tieng. Shortly after a briefing, two helicopters filled with journalists took off from Vientiane and landed on the runway at Long Tieng. They were then taken on a tour of the valley to view the devastation firsthand. After the tour, the journalists piled back into the choppers and were taken on the short flight to Skyline Ridge. But, just as they landed, the NVA opened up on the ridge with artillery and mortar rounds.

The journalists dove for cover and waited for the shells to stop raining down. The shelling continued for a while, and as soon as there was a lull, the journalists were quickly reloaded into the choppers and taken back to Vientiane. When they returned to their offices, they all contacted their home offices and filed their reports. As it turned out, they certainly got to see the war close up, but it was doubtful they got to see any actual NVA troops.

On January 26, 1972, The *Voice of the Nation* newspaper in Bangkok ran an article entitled, "Skyline Ridge Taken; Long Cheng Now Safe." The article stated,

"Government military sources said yesterday Laotian forces now fully control Skyline Ridge, which overlooks the city and is considered vital to the defense of Long Cheng (Long Tieng). The sources said government forces Monday reoccupied two positions called Charlie Tango and Charlie Delta which serve as helicopter landing zones on the eastern end of the ridge. The Laotian soldiers walked into the position without resistance after the enemy fire subsided, the sources said.

"At the moment, Long Cheng is clearly out of danger but the enemy is still in the area, an American source said. But both Laotian and American sources said a few enemy mortar rounds continue to fall on Skyline Ridge, which is adjacent to Long Cheng, the north-central Laotian base where the U.S. Central Intelligence Agency (CIA) trained, advised supported and paid Hmong regulars. The Americans moved most of their operations from the base when it came under intensive Communist pressure after the North Vietnamese overran the nearby Plain of Jars in mid-December 1971.

"Two weeks ago, North Vietnamese soldiers overran and occupied nearly all of Skyline Ridge and Radio Pathet Lao claimed falsely that Long Cheng had fallen. Monday night there were small clashes and mortar attacks at Sam Thong, seven miles northwest of Long Cheng but there was no significant damage, Laotian sources said. Some of the rounds hit Fire Base Thunder, two miles southeast of Sam Thong."

As the situation in northeastern Laos continued to deteriorate, the CIA arranged for still more Thai reinforcements and several additional battalions of RLG units from southern Laos to move in. By late January, the Lao and Thai troops had retaken Skyline Ridge from the NVA. But the cost of retaking Skyline was high: almost half of the defenders were killed or wounded. Later, in mid-March, the NVA sent tanks against Skyline. Some were stopped, but others made it to the ridges and fired down into Long Tieng. As mentioned previously, the Hmong defenders had always been terrified by the iron monsters, and for the most part they melted away into the trees when the tanks approached. Later, the NVA began firing the big 130mm guns towards Long Tieng again. By this time the dry season had arrived, and the NVA was ready to advance again on the ridges of Skyline above Long Tieng. By the end of the month, the NVA had taken the highest ridge on Skyline and were dug in to stay.

Between February and April 1972, the NVA changed their tactics regarding the use of their MiG aircraft in northern Laos. Instead of entering Lao airspace to engage the USAF, they would feint an engagement and then turn back to North Vietnam. But on February 21, the NVA began to take a dose of their own medicine when USAF Major Robert Lodge and First Lieutenant Roger Locher shot down their first MiG. Another MiG was downed a week later by Lt. Colonel Joseph Kittenger and First Lieutenant Leigh Hodgdon. A third MiG was shot down on March 30by Captains Fred Olmsted, Jr. and Gerald Volloy.

On March 13, 1972, in an article entitled, "Long Cheng under New Attack," the *Bangkok Post* related,

> "North Vietnamese forces, apparently beginning a new offensive campaign in northern Laos, launched heavy attacks yesterday against the defense perimeters of Long Cheng (Tieng) and Sam Thong bases near the Plain of Jars, informed sources said.
>
> "Several positions near Sam Thong fell to the North Vietnamese after intense mortar, and artillery rounds closed the Long Cheng air strip most of yesterday but North Vietnamese infantrymen did not penetrate the base. The bombardment also hit government positions atop Skyline Ridge, which overlooks Long Cheng, a base built by the U.S. Central Intelligence Agency to train and advise Hmong tribesmen fighting for the Government."

Also during the period of January through April 1972, the USAF stepped up its air sorties to focus on locating and destroying the powerful NVA 130mm artillery pieces and to disrupt construction of Route 54. A typical mission order involved approximately 60 aircraft, consisting of more than 30 F-4 Phantoms, six A-1 Skyraiders, six OV-10s, and about six gunships. Meanwhile, the Communists continued their slow advance. By early March, construction of Route 54 had been completed all the way up to Sam Thong, and the Communists began to bring up their armor and artillery. They commenced their attack on March 11, and the U.S. Embassy in Vientiane described the fighting as savage and bitter. The USAF tried to deter the Communists by sending in the B-52 bombers to hit over 100 targets in the Sam Thong/Long Tieng area, flying over 300 sorties in support of Thai and Hmong forces.

But by March 19, NVA troops from the 165 Regiment had been able to overcome and seize a helicopter landing pad on the west end of Skyline. Meanwhile, the NVA's 316 Division and 866 Independent Regiment were making preparations for a strike on the valley at Long Tieng. Hmong and Thai troops then counterattacked in an attempt to retake Skyline Ridge, and were able to seize a helicopter pad overlooking the road from Sam Thong.

Arriving soon after was a U.S. engineering team, with a load of anti-tank mines. The team seeded the area, including an adjacent road, with explosives. Sure enough, about a week later, the NVA decided to use that very road to initiate another attack on Skyline. During the advance, two of the three Russian tanks encountered the mines and they were disabled on the spot. The third tank turned around and departed, while the first two continued firing on Long Tieng until their ammunition was exhausted. Then the NVA fell back. A little while later, on April 2, 1972, the *Pacific Stars and Stripes* newspaper reprinted an article reported by UPI out of Vientiane entitled, "2 Red Tanks Blasted in Laos." Essentially, UPI had reported that two 30-ton Soviet made tanks had been destroyed and 50 North Vietnamese killed on Thursday, 30 March, in an abortive attack on a government position three miles from beleaguered Long Tieng. Military sources were also quoted as saying that three of the big tanks, carrying 85mm cannons, and hundreds of North Vietnamese troops launched the attack on a position called "Charlie Echo," about three miles northwest of Long Tieng.

The sources were also quoted as reporting the attack as a significant attempt to overrun Long Tieng, which had been under siege since January, and which had been severely battered twice that year. An American source reportedly said that two of the three tanks were disabled when they hit land mines between Sam Thong and Long Tieng, and that the disabled tanks were later destroyed by air strikes. Charlie Echo was on the western rim of Skyline Ridge, a key ridge just north of Long Tieng, where fighting had been going on since January 1972.

Meanwhile, on April 8, the United States resumed large-scale bombing raids over North Vietnam as a result of North Vietnam's invasion of South Vietnam. With their homeland under attack, the MiG aircraft left the friendly skies of Laos and returned to help defend Hanoi. Meanwhile, back at Udorn, Pat Landry was trying hard to get air support for Long Tieng, but most of the resources were still tied up in South Vietnam. After much wrangling and arm twisting, Landry was finally able to get a commitment for some B-52 strikes over northern Laos. He was also promised some AC-119K Stinger gunships. The B-52s arrived shortly thereafter, on April 10, and dropped their big bombs on the highest ridges at Skyline.

After the bombers left, the AC-119Ks moved in and began to rake the ridges with machine-gun fire. After the Stingers had expended all their ordnance, Hmong commandos went up on the ridge to finish off the remaining NVA. Fortunately, not many Communist fighters had survived the bombs and strafing, so the commandos finished off the rest in short order.

With the thumping General Tan had suffered at Skyline, he prepared to withdraw the bulk of his troops back to North Vietnam to rest and refit. As always, he planned to leave plenty of NVA troops behind to hold the turf they had already won. And, as usual at the end of each dry season, the NVA footprint in Laos had gotten bigger. While it was true that VP did enjoy some small victories each year, the NVA enjoyed larger ones. After all, Generals Tan and Giap had unlimited troops at their disposal, and plenty of weapons from China and Russia. They were patient, persistent, and calculating in their approach. They weren't looking for a quick win; they wanted a permanent victory in Laos and South Vietnam. On the other hand, VP had limited troops and limited resources, and the war was being run from the White House, where President Nixon was well aware that the American people didn't support the conflict.

With the rainy season approaching, General Tan continued his withdrawal from northern Laos. Before leaving, however, he decided to unleash one last barrage of 130mm artillery fire on Skyline Ridge and Long Tieng—and four NVA regiments remained in northern Laos to carry out Tan's orders. Once the heavy fighting tapered off, VP took the opportunity to rearm and retrain his Hmong guerrillas. A later assessment indicated that during the recent Communist offensive, tens of thousands of rounds of artillery had landed on Long Tieng, and the base had been devastated.

But, that didn't matter, because VP was already planning his next rainy season offensive. So as the NVA retreated, VP's scouts set out to locate the menacing 130mm gun emplacements. They were able to locate many, and mapped their coordinates for U.S. air strikes. The information was provided to the USAF in Thailand, and they went to work on the caves housing the big guns. By this time a new laser-guided bomb had been added to their arsenal, and once spotted no cave was safe. The way the weapon system worked was that when released from the aircraft, the bomb would literally seek out the entrance to the cave, enter, and locate the big gun before it exploded. Subsequent use of the weapon reportedly eliminated all but a few of the big guns.

At this juncture, with conditions on the ground in Laos continuing to deteriorate, National Security Advisor Henry Kissinger flew to Moscow in April 1972 for a secret meeting with Russia's leader, Leonid Brezhnev. During the meeting, Kissinger verbalized previous U.S. demands, and conceded that North Vietnam only had to withdraw the troops that had entered South Vietnam during the spring offensive. He did not even address the NVA troops already in South Vietnam and in Laos; in other words, mutual withdrawal was no longer a demand of the United States. Brezhnev listened to Kissinger's remarks, but essentially rebuffed his efforts, stating that he would not agree to exerting pressure on the North Vietnamese to end their offensive in South Vietnam and Laos.[106]

Meanwhile, back in Laos, the Secret War continued. By mid-May, General Lap had returned to northern Laos with elements from several battalions to act as a blocking force for VP's rainy season offensive. Vu Lap planned to turn the Plain of Jars into a strategic headquarters for year-round operations. The operational headquarters would be located near Khang Khay, and have at its disposal tanks, armored personnel carriers, artillery pieces, and Dac Cong commandos. With this objective in mind, the Communists began to harass the Lao forces in the area, frustrating all efforts by the Lao to establish a foothold around the Plain.

As the rains increased, the NVA rotated additional NVA units back to North Vietnam to rest. In fact, convoys of artillery could be seen headed north. Two regiments of the 312 Division had already moved out in April, and a third regiment joined them in May. With the three regiments gone and the weather deteriorating, hostile activity dropped off significantly. And, as he usually did during the rainy season, Vang Pao began to probe the NVA defenses looking for both weaknesses and ground he could retake.

As VP shuttled his troops around to probe the Communist positions, the 21st SOS Knives would usually participate in actually moving the Lao guerrillas from one location to the other, to expedite engagement of the enemy troops. On one such sortie on June 15, they were moving the Lao guerrillas from Ban Na to the vicinity of Khong Sedone, using eight CH-53 helicopters. The weather was deteriorating and a light rain was falling, so the plan was for the CH-53s to land in twos on the dirt airstrip, and while still moving, the guerrillas would exit the aircraft and the helicopters would then take to the sky and depart.

These types of landings were called "roll-on" landings; and while two of the eight helicopters were doing their roll-on landings, one aircraft hit a pothole in the airstrip, causing the rotor blades to strike the fuselage, disabling the aircraft. The crew got off the disabled aircraft, and boarded another helicopter. The aircraft (serial number 67-1625) was left on the airstrip and plans to lift it out the next day were made. But due to its size and weight, a giant Ch-54 "Sky Crane" would have to be located. A detail of local Hmong guerrillas were left to guard the aircraft, but during the night NVA commandos arrived at the site and engaged the local troops, causing them to flee from the site. The Communist commandos then attempted to blow up the helicopter by lobbing fragmentation grenades into and around it's exterior. The commandos then departed, probably thinking that they had permanently disabled the big aircraft; but a subsequent inspection determined that the aircraft was salvageable.

Over the next few days, helicopter mechanics assigned to USAF Special Operations were brought to the site, and they stripped out most of the removable parts. While the mechanics worked, Air America provided perimeter security. Understandably, they were very concerned for the safety of the mechanics, because the enemy was believed to be less than a mile from the site. At any rate, the mechanics stayed put and finished their job. The crippled bird was later lifted out by a U.S. Army Sky Crane and taken to Ubon Air Base. Over the next couple of months, the mechanics reinstalled all the parts that had been removed, and made other necessary repairs. Soon the aircraft was repaired, and returned to the 21ˢᵗ SOS at NKP for duty.[107]

During this same general timeframe, in Washington, D.C., on June 17, a security officer at the Watergate Office Complex was making his rounds when he discovered that the locks on several doors had been taped over, allowing the doors to be opened and closed without using a key. The officer didn't think much about it; he just removed the tape and continued on his rounds. An hour or so later, he discovered that the same doors had the locks taped over again. This time he knew something wasn't right, and called the local police. A short time later, the authorities arrived and arrested five men hiding in the offices of the Democratic National Headquarters. As history would later show, this was no ordinary burglary. The suspects were in possession of wiretaps and other electronic eavesdropping devices; inasmuch as this was a violation of Federal law, the FBI was called in, and assumed responsibility for additional investigation. Before long, it was learned that all five men worked either directly or indirectly for the White House. It was also learned that the burglars had also committed a variety of other crimes for their employers . . . and, as the investigation continued, all fingers began to point to President Nixon and his inner circle.[108]

Meanwhile, in June 1972, Vang Pao left Long Tieng and Laos without telling most of those around him where he was going. He flew to the United States, where he first met with Pop Buell, who was in the U.S. recuperating after a near-fatal heart attack. After meeting with Pop, they both flew to Washington to meet with politicians and military leaders at the Pentagon. They then traveled to CIA headquarters in Langley, VA for meetings with "The Agency." After meeting with the officials in Washington, Pop and VP were convinced that the U.S. would soon be pulling out of Laos. So, after completing their business in Washington, VP and Pop flew to Missoula, Montana, where three of VP's sons were attending school at Jerry Daniels' invitation. After visiting with his sons, VP returned to Laos, where he organized his traditional rainy season offensive.

While VP was in the United States on his brief visit, his headquarters at Long Tieng had been rebuilt by the CIA. The runway had also been repaired, and the civilians had begun returning as well. There weren't as many coming back this time, and many makeshift homes still sat empty after being abandoned when all hell had broken loose. Also, the number of CIA advisors had been reduced. Jerry Daniels was still at Long Tieng, and for that VP was thankful. Pat Landry had more Thai regiments brought in to support VP; and of course the Ravens were still there, flying every day and marking targets for bombing. As we have said before, they were the best of the best, and respected by all. So life at Long Tieng had somewhat returned to normal . . . but it would never be the lively place it had been in its heyday.

Later, in August 1972, two Hmong regiments reoccupied a part of the Plain of Jars and began to probe the NVA defenses. Pat Landry provided ample air support, but the young Hmong defenders were scared and they quickly retreated. Most of the young fighters were teenagers, under 15 years old, and were not mature enough to handle the rigors of war. They just didn't have the stomach for fighting. For his upcoming operation, VP had planned to use USAF helicopters, but government regulations precluded that from happening, because the huge CH-53 helicopters were limited as to what they could do without escort. As a result, only half of the Hmong assault group was deployed, and they were no match for the enemy artillery. A few months later, the Hmong returned to the Plain again, this time backed up by several Thai artillery batteries.

On August 27, an Air America C-123 "Provider" cargo aircraft carrying a crew of four, five passengers, and 13,500 pounds of palletized explosives crashed into a hill in the Nammeui Valley near Vang Vieng, killing all onboard. The aircraft was a total loss. At about the same time, the NVA initiated probes of their own, engaging the Hmong and Thai troops wherever they could be found. Pat Landry tried to help VP by sending more B-52 bombers to drop more large iron bombs into the craters that already existed on the Plain.

But the strikes didn't really deter the Communists, and with the weather deteriorating as the bombs fell, the NVA finally decided to pull back. As soon as the air support dropped off, however, they returned—and this time they brought Dac Cong Commandos and sapper teams. They immediately engaged the two Hmong regiments, and the B-52s came back, but the NVA did not budge. In any case, they were so close to the Hmong and Thai fighters that the aircraft had trouble finding good targets to hit.

In less than a week, the Hmong and Thai guerrillas retreated after suffering heavy casualties. But the NVA kept advancing, and again headed south towards Long Tieng. They marched until they were just a few miles from the ridges of Skyline, whereupon they stopped and dug in. They also brought in their heavy artillery for another siege. The CIA tried to help by focusing on interdicting the NVA supply lines and taking out the big guns, but somehow the supplies kept getting through, and the B-52s and fighter aircraft from Thailand couldn't take out the big guns in most cases.

On October 8, Kissinger once again secretly met with North Vietnamese officials, including Le Duc Tho[109], in Paris. During the meeting, Kissinger agreed to Hanoi's troops remaining in South Vietnam. He also agreed that South Vietnam, Laos and Cambodia would not be represented at the meetings, and that decisions regarding Laos would be made without input from Vientiane. But of course, no one told the Lao government about the back door deals being brokered by Kissinger in Paris. In late October 1972, it was announced that a tentative agreement had been reached by Hanoi and Washington. The agreement called for a ceasefire and a withdrawal of American combat troops from South Vietnam within 60 days. It also prohibited new troops from entering the war, and the agreement called for repatriation of prisoners. There was no mention of Laos or Cambodia, but it was inferred that agreements for those countries could be worked out later.

Unsurprisingly, the South Vietnamese leaders were furious that the agreement had been reached without their input. They refused to sign the agreement that allowed NVA troops to stay in the South. Slowly the agreement began to fall apart, and the negotiations stalled.

Meanwhile, back in Laos, fighting continued, and Pat Landry was able to acquire the services of General Dynamic's new F-111 "Aardvark." The Aardvark carried as much ordnance as an F-5 and F-105 combined, and it could bomb in any weather. The F-111 also offered a new capability with something called "radar beacon for offset bombing." The way it worked consisted of radar beacons deployed at key locations on the ground, used as offset aiming points for medium-altitude radar bombing. This technique could be employed within a 30-mile radius of a beacon, and would greatly assist the Ravens in calling for air strikes on suspected targets. But the best feature of this technique was that it could be used in all weather conditions.

To complement the new F-111s, the U.S. Air force installed radar beacons for offset bombing at Long Tieng and Bouam Long. One by one, the large NVA 130mm guns were found and eliminated by the Aardvark. The F-111 also assisted the defenders at Bouam Long, where they called it "Whispering Death" because the aircraft was very quiet; all that could be heard was a whooshing sound when it passed by. The first successful F-111 beacon bombing mission in support of Hmong defenders was flown on November 11, 1972. And, by November 30, more than 200 such missions had successfully delivered ordnance against targets in northern Laos. As confidence in the radar beacon bombing program grew, the number of F-111 sorties in Laos steadily increased, with more than 500 sorties being flown there during December 1972.

Also in December, 1972, UPI published an article entitled "Laos Reds Hurt Too Badly to Take Long Cheng—Gen." In the article; UPI quoted Vang Pao as stating that North Vietnamese troops would not be able to seize his mountain headquarters at Long Tieng during the current dry season. The article went on to say that VP's guerrillas had recently captured and destroyed two-thirds of the NVA supplies stockpiled on the Plain of Jars.

Figure 41. F-111 Aardvark
(Photo from the Public Domain)

The article also quoted VP as saying that the recent interdiction campaign had broken the back of a North Vietnamese effort to move against the CIA base at Long Tieng. The article did stipulate, however, that the NVA had long-distance 130mm artillery weapons that concerned the Hmong general. In addition to the information relating to Long Tieng, the article indicated that recent activity by VP's guerrillas had cut Route 7 leading from North Vietnam to Laos, and that at Ban Ban, the logistical base for the North Vietnamese, guerrilla troops had captured large quantities of Communist medical supplies, including stimulants that were provided to the North Vietnamese troops just before going into battle.

Meanwhile, on November 7, USAF Major John L. Carroll was flying a Raven FAC mission in his O-1 Bird Dog over Xiang Khoang Province when his aircraft was hit by ground fire, forcing him to land. Once on the ground, Major Carroll radioed the SAR helicopters of his intention to stay in the aircraft. Two SAR helicopters subsequently attempted a recovery, but intense enemy fire forced them to depart the area. The rescuers made a second attempt soon after, but were again driven away by enemy fire. Major Carroll was later classified as MIA. Many years later, it was learned that he had apparently died at the scene and was subsequently buried by the local villagers in the area. Efforts to recover Carroll's remains were successful, and he was returned to his family in 2007.[110]

Later, on December 24, 1972, USAF Captain Paul Vernon "Skip" Jackson III, Call Sign Raven 21, discovered large caches of NVA supplies hidden under trees while flying a FAC mission over the Plain of Jars. Jackson contacted the 7th/13th Air Force Command and Control Center in Udorn and requested jet fighters to destroy the hidden supplies. Shortly thereafter, four USAF A-7 "Slam" attack aircraft appeared overhead. One of the A-7s was flown by USAF Captain Chuck Riess.[111] Little did they know that Communist troops guarding the hidden caches were armed with 12.7mm and 14.5mm weapons, and would no doubt use them to protect their supplies.

Meanwhile, after briefing the fighters and marking the target with a smoke flare, Raven 21 cleared each of the fighters in hot to put bombs on the target. Fighters 1, 2 and 3 made their passes with deadly accuracy, resulting in large secondary explosions. Lining up last for his bomb run, Captain Reiss rolled in on the target—just as Skip Jackson's Cessna O-1 appeared in his windshield, directly in

Reiss's path. How Raven 21 had gotten into the wrong place is still unknown; in any case, Reiss maneuvered violently to try to miss Jackson's little

Figure 42. USAF A-7D
(Photo from the Public Domain)

observation aircraft as he came in hot on the target. Reiss's aircraft avoided hitting Jackson's directly, but their wingtips did touch, almost tearing the left wing off the Cessna. Reiss's A-7 had now become uncontrollable, and he ejected safely. At about this time Raven 20, piloted by USAF Captain Chuck Hines, had arrived over the scene. In the interim, Jackson's O-1 had, amazingly, landed in one piece on the ground, with him still inside the aircraft and the left wing of his aircraft missing. Unfortunately, Captain Reiss parachuted right into the waiting arms of the NVA, who took him prisoner, reportedly unharmed.

Captain Hines made several passes, and determined that Jackson was most likely dead inside his aircraft. Jackson's status was subsequently listed as KIA, and his remains were not recovered due to the presence of Communist troops in the area. Reiss was later marched overland to Hanoi and held in prison until the spring of 1973, at which time he was released with hundreds of other prisoners. The crash site where Skip Jackson went down has not yet been excavated, and Jackson's remains have not been recovered.

*   *   *

The year 1972 had been a devastating one for the Lao and the Americans who supported them. The NVA controlled all of northeastern Laos, except for Vientiane, Luang Prabang, Bouam Long, and Long Tieng. Air America lost at least six aircraft, and approximately 17 employees were killed in crashes. The USAF had lost the aircraft mentioned above and at least three AC-130 Spectre gunships. Washington was understandably worried, and the White House wanted the war to end sooner rather than later.

In order to jump-start the negotiations in Paris, President Nixon threatened to bomb North Vietnam. The North Vietnamese weren't impressed, and made no overture toward peace. Nixon's next move was to show force, and shortly thereafter, B-52s were winging their way to Hanoi loaded with large iron bombs. For 12 straight days, the bombs fell in North Vietnam. As additional encouragement, Nixon had given permission to target shipyards, docks, power plants and railroad yards. Meanwhile, the secret meetings between Kissinger and the North Vietnamese continued.

But Kissinger did not trust the North Vietnamese, and wanted to know their real intentions. In other words, were they negotiating seriously, or were they just using the peace talks as a smokescreen for their attack plans? No one knew for sure, and the White House wanted more information. The intelligence agencies were also unsure whether the Communists were being sincere in the peace talks, so everyone agreed that reliable information was needed badly.

As fate would have it, the CIA, in uncharacteristic style, had an idea. The Agency was aware of a telephone line used by the North Vietnamese military commanders to relay orders to the troops in the field. It was located near the city of Vinh, North Vietnam. They suggested that if the telephone line could be successfully tapped, the U.S. may be able to find out exactly what the intentions of the NVA were. The Agency also knew that the path of the line, and the fact that it was patrolled regularly, precluded access . . . except at one particular spot. That spot was some distance away from Vinh, where the line went straight up a cliff, over the summit, and down the other side of the cliff. It was believed that if the line was going to be tapped, it had to be at that location.

It was also believed that he only logical way to reach the summit and tap the phone line was by helicopter. But the problem with using a helicopter was that it could be very noisy, and could be heard approaching for miles around. To remedy that problem, the CIA needed a very quiet chopper. While they tried to locate one, the

Agency began training a group of Lao commandos for the anticipated wiretap mission. As luck would have it, the Hughes Aircraft Company in southern California had been working on just such a "quiet" helicopter, the Hughes OH-6A. The modifications consisted of adding an additional rotor blade, modifying the tips of the blades, and redesigning the tail rotor to reduce noise. A large muffler was also designed, along with several other gadgets allowing the pilot to vary the speed of the rotors in order to operate quietly. The Hughes effort appeared to be just what the CIA had been looking for, and with some additional improvement—such as larger fuel tanks to increase range, FLIR, night vision goggles, and long range navigation capability using LORAN-C—the helicopter just might work. So Hughes was contracted to develop and deliver two of the quiet helicopters.

Working on an accelerated schedule, the improvements were soon incorporated, and flight testing began shortly thereafter in early 1971 at Culver City, CA. Later, for security reasons, testing was moved to the famed "Area 51", a secret government test site near Tonopah, Nevada, to keep prying eyes from seeing the helicopter under development. There, the government was able to simulate conditions similar to those that the aircraft would experience on the actual wiretap mission. Later, after the bugs were worked out and the testing completed, two of the quiet helicopters were shipped to Taiwan. They were very similar to the Hughes 500 series helicopters, so they were conveniently listed as 500P-series helicopters. The common name for the 500 series helicopters in the field was "Loach," and they were already a common sight in South Vietnam.

With an acceptable helicopter developed, the CIA then came up with a plan to train and use Taiwanese pilots to fly the quiet helicopters on the wiretap mission. By using the Chinese pilots, the U.S. would have a level of deniability in the event the quiet helicopters were shot down and the pilots captured. In other words, if something went wrong, the Agency could point the finger at someone else, so as not to jeopardize the ongoing peace talks.

Meanwhile, two additional standard-configuration 500-series Loaches were purchased by Air America and delivered to Udorn Air Base. Upon arrival in Thailand, Air America began using the Loaches on routine missions in SEA, knowing the NVA had people watching and taking pictures. Air America wanted the Communists to get used to seeing the Loaches fly routine missions in Laos, thereby reducing the curiosity factor when, and if, the quiet helicopters were observed flying around the countryside.

Initial training of the Chinese pilots was completed in June 1972 in Taiwan. The two 500P quiet helicopters were secretly moved by USAF C-130 aircraft to a remote airfield in Thailand, where they were filled with fuel and flown to another remote airfield near Pakse, in southern Laos, identified only as PS-44. The airfield was already being used by the CIA and Air America, and a variety of helicopters came and went every day without drawing much of suspicion. A special hangar had also been constructed for the quiet helicopters, and access was limited to only a few people who had special clearance and access. Additional training of the Chinese pilots would be required, using the quiet helicopters, and it was decided that the 500Ps would only be flown at night to further shield them from view.

But just as soon as all the components of the mission were in place, things began to go wrong. For one thing, the Chinese pilots just weren't cut out for the task—and one of the quiet helicopters was lost in a crash during a training mission. So the Chinese were sent home and two Air America pilots with good credentials stepped in to fill the void, even though it would reflect badly on the U.S. if something were to go wrong on the mission.

By this time, the commandos selected to carry out the telephone line wiretap had been trained and were ready to go. There were even commandos

Figure 43. Hughes 500 Loach
(Photo from the Public Domain)

trained to protect the wiretap team. According to the plan, they would fly in a separate rescue aircraft during the actual mission. That way, they could extract the wiretap team if something went wrong on the upcoming mission. Another aspect of the wiretap mission that needed to be addressed was the fact that, in order to monitor the wiretap remotely, special electronic gadgets would be needed, including antennas, solar panels for power, and relays. In addition, the actual wiretap device had to be inconspicuous, so glass insulators were manufactured to duplicate the insulators already in use by the NVA. The fake insulators could even house the actual wiretap device.

Shortly thereafter, everything was ready, and the mission was scheduled for December 5, 1972. At the appointed time, the one remaining quiet helicopter took off and flew to a remote airstrip in Laos, where it was refueled. Afterward, two commandos climbed aboard and the helicopter took off again. The rescue team followed behind in a second Air America aircraft, at a safe distance in the event they were needed.

The mission was completed pretty much without incident, and the wiretap was successfully installed. When the device was activated, it began transmitting audio from the telephone calls between NVA generals. Of course, we don't know the actual substance of the conversations, but it was reported that Kissinger got the information he needed regarding their sincerity as related to the ongoing peace talks. And later, as history records, the peace agreement was signed in January 1973. The wiretap continued to operate successfully for several months before going silent. But it didn't matter then, because whatever it was that Kissinger needed, he already had it.

As 1972 drew to a close, the United States was quickly withdrawing from South Vietnam and northern Laos. As anticipated, the NVA and Pathet Lao were poised to close the net, ending the war once and for all, and were prepared to install puppet governments in South Vietnam and Vientiane. Meanwhile, the CIA continued its support of the Hmong guerrillas in Laos, and the U.S. State Department still maintained some semblance of the MAP program. Meanwhile, the U.S. was methodically drawing down its troops in neighboring Thailand as well. As the U.S. continued drawing down, the resentment against America began to build and slowly take hold. Suddenly, everyone could sense the inevitable.

Chapter 16

Collapse and Aftermath

On approximately December 22, 1972, the Communist forces in Laos launched an offensive that ultimately resulted in Thateng, Saravane, and Lao Ngam being overwhelmed and occupied by the enemy. The NVA then came together for a major assault on Pak Song. Unfortunately, at the time, many of the USAF units at NKP had been phased out, and the supporting troops had been either reassigned or sent home. The primary units remaining at NKP were the 21st SOS Knives, the 22nd SOS Sandys, the 361st Tactical Electronics Warfare Squadron (EC-47), and the Air Rescue and Recovery Service (ARRS).[112]

The U.S. Army Special Forces advisors also began to reduce the number of its personnel in both Thailand and Laos in late 1972. Prior to that time, the American soldiers had been providing training for the Thai and Hmong troops at bases in Thailand. But with the impending ceasefire and formation of a new coalition government in Laos, the U.S. Army personnel would not be needed; so they quietly returned to their parent organizations on Okinawa.

Meanwhile, several hundred Pathet Lao troops began probing RLG forces near Sala Phou Khoun, on the Plain of Jars, where two vital roads intersected. Route 13 ran north/south from Vientiane across the Plain, through Luang Prabang, and on into North Vietnam at Dien Bien Phu. Route 7 ran eastward across Laos from Sala Phou Khoun through Khang Khay and Nong Het, and then into central North Vietnam. As the probes became more forceful, the Lao government troops abandoned their equipment in place and retreated south along Route 13.

The FAR generals quickly developed a plan that called for a two-pronged attack to dislodge the Communists and retake the vital 7/13 road junction. First, a brigade of RLG troops would be airlifted to a position north of Sala Phou Koun, while several battalions would move over land towards the road junction from Vang Vieng. The battle plan wasn't a bad one, but like all such plans, it failed to survive contact with the enemy. At the appointed time, the battalions from Vientiane began to move northward—but the northern brigade, which was supposed to begin their march south, couldn't seem to get any momentum. Meanwhile, the group pushing northward continued to make good progress, and towards the end of the day on January 6 they were within 12 kilometers of Sala Phou Khoun. But the forward progress stopped when the battalion commander, RLA Colonel Khamphet Phamvilay, was killed by Communist gunners. The Lao troops then immediately turned around and headed back down the road in the direction of Moung Kassy.

To help stabilize the situation and reinforce the RLG troops, Vang Pao was asked to provide Hmong and Thai fighters for the operation. By January 10, three battalions were in place along Route 13. Two days later, a Raven FAC working in the area spotted two Russian tanks moving towards Moung Kassy with Communist infantry troops following along. Both tanks were subsequently destroyed by the Thai troops, but the RLG soldiers near Moung Kassy still refused to move.

Meanwhile, back in MR-2, VP's troops were taking a beating as 1973 began. Bouam Long was under constant siege, but the defenders were still holding on while the NVA pounded LS-32 with 130mm and 122mm artillery. The USAF flew sorties constantly to hopefully prevent any significant Communist ground attack, even as the Raven FACs tried to pinpoint the locations of the big guns for elimination. Hayden Curry, the new U.S. AIRA in Vientiane, wondered why the Ravens were having such difficulty . . . when suddenly, it occurred to him that the NVA troops, just like everyone else, were creatures of habit. They did the same thing over and over, as long as it worked. In other words, if we can't find the guns today, why don't we look for them where they were located last week?

Old aerial reconnaissance data was then pulled out of the filing cabinet and reviewed for the previous several weeks. Former artillery locations were identified on the maps, and the information was provided to both the Ravens and the aerial reconnaissance personnel at Udorn. Collectively, they went out to check these known locations—and sure enough, they began to locate the guns, because the NVA had simply moved them back to their original positions. From then on, when a gun was located, the information was passed to the Control Center at Udorn for targeting and elimination. Before long the guns were being destroyed, and the chokehold on Bouam Long was relaxed, just a bit.

Be that as it may, the Communists were still well-fortified in northern Laos, and they weren't going anywhere. They intended to stick it out and defeat the Lao and Americans at any cost. The Pathet Lao, on the other hand, lacked the stomach for combat, and began to seriously consider negotiating a peace deal directly with the RLG. After all, it was their country that was getting blown to bits. They suggested that a meeting take place between Souvanna and Souphanouvong. Actually, there had already been whispers and hints of peace, and the Pathet Lao had dispatched Phoumi Vongvichit to Vientiane back in October 1972 to explore the prospect of meaningful talks. It was also common knowledge that North Vietnam's lead negotiator had already told Henry Kissinger that peace would come to Laos within 30 days of a ceasefire in South Vietnam.

Later, on January 20, 1973, one of the last major combat assaults using USAF helicopters in Laos took place when seven CH-53 Knives out of NKP, and two Air America Chinook CH-47s, lifted in about 1,000 Hmong guerrillas to reopen the Vientiane/Luang Prabang highway at Sala Phou Khoun. During the lift, four of the choppers were damaged by ground fire; but the road was soon opened, and a fire support base was established to keep it open.

On January 27, the U.S., North Vietnam, South Vietnam, and the Viet Cong signed the Paris Peace Accords. Laos had been excluded from the event, but Kissinger later dispatched General Alexander Haig and the former Ambassador to Laos, Bill Sullivan, to Vientiane. Their job was to convince Souvanna Phouma to also sign the agreement. Shortly thereafter, they sat down with Souvanna, and he asked about assurances that North Vietnam would withdraw its forces from Laos. Unfortunately, Sullivan and Haig could not provide a satisfactory answer. They (mistakenly, as it turned out) believed that North Vietnam would withdraw their troops, but they did not know for certain when that day would be, so they could offer no such assurance to Souvanna. But then again, why would North Vietnam agree to withdraw their troops, when they had contended all along that they didn't *have* any troops in Laos? At any rate, Haig and Sullivan left the meeting empty-handed, because Souvanna refused to sign the agreement. Before the meeting ended, however, Haig and Sullivan reminded the Prime Minister that U.S. air support would most likely not be provided once the Peace Accords were implemented. Souvanna acknowledged the seriousness of the situation, and made it clear that he understood the message.

The Paris Accords called for "the United States, and all other countries, to respect the independence, sovereignty, unity, and territorial integrity of Vietnam as recognized by the 1954 Geneva Agreements on Vietnam." The inclusion of this statement was somewhat of a victory for North Vietnam, because it did not describe their war against South Vietnam as one of foreign aggression. The Accords specified that there would be an in-place ceasefire. All forces would hold their positions and only resupply their troops with consumables. Then the U.S. troops would withdraw within 60 days, along with all other foreign soldiers. All POWs would be released, and all Secret War participants would assist in repatriating the remains of the dead. There were also negotiations planned between Saigon and the Viet Cong, leading to a decision by the people of South Vietnam as to their political future. Finally, the reunification of Vietnam was to be carried out peacefully.

When President Nguyen Van Thieu of South Vietnam was briefed on the accords, he was furious because he had not been consulted prior to the agreements being reached in Paris. He accused Kissinger and Nixon of going behind his back, and he declined to sign the document.[113]

Meanwhile, back on the ground in northern Laos, the NVA launched yet another attack on Bouam Long. The attack began at night with a MiG strafing the site and dropping bombs. VP sent four T-28 aircraft to help the defenders at the site, but as the Trojans approached, the NVA gunners opened up on the aircraft, causing the pilots to become confused and frightened. On the first pass, the T-28s dropped their loads wide. Their next runs were at higher altitudes . . . and the bombs didn't reach their targets at all. On the following day, the site was socked in with fog and clouds, but the FB-111s came anyway. For days the mountains shook as the Aardvarks dropped their bombs with deadly precision. The NVA couldn't figure out how they were being hit with such accuracy when the weather was so bad; all they could hear was the whooshing sound as the Aardvarks passed by. The NVA then retreated.

Further to the northwest, the beginning of the end was also taking place at Nam Yu. As mentioned earlier in the story, over the years,

Nam Yu had been used primarily as a jumping-off point for CIA teams being sent into China to conduct intelligence-gathering missions. The CIA also used the strategic location to monitor China's progress as they constructed the "Chinese Road," and USAID had conducted refugee assistance from a compound in the area. But by the latter part of 1972, Washington had lost interest in the Chinese Road, believing that it wasn't a big threat to America's activities in Laos after all.

The fireworks later began on February 1, when Pathet Lao soldiers torched the USAID compound, sending a clear signal that the CIA compound was next. The CIA personnel hastily began destroying classified documents and materials as they radioed for reinforcements. On February 2, aircraft from Air America began bringing in reinforcements and heavy weapons. But by first light on the following morning, Communist soldiers were at the perimeter of the CIA compound. The Thai and Lao defenders did their best to hold off the attackers, but slowly and methodically, the Communists began to overpower the defenders. RLAF and U.S. fighters soon arrived and flew air support missions in hopes of discouraging the Communists, but the enemy kept advancing.

Towards the end of the day on February 3, the CIA contacted the USAF and asked for the Knives from NKP to come and evacuate the defenders from Nam Yu. Soon the large USAF CH-53 helicopters began arriving and shuttling out the defenders. Having lost the capability to conduct intelligence activities there, the CIA case officers left Nam Yu on one of the last helicopters. After all Lao and Thai personnel had been removed, RLAF T-28 aircraft showed up and bombed the CIA compound to destroy all the weapons and equipment. Nam Yu had been lost, this time for good.

On February 5, an EC-47 electronic monitoring aircraft from the USAF Security Service (Baron 52) disappeared over Saravane Province in southern Laos while listening to and recording Communist radio transmissions. Seven USAF personnel were aboard the aircraft when it disappeared. An airborne search was subsequently undertaken, and the downed aircraft was located. Upon conducting a ground search at the crash site, rescue and recovery personnel found the charred remains of three or four of the missing airmen. Upon further examination and evaluation, it was determined that all personnel onboard the aircraft had most likely perished in the crash, even though their remains were not found.

Later, however, a radio transmission was intercepted by a monitoring station, indicating that several of the airmen had survived the crash. It was believed they were being moved to North Vietnam. Over the next several years, reports were received indicating that some of the surviving airmen were being held in southern Laos, but it was later determined that the stories had probably been fabricated. Much later, in November 1992, a joint U.S. and Lao recovery team traveled to the area where Baron 52 crashed, and excavated the site. Remnants of the crash were still there, though little additional evidence was found. But it was still the belief of crash experts that all personnel onboard the EC-47 would have most likely perished on impact or in the subsequent fire.

While we're on the subject of southern Laos, things were beginning to fall apart there as well. The Communists initiated an attack on Pak Song on February 8, led by about a half-dozen Russian tanks. The RLA commander on the ground quickly called for Spectre, and soon the gunship was overhead. But new rules of engagement required the gunship to obtain clearance from the AOC at Savannakhet prior to opening fire on the enemy. Unfortunately, that process took about thirty minutes—and by the time the gunship received clearance to engage the enemy, the tanks and NVA troops had already overrun the defenders. When the 7th Air Force commander, General John Vogt, Jr., found out about the debacle, he personally investigated. He also traveled to Pakse and assured the RLA generals that he would personally oversee the retaking of Pak Song. General Vogt then laid out a very detailed plan using B-52 bombers and fast-moving jet fighters, and as many airborne tankers as necessary to retake the site. The idea was to use air power exclusively, eliminating any further decimation of Lao ground troops. The operation was subsequently undertaken, and by February 12, the Lao flag was flying over Pak Song again.[114]

In February 1973, Henry Kissinger flew to Vientiane to personally talk to Souvanna Phouma, who still hadn't signed the ceasefire agreement. Kissinger thought he could get the Prime Minister to sign the Peace Accords, and then he would fly on to Hanoi to wrap up his work. But Souvanna still wouldn't sign. While in Laos, Kissinger discovered that North Vietnam still hadn't withdrawn any of its troops; in fact, the NVA had brought even more troops into Laos. He then flew to Hanoi demanding answers. The government in Hanoi informed Kissinger that they would withdraw troops only after new governments had been installed in Cambodia and Laos. In other words, they wanted Communist governments installed.

Meanwhile, after Kissinger's unsuccessful meeting with Souvanna, negotiations between the Royal Laotian Government and the Pathet Lao finally got underway. Hanoi, fearing that with the ceasefire in South Vietnam America might send troops to Laos, pressed the Pathet Lao to reach an agreement quickly. But the Rightists were reluctant to agree. In order to pressure them to sign, the U.S. delayed food and equipment shipments to Laos, and withheld their monetary allotments as well. Meanwhile, on February 12, 40 U.S. POWs were allowed to leave Hanoi onboard a C-141 transport. Over the next several months, a total of 591 American prisoners were released by the Communists.

A little while later, on February 21, 1973, the Pathet Lao, Neutralists, and Rightists finally signed an Agreement on "The Restoration of Peace and Reconciliation in Laos." The agreement called for an immediate ceasefire. Vientiane and Luang Prabang were to become neutral cities, with both Communists and non-Communists sharing the administration. There would also be a new coalition government, the Provisional Government of National Union (PGNU), with the Prime Minister (Souvanna) having executive power. The new National Political Consultative Council (NPCC) would hold legislative power. Other details were also to be negotiated. Once the new government was up and running, all foreign troops would have 60 days to leave the country.

On the following day, as anticipated, General Vogt announced that all U.S. air power would be withdrawn from Laos effective at noon on that date. In less than an hour after the announcement, the NVA swept over Pak Song and the Bolovens Plateau, driving out Lao government forces. In retaliation, the B-52 bombers were summoned and conducted more raids against the Communists, but no other follow-up action was taken by the United States. And, with that event, Southern Laos was pretty much handed over to the Communists.

Meanwhile, back in MR-2, it was business as usual, with Vang Pao conducting an operational meeting with the Ravens, the CIA advisors and other staff members. At the meeting, VP was quoted as saying, "You know, you can sit down with the Communists at the table and you can talk to them. They will nod their heads and smile politely, talk to you, agree to anything, but under the table they will always be kicking you." The meeting then continued, and everyone understood the Hmong had been sold out. But they still held out hope that when, and if, things got really bad, the U.S. would do the right thing and help the Hmong find a better place to live in safety. After all, we owed them that much.

Shortly after his operational meeting, VP received an unsigned, typed communication at his headquarters in Long Tieng. The document officially notified him that the USAF would cease all air support at 1200 hours on that date, and that they were under instructions to clear Lao air space at that time. At 2:30 P.M. that same day, one of the outposts defending Long Tieng fell, and the others were under heavy attack.

With a ceasefire in place, the U.S. military presence would decrease dramatically over the coming months. To help that process along was U.S. Army Major General Richard Trefry, the newly assigned Deputy Chief, JUSMAGTHAI. Trefry would not only oversee Project 404, but he would also become the Defense Attaché in Vientiane, and be responsible for both AIRA and ARMA. His job in Laos was to reduce the number of U.S. military advisors and, at the same time, help the RLAF and RLA become more self-sufficient. Also, General Trefry would assume responsibility for the Requirements Office (RO) at the U.S. Embassy in Vientiane. Inasmuch as the RO managed the MAP budget, it was a logical move; but there wasn't much time to get everything done. The Ravens were scheduled to deactivate and leave the country by the end of June 1973, turning over all FAC duties to the RLAF. Air America was also scaling back, and the RLAF would have to assume ownership and responsibility for the aircraft transferred to Laos by the Company. H-34 helicopters would also be turned over to the RLAF, so even more Lao pilots and mechanics would need to be trained. Knowing his plate was full, Trefry dived right in and began getting the job done.

Meanwhile, NVA troops and Soviet advisors continued to flow into Laos.

On the civilian side of the equation, the CIA would need to take the necessary steps to integrate the Hmong guerrillas and VP into the RLA. As a first step, the SGUs would be renamed Lao Irregular Forces (LIF). The eventual plan was to have the Hmong guerrillas report to

VP under the FAR, and that transition was supposed to be completed by June 1973. The Thai troops were then formed into SGUs. At that time they numbered about 15,000, but that number decreased as desertions began to take place. And, of course, ultimately, the plan was to send all Thai personnel home within 12 months.

After the ceasefire agreement, violations continued to occur; they were daily at first, and then slowly tapered off. At this point in time, Laos was a torn and divided country, and everybody was tired of fighting. Without air power, the Hmong had no desire or reason to fight. VP's irregulars were slowly merged into the Army. But they no longer received combat pay, and their wage scale was decreased to coincide with the RLA pay scale. Also, Long Tieng had finally lost its luster. It wasn't a booming war-time city any longer. Petty crimes increased due to shrinking paychecks and nothing to do. Robberies became commonplace and there were the occasional murders, believed to be reprisal killings.

As March 1973 arrived, sporadic fighting continued in northern Laos, but for the most part Lao and NVA troops maintained a defensive posture. In April, Ambassador Godley was scheduled to leave Laos for reassignment. As he planned his departure, he asked Washington for guidance that he could pass on to those State Department employees remaining in Laos. The ambassador was essentially told to tell them to maintain the status quo. He dutifully passed the message to all embassy personnel, who in turn relayed the message to the RLG and Hmong forces. But, that didn't mean offensive operations weren't being conducted in Laos by the U.S. and North Vietnam, because they were in fact taking place. Covert operations were occurring under the radar screen, just as they always had. Sources still needed to be debriefed, wiretaps had to be serviced, and spies had to be tasked and paid. In other words, the Secret War continued, but on a reduced scale.

In the latter part of March, the U.S. began to press both the North Vietnamese and the Pathet Lao for release of all U.S. POWs captured in Laos. But would the Pathet Lao honor the agreements made by North Vietnam? No one could be sure, and to further complicate matters, no details had been worked out between the Communists and the U.S. as to the procedures for prisoner exchanges. On March 26, it was announced that eight prisoners held in Laos would be released in Hanoi on March 28. Then, on

March 27, the Pathet Lao sent the U.S. Embassy in Vientiane a note indicating that with the release of the eight personnel, their obligation would be fulfilled.

U.S. officials were dumbfounded at this development, and tried in vain to get the Pathet Lao to discuss the issue. Formal discussions and communications resulted in only generic responses from the Communists, indicating that officials in Sam Neua were reviewing the requests for prisoner release. The North Vietnamese apparently smelled a rat, and quickly tried to disassociate themselves from the POW issue in Laos. In fact, they insisted that the release of U.S. POWs in North Vietnam, and the withdrawal of U.S. troops from South Vietnam, proceed on schedule as a completely separate issue. And of course all the parties, except the Pathet Lao, acknowledged that U.S. POWs were still being held in Laos.

At this juncture, let's step back and examine what we know about the POW issue, and see if we can come up with a possible explanation as to why only eight U.S. POWs captured in Laos were released in 1973. We know that the total number of U.S. personnel classified as either MIA or POW exceeded 500. Being realistic, we can assume that a fair number would have perished in their aircraft as the machines impacted the ground. We can also assume that many airmen sustained injuries during bailout or while crashing; that would have most likely decreased their chances for survival while in captivity, given a lack of proper medical care. We also know that the Pathet Lao despised Americans, especially those who flew over their villages trying to kill them with bombs and machine gun fire, and they did not hesitate to execute captured Americans based upon the slightest provocation. To be blunt, they would simply put a gun to the head of a prisoner and pull the trigger without hesitation. Their hatred for Americans was just that intense.

We must also ask ourselves if there would be any rational reason for the Communists to keep POWs incarcerated after the signing of the Vientiane Agreement. Personally, I don't think so. The Pathet Lao had won the ultimate prize, and that was domination of Laos. Why would they need to keep the prisoners as bargaining chips when China, Russia and North Vietnam were all courting Laos with plenty of aid and equipment? In other words, they didn't need, or probably want, aid from the U.S., given the strings that were always attached—and the fact that there would need to be Americans in

Laos to administer the aid dollars. No, they wanted the U.S. out of their country completely, and gone forever.

To sum up the plight of the U.S. POWs in Laos, many died in combat related crashes or injuries. The Communists executed many others, and a fair number were killed while trying to escape. Many others probably died in captivity due to illness, poor nutrition and a lack of medical care. The Pathet Lao hated the Americans and probably would have had no qualms about expediting the demise of the few prisoners who have survived against all the odds prior to the ceasefire. And, remember, dead men don't talk.

But getting back to 1973: in the month after the ceasefire, the NVA attacked the Lao troops at Tha Vieng in April, capturing two Thai soldiers. Three days later the town fell. Souvanna Phouma objected publicly and asked the United States to intervene. The USAF later sent a two man Combat Control Team (CCT) to a mountaintop near Tha Vieng. There they placed a directional beacon device that would allow precise U.S. bombing coordinates. Early the next morning, a trio of B-52 bombers flew over the area and dropped large iron bombs on the NVA. That evening, a second wave of B-52s came and finished the job. Having completed their assignment, the CCT quietly left the area. The event was significant because it would be the last air support received from the United States Air Force. Notwithstanding, the NVA later took Muong Soui, Sala Phou Khoun and Tha Vieng.

Meanwhile, on May 7, Emmet Kay, a civilian pilot employed by Continental Air Services (a contract cargo hauler) was flying a Pilatus Porter aircraft on a routine mission, transporting Hmong guerrilla troops to an airstrip near the Plain of Jars. No enemy contact was anticipated, since hostilities had officially ended. Upon reaching the village where he was to deposit the troops, Kay made a pass over a village to visually check out the airstrip. Everything appeared to be normal on the ground, and Kay did not observe any signs of danger. Shortly thereafter, however, while positioning for landing, Kay took small arms fire from the ground, and the aircraft sustained damage to the extent that he thought it best to initiate a controlled crash landing. He found a suitable location and put the aircraft down without injury to himself or any of his passengers. Upon deplaning, however, Kay and his group were immediately surrounded and taken into custody. Soon, they found themselves prisoners of the Pathet Lao. The prisoners were then marched to a cave complex in northern Laos, where Kay was separated from the rest of the group and imprisoned briefly. A few days later, he was transported to North Vietnam.

After spending a few weeks in North Vietnam, Kay was debriefed and then returned to another cave prison in northern Laos, where he remained for over a year. Oddly enough, during the time he was imprisoned, Kay was treated rather humanely, but understandably contracted dysentery and other digestive system ailments. He was allowed to write to his family and his employer, and even received supplies and other goods from Continental Air Services while in custody. Finally, Kay was released to U.S. control on September 18, 1974. Upon return to friendly hands, Kay was again debriefed. He related that while being held prisoner, he recalled not seeing any other Americans in captivity, but was told by some of his captors that many U.S. POWs were still being held in northern Laos.

Also in May 1973, in unrelated events, the U.S. Congress learned that President Nixon had authorized the bombing of Cambodia back in 1970, and that the bombing had continued into 1973 without the knowledge of, and approval by, the Congress. In fact, it was alleged that the President had directed others below him to hide the facts from the lawmakers. In June, Congress retaliated by passing legislation directing a halt to the bombing. Nixon vetoed the legislation, but in November Congress overrode Nixon's veto.

Meanwhile, back in Laos on June 28, a Memorandum of Understanding relating to Thai SGUs and equipment was signed by Lao and U.S. officials. The agreement called for a phased and orderly program to effect the deactivation of the SGUs during the period of June 21, 1973 to June 1974. The agreement also called for the removal of all non-Lao personnel connected with the SGUs.

By August, all American military action in Laos had ceased. The Ravens were gone, and Air America was to reduce its fleet significantly. Of course, the military personnel who had been disguised as "Air Attachés" also left Laos, as did most of the military advisors. The only two agencies remaining in Laos were the State Department and USAID. All remaining military personnel, if retained, would be transferred to the Defense Attaché Office. And, as called for in the accords, the Thai military and mercenary soldiers were to be returned home.

As the summer of 1973 dragged on, talks continued regarding the formation of a coalition government in Laos. Some agreements had been reached regarding Vientiane and Luang Prabang, but many FAR officers were disturbed about the future of Laos under a mixed Pathet Lao/FAR coalition government. Some of the FAR officers even traveled to Bangkok to discuss their concerns with former colleagues who had previously grown weary of the fight and moved to Thailand in exile.

It was not exactly clear who the officers talked to, but it was common knowledge that the Thai government was unhappy about the possibility of the Pathet Lao coming to power in Laos. At any rate, Thao Ma's name was beginning to be mentioned in Vientiane again. By mid-August 1973, there were also quiet whispers about Thao Ma returning to Laos to initiate a coup, at the encouragement of Phoumi. Later, on August 20, Thao Ma and his supporters quietly crossed the Mekong River during the night, from Thailand into Laos, arriving in Vientiane very early the next morning, well before the sun came up. A few hours later, residents of the capital city awoke to unfamiliar sounds as Thao Ma's followers began to hand out blue-and-white ascots to supporters. Many donned the ascots immediately, including airport workers at Wattay. Thao Ma's supporters then took over the National Bank, the radio station, and the airport.

Thao Ma and six of his loyal pilots arrived at Wattay around noon and commandeered several T-28 aircraft, as other followers read a communiqué on the air at the radio station. Thao Ma and his pilots were soon in the air over nearby Chinaimo Air Base, dropping bombs. Government forces quickly responded; Thao Ma's T-28 fighter was fired upon, causing it to crash. The former general survived the crash, and was quickly arrested and turned over to General Abhay Kouprasith. At that point, the coup quickly fizzled. Thao Ma was reportedly confronted, at which time he became verbally combative and was shot once in the head, either by Kouprasith or one of his underlings; but in any case, the little general did not die straight away. In fact, he continued to berate his captors. He was then reportedly shot again—and then gutted. Afterwards, his body was reportedly tossed into the Mekong River. Approximately 60 of Thao Ma's followers were also reportedly executed, and the coup ended by sundown that same day.[115]

The citizens of Vientiane were not surprised the coup had taken place, since it had been rumored for days, and the Pathet Lao had even broadcasted the news 12 hours before the actual attempt. In any case it was widely known that citizens were upset because Souvanna had sided with the Communists, granting them too much authority in the new government. But if every dark cloud has a silver lining, perhaps Thao Ma's coup was the catalyst to move the Lao towards unification. On September 14, a ceasefire agreement called the Vientiane Accords was signed by all factions, allowing the country to move forward in forming a new coalition government. The agreement called for the withdrawal of all foreign troops from Laos within 60 days of the creation of the new coalition government. It also called for the release of all POWs within that 60-day period. The U.S. held up its end of the agreement, and met the deadline; but North Vietnam, of course, did not remove all its troops. In fact, only a few thousand returned to Hanoi.

This agreement was very important to the United States, because it called for the immediate release of all POWs held in Laos by the Pathet Lao, and required the Communists to assist in recovering the remains of all POW/MIAs who perished, either in combat or in captivity. Also, according to Kissinger, he had received assurances from the North Vietnamese in Paris that the prisoners held in Laos would be released at the same time the prisoners in North Vietnam were released. That release was to take place by March 28, 1973.

But, as we now know, only eight prisoners reportedly captured by the Pathet Lao in Laos and later moved to North Vietnam were released on that date. It was later learned that upon arrival in the Hanoi area, the eight prisoners had not been integrated with the other U.S. POWs; they were held in separate facilities.

Later, in August 1973, combat air operations from Korat and Utapao Air Force Bases in Thailand were halted. Electronic surveillance, air intelligence and gunship (AC-130) operations, however, continued from Korat until February 1976. The Thai Air Force then assumed control of the base, continuing some operations from Korat. In fact, the base is still open today, and is used by the U.S. periodically to conduct air combat exercises.

Meanwhile, on October 12, 1973, two Russian AN-12 transports landed at Wattay Airport after taking off from Gia Lam Air Base in North Vietnam. When the aircraft rolled to a stop, soldiers of the

Pathet Lao, 206 Public Security Battalion emerged from the aircraft. Not wanting to be left out, the Chinese also airlifted a group of their own soldiers into the royal capital at Luang Prabang. By the end of the year, more Pathet Lao soldiers arrived, ultimately reaching battalion strength. Of course, the purpose of bringing Pathet Lao and Chinese soldiers directly to Vientiane was to show the citizens that the Communists were now in charge, and would police the daily activities of the Lao citizens in the business capital. Heretofore, the citizens had pretty much been immune to the war, and had experienced no direct contact with the Communists. But, that was about to change.

Meanwhile, the NVA quietly began to return more of its regiments to North Vietnam. On November 6, 1973, the U.S. Congress passed the War Powers Act of 1973, authorizing the president to send U.S. armed forces into action abroad only after authorization by Congress, or if the U.S. was already under attack or under serious threat of attack. The resolution required that the President notify Congress within 48 hours of committing armed forces to military action, and forbade armed forces from remaining anywhere outside the United States for more than 90 days without an authorization of the use of military force or a declaration of war. In December, Congress also passed the Foreign Assistance Act, requiring that all U.S. aid to Laos to be administered by the Department of State effective in October 1974, cutting the Department of Defense completely out of the picture. But only about $100,000,000 dollars were set aside; and even as U.S. aid was slashed by two-thirds, the new U.S. Ambassador to Laos, Charles Whitehouse, was directed to maintain a strong non-Communist posture. Whitehouse was also instructed to provide Souvanna with assistance during the transition period to a coalition government.

With the end of the Secret War in sight, the Hmong guerrilla fighters would have to return to subsistence farming to make a living and provide for their families—but the task would be formidable, because there were no longer farm animals available, and all the farm tools previously used were long gone. Therefore, in order to assist in the transition from war-fighting to farming, the U.S. provided funds to develop various farm projects, including raising livestock, chickens and swine. In addition to start-up funds, a bank was established, and technical experts were brought into Laos to assist in the transition.

Farm Service Centers were later established, and all projects were managed by the Xiengkhouang Development Corporation, which was staffed by indigenous personnel. The projects funded by the U.S. were not designed to require long-term oversight by the Americans, and it was later reported that the effort appeared to be successful.

On February 14, 1974, Secretary of State Henry Kissinger issued a policy directive requiring the U.S. Embassy in Laos to provide effective military assistance to Souvanna Phouma. The assistance was to continue until a new coalition government was formed. A short time later, during the first week of April, the Rightists, the Pathet Lao, and the Neutralists finally reached an agreement to form a new coalition government. It was constituted as the Provisional Government of National Union (PGNU). Souvanna remained as the Prime Minister, and Souphanouvong was named to head a newly created portfolio called the Joint National Political Council, putting him on a more equal footing with Souvanna. Cabinet posts were then assigned with equal representation from the factions, and a deadline of June 4, 1974 was established for the withdrawal of all foreign military personnel, which would mean the end of the line for Thai military personnel serving in Laos.

At about this same time, Souphanouvong emerged from hiding; and with the Pathet Lao in control, he was an instant hero. They even held a parade for the Prince, and the streets were crowded with young people jockeying for position to see him. After the parade, Souphanouvong gave a short speech, and then with much fanfare got into a car, and his motorcade drove away. With that event, he immediately became the de facto leader of the Pathet Lao. Many people then scratched their heads, wondering how a man who had spent the last ten years hiding in a cave could all of a sudden become a leader.

Meanwhile, by June 1974, most of the Air America people had left Laos, and their maintenance facilities were sold. Likewise, the CIA had to significantly reduce the number of advisors in Laos. Most of the paramilitary officers soon found themselves out of work and on their way back home to the States. Some went to nearby Bangkok to contemplate their next move. Still others had been in Laos for many years, and just didn't want to go home and have to deal with all the anti-war sentiment. Pat Landry transferred, and the Udorn CIA facility was practically empty. By then Pop Buell had retired, after suffering a major heart attack. He was never the same again; the war had depleted him of all his energy. But he was still around, working with children at a home for the blind in Vientiane.

Across the river in Thailand, things were also changing. Most of the warplanes and personnel had left the country with very few troops and support personnel remaining. The instant cities that had sprung up around the military bases during the war were mostly vacated; the bars, shops and restaurants were empty. One by one the bases closed down, and looting became the order of the day. Everything that wasn't nailed down was taken first; then the stuff that *was* nailed down was taken. In the end, all that remained at most locations was an unused air field, stacks of PSP, and crumbling asphalt streets. All the structures that could be disassembled were taken apart and removed. What used to be a barracks later became a bungalow, or a schoolhouse in a nearby village. Before long, the jungle and the snakes, returned to reclaim the land.

On August 8, 1974, President Nixon, facing impeachment, announced in a nationally televised address that he would resign the presidency effective at noon the following day—even though he still denied any involvement in the Watergate debacle. Early the next morning, on August 9, Gerald Ford assumed the office of President. The new president granted Nixon a full and unconditional pardon on September 8. Meanwhile, back in Laos, Souvanna left Vientiane for several months of medical convalescence in Paris, at the invitation of the French government.

Also in September 1974, an American citizen, thought to be a tourist, was apprehended by the Pathet Lao. He was Charles Dean, brother of former Vermont governor Howard Dean, and he was taken into custody along with an Australian friend by the name of Neil Sharman. The two travelers had reportedly been traveling from Vientiane to Thakhek, Laos when detained at a Communist checkpoint. The two travelers were taken to a nearby Pathet Lao holding facility, and later moved by road to another detention facility in the Sam Neua area. They were interrogated at length, with Dean and Sharman insisting that they were merely tourists seeing the country and taking photographs. But it was fairly clear that the Pathet Lao were convinced the two were employees of the CIA.

The news of Dean's apprehension soon reached family members in the United States, who traveled to Vientiane to negotiate his release. The effort was unsuccessful, and in December 1974, Dean and Sharman were placed in the back of a truck, reportedly for transport to North Vietnam; but just prior to reaching the border, the pair were removed from the vehicle and summarily executed. It was not known why they were executed, because neither was known to be in the employ of the U.S. government. Shortly after Dean and Sharman were killed, attempts to obtain Charles Dean's remains were initially unsuccessful. But at least one publication indicated that Dean's remains were ultimately returned, and that he was buried with full military honors.[116]

As 1975 began, much of the U.S. activity in Laos had ceased, and excess equipment and people were being moved to other locations in SEA. The plan was to slowly remove U.S. personnel in the hopes that the newly formed coalition government could hold the country together until the personnel relocations had been accomplished. In other words, the idea was not to leave entirely, but to retain an American presence in Laos until the intentions of the Communists became fully known.

In Laos, the Pathet Lao's strategy was threefold. First, they would organize popular dissent against the old regime in the form of riots and demonstrations. Next, Pathet Lao personnel would instigate mutiny in the Army units. And, lastly, the Pathet Lao would use intimidation techniques against the local authorities to get them to come over to their side, thereby severing the ties between the rural population and the old government officials. Slowly, their plan began to come together—with the only obstacle in their path being General Vang Pao, who still continued to fight.

In neighboring Vietnam, 1975 would become a very busy year. In the second half of 1974, North Vietnamese General Van Tien Dung, Chief of the General Staff and NVA leader at Dien Bien Phu in 1954, chaired a meeting in Hanoi to discuss plans for the upcoming year. All the NVA generals were there. They discussed strategy and direction, and presented their ideas for the 1975 campaign to consolidate North and South, Vietnam. It was finally decided that the campaign would start in the Central Highlands, the northernmost part of South Vietnam. General Dung was optimistic and believed that the NVA would make good progress, but just how much could not be determined. Dung hoped that the campaign could be completed before the end of 1975, but was prepared to continue into 1976 if necessary.

Meanwhile, on March 5, 1975, the CIA and U.S. Army Intelligence published a joint memorandum indicating that South Vietnam could contain the NVA through the dry season and into the following year. But little did they know just how wrong their assessment was, because General Dung was about to pounce. Dung's plan was to attack first at Ban Me Thout, and then push south towards Saigon. And, that's exactly what he did on March 10. Ban Me Thout quickly fell, and the South Vietnamese soldiers began a hasty retreat southward. They hoped to regroup further south and stop Dung's advance, but there would be no stopping him.

By April 9, the NVA had reached Xuan Loc, the last line of defense north of Saigon. The South Vietnamese put up a stiff resistance there, but after several days of fighting, the NVA got the upper hand and the city fell. On April 21, South Vietnam's President Thieu resigned, loaded his worldly possessions in a borrowed U.S. cargo aircraft, and flew to Clark Air Base in the Philippines—the first stop on his way to exile. Theiu had reportedly pleaded with Washington for help, but by this time, President Ford had pretty much written off South Vietnam. His directions to U.S. generals in Saigon were to stall the South Vietnamese, while making them think that more funds would be forthcoming. But there was no stalling the NVA. They continued their march southward to Saigon, taking everything in their path and wiping out all resistance. On April 30, 1975, Saigon fell. The North Vietnamese immediately changed Saigon's name to Ho Chi Minh City, in honor to their hero.[117]

Meanwhile, back in Laos, 1975 had begun with ominous signs. All public meetings and demonstrations were banned. Becoming nervous, many influential business and political leaders began to quietly move their assets and families to Thailand, France and the United States. And, from their stronghold on the Plain of Jars, the Pathet Lao troops, supported by NVA soldiers and artillery, began advancing toward Vientiane. By late April, the Communists had taken the government installation at Sala Phou Khoum, opening up Route 13 towards Muang Kassy. By this time, the Pathet Lao had already heard about the fall of Saigon, and believed that victory in Laos was now within their reach. Meanwhile, more Rightists and RLG personnel continued to leave Laos, as the Pathet Lao quickly took over the Ministry of Defense. With this move, the RLA was no longer able to put up a defense against the Communists.

Now emboldened, the Pathet Lao took over all the major towns, and the population panicked as Vang Pao led his troops into exile in Thailand. At least a third of the country's population fled, and the Pathet Lao simply walked into Vientiane and took control in August 1975. For the next few months there was relative calm in Laos, as other countries offered aid and reconstruction personnel. Soon, Soviet engineers and other advisors from Eastern Bloc countries began to flow into Laos to fill the void left by the Americans.[118]

The King of Laos abdicated on December 2, 1975, and Souvanna Phouma resigned. The Lao People's Democratic Republic (LPDR) was then proclaimed, with Souphanouvong as its token President. Kaysone Phomvihane was installed as the Prime Minister, and he, in effect, ruled the country. Non-Communist newspapers were shut down, and the government agencies were purged of pro-Western supporters. Re-education camps began to open in many parts of Laos, and thousands of Lao citizens were carted off to these camps for detention. Many did not return from the camps, and others were held for many years before being released.

As far as Washington was concerned, the Southeast Asian debacle was over, with Laos being discarded into the dustbin of history along with Vietnam and Korea. But for the Hmong left behind in Laos, the story did not end.

Epilogue

As 1974 ended and 1975 began, the Secret War in Laos was winding down. There were still some pockets of resistance, but for the most part, hostilities had subsided. By May, the Pathet Lao had won what they viewed as the ultimate prize: the control of Laos. But it had been a costly undertaking for all parties involved. The United States had spent hundreds of millions of dollars annually on the war effort, and two million tons of ordnance had been dropped on Laos during the war. But much of that ordnance had not exploded, and remained a threat. In the conflict, the U.S. had lost approximately 600 U.S. personnel from about 1963 to 1975. Some were killed in action (KIA), others were missing in action (MIA), and many were believed held prisoner by the Pathet Lao and North Vietnamese as POWs. The combined losses of fixed-wing aircraft for the U.S. Navy, Air Force and Marine Corps in the skies over Laos totaled almost 500.[119] Dozens of U.S. military personnel were also killed on the ground in Laos while supporting the RLA, RLAF and Hmong SGU units, and the death toll for the Hmong exceeded 12,000.

We should also remember the brave men and women of Air America, Bird and Son, and Continental Air Services, who also sacrificed to support the Hmong guerrillas during the war, and sometimes gave their lives in the effort. They lost almost 250 personnel and many aircraft to hostile fire. But by 1975, most of the employees of the contract airlines had moved on to other opportunities. Many are still flying in support of other countries fighting for their freedom.

Even though the North Vietnamese government denied ever having troops in Laos, they continued to return to Laos on a regular basis for several years after the war to repatriate the remains of the thousands of NVA soldiers killed there. The Chinese, on the other hand, did not lose a significant number of military personnel in Laos, because they had mostly provided material aid to the Pathet Lao during the war, in the form of food, arms, ammunition, and medical supplies. They did not have actual ground combat units in Laos, even though they did provide some advisors.

As the United States withdrew from Laos in 1975, substantial numbers of advisors from other Communist countries poured into the country to fill the void thereby created. The U.S. was not permitted to retain advisors in Laos after 1975; but America was able to retain its embassy in Vientiane, along with a limited number of personnel to pursue the issue of U.S. POW/MIA personnel believed still held in Laos; and of course, the U.S. continued to provide limited financial aid to the war-torn country.

For a brief period after the war, things were relatively quiet in Laos. There were very few aircraft flying overhead, and the constant rumble of exploding bombs and artillery fire had pretty much subsided. Outwardly, everything appeared peaceful; but behind the scenes, there was a great deal of activity underway by the Lao People's Revolutionary Party (LPRP) in their quest to undermine and take over the government. It was during this period of time that many affluent Lao families in Vientiane elected to quietly slip across the Mekong River into the safety of Thailand. Thousands of Hmong personnel loyal to Vang Pao and the United States also began a hasty retreat to Thailand. As mentioned in Chapter 16, VP and a thousand or so of his most loyal followers were among the first refugees to arrive in Thailand.

The United States had already paved the way for their arrival by assisting the Thai government in converting a vacant military installation into a temporary settlement for the Hmong. Utilizing existing buildings, barracks and other facilities, the Hmong were able to settle in and prepare for relocation to the United States, France, Australia, or wherever they could receive assistance and permanent residence. The U.S. Embassy in Bangkok quickly ramped up its staff to process the Hmong families for resettlement to their new homes, by expediting the completion of all the required documentation.

Meanwhile, after assuming power in Laos in 1975, the LPRP continued to espouse its Marxist-Leninist doctrine and their intent to create a new socialist society. Their goals were to achieve socialist transformation, with so-called socialist construction. They claimed to have won the national democratic revolution by winning a "people's war" with a peasant alliance under the leadership of the LPRP. As a token gesture, the recently formed coalition government in Laos was retained for a brief period of time even though it was ineffective at best. King Savang Vatthana and his family were temporarily allowed to remain in Luang Prabang, with the king given a token title as an advisor to President Souphanouvong.

But any pretensions that Laos' new Communist government was anything but totalitarian soon fell by the wayside. Conversations about freedom of expression quickly ceased, and newspapers with views differing from those of the government were closed down. Then the purges began within the Coalition government, and many government and police officials were carted off to the re-education centers. As personal freedoms disappeared, still more Lao citizens began to flee: they simply boarded up their property and crossed the river into Thailand.

In December 1975, the King abdicated. He and his family were soon rounded up and taken to a re-education center in northern Laos.

Meanwhile, the RLG officers, high-level civilian governors, and district chiefs were also rounded up and transferred to northern Laos, where they were held in so-called "seminar camps." The LPRP also rounded up thousands of others they labeled as social deviants: prostitutes, drug addicts, gamblers, thieves, orphans and malcontents. All told, the number of detainees rapidly climbed to more than 30,000. Some were held for only a few months, some for several years, with some being held as long as ten years while the LPRP attempted to convince them to become loyal Communists.

Initially, there were a half-dozen or so re-education camps in northern Laos. They were simply identified by numbers, beginning with "1" and ending with "6." The most notorious was Camp 1, near the town of Sop Hao. This particular reeducation center was nothing more than a maximum security prison designed to hold the most incorrigible leaders from the former Lao Republic. The irony of the situation was there was no reeducation taking place. The inmates were starved to death and forced to work on hard-labor projects, like road construction, bridge building, and clearing of unexploded ordnance. Many either starved to death or died from dysentery. If either of those options didn't result in death, the Pathet Lao would simply execute the prisoners at the rate of one or two each day.

As the number of detainees increased in the prison system, more prisons had to be constructed. Some were built near Vientiane and in central Laos. Later, still more prisons were built in the southern part of the country. Petty criminals, prostitutes, and lower-ranking military personnel were selected for re-education into the Communist doctrine. If any detainee rejected the re-education process, he or she would be transferred to Camp 1 for final disposition.

The King, Queen, other royal family members, and most of the former Lao military hierarchy all died at Camp 1. Like the other prisoners there, they starved to death, died of disease, or were executed at the hands of the Pathet Lao.

As the LPDR continued to tighten their grip on Laos, tens of thousands of refugees crossed the Mekong River into Thailand, quickly inundating the refugee system. Soon, all the available facilities were overcrowded, and new refugee camps had to be built as quickly as possible. The Lao refugees were crammed into cramped quarters, and were not allowed to leave the camps. The U.S. provided funding to reimburse the Thai government for maintaining the refugee camps, but relations between the Hmong and the Thai became strained. The Thais were fearful that even more Hmong would seek refuge in Thailand; and the bigger question was, would North Vietnam retaliate against Thailand for providing sanctuary to the Hmong? No one knew the answer for sure, but it appeared that no such intentions were being considered by the Communists.

Later, with so many of the Hmong biding their time in the refugee centers while awaiting sponsors in other countries, they became candidates for the resistance movement. VP and other former Lao generals quickly recruited resistance fighters and sent them on cross-border raids into Laos. Of course, these pinpricks did not seriously threaten the LPDR, but dealing with the resistance did require quite a bit of time and money. The resistance fighters would blow up bridges and roads and interrupt communications lines, among other acts of sabotage. But as time passed, relations between Laos and Thailand slowly improved, and the cross-border raids began to diminish. Meanwhile, the Hmong guerrillas and their families continued to flow into Thailand, and the refugee population swelled.

During the summer of 1975, VP and his family departed Thailand for France, and then moved on to permanent exile in America. With the assistance of the U.S. Government, they initially settled in Montana on a small ranch. Many refugees soon followed VP to America and a new life. But VP did not sit around and watch the grass grow: he immediately swung into action, seeking support for the Hmong resistance fighters left behind in Laos. Naturally, he turned to his old benefactor, the United States. At the time, America was already providing arms and money to the resistance in Cambodia, so some of the money from that effort was diverted to the resistance in Laos. VP then began making frequent trips to Thailand, where he met with the resistance to discuss strategy and tactics. But it wasn't long before Thai government officials began to worry about the Hmong resistance operating from Thai soil.

The issues that influenced the Thai Government's reluctance to support VP's resistance fighters were twofold. First, public opinion in SEA had begun to change. The United States was not looked upon favorably any longer, based upon the debacle in Laos and South Vietnam. Secondly, with the Communists taking over Vietnam and Laos, there wasn't much to stop them from punishing Thailand for supporting VP and the Americans. And, at that juncture, Thailand did not care to test the Communists.

Meanwhile, in the U.S., the Lao refugees were rapidly settling in and getting established. But the Hmong had no intentions of becoming permanent residents of the United States. Their goal was to retake their country from the Communists and return home to their mountains. So VP and the others later formed the United Lao National Liberation Front (ULNLF) to support the Hmong resistance in Laos. The ULNLF was also known as "Neo Hom." The Neo Hom had two objectives: to break the silence and inform the world about what was taking place in Laos, and to obtain support for the Neo Hom resistance in Laos.

Soon, public officials in Washington were being visited by VP and others beating the drum for funds to support the ULNLF. The Lao settlers in America were also asked to dig deep into their pockets to help fund the resistance in Laos. They contributed what little they could, and every little bit helped. But as the resistance began to heat up, China, North Vietnam and the Soviet Union began to apply pressure on Thailand to discontinue support to the Hmong resistance. Feeling the heat, the Thai government began to discourage Neo Hom activities in Thailand. Support in the U.S. government also began to wane, because America was already embroiled in new conflicts in other parts of the world. The U.S. even went so far as to enact legislation making it a federal crime for private persons to provide assistance to the guerrillas. The law essentially curtailed VP's and the Neo Hom's support of the resistance in Laos, and would later be used against VP himself.

Meanwhile, back in Laos, a new one-party government had been installed. It consisted of a President (Soupannavong), who was also Secretary General (leader) of the party. Under the President was the Prime Minister. Government policies were determined by a nine-member Politburo and a forty-nine member Central Committee. While there was resistance to the LPDR and its one-party domination of power, the Lao citizens at large initiated little resistance, given their passive nature. They just accepted the new order, because they had no other alternative. Lao Communist officials did not hesitate to justify their rationale for one-party rule. They said that the country was too underdeveloped, that the citizens were not sufficiently educated to make choices as to who should rule, and that the people could not understand a government ruled by multiple parties in any case. The LPDR also explained that one-party rule was necessary in order to continue economic growth.

Some educated Lao citizens have begun to speak out in recent years, however, and have conducted some protests. But even with the break-up of the Soviet Union and other Communist countries, Laos remains Communist. One would think that the Lao intellectuals would have attempted to rally the citizens into challenging the Communists in Laos, but that hasn't happened. In fact, the Politburo has remained united. By the late 1980s, human rights advocates in Laos did begin to gain some ground in obtaining more individual liberties. Most of the re-education centers were closed, and the last of the surviving detainees were merged back into society.

Later, with support for Communism waning in the Soviet Union and economic hard times in Vietnam, the LPDR had to look outward to survive. Relations with other countries in the Southeast Asia region were encouraged; and beginning in April 1994, Lao citizens with identification cards and tourists with passports and visas could travel freely within Laos, except to certain restricted zones like Long Tieng. In recent years, travel to and from Thailand has also been encouraged. Tourists to Laos from the United States and Europe are now welcomed guests, and the government has even allowed guided tours of some of the Pathet Lao caves in northern Laos.

The relationship between Thailand and Laos has been an on again/off again situation for the three decades since Laos became a Communist country. In recent years, Thailand has stopped supporting the Hmong resistance completely and discouraged refugees, improving relations even more. Relations between Laos and North Vietnam have remained strong since the war, but relations with China have ebbed and flowed. If you recall, China was the main contributor for arms and supplies during the war, while North Vietnam provided the foot soldiers and manpower to fight the war; but once the war was over, Laos did not feel any need to remain close to China.

Nonetheless, China has persisted, and the LPDR finally ordered Peking (Beijing) to remove all their troops and workers from Laos, just as soon as all road construction projects were completed. China complied, and immediately began to provide guns and ammunition to VP's resistance fighters left behind in the jungles of Laos. Not surprisingly, the construction of roads in Laos by China slowed down considerably, allowing them continued access to the country.

Laos' relations with the Soviet Union also remained strong until the early 1980s, when Communism began to lose its grip in Europe and funding from the Soviets quickly dried up for Laos and North Vietnam. The Soviet Union then withdrew most of its embassy personnel from SEA. This left Laos no choice but to once again cozy up to China for aid and technology. Presently, China and Thailand provide most of the aid to Laos, with North Vietnam also providing what it can.

From an economic standpoint, when the Secret War ended, the newly-formed LPDR found itself with a bankrupt state. Heretofore, aid from the United States had provided the stimulus for the economy, but the majority of assistance from America was no longer available. The LPDR therefore felt it had no alternative but to impose taxes on agriculture. The result was animosity among the simple farmers, the very group that the LPDR claimed to represent. The Party then realized that they would have to move slowly in reforming the economy. In 1978, following Hanoi's lead, the LPDR launched a program to collectivize agriculture. But the environment in Laos, and the mindset of the indigenous Lao, did not bode well for such a move, and so collectivization quickly fizzled; a year or so later, the government announced an end to the policy. By 1980, fewer than five percent of the collectives were still operating. Also by 1980, it became clear that the economic reforms still had not been effective, and the LPDR initiated new economic reforms in a program called the New Economic Mechanism (NEM), decentralizing administrative controls on pricing, production and wages.

In the years following the creation of the NEM, the Lao government encouraged private enterprise, and relaxed centralized control over it. It took several years, however, for legislation to catch up with the economic reforms. During the 1980s, the LPDR continued to encourage agriculture through private ownership, and also encouraged private business enterprises. With the privatization of state enterprises, commercial business did improve and expand, but unfortunately laws and regulations to support market institutions and private property rights lagged far behind. By the early 1990s, bankruptcy and liquidations laws had been passed. Some of the Lao businessmen who fled in 1975 slowly began to return, and have since reopened their shuttered businesses.

Laos also reached out to the United Nations for development aid. The UN responded, but reminded the LPDR that the country needed to draft a constitution guaranteeing individual rights in order to continue receiving aid. Finally, on August 14, 1991—after 16 years of lip service—the Supreme People's Assembly (SPA) finally adopted a constitution. The new constitution purported to guarantee freedom of speech, and petition, and it talked of equality among ethnic tribes and respect for religion, including Buddhism. Also, the State agreed to protect the right of private ownership, with the goal of transforming the economy into one of good production.

With a new constitution and aid from the United Nations, dollars flowed in, the Lao economy steadily improved until 1997, when a financial crisis engulfed Thailand. And, inasmuch as the economy of Laos and Thailand were intertwined, the currency of both countries began to slide. Unfortunately, the single party system in Laos also became an obstacle to economic development. Understandably, the economy continued to struggle through the late 1900s, but began to improve with the dawn of the twenty-first century. But even as the economic situation began to improve, the government lagged behind in instituting the necessary financial systems to support the expanding economy.

Today, the LPDR still depends on aid from other countries. From 1975-1978 alone, Laos received more than $200,000,000 in technical assistance and commodity aid from other countries. This overdependence on foreign aid continued into the 1980s, when it was estimated that almost 80% of the annual Laotian revenue came from aid. Most has been provided by the International Monetary Fund (of which the United States is the primary contributor, ironically). The U.S. has also provided shipments of food and medicine to Laos, with the stipulation that the LPDR provide assistance in recovering the remains of U.S. servicemen killed or missing in Laos during the Secret War.

But, it's one thing to quote facts and figures, and quite another to hear from an unbiased American who actually spent time in Laos after the Communist takeover. That's exactly what we're going to look at next. In 1997, half a world away from Laos, a graduating senior at Princeton by the name of Brett Dakin noticed a job posting on a bulletin board at the university. It announced that a job existed for an American in Laos at the National Tourism Authority (NTA). The job posting provided very little information, but it did pique Dakin's interest—and the university had agreed to provide a stipend for room and board to the successful applicant. Out of curiosity, Dakin applied for the position, but didn't think much more about it until he learned that he had been accepted. After graduation in 1998, he set off on his journey to Laos, not really knowing what to expect. Upon arrival in Laos, he resided in Vientiane, the business capital of Laos, for approximately two years, and lived entirely on the local economy and even learned the Lao language.

Dakin lived in an ordinary neighborhood with other Lao citizens, eating at the same restaurants. He made friends with the Lao and other foreigners like himself, and traveled into the countryside at every opportunity to discover and experience the new Communist country. He resided in Laos until 2000, at which time his contract ended and he returned to the United States. Afterward he wrote a book entitled *Another Quiet American: Stories of Life in Laos*, which was published by Asia Books in 2003.

The book provides an outsider's observations of a country that embraced Communism and tried to make it work. It explains how Laos struggled after the United States pulled out in 1975, and how little progress was made in successfully implementing the Communist model. Dakin observed that few roads were paved in Vientiane, and that Wattay Airport had not been substantially modernized since the Americans left in 1975. In addition to little progress being made in the infrastructure of the country, and little stimulation to the economy, the government was hardly even capable of conducting day-to-day business. Corruption still ran deep; most of the income from the few export industries in operation, like logging, was siphoned off by the former Pathet Lao generals running the country. In some government offices like the NTA, where Dakin worked, there were only a few computers available, and at times they didn't even have ink cartridges for the printers. He found it odd that the very office promoting tourism had great difficulty even communicating with the outside world.

In his book, Dakin also talked about the ordinary people who went about their daily lives, unaware of what the government was doing and how it would affect them. These simple people had seen the French and Americans come and go from their country, leaving it better off in some cases, worse off in others. These ordinary people did not appear to be concerned about what was happening in Washington or Hanoi, but were completely consumed by their own traditions and culture. They also held strong in their belief that Buddha would take care of them, and that whatever else happened was simply beyond their control. They lived in the moment and tried to make the best of it. But should we be surprised at their behavior, when they had no say in how the country was being run, and knew little of what was going on outside Laos?

During the twenty-five years that have passed since the Communist took over, most of the former Pathet Lao leaders have died, resulting in a softening of the government's hard-line view towards noncommunist nations. As a result, Laos is beginning to reach out to the rest of the world. Relations between Laos and Thailand have also improved significantly; trade takes place freely between the two countries, as Laos becomes an increasingly vibrant market for goods from Thailand. Soon Laos will be providing most of the hydroelectric power to Thailand. If managed correctly, the income from the venture could very well bring Laos considerable wealth and power, and this could result in a win-win situation for both countries.

And then there's China, which has completed many highway projects in Laos, providing a valuable conduit for goods to flow between the two countries. Vietnam is still a good friend to Vientiane, but can contribute little from a military standpoint. In fact, it is a very poor country today. Russia has also provided aid to Laos, but since the break-up of the old Soviet Union, that support has diminished significantly. There are some Russian aircraft still present on the airfield near Vientiane, but it's not a real air force. Some of the aircraft may be capable of flying, but their ability to *fight* is a completely different issue. What China will do in the future is anyone's guess, but they certainly have the capability to take over Laos and Vietnam with relative ease. The Lao and the Vietnamese are well-aware of that fact, and live with that knowledge every day. And we know the history of Laos: they were not, and are not, a war-like people.

As far as the POW/MIA issue goes, their status remains unresolved for the most part. The United States is still very active in trying to locate the Americans left behind in Laos; the LPDR does allow access, but very little assistance. Some remains have been recovered and repatriated, but many areas remain off-limits. And, of course, one nagging question still remains: why hasn't the LPDR made a full accounting of the missing? For one thing, it's more beneficial, financially, if they don't; because as long as we have people in Laos looking for the prisoners and the missing, money will continue to flow into the country in the form of aid. Also, at this juncture it would be incredibly embarrassing for Laos to admit that they held POWs after the Secret War ended. If they admitted that fact, it could seriously jeopardize their fragile reputation in the international community. So it's much more advantageous for them to just remain silent and let the United States continue its work in locating and returning the remains of the POW/MIA on a piecemeal basis. And, remember, dead men don't talk.

By now, you're probably wondering what happened to Vang Pao and the loyal followers who were able to safely get out of Laos before the Communists took over. We've already addressed the issue of the Neo Hom, and VP's determination to keep that effort going—but where he is today, and what is he up to? Actually, VP is alive and well, living in southern California. He's still determined to return to Laos with his Hmong followers and live in peace; in fact, he promised that he *would* return in early 2010, but as of this writing, that promise is yet to be fulfilled. It's not because he isn't trying, because he is. It's just that he has been unable to obtain permission from either the LPDR or the government in Thailand to return to the region—and in fact, both countries appear to be very much against such an experiment.

To complicate matters, VP and several of his followers were arrested in 2005 by the U.S. Bureau of Alcohol, Tobacco, and

Firearms (ATF) for allegedly attempting to purchase arms and other war-making materials for the Hmong resistance in Laos. The charges against VP were reportedly dropped by the U.S. government in 2009, but several of his followers must still face the charges against them.

It will be interesting to watch as events continue to unfold in Laos. Many questions remain. What is China's real master plan for Laos when the last of the old Pathet Lao leaders die? We don't know, but I'm sure China has such a plan prepared. Vietnam can only stand back and watch, because like circumstances will affect their country as all the old Viet Minh leaders pass on to their eternal rewards. One thing we do know is that there's not a strong base in Laos from which to choose new people who can lead the country. Despite the horrors of the Secret War, the Lao were, are, and probably always will be passive in nature, not prone to conflict and bold moves. But there's nothing wrong with that: in fact, the world could learn much from the easygoing Lao people. We need a world where peace prevails, and where people can live in harmony. And perhaps China's strategies all along was to just wait until the time was right, and then offer a helping hand when the people of Vietnam, Laos and Cambodia have no other country to turn to.

In the final analysis, the United States let Laos down; we failed to live up to our agreements with them. Hundreds of missing Americans from the Secret War have not yet come home. Families wait, Americans wonder, and the Lao remember. We can only continue to wait and watch as events in Southeast Asia unfold.

After all the fighting and dying, one wonders what life in Southeast Asia would have been like today if President Eisenhower had decided to exercise the ultimate option in 1954, and had dropped a few well-placed atomic bombs on North Vietnam. If that event had taken place, there might have never been a Vietnam War, or a Secret War in Laos. Vietnam, Laos and Cambodia might have become thriving countries . . . and the U.S. itself might not have been torn apart from the inside by the strife and unrest that resulted from the war. Had the United States exercised the ultimate action in 1954, China may have responded militarily, but it's doubtful that they would have been successful—because a few more well-placed atomic bombs could have eliminated any will to fight on the part of the Chinese.

In the bigger picture, our defeat in Vietnam and Laos has made us a weaker nation, still divided by that conflict. The rest of the world also remembers how we let our allies down, and our weakness has emboldened terrorists around the world. Sadly, we will never know how things would have turned out if we had taken bold decisive action in 1954. But some things haven't changed, because the United States is currently consumed by the War on Terrorism and the war in Afghanistan, which is similar in many ways to the Secret War in Laos. But there will always be wars to fight, causes to champion, and evil forces to eliminate. And, we, the ordinary citizens, of the world will continue to live our lives in the hope that things will get better.

God bless America, and all mankind.

References

Books

Bailey, Lawrence R., Jr., with Ron Martz. *Solitary Survivor: The First American POW in Southeast Asia.* Brassey: Washington, D.C, 2003.

Conboy, Kenneth, with James Morrison. *Shadow War: The CIA's Secret War in Laos.* Paladin Press: Boulder, 1995.

Curry, Robert. *Whispering Death: Our Journey With the Hmong in the Secret War for Laos.* iUniverse: New York, 2004.

Dakin, Brett. *Another Quiet American: Stories of Life in Laos.* Asia Books: Bangkok, 2003

Davis, Charles O. *Across the Mekong: The True Story of an Air America Helicopter Pilot.* Hildesigns: Charlottesville, 1996.

Dorr, Robert F. *Chopper: A History of American Military Helicopter Operations from WWII to the War on Terror.* Berkley: New York, 2005.

Doyle, Edward, and Samuel Lippsman. *Setting the Stage: The Vietnam Experience.* Boston Publishing: Boston, 1981.

Fall, Bernard B. *Street Without Joy: A Poignant, Angry, Articulate Book on the French Debacle in Indochina.* Stackpole: Mechanicsburg, 1994.

Gup, Ted. *The Book of Honor: Covert Lives and Classified Deaths at the CIA.* Doubleday: New York, 2000.

Halliday, John T. *Flying Through Midnight: A Pilot's Dramatic Story of his Secret Missions Over Laos During the Vietnam War.* Scribner: New York, 2005.

Hathorn, Reginald. *Here There Are Tigers: The Secret Air War in Laos, 1968-69.* Stackpole: Mechanicsburg, 2008.

Lederer, William J. *A Nation of Sheep.* W.W. Norton: New York, 1961.

McCoy, Alfred W. *The Politics of Heroin: CIA Complicity in the Global Drug Trade.* Lawrence Hill: Chicago, 1991.

Merritt, Jane Hamilton. *Tragic Mountains: The Hmong, the Americans, and the Secret Wars for Laos, 1942-1992.* Indiana University Press: Bloomington, 1999.

Morrison, Gayle L. *Sky Is Falling: An Oral History of the CIA's Evacuation of the Hmong from Laos.* McFarland: North Carolina, 1999.

Nyc, Frederick F. III. *Blind Bat: C-130 Night Forward Air Controller, Ho Chi Minh Trail.* Eakin: Austin, 2000.

Prados, John Safe for Democracy: *The Secret Wars of the CIA.* Ivan R. Dee: Chicago. 2006.

Prados, John. *The Sky Would Fall: Operation Vulture, The Secret U.S. Bombing Mission to Vietnam.* Dial Press: New York, 1983.

Pratt, John Clark. *The Laotian Fragments.* Viking: New York, 1974.

Quincey, Keith. *Harvesting Pa Chay's Wheat: The Hmong and America's Secret War in Laos.* EWU: Spokane, 2000.

Robbins, Christopher. *The Ravens: The Men who Flew in America's Secret War in Laos.* Crown: New York, 1987.

Robbins, Christopher. *Air America: The Story of the CIA's Secret Airlines.* Putnam: New York, 1979.

Schanche, Don A. *Mister Pop: The Adventures of a Peaceful Man in a Small War.* David McKay: New York, 1970.

Schemmer, Benjamin F. *The Raid: The Son Tay Prison Rescue Mission.* Ballentine: New York, 2002.

Schlight, John. *A War Too Long: The History of the USAF in Southeast Asia.* U. S. Air Force: Washington, D.C., 1996.

Secord, Richard. *Honored and Betrayed: Irangate, Covert Affairs, and the Secret War in Laos.* John Wiley & Sons: New York, 1992.

Shultz, Richard H., Jr. *The Secret War Against Hanoi: Kennedy's and Johnson's Use of Spies, Saboteurs, and Covert Warriors in North Vietnam.* Harper Collins: New York, 1999.

Stevenson, Charles A. *The End of Nowhere: American Policy Toward Laos Since 1954.* Beacon Press: Boston, 1973.

Sutton, Richard O. *Operation White Star.* Daring: Canton, 1990.

Tilford, Earl H., Jr. *Search and Rescue in Southeast Asia: The United States Air Force.* U.S. Air Force: Washington, D.C., 1992.

Warner, Roger. *Shooting at the Moon: The Story of America's Clandestine War in Laos.* Steerforth: South Royalton, 1996.

Weldon, Charles, M.D. *Tragedy in Paradise: A Country Doctor at War in Laos.* Asia Books: Bangkok, 1999.

Yenne, Bill. *Attack of the Drones: A History of Unmanned Aerial Combat.* Zenith Press: China, 2004.

Documents

Anthony, Victor B. and Richard R. Sexton. *The War in Northern Laos (1954-1973): The United States Air Force in Southeast Asia.* USAF, 2001.

Blaufarb, Douglas S. *Organizing and Managing Unconventional War in Laos (1962-1970).* Rand Corporation, 1971.

Blout, Lt. Colonel Harry D. *Air Operations In Northern Laos (1 Apr-1 Nov 70): A Project CHECO Report.* USAF, 1973.

Burch, Lt. Colonel Robert M. Command and Control (1966-1968(: A Project Checo Report. USAF (undated).

Burch, Major Robert M. *The ABCCC in SEA: A Project CHECO Report.* USAF, 1968.

Butler, Jimmie H. *College Eye: A Project CHECO Report-Selected Excerpts.* USAF 1969.

Collins, Captain Charles V. *Herbicide Operations In Southeast Asia July (1961-June, 1967): A Project CHECO Report.* USAF, 1970.

Elder, Major Paul W. *Buffalo Hunter (1970-1972): A Project CHECO Report.* USAF,1970.

Futrell, Robert F., assisted by Martin Blumenson. *The Advisory Years to 1965: The U.S. Air Force in Southeast Asia.* USAF, 1967.

Hoadley, Daniel S. *"The Junkyard Air Force": The A-26A Nimrod In Combat Over Laos (1966-69).* Educational Submission, 1993.

Knox, Captain Thomas R. *Corona Harvest, Waterpump, 1964-1965.* USAF, 1973.

Leary, William M. *CIA Air Operations in Laos (1955-1974): Supporting the Secret War.* CIA, 1972.

McCrea, Michael M. *U.S. Navy, Marine Corps, and Air Force Fixed-Wing Aircraft Losses and Damage in Southeast Asia (1962-1973).* U.S. Navy, 1969.

Liebchen, Captain Peter A.W. *MAP Aid To Laos (1959-1972): A Project CHECO Report.* USAF, 1992.

Porter, Captain Melvin F. *Second Defense of Lima Site 36: A Project CHECO Report.* USAF, 1967.

Porter, Captain Melvin F. *Commando Vault: A Project CHECO Report.* USAF, 1981.

Unknown. Cable Authorizing Air Strikes on Laos Infiltration Routes (#83). U.S. Department of State and Department of Defense. 1968.

Unknown. *The Battle for Skyline Ridge (1971-72): The CIA and the "Secret War in Laos."* USAF, date unknown.

Vallentiny, Captain Edward. *The Fall Of Site 85: A Project CHECO Report.* USAF, 1993.

Vallentiny, Captain Edward. *USAF Operations from Thailand (Jan.1967 To Jul. 1968): A Project CHECO Report.* USAF, 1976

Van Staaveren, Jacob Interdiction in Southern Laos (1960-1968). USAF, date unknown.

Websites

http://aviation-safety.net/database
http://countrystudies.us/laos
http://firefly33.com
http://gandarmount.wordpress.com
http://wgordon.web.wesleyan.edu
www.1stmob.com
www.ac-119gunships.com
www.af.mil
www.af.mil/bios
www.afa.org
www.aiipowmia.com
www.aircommandos.org
www.airwarvietnam.com
www.arlingtoncemetery.net
www.b-57canberra.org
www.chancefac.net
www.combatweather.org
www.defenselink.mil
www.ec47.com
www.globalsecurity.org
www.ibiblio.org
www.limasite85.us
www.nationalmuseum.af.mil
www.nationsencyclopedia.com
www.nexus.net~911gfx/aircraftlosses.html
www.ov-10bronco.net
www.pacom.mil/jtffa.htm
www.pjsinnam.com

www.pownetwork.org
www.psywarrior.com
www.scopesys.com
www.specialoperations.net
www.spyflight.co.uk/rf4c.htm
www.taskforceomegainc.org
www.usvetdsp.com
www.vietnam.ttu.edu
www.vietnamgear.com
www.vietnamwar.com
www.virtualwall.org
www.wikipedia.org

Endnotes

Introduction

[1] *Nation of Sheep* explains America's flawed foreign policy approach at home and abroad. Lederer was also an associate author of another popular book around that same time, *The Ugly American*, which pointed out how the United States could improve its image abroad. As well as being an author, Lederer was a West Point graduate and served in the U.S. Navy in Southeast Asia.

Chapter 1

[2] The term *Viet Minh* means "League for the Independence of Vietnam." Described as a national liberation movement, it was formed by Ho Chi Minh in 1941 to seek independence from France, and to oppose the Japanese occupation. As strange as it may seem, the Viet Minh was initially funded, in part, by the United States. In fact, Ho Chi Minh was a paid asset of the forerunner to the CIA, the Office of Strategic Services (OSS).

[3] Bernard B. Fall was a recognized journalist and scholar who traveled extensively with the French during the First Indochina War, and later with the United States in South Vietnam. He wrote many books and articles about Southeast Asia. He lost his life in South Vietnam while accompanying U.S. Marines on a routine patrol in 1967, when he stepped on an Improvised Explosive Device (IED) planted by the Vietcong. *Street without Joy*, published by Stackpole Books in 1964, describes the final days of the First Indochina War. Fall also wrote *Hell in a Very Small Place* (Dien Bien Phu), also published by Stackpole Books.

[4] Though as luck would have it, early on in the war, in what was called "Operation Lea," French paratroopers dropped right on top of a village where Ho Chi Minh was hiding out. Ho would have been captured, but just minutes before the arrival of the French, he had escaped into the jungle. Needless to say, the French were never lucky enough to come that close to capturing Ho again.

[5] Aid or way stations were strategically located alongside the trails throughout areas of conflict. The stations contained medical equipment,

personnel, food, water, supplies and ammunition. The Viet Minh had dedicated personnel whose sole job was to provision and preserve the way stations. They also had dedicated forces to patrol and keep the trails and way stations safe.

6   This was odd, because the trail through Dien Bien Phu was neither the only viable way of entering Laos, nor was it the most direct route. There were other, more direct points of entry.

7   Upon assuming the office of President, Eisenhower was determined to balance the government's out-of-control budget. One of his ideas was to make the Army smaller and lighter, and the Navy and Air Force more powerful in the event that atomic weapons needed to be used against enemies. Ike believed that the use of atomic bombs would greatly shorten the length of future wars and conflicts. I mention this because of an operation in the planning stages at the time called "Operation Vulture."

8   For complete details of the battle of Dien Bien Phu, read Bernard B. Fall's *Hell in a Very Small Place*.

9   The United States refused to participate in the talks, and declined to recognize the accords that were reached there.

Chapter 2

10   As mentioned in Chapter One, very few made it out, most disappearing mysteriously along the way.

Chapter 3

11   CAT was later renamed Air America.

12   The first Green Berets assigned to the PEO as advisors were part of what was called Operation Hotfoot. These soldiers wore civilian clothes and were referred to as "Mister." They were officially classified as technicians. Their role, however, was to train, equip and mentor guerrilla forces. They were not officially allowed to take up arms against the Communist forces in Laos, except in situations requiring them to protect their own lives.

13   In conjunction with SEATO, Joint Task Force 116 was deployed from Okinawa to Thailand. The Task Force included a US Marine Battalion Landing Team (BLT); the battle groups, Infantry troops, and supporting elements under a detachment of the Logistical Command, which also

included elements of Aviation Company (Caribou); a Field Hospital; and a Signal Company. As necessary, the other U.S. military services would provide specialists to the JTF as needed.

14   IVS was contracted to USAID to train Lao farmers in various agricultural projects.

15   Telegrams from this period were usually written in a cryptic fashion, and the rules of grammar, punctuation and form did not always prevail. For the sake of brevity, some material in the telegrams was left out.

16   The SC-47 was a converted C-47 transport aircraft with special cameras and other related gear installed to conduct surveillance and photographic reconnaissance. Other variants were the EC-47, RC-47 and VC-47, to name a few. Inasmuch as this was a versatile aircraft, it was reconfigured as necessary, depending on mission requirements.

17   This problem would be corrected in later MAP budgets, when funds for fourteen T-28s (configured as strike aircraft) were included.

18   Some sources indicate that this meeting took place on March 13, 1961. A review of the White House Diary for the month of March 1961 indicates the meeting was most likely held on March 6. On March 13, the President's day was pretty much taken up by a visit from the head of a European country.

19   In any case, the obsolete T-6 (built in 1937) could carry only two rockets and enough machine gun ammunition for 16 seconds of firing, and had a top speed of just 140 knots.

20   Actually, the French hadn't been in a position to negotiate anything, considering that they lost the battle, and many of their own people were also POWs in North Vietnam.

21   As mentioned earlier, White Star personnel were actually U.S. Army Special Forces professionals. For some light and informative information on Operation White Star, consult *Operation White Star* by Richard O. Sutton, Daring Publishing, 1990.

22   Inasmuch as there were few improved roads in Laos and no other means of surface transportation, the only practical way to deliver supplies, equipment and troops was by air, using the Lima sites.

23   The U.S. Air Force personnel killed in the crash of the SC-47 (or EC-47, as it was also reported), were 1Lt. Ralph Magee (Pilot), SSgt. Alfonse Bukowski, SSgt. Frederick S. Garside, 2Lt. Glenn Matteson, SSgt. Leslie Sampson, and 1Lt. Oscar Weston (Co-Pilot).

24   The above quoted telegram is unusual in substance. It hits hard and gives specific instructions to U.S. personnel in Laos. This telegram literally

took the gloves off, and gave the embassy personnel the authority they needed to get the job done. The reader can well imagine the impact this telegram had when it arrived at the embassy in Vientiane.

25 The IVS residence where Captain Moon was held and executed was the same house used by IVS when Pop Buell came to Laos. It was located in the village of Lhat Houang.

26 Padong was an old French trading post that had been constructed and used as an opium trading base. It had several permanent structures and a dirt airstrip.

27 Early on in the Secret War, it was customary for the attackers to leave an avenue of escape from the battleground so noncombatants could escape to safety.

28 The names of the pilots were reportedly Walter Wizbowski and Charles Mateer. The H-34 also carried a mechanic, but there was no mention of his status. There was also a MAAG advisor on the aircraft who was wounded in the crash, but no additional information was provided about him, either.

29 Thao Ma was pressured by Generals Kouprasith Abhay and Ouane Rathikone to provide transport for their drug trade. These two generals wanted access to all C-47 aircraft under Thao Ma's control to smuggle gold and opium. They offered him $2,000 a week if he would cooperate, but he turned them down flat. The two generals then maneuvered to oust him from his command. Sadly, the CIA Chief of Station, Ted Shackley, approved of the plot, considering it a small price to pay for the two generals' cooperation in the Secret War.

Chapter 4

30 George Doole retired from Air America in 1971 and accepted employment at Evergreen International Aviation Company. He passed away anonymously on March 9, 1985 in Washington, D.C. He didn't tell anyone that he was sick, and when he died there was no obituary written. Nor was there was a memorial service, or flowers at his graveside service in his hometown of Liberty, Illinois.

Chapter 5

31 Landry had arrived in Laos in March 1961 with Anthony Poshepny (also known as Tony Poe), Tom Fosmire, Jack Shirley, and Tom Ahern.

32   You can read more about Doc Weldon and his amazing story in his book *Tragedy in Paradise: A Country Doctor at War in Laos*. Doc was always in the thick of the fight, along with Pop Buell, as the two worked tirelessly to help the humble and proud Hmong people in their struggle against the Communists.

33   Other sources cite the date of this incident as November 22 or November 29, but the best evidence suggests that it was November 27, 1962.

34   It should be mentioned that the effort to support Kong Le and Phoumi was in no way connected to the counterinsurgency program administered by the CIA and Vang Pao. The two programs were administered separately. The goal was the same, however, and that was to defeat the Communists and run North Vietnam out of Laos.

35   The information regarding Pop Buell is included here only because it differs from the information reported by more reliable sources. As mentioned in the introduction to this book, facts were often reported incorrectly when events about the Secret War in Laos were recorded.

Chapter 6

36   Bacci is a ceremony to celebrate a special occasion. It could be a marriage, homecoming, birth, or a local holiday. It includes flowers, food, chants to Buddha, and the tying of strings around the wrists of the attendees. The strings represent continuity, friendship, and permanence.

37   This was the first time USAF pilots were used directly as FACs in support of ground forces in northern Laos.

38   Heretofore, the Huskies had mostly been used to rescue airmen trapped in downed aircraft during routine operations. They were not designed to be used in combat, and had no long-range capability.

39   In 2005, a declassified National Security Agency report indicated there were no North Vietnamese patrol boats in the area when the *U.S.S. Maddox* opened fire on August 4. This conflicts with other accounts indicating that the *Turner Joy* opened fire, not the *Maddox*. At any rate, the report concluded there was no provocation. U.S. Naval aviators over the area on that night had also reported no patrol boats in the area.

40   The HH-43 Huskies did not have the fuel range to fly nonstop from NKP to northern Laos, so crews loaded 55-gallon drums into the helicopters

and literally pumped fuel from the drums to the fuel tanks during flight in order to reach their destination.

[41] The dual nature of the war in Laos resulted in the expression "Parallel War" being adopted when describing the two efforts.

[42] The AGM-12 Bullpup missile was developed in 1962, and carried a 250-pound warhead. It was roll-stabilized and visually guided by the pilot or weapons operator, using a tracer on the back of the missile to track the weapon in flight while using a control joystick to steer it to the target using radio signals. It was initially powered by a solid fuel rocket motor.

[43] It was immediately apparent that Washington didn't understand its adversary. Ho Chi Minh had no intention of ending the war; the Viet Minh were in it for the long-haul. The French never understand that, and similarly, those prosecuting the war for the U.S. never got the point that conventional bombing wasn't the answer.

[44] The HH-43 operated at a ceiling of 25,000 feet with a range of 185 miles, and flew at a maximum speed of 120 mph. In other words, they were large targets in the sky.

[45] The term "sheep-dipping" originally referred to the dipping of sheep in a liquid insecticide solution to protect them from being bitten and infected by insects. The meaning of the term as it was used during the Secret War in Laos referred to taking U.S. military personnel and disguising them as U.S. civilians to give the appearance of compliance with the Geneva Accords of 1962, which restricted the assignment of U.S. military personnel in Laos.

[46] Since the early 1990s, numerous sites where the aircraft could have gone down have been investigated by the Department of Defense, and potential eyewitnesses were interviewed. In November 2004, the actual crash site was located and human remains were recovered. The remains were subsequently identified as those of Captain Baker and Captain Lewis. Aircraft fragments, specifically identifying the downed aircraft, were also found at the crash site.

[47] Bango was the call sign for the F-4 Phantoms, and Whiplash was the call sign for the F-105 Thunderchiefs.

[48] In 1965, China began construction of a road from their border through the northern part of Laos. The road passed through Moung Sing in Northwest Laos to Nam Tha, then down to Moung Sai. From Moung Sai it followed the Beng River southward to Pak Beng on the Mekong River. The Lao government didn't quite know why the road

was being constructed, but they didn't protest China's presence in Laos. China described the road as a humanitarian project, but the Lao remained cautious. The Thai government was against the road being constructed, but they were not in a position to do anything about it. As construction of the road progressed, the Chinese installed antiaircraft weapons to protect their workers. Any and all aircraft that came near the road were fair game, and the gunners would not hesitate to open fire. The U.S. avoided the area and restricted air operations near the road.

49 As mentioned earlier, the crews of the HH-43s placed a 55 gallon drum of fuel in the back of each helicopter, along with a hand pump allowing the crew to manually pump fuel from the barrel into the onboard fuel tank in order to extend the range of the HH-43, allowing it to reach LS-36.

50 The estimated range of the CH-3 aircraft was about 450 miles. Its cruising speed was 144 mph and it could carry a payload of approximately eight thousand pounds. Its operating ceiling was 11,000 feet. Reports regarding armor plating on the loaned CH-3s differed, with some reports indicating that that were armor plated, and others indicating they were not.

51 USAF rescue helicopters stood alert on most days at LS-36 and LS-20A to effect rescues as required. The helicopters would arrive early in the morning and stay at the site until sunset, when they would depart to the safety of nearby Thailand. Under some circumstances, the helicopters could remain overnight if authorized.

52 In mid-July 1962, a decision was made in Washington to transfer responsibility for the CIA's paramilitary programs in Vietnam to the U.S. military. The plan called for MACV to lead the effort utilizing a variety of covert operations directed against Hanoi. The objective of the operation was to cause the Communist leadership to divert resources from its insurgency in South Vietnam to deal with the threat posed by the penetrations by the United States. The belief was that over time, the insurgency would stop. The effort was called OPPLAN34-A, and it led to the creation of the Studies and Operations Group (SOG), a euphemism for the Special Operations Group (Green Berets). For additional information about OPPLAN34-A, see *The Secret War against Hanoi* by Richard H. Shultz, Jr. (Harper Collins, 1999).

53 A separate, unofficial source claims the two HH-43s were launched from NKP, Thailand. Neither was armor-plated.

54   As you may recall, LBJ was under the impression that at some point, the NVA would tire of fighting and agree to peace talks. So he would occasionally halt the bombing. The NVA weren't interested in peace, but they looked forward to the bombing halts because the halts gave them time to repair damage and restock their positions with ammunition and supplies.

55   Most TACAN units were more or less automated, and did not require the constant presence of technicians. The units did require occasional periodic maintenance, though, and some older model TACAN stations did require attendants.

56   The AC-47 was a converted C-47 military cargo plane, retrofitted with mini-guns and illumination flares on the port side of the aircraft. It is believed that this was the first time the AC-47 was used in combat in Laos.

57   Napalm is a mixture of benzene, gasoline and polystyrene. When the napalm canisters hit the ground, the momentum of the bomb causes an explosion, resulting in everything in its path being consumed by gelatinous balls of fire. The substance sticks to the skin and clothing, immediately resulting in third degree burns. The napalm also sucks all the oxygen out of the air when it explodes, making it extremely hard to breath.

58   The old Hmong ritual consisted of every person drinking from a cup of the same purified water. Drinking from the cup signified that each person was cleansed of past aggressions. This ritual also got everyone on the same sheet of music again, and all was forgiven.

59   It was not uncommon for POWs to be moved frequently while in captivity. One former prisoner recalled being moved approximately nine times during his period of incarceration.

60   Colonel Aderholt was on long term assignment to the CIA from the USAF, and was considered to be an expert in logistics acquisition. He could always be counted on to find and deliver the necessary implements of war. Early on in the Secret War, he was the first to deliver aircraft, bombs, weapons, ammunition and explosives to Vang Pao and his men.

Chapter 7

61   Lamplighter was the call sign for a C-130 aircraft used to drop illumination flares over required locations. The aircraft could also be used as a FAC aircraft under certain circumstances. The Lamplighter

aircraft were permanently assigned to Naha Air Base, Okinawa, and flew flare missions on a temporary duty basis from Ubon Air Base, Thailand. When flying over the southern portion of Laos (Steel Tiger), their call sign was "Blind Bat." When flying missions over North Vietnam and northern Laos, their call sign was "Lamp Lighter."

[62] The TSQ-81 radar equipment was developed and manufactured by the Reeves Instrument Corporation, Long Island, New York, and was a follow-on to the MSQ-77 Bomb Scoring System. The TSQ-81 was specifically developed to allow radar equipment technicians to direct bombs in any weather, directly onto the target. Of course, the TACAN unit was used for tactical air navigation.

Chapter 8

[63] "Raven" was the call sign for the FACs in Laos. The name was chosen based upon the many myths about the birds of prey of the same name. Ravens were considered to be the smartest and most cunning of birds, and were admired for their keen sense of perception.

[64] The mortality rate for the Ravens was estimated to be about fifty percent.

[65] There have been at least two books written about the Ravens: *The Ravens*, by Christopher Robbins, and *The Laotian Fragments* by John Clark Pratt.

Chapter 9

[66] The International Opium Commission's meeting in 1909, in Shanghai, represented the first steps toward international drug prohibition.

[67] A kilogram is roughly equivalent to a U.S. weight of 2.2 pounds.

[68] The information regarding the critiques of Mr. McCoy's books is available in the public domain.

Chapter 10

[69] The Muscle Shoals program was later renamed Igloo White, and the control facility at NKP was first called Blue Chip, and, later, Task Force Alpha.

[70] It should be noted there were conflicting reports concerning this incident. First, it was reported that both AN-2 Colts were downed by

ground fire. Another report indicated the helicopter chasing the Colts was a Bell 205 helicopter, and not a UH-1. The Bell 205 is a civilian version of the Bell UH-1 military helicopter.

71 On pages 181-205 of a book entitled *Military Region 2, Several Battles During the War of Liberation, 1945-1975, Vol. III,* published by the People's Army of Vietnam Publishing House, Hanoi, 1996, the following information is provided in a paragraph labeled "Summary": "Given the terrain features of Pha Thi, the deployment of enemy forces (Hmong, Thai and Americans), troop strength and firepower, defensive fortifications, and the enemy's operational procedures, it was obvious that it would be difficult to use a large attack force and hard to develop firepower. However, if we used the small size of a sapper force and appropriate tactics, we could achieve victory and a higher level of combat effectiveness."

72 The northwestern approach of the mountain was the area containing the footpath. From this approach, it was possible to climb and walk up the mountain to the summit. But it was difficult, and dangerous.

73 According to the reference mentioned previously, the NVA base of operations was in the vicinity of Muong Cau and Huoi Muoi in Moung Son District, a Pathet Lao liberated zone about 40 kilometers northwest of Pha Thi. The reference also indicated that on December 18, 1967, one eight-man sapper cell had reconnoitered Pha Thi. The cell conducted terrain reconnaissance, reconnoitered the enemy situation, searched for a concealed route of movement, and confirmed that the enemy command post was in the Pha Thi area. On January 22, 1968, two NVA reconnaissance cells resolved to do whatever it took to climb to the summit of the mountain and probe the radar navigation site. The cells did later climb to the top and reconnoitered the radar navigation site, as well as the Thai defenders' area, and the helicopter pad where CIA and Hmong forces resided and worked.

74 It was later realized that the flares from the Lamplighter may have actually aided the sappers by providing more visibility as they climbed the cliff.

75 The USAF technicians at the site were not trained combatants. At best they would possess minimal knowledge of firearms, but it was doubtful that they knew how to use any other weapons, or had received any training in hand-to-hand combat.

76 JTF-FA later became what is known today as the Joint POW/MIA Accounting Command (JPAC).

[77]   For an in-depth analysis of the events leading up to fall of LS-85 and information developed years later, please read Dr. Timothy Castle's book, *One Day Too Long.*

[78]   It's interesting that Momyer would point fingers at the embassy, when he personally disapproved the evacuation of the USAF personnel just hours before they were killed. At that time, the CIA had provided a report indicating that attack on the radar navigation site was imminent.

[79]   Bill Lair did not appear to be the sort of person who did things on a grand scale, with a large cast of players. Some viewed his approach as being pragmatic and methodical; he was known for thinking things through and initiating small actions to chip away at the Communists. But the fact was that the war had evolved into something much larger, requiring different tactics and bold action. Lair was, however, the right man at the right time, and he did an excellent job while assigned in Laos and Thailand.

[80]   The artificial horizon, or attitude indicator as it is also called, is a primary flight instrument used to inform the pilot of the orientation of the aircraft relative to the earth. Vertigo is a type of dizziness associated with a balance disorder. A person experiencing vertigo in an aircraft doesn't know which way is up or down. Vertigo can take place when a pilot can't see the sky above or the ground below to use as a reference.

[81]   A standard USAF SAR called for two rescue helicopters. One aircraft would be designated as the "Low" bird, and the other would be referred to as the "High" bird. The Low bird was the primary rescue aircraft, with the High bird serving as the back-up aircraft in the event one helicopter was insufficient for the rescue. If the primary became damaged or was shot down, the High bird would become the Low bird to rescue everybody on the ground.

Chapter 11

[82]   For additional information about the OV-1, read *Whispering Death: Our Journey with the Hmong in the Secret War for Laos*, by Robert Curry.

[83]   Some sources indicate that Vang Pao was the one pushing for a strike on the Chinese mission, not Souvanna. At any rate, the Chinese needed to be punished, it was felt, because they were the ones providing AK-47s and ammunition to the Pathet Lao.

[84]   As you may recall, Ambassador Godley had recently predicted this same scenario.

85   Official documentation conflicts regarding who developed Operation About Face, as both the USAF and Vang Pao took credit.

86   During Operation About Face, the U.S. bombing campaign included the use of Combat Skyspot (Bomb Directing Central Radar), LORAN-D (a terrestrial radio navigation system), and offset aiming points systems (Commando Nail), allowing all-weather bombing with greater accuracy.

87   U.S. pilots were prohibited from bombing in the buffer zone. Knowing that, the NVA would often stage their war supplies in the zone, because they felt it was safe to do so.

Chapter 12

88   Arc Light involved USAF B-52 bombers out of Anderson Air Base in Guam. Arc Light operations were most often close air support bombing raids of enemy base camps, troop concentrations, and supply lines.

89   The BLU-82 was developed under a program called Commando Vault that ran from November, 1967 to the latter part of 1970. Various payloads and detonation methods were used, depending on the objective.

90   One official report indicated that the NVA attack on May 15, 1970 was compromised when a Communist soldier stepped on a mine, alerting the defenders at LS-32 of the NVA's intention to attack.

91   The raid on Son Tay will be covered in-depth in a chapter to follow.

92   There is some disagreement concerning the actual number of RF-101 aircraft lost in Southeast Asia, but the number is believed to have been between 32 and 35.

Chapter 13

93   As of July 1967, the Scatback courier was no longer required to transport reconnaissance photographs, because a new system, "Compass Link," was established. Using a satellite relay system, reconnaissance photos could be transmitted electronically to Washington, D.C. in minutes.

94   The cost of one drone was approximately $200,000.

95   The flight engineer and PJ both survived and both were returned to duty after they had sufficiently mended. Both were recognized for their heroic efforts.

96 A similar program, "Blue Tree," was authorized for U.S. military aerial reconnaissance over North Vietnam.

Chapter 14

97 The reason for disassembling the mock-up of the village every night after training was because every day, a Soviet reconnaissance satellite orbited earth on a path over Eglin Air Force Base, at which time it would photograph activities and objects on the ground. The planners did not want them to see the mock village.

98 Other information indicates that President Nixon was not available for the meeting on October 8, 1970, and that he was briefed at a later date and approved the mission.

99 For more information about the Son Tay Raid, see the excellent book *The Raid* by Benjamin Schemmer, which provides an in-depth analysis of the operation. Another book, *At the Hurricane's Eye* by Greg Walker, also discusses the raid. Numerous government documents pertaining to the subject of Son Tay have been declassified, and are now available in the public domain.

Chapter 15

100 The CIA's budget for 1971 to support the Hmong guerrillas was approximately $70,000,000.

101 Operation Lam Son 719 was the brainchild of U.S. Army General Creighton Abrams, General Westmoreland's replacement in Saigon. Abrams' idea was to have the South Vietnamese Army push into Laos and cut the Ho Chi Minh Trail, depriving the NVA of much-need war supplies in South Vietnam. Most of the U.S. air power in Southeast Asia was diverted from other missions to support Lam Son 719. Abrams' plan may have looked good on paper, but within a few days after initiating the fight using 16,000 soldiers, the South Vietnamese were overpowered and had been slaughtered by 36,000 NVA regulars. With that whipping, Abrams had been officially welcomed to Vietnam by Ho Chi Minh.

102 Intelligence indicates that some of Dac Cong had been specifically tasked to eliminate the Ravens during the attack at Long Tieng.

103 Some sources indicate that this event took place on March 9, and others indicate that it was March 1, 1971.

[104] Some sources identify this gunship as an AC-47 Spooky; however, 7/13th Air Force sources list it as an AC-130 Spectre.

[105] Other accounts of the event indicated that one F-4 was shot down by artillery over Sam Neua, another was shot down by the MiG-21, and the third ran out of fuel. While the facts of what happened are not completely clear, what does seem consistent is that three F-4 Phantoms were lost that afternoon.

[106] Details regarding specific issues discussed by Kissinger and Brezhnev in April 1972 can be found in the National Archives at the Nixon Presidential Library.

[107] Aircraft 67-1625 would go on to serve the United States with distinction. On May 2,1999, using the call sign "Chalk 2," this aircraft was one of several used in the rescue of "Hammer 34," a USAF F-16 pilot downed over Serbia during Operation Allied Force. It also saw service during the war in Iraq. It was lost on November 23, 2003 while assigned to the 21st SOS during Operation Enduring Freedom, flying with the call sign "Beatle 12." On her last mission, she suffered compressor stall during take-off from a forward operating location. The helicopter crashed and was destroyed, and all personnel onboard were lost.

[108] This debacle became known simply as "Watergate," and before it was over, heads were certainly going to roll.

[109] Le Duc Tho was a Vietnamese revolutionary, general, diplomat and politician. He helped form the Indochinese Communist Party in 1930 and oversaw the Communist insurgency that began in 1956. In the early 1970s, he and Henry Kissinger engaged in secret talks that reportedly led to a ceasefire and the Paris Peace Accords.

[110] Other information has subsequently been received from a former Air America source, who related that Carroll landed his aircraft on the Plain of Jars after sustaining aircraft damage from Communist gunners on the ground. Upon landing, the enemy was reportedly all around Carroll, and apparently he somehow suffered a fatal head wound. Also according to the source, rescuers could see Carroll's body and the apparent head wound, but could not recover his body due to heavy ground fire.

[111] Another official USAF report listed Reiss' aircraft as an F-4 Phantom, not an A-7 as first reported. It could have been either, however, because the F-4 operated daily in northern Laos, and the A-7s were also active, having replaced the A-1 Skyraiders on November 7, 1972 at NKP. The A-7 was a single-engine attack aircraft that cruised at over five hundred

miles per hour, had a maximum range of two thousand miles, and could carry a variety of missiles and up to 20,000 pounds of bombs.

Chapter 16

[112] These units would continue operations until the base closed down completely in June 1975.

[113] The accords were signed by Tran Van Lam, Minister of Foreign Affairs and the Republic of South Vietnam's representative at the Paris Peace Talks.

[114] General Vogt reminded Ambassador Godley that if and when the RLG and Pathet Lao signed a ceasefire agreement, USAF air power would be withdrawn and Pak Song would most likely be retaken by the Communists. (And that's exactly what happened).

[115] Because there are several variations of the story about which shot Thao Ma and what happened afterward, we can never be sure exactly what did take place. What we know for sure, however, is that Thao Ma was killed that day, after his failed coup.

[116] Like many other events reported in Laos, the information regarding Dean and his capture varied, based upon the source(s) of the reports. It is known, however, that he was detained by the Pathet Lao in 1974 and did not return alive.

[117] General Dung's star continued to shine for several years after the Vietnam War, and he was appointed Minister of Defense in 1980. Later, however, he was dropped from the Politburo and labeled as being "too autocratic" by the reform movement. Dung then quietly retired, and later passed away on March 17, 2002 after a long illness.

[118] For specific information relating to the fall of Laos and Vang Pao's exit to Thailand, I recommend Gayle L. Morrison's excellent book, *Sky Is Falling: An Oral History of the CIA's Evacuation of the Hmong from Laos.*

Epilogue

[119] During the Secret War in Laos, the United States flew more than 40,000 air combat missions in support of indigenous troops.